1999

DISCOURSE AND COGNITION

BRIDGING THE GAP

edited by
Jean-Pierre Koenig

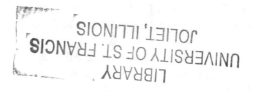

CENTER FOR THE STUDY OF
LANGUAGE AND INFORMATION
STANFORD, CALIFORNIA

Library of Congress Cataloging-in-Publication Data
Discourse and cognition: bridging the gap / edited by Jean-Pierre Koenig.
        p. cm.
   Based on papers presented at the 2nd Conceptual Structure,
Discourse, and Language Conference, which was held Apr. 1996,
University at Buffalo.
   Includes bibliographical references and index.
   ISBN 1-57586-115-1 (alk. paper). – ISBN 1-57586-114-3 (pbk. :
alk. paper)
   1. Discourse analysis—Psychological aspects. 2. Psycholinguistics.
3. Semantics. 4. Metaphor. I. Koenig, Jean-Pierre. II. Conceptual
Structure, Discourse, and Language Conference (2nd : 1996 : University at Buffalo)
P302.8.D573 1998
401'.41—dc21   98-24184
                                                        CIP

Contents

Part III
Metaphors   165

Part IV
Mental Spaces   253

Preface

This book grew out of the second *Conceptual Structure, Discourse, and Language* conference (CSDL) held at the University at Buffalo in April 1996. The conference was organized by Leonard Talmy and myself with the intention of bridging the gap between scholars interested in the cognitive and discursive underpinnings of language.

Despite their diversity, a general thread unifies the topics the thirty odd chapters of this volume cover: what is the relation between linguistic structure, language use, and general cognition? These language-external connections to linguistic structure include more traditional areas such as discourse factors and conceptual structure (including conceptual metaphors), as well as pragmatics, computational modeling and psycholinguistics. But many of the papers go further, into uncharted territory, exploring metaphorical gestures, conceptual structuring in the use of ASL, or the analysis of mathematical thoughts.

Two groups of papers fall within strong traditions in the 'cognitive linguistics' community: metaphor analysis and the theory of mental spaces. But interestingly enough, only one paper deals with traditional metaphor analysis, Grady's reanalysis of Reddy's well-known conduit metaphor. His reanalysis exemplifies a new approach to conceptual metaphors in which metaphorical mappings are broken down into "primary metaphors" that are directly experientially grounded; what used to be called *a* metaphor such as "the conduit metaphor" now becomes the result of composing these more primitive mappings. Other papers cover more novel areas. Cienki's paper discusses metaphoric gestures and emphasizes their theoretical importance in motivating the conceptual nature of metaphors by preventing an over-reliance on *linguistic* data. Taub's paper examines the relationship between the event-structure metaphor and auxiliaries. She concludes that, contrary to what is often assumed in grammaticization theory, the former does not directly motivate the latter; rather they are both grounded in our common experience with body movements and sensations. Lakoff and Nuñez's paper follows on George Lakoff's recent use of metaphor analysis tools in the study of cultural phenomena (including politics and academic traditions.) In this provocative paper, they begin to analyze conceptual metaphors used in Mathematics and suggest that Mathematics is not as disembodied as our 20th century, mathematical logic inspired tradition claims. Finally, Barnden presents a computational system (ATT-Meta) which reasons about mental states whose descriptions are metaphorical, thus illustrating how the analysis of conceptual metaphors can be applied to real world inferencing systems.

The second tradition healthily represented in this volume is Gilles Fauconnier's theory of Mental Spaces and the more recent 'blending' framework. Mushin's paper proposes a revision of the mental spaces theory into a more multidimensional approach so as to account for narrative viewpoints. Huumo's paper uses mental spaces to account for existential and locative inversion constructions while Irandoust argues that French imperfective past tense is not a temporal anaphor, but must be interpreted relative to more general reference frames for episodes. Two papers discuss fundamental questions in 'blending' theory: what makes for a 'good' or 'bad' blend, what are examples of constraints on conceptual blending? In their first paper, Fauconnier and Turner proposes several general principles by which optimal blends abide, while their second paper illustrates how these principles apply in the interpretation of counterfactuals, an area of primary interest in the theory of Mental Spaces since its earliest days. As in the case of metaphors, a couple of papers branch out of traditional linguistics description to apply the theory to new areas. Fridman-Mintz and Liddell's paper illustrate Mental Spaces construction in ASL and show how the availability of an actual physical grounding for their construction allows information to be encoded which is not available in the case of spoken language and 'ungrounded' mental spaces. Finally, Robert uses the 'blending' framework to study how mathematical proofs are conducted. As Lakoff and Nuñez did, Robert suggests that mathematical concepts are grounded in everyday image-schemata contrary to the formal Hilbertian tradition.

Several papers deal with the interface between semantics and pragmatics. Some address the issue of the relation between meaning and Gricean principles or Speech Act theory. Koenig and Benndorf's paper argues that the lexical semantics of the German conjunction *aber* makes reference to Gricean inferential processes, contrary to the traditional hypothesis of a strict separation between semantics and pragmatics. Byrne illustrates the link between semantics and pragmatics in the conditions of use of generic objects in Spanish; their occurrence depends on both the lexical semantics of the verb and the speaker's pragmatic knowledge. Schwenter discusses uses of *si* in realis context in Spanish and suggests that 'conditionality' is not primarily linked to irrealis, but to a more pragmatic notion of non-assertion. Other papers tackle the correspondence between syntax and information structure. Polinsky discusses several object asymmetries in the double object construction and proposes to account for them through the information structure associated with the construction. Lambrecht and Michaelis use information structure to provide an algorithm to predict sentence accents in questions. Finally, several papers discuss the relation between lexical or grammatical structure and discourse factors. Kirsner and van der Kloot use both textual and psychological evidence to discuss the pragmatic underpinnings of the relationship between locative expressions and agency at the root of the historical evolution of the English progressive. Schilperoord and Verhagen argue that syntactic criteria are insufficient for a proper break down of texts into discourse units; attention must also be paid to the conceptual dependencies that hold between clauses. Braun looks at language use in a language without grammatical gender (Turkish) and finds evidence of the presence of gender categories even when no grammatical markers of gender are present.

As expected, many papers center on the role of conceptual structure in the description or motivation of linguistic structure. Goldberg tackles the difficult problem of what constitutes a single event, or more precisely what kinds of event relations can be packaged together to make up a 'single semantic predication.' Farrell discusses a very interesting pattern of number marking in Brazilian Portuguese and shows how the interactional properties of objects can motivate the use of singular number marking for 'objective' pluralities. Fong argues that Finnish State Cases have a temporal interpretation (they temporally place location relations prior to or later than the event described by the verb with which they co-occur) while Fong and Poulin go back to Talmy's typological semantic classification. They argue that the primary difference between verb- and satellite-framed languages such as English and French respectively is that the former *requires* the verb to lexically encode an accomplishment; the latter, by contrast, allows for template augmentation whereby the meaning of activity verbs extends to an accomplishment reading. Harris presents evidence from both semantic priming and letter detection tasks in favor of an idiom or common word combinations level of representation above the mere word-level of representation. Finally, two papers tackle historical issues. Langacker further discusses the role of subjectification in grammaticization in motivating two salient properties of highly grammaticized forms, 'transparency' (roughly equivalent to the notion of semantic neutralization) and meaning 'overlap' with co-occurring elements. Ariel discusses the interaction between universal principles governing successful communication and *ad hoc* factors in the variable evolution of three (person) inflectional paradigms in Hebrew.

I hope this short overview will suggest to the prospective reader that our attempt at bridging the gap between research in discourse analysis, conceptual structure, and general cognition was successful. Let me finish with a few words of thanks to those who made the conference possible, Carole Orsolits, Pat Waldron, and the graduate students from the University at Buffalo. Without them none of this would have taken place. Let me also thank the anonymous reviewers for contributing their time to review all the papers that were submitted as contributions to this volume. The quality of this book owes a great deal to their generous efforts.

Part I

Conceptual Structure and Grammar

The Conceptual Basis of Number Marking in Brazilian Portuguese

PATRICK FARRELL

University of California, Davis

1. Introduction

Grammatical descriptions of the Portuguese language and even studies focusing specifically on number typically provide elaborate accounts of the rather intricate allomorphy associated with plural marking on nouns and agreeing adjectives. As for the conceptual basis of the singular/plural distinction, however, they do not go much beyond noting, as in Barleta de Morais 1992, that "a primeira forma indica um só elemento e a segunda, mais de um" (the first form designates only one element and the second, more than one). It might seem natural to assume that number marking has a more or less intuitively obvious and largely language-independent rationale, at least across Indo-European languages. As in related languages, the singular noun *livro* 'book' refers to one book and its plural counterpart *livros* to more than one. Although many such regular correspondences hold for contemporary spoken Brazilian Portuguese (henceforth BP), there are also certain very common

* Thanks are due to Carlos Faraco, Adam Karp, Almerindo Ojeda, and Scott Rex for discussing the issues with me, and Violette Farrell, Carlos Faraco, Maria Bulgacov, and Rejane Tavares de Lima for contributing native-speaker intuitions.

3

situations in which plural marking is not used, contrary to what a speaker of Spanish or English, for example, might expect. In the following examples, which would be used in the same circumstances in these three languages, the BP nouns *laranja* 'orange' and *sapato* 'shoe' are in the singular form (with no overt marker of number), as are all of the agreeing elements.[1]

(1) a. Eu vou comprar a laranja. *BP*

           Literallly: 'I'm going to buy the orange.' (i.e., 'oranges')

     b. Voy a comprar las naranjas. *Spanish*

           'I am going to buy the-PL orange-PL.'

     c. I'll buy the oranges. *English*

(2) a. Este sapato está sujo. *BP*

           Literally: 'This shoe is dirty.' (i.e., 'this pair of shoes')

     b. Estos sapatos están sucios. *Spanish*

           'this-PL shoe-PL are dirty-PL.'

     c. These shoes are dirty. *English*

Examples such as these show that there is no language-independent meaning of the singular/plural distinction, such that useful grammars of BP and English could simply specify that there is such a distinction and provide the morphological and phonological details of plural marking.

The main goals of this paper are to provide an analysis of the semantics of the singular/plural distinction in BP and, in so doing, to elucidate the systematicity of such cross-linguistic differences as are illustrated by the examples in (1)–(2) and the conceptual motivations underlying them. Drawing on certain ideas from cognitive grammar (Langacker 1991), the categories of singular and plural in BP are characterized as having the structure of hierarchically organized RADIAL CATEGORIES in the sense of Lakoff 1987. It is possible to isolate highly abstract overarching meanings and prototypical instantiations of these meanings. Various other senses of singularity and plurality can be characterized as motivated extensions from the prototypical meanings. Although the categories of number may have the same overarch-

---

[1] As Carlos Faraco has pointed out to me (personal communication) the inflectional -s found on plural nouns, like that found on the first person plural forms of verbs, is often dropped in very casual speech, provided that the plurality is otherwise marked somehow (a plural agreeing article or verb, or a numeral quantifier, for example). This is clearly a distinct phenomenon from the singular categorization of nouns designating "pluralities" considered here, which is not limited to casual speech, occurs with speakers who do not otherwise drop inflectional -s, occurs without plurality being marked in some other way, and in fact involves singular agreement.

ing and core meanings in BP, English, and other languages, BP differs concerning the internal structuring of these categories and how certain entities are conventionally conceived of in terms of the relevant conceptual distinctions.

2. Some Fundamental Distinctions

I begin with the assumption that physical objects are prototypical of the universal linguistic category NOUN, which can be defined as PROFILING a region in some domain (Langacker 1987b, 1987a, 1991). Common nouns in BP, as in English, divide into three main classes, whose conceptual bases are illustrated by the diagrams in Figure 1 (based on Langacker 1991: 78).

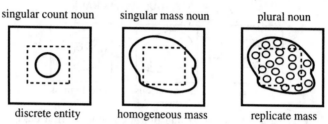

Figure 1. Main classes of common nouns

A singular count noun, such as *livro* 'book', profiles a DISCRETE ENTITY, which can be defined as a region that is bounded within the scope of predication (i.e., the perspective taken on a scene) in some domain, such as physical space. In Figure 1 and elsewhere, domains are indicated by solid rectangles, regions within a domain (or entities) are indicated by drawings thereof, and the scope of predication by a dashed rectangle. A singular mass noun, such as *barro* 'mud', profiles a HOMOGENEOUS MASS, i.e., a region that is unbounded in the scope of predication in some domain and whose internal composition is conceived of as uniform, in spite of the fact that it may be particulate at some level of perceptual or intellectual analysis (as in the case of *areia* 'sand'). A plural noun, such as *livros* 'books', profiles a REPLICATE MASS, i.e., a region that is unbounded within the scope of predication within some domain, while being composed of a conglomeration of highlighted discrete entities (or subregions).

There is a conceptual similarity between singular count nouns and singular mass nouns, since both profile a region whose internal particulateness is not highlighted. This similarity is sufficiently salient as to motivate inclusion of both within the singular category. There is also a conceptual similarity between singular mass nouns and plural nouns, since both profile unbounded regions. This similarity is grammatically reflected in the possibility of using only these kinds of noun without a determiner (in specific contexts), as in *Eu vi barro/livros/*livro na mesa* 'I saw mud/books/*book on the table.'

The categories of singular and plural in BP can be characterized as shown in Figure 2, in which lines with a single arrow indicate the relationship of INSTANTIATION, wherein a more fully elaborated image schema is a particular instance of a more general image schema, and lines with a double arrow indicate conceptual similarity among schemas.

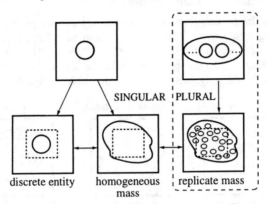

Figure 2. The singular and plural categories: first pass

Discrete entities and homogeneous masses instantiate the highly abstract singular image schema (one region in some domain); replicate masses instantiate the highly abstract plural image schema (more than one entity in a region in some domain).

3. Mass Concepts

There appear to be three keys to understanding the routine use of a singular noun in cases such as the following:

(3)   a.   Eu vou comprar a *laranja*.

'I'm going to buy the orange.' (i.e., 'oranges')

b.   Acabou o *fósforo*.

'Ran out the match.' (i.e., 'The matches ran out.')

c.   A *maçã* está bonita hoje.

'The apple is beautiful today.' (i.e., 'the apples are')

First, the objective particulateness of masses is not in and of itself a determining factor in their categorization. There are many relatively coarse-grained and highly particulate substances for which singular mass nouns are regularly used in BP (*feijão* 'beans', *aveia* 'oats', *gente* 'people', etc.).[2]

---

[2] The same is of course true for English, although the lines are drawn somewhat differently (see Wierzbicka 1985, McCawley 1975).

Although the boundary between them is not a clear one, it is perhaps useful to distinguish two kinds of homogeneous masses, according to degree of perceived particulateness. The constituent particles of what are conceived of as NONPARTICULATE MASSES, of which *barro* 'mud', *ar* 'air', and *água* 'water' are good examples, are imperceptible; those of PARTICULATE MASSES are not. The former remain the same substance under division to the point of some entity beyond ordinary sensory experience, such as the individual molecule. The latter have readily perceived constituents: the individual human being with *gente*, the *grão de feijão* 'grain of bean', and so forth.

Second, the same objective scene can be construed in subtly different ways that may correspond to different linguistic expressions. For example, either *lumber* or *boards* can be used to refer to a stack of boards. *Lumber* seems to evoke a construal of the scene in which the particulate nature of the mass is less salient than with *boards* (Langacker 1991: 78). Thus, in my terms *lumber* is a singular mass noun that designates a substance construed as a particulate homogeneous mass; *boards* is a plural noun that designates the same substance construed as a replicate mass. The conceptual difference is simply one of highlighting: the constituent particles of the mass are highlighted only in the case of *boards*. The grammatical correlate of this difference is that only *boards* contains a stem which itself designates a discrete entity. The pair of nouns *gente* 'people-SG'/*pessoas* 'person-PL' is an example of the same phenomenon in Portuguese.

Third, singular nouns may be polysemous. Just as verbs such as *open* and *break* can be used with either causative or inchoative meanings, singular nouns such as *cake* and *rock* have either a discrete entity or homogeneous mass meaning (*We ate cake/a cake, I carved my initials in rock/a rock*), depending on how the entities are construed with respect to scope of predication. As shown in Figure 3, if the scope of predication is smaller than the entire region corresponding to the discrete entity sense of *cake*, the entity is conceived of as a nonparticulate mass.

Figure 3. Two senses of *cake*

There are also nouns such as *seed* that give count and mass readings in a somewhat different way. In the case of *We planted a seed, seed* is used as a count noun, designating a single discrete entity. In *We bought some seed, seed* is used as a mass noun that designates a particulate homogeneous mass consisting of more than one of the entity designated by count noun *seed.*

Thus, a mass consisting of seeds can be construed either as a replicate mass (*We bought some seeds*) or as a non-replicate mass. In the latter case, the singular form of the noun is used. The two senses of the singular noun *seed* are shown in Figure 4.

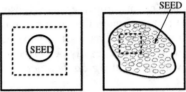

Figure 4. Two senses of *seed*

Now, the use in BP of singular nouns such as *laranja* 'orange', *fósforo* 'match', and *maçã* 'apple' to designate masses consisting of conglomerations of discrete entities (oranges, matches, apples, etc.) can be seen as a simple manifestation of the phenomenon illustrated by *seed*. That is, the singular forms of these nouns are polysemous in the way shown in Figure 4: they have both a discrete entity sense (*Eu tenho uma laranja/um fósforo/uma maçã* 'I have an orange/a match/an apple') and a particulate homogeneous mass sense, as illustrated by the examples in (3).

Nouns of this kind can of course be pluralized, in which case they designate a replicate mass consisting of more than one of the discrete entity that the singular noun designates. As expected, there are situations in which speakers can choose between a plural or singular form of the noun. For example, in speaking of a display of apples at a store, either of the following utterances is possible:

(4) a. Que maçã bonita!

    'What beautiful apple!' (i.e., 'apples')

  b. Que maçãs bonitas!

    'What beautiful apples!'

However, as predicted under the proposed analysis, according to which the choice correlates with a certain kind of conceptual distinction, it is necessary to use the plural noun in a situation in which a few apples are spread out on a table (*Pega as maçãs da mesa* 'Take the apples from the table') and much more natural to use the singular noun in speaking, for example, about buying a bag filled with an indeterminate number of apples (*Eu vou comprar maçã no supermercado* 'I'm going to buy apple—i.e., apples—at the supermarket'). Not surprisingly, numerical quantification forces use of the plural form (*Estas sete maçãs são minhas* 'These seven apples are mine'/*Esta sete maça é minha* 'This seven apple is mine'), presumably because a numerically quantified NP profiles a specific subset of the highlighted entities that constitute the region designated by the modified noun.

The kind of polysemy displayed by singular *laranja, fósforo,* and *maçã* is quite general and, I believe, essentially predictable. Importantly, this phenomenon does not depend on the physical, "objective" properties of things. Rather, it can only be understood in terms of their INTERACTIONAL PROPERTIES (Lakoff 1987), i.e., in terms of how they are used and experienced in routine human interactions with them. The nouns that work like *laranja* with respect to number marking designate physical objects which we deal with in a bundling way, whereby a conglomeration is created whose exact number of constituents is experienced as less important than its overall volume or weight. Thus, the mass sense of a singular noun that is basically a count noun is available (in amenable situations) for things that are typically bought and sold (or otherwise dealt with) by the gram or kilogram or by the container or bunch, including fruits and vegetables of all kinds and matches, rocks, nails, and all manner of similar objects.

The fact that the choice between plural and singular marking on nouns in the *laranja/fósforo* class is constrained by discourse context (for example, buying an indeterminate quantity vs. picking up a few scattered items) and by linguistic context (presence vs. absence of a numerical quantifier) shows that the singular/plural distinction cannot be said to be simply optional in BP. This claim is further supported by the fact that in referring to objects consisting of more than one discrete entity plural marking may not be omitted with nouns designating things that do not have appropriate interactional properties. For example, cars and hammers are typically dealt with and experienced in a more individualistic way than oranges and matches. We ordinarily deal with them on a one-by-one basis or in groups determined by numerical quantification rather than by weight or volume. Correspondingly, (5a) can only be used in reference to a single car; a display of cars on a dealer's lot would require (5b), with overt plural marking.

(5) a. Que carro bonito!

'What (a) beautiful car!'

b. Que carros bonitos!

'What beautiful cars!'

Similarly, (6a) is an acceptable way of expressing only a plan to buy one hammer; (6b), with plural marking, is the way to express a plan to buy several hammers, presumably because the internal structure of masses comprised of hammers is automatically construed as replicate due to the ways in which we ordinarily buy them (by specific numbers rather than by volume).

(6)   a.   Eu vou comprar o martelo.

'I'm going to buy the hammer.'

b.   Eu vou comprar os martelos.

'I'm going to buy the hammers.'

4. Pair and Group Concepts

The proposed analysis, thus far, is that BP is liberal in its use of singular nouns to refer not only to a discrete entity but also to masses consisting of conglomerations of this discrete entity. This analysis does not, however, account for all of the uses of singular nouns in BP for what might be considered pluralities. In a nutshell, the analysis for the remaining cases is that pairs and groups are taken as instantiating the discrete entity image schema and may, therefore, be referred to by a singular noun.

To begin with, it is important to note that for discrete entities comprised (wholly or in part) of two functionally essential and highly salient symmetrical parts, a singular count noun is invariably used in BP. Examples include *tesoura* 'scissor (= pair of scissors)', *calça* 'pant (= pair of pants)', *pinça* 'tweezer (= tweezers)', *alicate* 'plier (= pair of pliers)', *binóculo* 'binocular (= binoculars)', and *algema* 'handcuff (= pair of handcuffs)'. The use of this class of nouns is illustrated in the following examples, which show that the singular form of the noun designates what in English is construed as a pair and the plural form designates only multiple pairs.[3]

(7)   a.   Eu comprei uma calça nova/uma algema boa.

'I bought a new pant/a good handcuff (= a pair).'

b.   Eu comprei umas calças novas/umas algemas boas.

'I bought some new-PL pant-PL/some good-PL handcuff-PL.'
(= pairs)

The conceptual basis for the inclusion of such objects within the singular category seems clear. Although they can be viewed as instantiating the

---

[3] Even nouns in this class ending in an *s* that is a marker of plurality etymologically (*óculos* 'eyeglasses') or in the source language of a borrowing (*shorts* 'shorts'/*jeans* 'jeans') are treated as singular. A general irregular feature of Portuguese number marking is that nouns ending in *s* that are not stressed on the final syllable have no overt plural marking (for example, *um ônibus* 'a bus'/*uns ônibus* 'some busses'). It is therefore easy to see how a final *s* on a noun such as *óculos*, which is historically the plural of *óculo* from the Latin word for 'eye', could be reanalyzed as part of the root rather than a plural marker. According to Barleta de Morais 1992, grammarians prescribe—to little avail—againgst treating *óculos* as singular.

plural image schema of Figure 2, by virtue of their internal multiplicity, their overall structure forms a bounded region within the scope of predication in the domain of physical space, making them also instantiations of the discrete entity schema.

English presumably differs from BP in that the plural category is structured to include the paired-part entity concept, which is an equally reasonable way of drawing the line between the singular and plural categories.[4]

What scissors, pants, handcuffs, etc. have in common is that they are comprised primarily of a pair of physically united symmetrical objects. There are also symmetrical discrete entities that function together as pairs, without however being physically united. Footwear is a good example. Shoes, boots, sandals, socks, and similar objects are experienced primarily as objects that form pairs. We rarely wear and probably never purchase one sock or one shoe. When one member of a pair of socks or shoes is lost, the whole pair becomes virtually useless and is likely to be discarded. With this in mind, it is not difficult to understand why nouns designating footwear of all kinds in BP are singular in form, whether they are used for a pair of objects or a single object. That is to say, example (8a) is ambiguous; it can be used either if one member of a pair of shoes/socks/boots or an entire pair is found in the car.

(8)   a.   Eu achei um sapato/uma bota/uma meia no carro.

          'I found a shoe/a boot/a sock in the car.'

    b.   Eu perdi um pé daquele sapato.

          'I lost one foot of that shoe.' (i.e., 'one shoe of the pair')

The singular noun most often refers to a pair. To speak of one of the shoes forming a pair and avoid the kind of ambiguity displayed in (8a), it is possible to use the noun *pé* 'foot' in the construction illustrated in (8b).

Thus, the singular noun *sapato*, like all others designating footwear, has two senses, as shown in Figure 5.

Figure 5. Two senses of *sapato*

---

[4] In early Portuguese (see Nunes 1945: 232), and possibly in other contemporary dialects, plural forms are used for at least some entities with paired parts (including handcuffs, scissors, and various sorts of leg-covering clothing), suggesting that BP has restructured the categories of number in such a way as to shift the paired-part entity concept to the singular category.

The plural form of such nouns also has two senses, corresponding to the replicate mass construals of the two senses of the singular form. That is, *sapatos*, for example, can be used to designate multiple pairs of shoes (*Eu comprei dois sapatos novos* 'I bought two new shoes (= 2 new pairs of shoes)) or multiple individual members of shoe pairs (*Eu vi um monte de sapatos no lixo* 'I saw a bunch of shoes in the garbage').

The analysis that I wish to suggest is that footwear is conceived of in a way that is similar to paired-part entities such as *calça* 'pants', *tesoura* 'scissors', *óculos* 'glasses', and other similar singular nouns. There is, thus, an entity-pair image schema that differs from the paired-part entity schema only in that its constituents form a bounded region not in physical space but in the domain of function, as illustrated in Figure 5. By virtue of the similarity, the entity-pair image schema is included in the singular category.

The kind of polysemy displayed by *sapato* and other nouns for footwear occurs also with the nouns *luva* 'glove', *brinco* 'earring', and with terms for body parts that come in pairs, including *pé* 'foot', *mão* 'hand', *lábio* 'lip', *sobrancelha* 'eyebrow', *seio* 'breast', and *ombro* 'shoulder'. The following examples show that a singular body-part term can be used with either a discrete entity sense (b-examples) or with an entity-pair sense (a-examples).

(9)   a.   Você precisa lavar a mão/as mãos.

        'You need to wash the hand/the-PL hand-PL.' (i.e., 'your hands')

      b.   Eu cortei a mão.

        'I cut the hand.' (i.e., 'my hand')

(10)   a.   A Júlia queria sentar no meu ombro/nos meus ombros.

        'Julia wanted to sit on my shoulder/on my-PL shoulder-PL.' (i.e., 'straddling my neck')

      b.   Eu estou com dor no ombro direito.

        'I have a pain in my right shoulder.'

Although it is often less natural, a plural noun may be used in situations for which a singular noun with the entity-pair sense is appropriate. The entity-pair sense is readily evoked when such nouns are used in talking about routines that typically involve the designated body parts functioning or being experienced together (washing feet, checking hands for cleanliness, sitting on shoulders, etc.). For routine activities in which a single member of a body part pair is typically involved, the singular noun has only its discrete entity sense. For example, the activity of raising a hand to indicate presence in a group typically involves only one hand. Thus, under ordinary circumstances, the order *Levanta a mão* 'raise the hand (i.e., your hand)' can only be carried out by raising either the left or right hand—not both.[5]

The image schemas for paired-part entities and entities that function as a pair are actually best characterized as instantiations of more general schemas, i.e., those for grouped-part entities and entities that function as a group. Stairs and bleachers are good examples of discrete entities that consist of functionally essential and highly salient symmetrical parts. They differ from such entities as scissors and pants in that they typically have more than two of the key parts. Not surprisingly, in BP the nouns for these objects are treated like those for scissors and pliers, i.e., they are singular in form (*escada* 'stairs' and *arquibancada* 'bleachers'). Similarly, the singular forms of certain nouns naming entities, including body parts, that come in groups larger than pairs, can have an entity-group sense that corresponds to the entity-pair sense of nouns such as *sapato* 'shoe', *pé* 'foot' and *mão* 'hand'. In particular, the singular forms of nouns such as *chave* 'key', *dente* 'tooth', and *unha* 'fingernail' can be used either in reference to a single key, tooth, or fingernail or a set of the same, as illustrated by the following examples.

(11)   a.   Eu perdi a chave dessa porta.

          'I lost the key for this door.'

       b.   Onde você deixou a minha chave.

          'Where did you leave my key.' (i.e., 'my set of keys')

(12)   a.   Eu quebrei uma unha.

          'I broke a fingernail.'

       b.   Eu preciso pintar a unha.

          'I need to polish the fingernail.' (i.e., 'my fingernails')

(13)   a.   A Júlia perdeu um outro dente.

          'Julia lost another tooth.'

---

[5] The entity-pair construal of objects that function in pairs has apparently become highly conventional with body part coverings and is becoming so with body parts. The extension of the entity-pair image schema to nouns designating body-part pairs is presumably due in part to the conceptual metaphor BODY PART COVERINGS ARE THE BODY PARTS THAT THEY COVER, which manifests itself otherwise in the expression *um pé da bota* 'one foot of the boot (i.e., one boot of the pair)' and in the shift in meaning for the word *óculos* (Latin 'eyes' > Portuguese 'glasses'). This metaphor is manifested in English in the expressions *pant legs* and *four eyes* 'person who wears glasses'. That is to say, it is natural to treat *mão* and *pé*, for example, in the same way that *luva* and *bota* are treated grammatically, because gloves and footwear are largely understood in terms of hands and feet.

b. Eu já escovei o dente da Júlia.

'I already brushed the tooth of Julia.' (i.e., 'Julia's teeth')

As with entities that form a pair, this sense is evoked specifically in situations in which the entities are typically experienced as a group.

5. Summary and Conclusions

The proposed analysis of the categories of number in BP is summarized in Figure 6. Each category contains a highly abstract image schema (an overarching meaning) that the various specific meanings of singular and plural marking can be seen as instantiating: one region in some domain in the case of the singular category and more than one entity in a region in some domain in the case of the plural category. The prototypical instantiation of the plural schema is the replicate-mass schema; that of the singular schema is the discrete-entity schema. Other senses of singularity are related to the prototype by similarity links or by the relation of instantiation.

The initially surprising use of singular nouns in cases such as *Eu vou comprar a laranja* 'I'm going to buy the orange (i.e., oranges)' and *Este sapato está sujo* 'This shoe (i.e., pair of shoes) is dirty' is attributable to rather small but highly significant differences between BP and English and other languages in this conceptual domain. To begin with, although the categories of number in English, for example, could be said to be organized around the same basic image schemas (plausibly members of a universal set of available number concepts), the boundaries between the two categories are drawn somewhat differently. Most importantly, the entire set of related schemas for grouped-part entities and entity groups are included in the plural category in English. Given that these are all equally reasonably viewed as instantiations of the discrete entity schema, it is understandable that they fall within the singular category in BP. Thus, BP uses a singular form of the noun associated with the concept SHOE for the concept SHOE PAIR as well. Furthermore, although particulate masses in both English and BP are conventionally conceived of as homogeneous rather than replicate and are therefore associated with singular nouns, BP is much more liberal with respect to this matter. That is, in addition to allowing homogeneous mass construals of particulate substances such as rice, corn, and seed, BP systematically allows such a construal for masses created from all kinds of entities, provided that their number of constituents is experienced as being less significant than their overall volume or weight. Thus, a singular noun is appropriate for oranges and potatoes bought by the kilogram as well as for many kinds of objects that are typically experienced in terms of bundles or conglomerations of a similar kind.

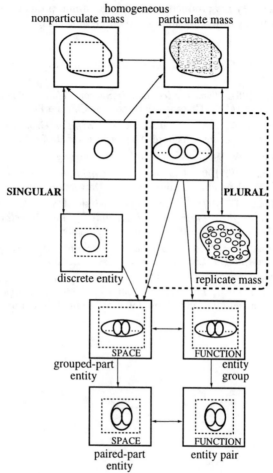

Figure 6. The singular and plural categories in BP: final pass

Among the general conclusions that can be drawn are the following. First, the categories of number can be insightfully characterized as radial categories: similarity links between various concepts explain their inclusion in the singular category. Second, the relevant categorization of objects depends not so much on their physical properties as their interactional properties: bunches of oranges and matches are conceived of as a singularity because we deal with them in a bundling way; hands and teeth are treated as a singuarity because we experience them as functional units. Third, the concepts "one" and "more than one" are not entirely given to us by "objective" reality. Rather they are products of the human mind, projected onto reality in different ways by different cultures and different languages.

References

Barleta de Morais, Clóvis. 1992. O número dos nomes em português. *Alfa* 36.177–188.

Lakoff, George. 1987. *Women, Fire, and Dangerous Things: What Categories Reveal about the Mind.* Chicago: University of Chicago Press.

Langacker, Ronald W. 1987a. *Foundations of Cognitive Grammar, Volume I: Theoretical Prerequisites.* Stanford: Stanford University Press.

Langacker, Ronald W. 1987b. Nouns and Verbs. *Language* 63.53–94.

Langacker, Ronald W. 1991. *Foundations of Cognitive Grammar, Volume II: Descriptive Application.* Stanford: Stanford University Press.

McCawley, James D. 1975. Lexicography and the Count-Mass Distinction. *Proceedings of the Fourth Annual Meeting of the Berkeley Linguistic Society,* 314–321. University of California, Berkeley.

Nunes, José Joaquim. 1945. *Compêndio de gramática histórica portuguesa: Fonética e morfologia.* Lisbon: Livraria Clássica Editora.

Wierzbicka, Anna. 1985. Oats and Wheat: The Fallacy of Arbitrariness. In John Haiman, ed., *Iconicity in Syntax, Typological Studies in Language, Vol. 6,* 311–342. Amsterdam and Philadelphia: John Benjamins Publishing Company.

Space and Time in the Semantics of the Finnish Case System*

VIVIENNE FONG
Stanford University

1 Introduction

The myriad functions of the Local Cases in Finnish have generated numerous discussions and analyses (Itälä 1984, Leino 1990, Huumo 1995, *inter alia*). Fong (1997b) argues that the Directional Local Cases have a temporal intepretation, which captures the range of verbs Directional Locative predicates systematically occur with. In this paper, I extend this idea to the interpretation of the Finnish State Cases. I show that the Directional Local Cases pattern with the Elative and Translative State Cases, in depicting locations or states that hold at time intervals anterior or posterior to the event time denoted by the verb. The non-directional Local Cases in turn pattern with the Essive State Case; they predicate locations or states that hold only for the duration of the state or event denoted by the verb.

The distribution of the Local and State Cases in Finnish can thus be unified from the perspective of the temporal intervals these Case suffixes denote, in relation to the temporal (event) structure of the verbs they combine with. This analysis motivates temporal meaning in both the Local and State Case systems, and demonstrates that temporal relations are neither secondary to, nor derived from, spatial meanings.

2 The Semantics of Case

2.1 Overview of the Finnish Case System

The Case paradigm for Finnish nominals is given in Table 1.[1] The interpretation of the Local and State Semantic Cases will be discussed below. The Local Cases are the Inessive, Illative, Elative, Adessive,

---

*I am grateful to Arto Anttila, Melissa Bowerman, Adele Goldberg, and Paul Kiparsky for comments and discussion. I owe Arto Anttila and Paul Kiparsky another round of thanks for language consultation.

[1] Classification adapted from Karlsson (1987), Vainikka (1989), Blake (1994). The Case meanings given in Table 1 and in the glosses follow traditional definitions (see, for example, Karlsson (1987)).

Allative, and Ablative. The State Cases are the Essive, Translative, and Elative.[2]

Case	Form (Singular)	Notes
NOMinative	-∅	
PARtitive	-a/-ta/	
ACCusative	-n, -∅	
GENitive	-n	
ESSive	-na	expresses a temporary state/function
TRAnslative	-ksi	expresses the end point of a movement/change
ABEssive	-tta	'without'
COMitative	-ine	'with, accompanied by'
INStructive	-n	'(instrumental) with, by'
LOCAL CASES (Non-directional)		
INEssive	-ssa	'in'
ADEssive	-lla	'at/on'
(Directional)		
ELAtive	-sta	'out of'
ILLative	-(h)Vn/-seen	'into'
ABLative	-lta	'from/off of'
ALLative	-lle	'to/onto'

TABLE 1 The Case Paradigm for Finnish Nominals

2.2   The Local Cases

The six Local Cases in Finnish form a sub-system of their own, sharing the basic function of expressing location.

In traditional grammars, the Directional Local Cases (the Illative, Elative, Allative, and Ablative) are considered to have an additional path or directional meaning. However, the Directional Locatives (DLs) also systematically occur with verbs which denote neither motion nor change of state—for example, *jättää* 'leave', *löytää* 'find', and *unohtaa* 'forget' (1).

---

[2] In the historical development of the State Cases, there was a gap left by the Partitive Case, which in contemporary Finnish is filled by the Elative Case (Leino 1990). So the Elative has both locative and state functions.

(1)   a.   Jät-i-n   avaime-t auto-on/*auto-ssa.
           leave-PAST-1P key-PLU car-ILL   car-INE
           'I left the keys in (lit. 'into'/*'in') a/the car.'

       b.   Löys-i-n   kirja-n   laatiko-sta/*laatiko-ssa.
           find-PAST-1P book-GEN box-ELA   box-INE
           'I found a/the book in (lit. 'out of'/*'in') a/the box.'

       c.   Unohd-i-n   kirja-n   auto-on/*auto-ssa.
           forget-PAST-1P book-GEN car-ILL   car-INE
           'I forgot a/the book in (lit. 'into'/*'in') a/the car.'

A cross-linguistic generalization of locative predication needs to explain why in Finnish, the so-called 'directional' locatives occur with such verbs, while in English, only the non-directional locatives are possible (see (2)).[3]

(2)   a.   I left the keys in/*into the car.

       b.   I found the book in/*out of the car.

       c.   I forgot the book in/*into the car.

Dahl (1987) suggests treating verbs like 'remain' and 'leave' as borderline cases between location and direction. On the one hand, these verbs pattern with motion verbs (e.g., 'move') in encompassing at least two points in time; on the other, they pattern with state verbs (e.g., 'be situated', 'sit') in involving only a single location. Finnish 'remain' (*jäädä*) patterns like a directional verb, and takes a goal as complement, expressed by DL Case. English, however, treats 'remain' as a state verb, which does not take goal complements. To account for why Finnish 'remain' takes goal complements, Dahl also claims that Finnish defines goal as "the point at which some object is situated as the result of what is said to take place," whereas English defines goal as the final point of a movement (Dahl 1987:153ff). As such, "in the grammar of Finnish, there will be a rule to the effect that if something suits [the goal definition for Finnish], the noun phrase...that refers to it will be marked with one of the directional cases."(Dahl 1987:154)

However, notice that sometimes, goals are expressed by Direct Objects, in Accusative or Partitive Case:

(3)   a.   Tuovi   saavutt-i   maali-n.
           Tuovi-NOM reach-PAST-3SG goal-ACC
           'Tuovi reached the goal.'

---

[3] See also Dahl (1987) for a comparison of these languages with Russian, which has Directional Locative Cases, but unlike Finnish, uses the non-directional ones with such verbs.

LOC(IN)	LOC(AT)	holding at time
INESSIVE	ADESSIVE	
ILLATIVE	ALLATIVE	$t_0 \ldots t_n$
ELATIVE	ABLATIVE	$t_{-n} \ldots t_0$

TABLE 2 Time intervals in which DLs hold

b. Tuovi   tavoittel-i   täydellisyytt-ä.
    Tuovi-NOM strive-PAST-3SG perfection-PAR
    'Tuovi strove for perfection.'

Since Goal is a semantic/conceptual category as opposed to a morphological one, Dahl's theory of goal meanings, formulated to account precisely for the fact that 'remain' takes goal complements, does not in the end explain why 'remain' takes DL complements.[4] Therefore, it is unclear why we should assume that 'remain' takes goals in Finnish but not in English, and that the definition of goal is different in the two languages.

In contrast, Fong (1997b) argues that the lexical meanings and entailments of verbs like 'leave', 'remain', 'forget', and 'find' are identical in both English and Finnish, and the languages only differ in the meanings of the English locative prepositions and the corresponding Finnish Cases.[5] Unlike the English prepositions *into* and *out of*, the DL Cases do not encode a path meaning, which is interpreted as involving a notion of change from one region to another.[6] Instead, DL Cases can be defined as predicating locations at time intervals anterior/posterior to the event time denoted by the verb.[7] The time intervals in which the DL Cases can be evaluated are given in Table 2.[8]

Having temporal interpretations for DLs captures their systematic occurrence with motion, cognition, change of state, and aspectual verbs. Verbs like 'leave' and 'find' do not cause the Object to undergo a change of location or state, but they do entail that the Object is in a particular

---

[4] Note that 'remain'-type verbs do not take "goals" in Accusative Case:
(i)   Tuovi   jä-i   *huonee-n/ huoneese-en.
        Tuovi-NOM remain-PAST-3SG room-ACC room-ILL
        'Tuovi remained *room/in (lit. 'into') the room.'

[5] For a fuller exposition of the arguments, see Fong (1997b).

[6] See Dowty (1979) and Wunderlich (1991) for one way of representing the semantics of path prepositions in English.

[7] More recently, Fong (1997a) provides an analysis of DL meanings that generalizes to the distributions of DLs as modifiers of nouns, as well as verbs. Here, I am concerned only with DLs occuring with verbs, and so will only deal with the temporal domains that verbs and DL predicates operate in.

[8] In the time intervals, t_0 is the culmination point of the action denoted by the verb.

location before, or after, the action takes place. The DLs hold at just such a time interval anterior or posterior to the culmination of the action. Because they do not encode path meanings, they do not conflict with the meanings of such verbs.

Aspectual verbs like *ruveta* 'begin' and *lakata* 'stop' take verbal complements that are suffixed with Illative and Elative Case, respectively (4). Aspectual verbs like 'begin', for example, describe the onset of an event. The Illative predicate holds at times posterior to the time of 'beginning', and is predicted to be compatible with the meaning of 'begin'.

(4)   a.   Vieno   rupea-a   luke-ma-an.
               Vieno-NOM begin-3SG read-INF-ILL
               'Vieno begins reading.'
        b.   Vieno   lakka-a   luke-ma-sta.
               Vieno-NOM stop-3SG read-INF-ELA
               'Vieno stops reading.'

With change of state verbs like *rikkoa* 'break', any path meaning associated with DL predication is an implicature that is defeasible. For example, the Ablative predicate in (5) denotes the location of the vase prior to its breaking. This reading holds in a context where the broken pieces remain on the shelf after the breaking event, thus showing that any path interpretation (of the vase falling off the shelf) is indeed an implicature.[9]

(5)   Kissa   rikko-i   maljako-n hylly-ltä. Palase-t
        cat-NOM break-PAST-3SG   vase-ACC shelf-ABL piece-PLU
        jä-i-vät   hylly-lle.
        remain-PAST-3PLU shelf-ALL
        'A/The cat broke a/the vase off a/the shelf. The pieces remained on the shelf.'

As for the Inessive and Adessive Cases, these do not have temporal interpretations, and are similar to English *in*, for example. In (6), the Inessive locative just depicts the location where the action denoted by the verb is carried out.

---

[9] With motion verbs, DL predication gives an unequivocal path reading (see (i)). Here, I assume that Finnish motion verbs can express a change or transition through time (cf. Verkuyl (1978)). The DL predicate is compatible with this meaning of change encoded in the verb, by depicting the location of the moving entity at an anterior or posterior time, in relation to the event time when the transition happens.

(i)   Kissa   hyppäs-i   hylly-ltä. (#Se   jä-i   hylly-lle.)
        cat-NOM jump-PAST-3SG shelf-ABL   it-NOM remain-PAST-3SG shelf-ALL.
        'A/The cat jumped off a/the shelf. (#It remained on the shelf.)'

(6) Sointu   kanto-i   kirja-a   Tukholma-ssa.
     Sointu-NOM carry-PAST-3SG book-PAR Stockholm-INE
     'Sointu was carrying a/the book (around) in Stockholm.' *or*
     'Sointu carried a/the book in Stockholm.' (*habitual reading*)

Since the Illative/Allative predicates hold at a time after the event time denoted by the verb, this predicts that the predicates occur in constructions which entail a location posterior to event time, but the Inessive/Adessive ones do not. Supporting evidence comes from examples where the locative is to be interpreted as a (final) destination, instead of as the location in which the event takes place. First, contrast (7), where Stockholm is the destination the book is being carried to, with (6), where the city is the location in which the carrying takes place.

(7) Sointu   kanto-i   paketti-a   Tukholma-an.
     Sointu-NOM carry-PAST-3SG parcel-PAR Stockholm-ILL
     Intended reading: 'Sointu was carrying a/the parcel to (lit. 'into') Stockholm.'

Second, when a verb like *pysähtyä* 'stop' occurs with an Inessive locative as in (8a), the sentence means that there was a stopping in Huittinen before the bus moved on to another destination.[10] When the verb occurs with an Illative locative, however, the sentence means that the bus remained in Huittinen after stopping (8b).

(8) a. Bussi   pysähty-i   Huittisi-ssa   ennen
         bus-NOM stop-PAST-3SG Huittinen-INE before
         saapumis-ta Helsinki-in.
         arrival-PAR Helsinki-ILL
         'A/The bus stopped in Huittinen before arrival in (lit. 'into') Helsinki.'

     b. Bussi   pysähty-i   Huittisi-in   (#ennen
         bus-NOM stop-PAST-3SG Huittinen-ILL   before
         saapumis-ta Helsinki-in).
         arrival-PAR Helsinki-ILL
         'A/The bus stopped in (lit. 'into') Huittinen (#before arrival in (lit. 'into') Helsinki).'

Further evidence comes from resultative constructions, which depict a resultant change of state or location of the Object. Here again, the DL Case appears on the resultant locative predicate (9).

---

[10] Itälä (1984) describes this type of Inessive locative as a place viewed as an intermediary stop between two other places.

(9)   Maanviljelijä ampu-i   ketu-n   metsä-än/*metsä-ssä.
       farmer-NOM shoot-PAST-3SG fox-ACC forest-ILL   forest-INE
       Intended reading: 'A/The farmer shot a/the fox, and the fox
       remained in a/the forest after the shooting.'

In addition, compare the DL Case on verbal predicates (in (4)
above) with the Inessive Case on an infinitival verb in (10) (from Huumo (1995)) below. In (10), the infinitival Inessive has a progressive
sense, depicting an ongoing activity (Huumo 1995), which concurs with
the interpretation of Inessive predicates as holding at event time. Example (11) shows that the Inessive Case on infinitival verbs and locative
predicates are ill-formed with a verb like *jäädä* 'remain', which patterns
with 'leave' verbs.

(10)   Elmeri   on   meditoi-ma-ssa   komero-ssa.
       Elmeri-NOM be-3SG meditate-INF-INE closet-INE
       'Elmeri is meditating in the closet.'

(11)   Vieno   jä-i   meditoi-ma-an/
       Vieno-NOM remain-PAST-3SG meditate-INF-ILL
       *meditoi-ma-ssa   komero-on/*komero-ssa.
       meditate-INF-INE closet-ILL   closet-INE
       'Vieno remained meditating in the closet.'

2.3   The State Cases

The Essive Case is described as expressing "a (temporary) state or
function, sometimes circumstances, conditions, or causes." (Karlsson
1987) The examples below show that Essive predicates hold for the
duration of a state, but not at times anterior/posterior to the time the
state holds. In (13), the state of being ill is bounded by the durative
adverbial 'three weeks'.

(12)   Toini   on sairaa-na.
       Toini-NOM be ill-ESS
       'Toini is ill.'

(13)   Toini   oli   sairaa-na kolme viikko-a.
       Toini-NOM be-PAST-3SG ill-ESS   three week-PAR
       'Toini was ill for three weeks.'

The example in (14) (from Karlsson (1987)) shows the Essive co-
occurring with the Inessive locative. This is to be expected, since both
these Cases are treated here as holding for the duration of the state
denoted by the verb.

(14)   Heikki   on Jämsä-ssä lääkäri-nä.
       Heikki-NOM be Jämsä-INE doctor-ESS
       'Heikki is (working as) a doctor in Jämsä.'

The Translative Case usually expresses "a state, property, function or position into which something/someone enters, or the end point of a movement or change" (Karlsson 1987). It occurs with verbs of change of state (15–16), and also with verbs in the resultative construction, where the predicate depicts the resultant state (17).

(15) Toini   tul-i   sairaa-ksi.
      Toini-NOM become-PAST-3SG ill-TRA
      'Toini became ill.'

(16) Hän muuttu-i   touka-sta   perhose-ksi.
      s/he change-PAST-3SG caterpillar-ELA butterfly-TRA
      'S/he changed from a caterpillar into a butterfly.'

(17) Ravist-i-n   mato-n   puhtaa-ksi.
      shake-PAST-1SG carpet-ACC clean-TRA
      'I shook a/the carpet clean.'

One might conclude that the Translative Case encodes a meaning of change, comparable to the use of the English *into* in the translations of the above examples. But notice that the Translative Case also occurs with verbs that do not denote change, such as *jäädä* 'remain' (18).

(18) Toukka   jä-i   touka-ksi.
      caterpillar-NOM remain-PAST-3SG caterpillar-TRA
      'A/The caterpillar remained a caterpillar.'

Also, the Translative occurs with verbs like *jättää* 'leave' in depictive predication. Contrast the depictive use of the Translative predicate in (19a), with the ill-formed context which forces it to be interpreted as resultative predication in (19b).

(19) a. Lasi   oli   tyhjä. Jäti-n   lasi-n
          glass-NOM be-PAST-3SG empty leave-PAST-1P glass-ACC
          tyhjä-ksi.
          empty-TRA
          'The glass was empty. I left it empty.'

      b. Lasi   oli   täysi. #Jäti-n   lasi-n
          glass-NOM be-PAST-3SG full   leave-PAST-1P glass-ACC
          tyhjä-ksi.
          empty-TRA
          'The glass was full. I left it empty (i.e. the result of my leaving the glass was that it became empty).'

So the Translative Case behaves like the Illative/Allative Cases with respect to verbs like 'leave' and 'remain'—verbs which do not have change or path meanings. Notice also that the Translative and Illative Cases co-occur in resultative constructions (20).

STATE	LOC(IN)	LOC(AT)	holding at time
ESSIVE	INESSIVE	ADESSIVE	
TRANSLATIVE	ILLATIVE	ALLATIVE	$t_0 \ldots t_n$
ELATIVE	ELATIVE	ABLATIVE	$t_{-n} \ldots t_0$

TABLE 3 Time intervals shared by State and Local Cases

(20) Maanviljelijä ampu-i   ketu-n metsä-än kuoliaa-ksi.
      farmer-NOM shoot-PAST-3SG fox-ACC forest-ILL dead-TRA
      Intended reading: 'A/The farmer shot a/the fox dead, and the
      fox remained in a/the forest after the shooting.'

Therefore, the Translative Case can be seen as encoding a time
period after the culmination point of the event, just like the Illa-
tive/Allative Cases. This ensures that the Translative predicate does
not conflict with verbs like 'leave' and 'remain'; nevertheless, the predicate is still interpretable as denoting resultant states with verbs like
'become' and 'change', because the predicate holds for a time after the
event time.

The Elative Case has a dual function. In its State use, it is the
converse of the Translative, encoding a time interval before the culmination point—the same temporal interpretation as its DL counterparts,
the Elative and Ablative. In (16) above, the Elative predicate depicts
the state prior to the change.

3   Relating the State and Local Cases

The classification of the State and Local Cases using a temporal interpretation groups certain State Cases with the Local ones, as summarized in Table 3. The time $t_0 \ldots t_n$ picks out the Illative, Allative and
Translative Cases, and the time $t_{-n} \ldots t_0$ picks out the Elative (Local
and State) and Ablative Cases.

This relation between the State and Local Cases in fact finds support from the historical development of the Local Cases in Finnish.
Inessive and Adessive come from local suffixes (-s- 'in', -l- 'at', respectively) combining with Essive -na, and the Elative and Ablative from
the combination with the Separative -ta (Hakulinen 1961, Leino 1990).

We have seen that the Illative and Translative Cases share the temporal interpretation of denoting intervals posterior to the event time.
How do they differ? The Illative occurs with verbal predicates (see (4),
for example), and with Noun Phrases denoting, or interpretable as location (1). The Translative occurs with adjectival predicates (17) and
with non-locational Noun Phrases (18).

As for the Inessive and Essive Case forms, it seems that the Essive occurs with adjectival predicates, while the Inessive occurs with nominal ones, in the minimal pairs below:

(21) a.   Toini   on   sairaa-na/*sairaa-ssa.
           Toini-NOM be-3SG ill-ESS   ill-INE
           'Toini is ill.'
      b.   Toini   on   flunssa-ssa/*flunssa-na .
           Toini-NOM be-3SG flu-INE   flu-ESS
           'Toini has the flu.' (lit. 'Toini is in flu')

4 Conclusion

In the above discussion, I have shown that the Local and State Cases in Finnish have systematically similar distributions. In particular, the DL Cases and the Translative/Elative State Cases fall into categories denoting anterior or posterior time intervals with respect to the event time denoted by the verb. The analysis motivates temporal meaning as basic to the semantics of these morphemes. This view differs from the common assumption that temporal relationships are derived from spatial ones (attested in diachronic analyses (Traugott (1975), for example)). This paper shows that, from a synchronic perspective, temporal meanings are central to the proper interpretation of these Case morphemes.

References

Blake, Barry J. 1994. *Case.* Cambridge: Cambridge University Press.

Dahl, Östen. 1987. Case Grammar and Prototypes. In *Concepts of Case,* ed. René Dirven and Günter Radden. Tübingen: Gunter Narr Verlag.

Dowty, David R. 1979. *Word Meaning and Montague Grammar.* Dordrecht: Reidel.

Fong, Vivienne. 1997a. A Diphasic Approach to Directional Locatives. Paper presented at Semantics and Linguistic Theory 7, Stanford University, to appear in proceedings.

Fong, Vivienne. 1997b. A Temporal Interpretation for Locative Case. *Proceedings of WCCFL* 15:145–159.

Hakulinen, Lauri. 1961. *Suomen kielen rakenne ja kehitys.* Helsinki: Otava. 2nd edition. [The Structure and Development of the Finnish Language].

Huumo, Tuomas. 1995. Bound Domains: A Semantic Constraint on Existentials. *SKY: Yearbook of the Linguistic Association of Finland* 7–46.

Itälä, Marja-Leena. 1984. *Die lokosemantischen Interrelationen zwischen Verb und Lokativbestimmung.* Turku: Turun Yliopisto.

Karlsson, Fred. 1987. *Finnish Grammar.* Porvoo: Werner Söderström Osakeyhtiö. 2nd edition.

Leino, Pentti. 1990. Spatial Relations in Finnish: A Cognitive Perspective. *Stockholm Studies in Finnish Language and Literature* 6:117–152.

Traugott, Elizabeth Closs. 1975. Spatial Expressions of Tense and Temporal Sequencing: A Contribution to the Study of Semantic Fields. *Semiotica* 15(3):207–230.

Vainikka, Anne M. 1989. *Deriving Syntactic Representations in Finnish.* Doctoral dissertation, University of Massachusetts, Amherst.

Verkuyl, Henk J. 1978. Thematic Relations and the Semantic Representation of Verbs Expressing Change. *Studies in Language* 2:199–233.

Wunderlich, Dieter. 1991. How do Prepositional Phrases fit into Compositional Syntax and Semantics? *Linguistics* 29:591–621.

Locating Linguistic Variation in Semantic Templates

VIVIENNE FONG AND CHRISTINE POULIN
Stanford University

1   Introduction

Any theory of how verb meaning relates to verb syntax must account
for why particular verb classes can occur in a range of syntactic frames.
Lexicalist theories assume that verbs with multiple meanings have multiple lexical semantic representations (Pinker 1989, Rappaport Hovav
and Levin 1995a). Levin and Rappaport Hovav give verbs an articu-
lated lexical semantic representation in the form of predicate decomposition, which consists of primitive predicates and constants. Constants
represent the idiosyncratic elements of meaning, distinguishing among
the members of a given verb class. Specific combinations of primitive
predicates represent the structural aspect of verb meaning, defining the
major semantic classes of verbs. The various combinations of primitive
predicates constitute the basic stock of lexical semantic templates of a
language. Levin and Rappaport Hovav argue that (i) templates may be
freely augmented to other possible templates—for example an Activity
template can be augmented to an Accomplishment template (cf. (1a)
and (1b)) and (ii) a verb can be associated with more than one semantic template—for example, a single verb can be associated with both
Activity and Accomplishment templates.

(1)   a. [x ACT]
       b. [[x ACT] CAUSE [y BECOME AT LOCATION]]

This approach explicitly locates the difference in verb meanings in the
semantic templates, and raises the issue of how languages differ.[1]

---

[1] Contrast this approach with constructional frameworks (most notably Hoekstra
(1992) and Goldberg (1995)), where verbs with multiple meanings have 'core' meanings that are compatible with more than one syntactic structure. While lexicalist
theories assume that verbs have structured lexical semantic representations that indicate their argument structure, constructional approaches assume that elements of
meaning reside partly in the verbs themselves, and partly in the syntactic constructions, so that the meaning of a verb in a given use is derived compositionally from
the meaning of the verb and the construction (Rappaport Hovav and Levin 1996).
In this paper, we will not deal with the differences between the two approaches.
Rather, we show that the lexicalist approach gives us a way of articulating the difference between English and French, based on Levin and Rappaport Hovav's idea
of template expansion.

Talmy (1985, 1991) proposes a bipartite typology of languages on the basis of whether they are "verb-framed" or "satellite-framed". With reference to how verbs express the notion of PATH, verb-framed languages map PATH onto the verb, while satellite-framed languages map PATH onto the verb's satellites.[2] According to Talmy, French behaves like a verb-framed language, and English like a satellite-framed one.

In this paper, we show that French in fact takes PATH satellites. However, the difference between French and English is that English allows template augmentation, but French does not. The evidence comes from the interpretation of manner of motion verbs as Activities and as Accomplishments (with a PATH interpretation), and also from resultative constructions in these two languages.

We find that French only allows Accomplishment readings in cases where either the verb or the locative predicate inherently encodes the BECOME predicate in the Accomplishment template. On the other hand, English allows an Activity verb to extend its meaning to incorporate the BECOME predicate in the Accomplishment reading.

2 From Activity to Accomplishment

A basic Activity template [x ACT (ON y)] can be integrated with constants like MANNER or PATH to give, for example, the template in (2a) [x ACT$_{<MANNER>}$ (ON y)]. (cf. Levin and Rappaport Hovav (1995)). It has been claimed that French verbs of motion can only integrate either PATH (e.g. *monter* 'go up', *reculer* 'go backwards') or MANNER (e.g. *courir* 'run', *nager* 'swim') but, unlike English, not both (see, for example, Talmy 1985, Jackendoff 1990). However, we show in section 2.1 that one class of nonagentive verbs in French does in fact integrate both MANNER and PATH, with a template like (2b).

(2) a. x ACT$_{<MANNER>}$
     b. x [BECOME AT LOCATION]$_{<MANNER>}$

In section 2.2, we show that while manner of motion verbs normally have MANNER readings only, a PATH reading can be forced by adding a prepositional phrase that unambiguously denotes PATH. Furthermore, the evidence we present falsifies the standard assumption in the literature that French manner of motion verbs cannot occur with goal phrases to give Accomplishment readings (see also Bouchard (1995) and Slobin and Hoiting (1994) for a similar view, and Slobin (1996) for discussion of Spanish).

---

[2] A satellite is defined as "the grammatical category of any constituent other than a nominal complement that is in a sister relation to the verb root" (Talmy 1991:486).

A common assumption in the literature on lexical aspect (e.g., Dowty 1979, Vendler 1957, Verkuyl 1972, Verkuyl 1993) and unaccusativity (e.g., Hoekstra 1984, Levin and Rappaport Hovav 1992, Rappaport Hovav and Levin 1995b, Van Valin 1990) is that English verbs of manner of motion have a dual aspectual classification. For instance, the verb *run* can be used as an Activity verb (*Kim ran*), or, when a goal phrase is added, as an Accomplishment verb (*Kim ran to school*). If we assume that the meaning of the Activity use is more basic than the meaning of the Accomplishment use, a verb like *run* would have a basic classification as an Activity verb and a derived classification as an Accomplishment verb in the presence of a goal phrase. This dual aspectual classification is available to all English verbs of manner of motion (e.g. *bounce, glide, slide, swim, wander*). Thus, in the English verb lexicon: (i) for a given manner of motion both Activity and Accomplishment meanings are available, and (ii) the same verb can be associated with the semantic templates associated with both meanings.

According to Carter (1988), Rappaport Hovav and Levin (1995b), Talmy (1985), and others, French differs from English in both respects. On the basis of examples like (3), they claim that French does not allow a manner of motion verb to appear with a goal phrase, and therefore the verb cannot receive an Accomplishment interpretation. Although (3a) is ambiguous in English, allowing either an Activity or an Accomplishment interpretation, its French equivalent in (3b) has only the Activity interpretation.

(3)   a. The mouse is running under the table.   (ambiguous)
       b. La souris court sous la table.   (non-PATH only)

Another preposition, *dans* 'in', also gives an Activity-only reading with this class of verbs:

(4)   La souris danse dans la maison.
       'The mouse is dancing in/*into the house.'

(3b) and (4) seem to show that French verbs of manner of motion only have a meaning comparable to the Activity sense of English verbs of manner of motion. However, there are in fact two ways in which French verbs can receive an Accomplishment reading: (i) the nonagentive manner of motion verbs encode both PATH and MANNER; (ii) a PATH meaning can be contributed by a PATH preposition.

2.1 Verbs incorporating manner and path

Contrary to the claim that French verbs of motion cannot incorporate both MANNER and PATH, nonagentive verbs are change of location verbs with the representation in (2b). In (5), the PATH meaning comes not from the preposition *dans* (as in (4)), but from the verb *rouler* itself.

(5)   La balle a roulé dans la boîte.
       'The ball rolled into the box.'

Other verbs in this nonagentive class include *basculer* 'topple over'/'tip over', *débouler* 'roll down', and *dégringoler* 'tumble down'.

(6)   Claude a basculé dans le trou.
       'Claude toppled over in/into the hole.'

(7)   Les ordures déboulèrent de la boîte métallique.
       'The trash rolled down from the metal box.'

(Queneau in *Le Petit Robert*)

(8)   Claude a dégringolé du toit.
       'Claude tumbled down from the roof.'

2.2   Path Prepositions

While manner of motion verbs normally have only MANNER readings, a PATH reading can be forced by adding a prepositional phrase that unambiguously denotes PATH—e.g., *vers* 'towards', *à travers* 'through'. Consider the examples in (9–10):

(9)   a. Le poisson a nagé vers la rive.
          'The fish swam towards the river bank.'
       b. L'enfant a couru vers sa mère.
          'The child ran towards her mother.'

(10)   a. Le poisson a nagé à travers la chute d'eau.
          'The fish swam through the waterfall.'
       b. L'oiseau a volé à travers le feuillage.
          'The bird flew through the foliage.'

In addition, the examples in (10) falsify the standard claim in the literature that French manner of motion verbs cannot occur with goal phrases to give Accomplishment readings. Rappaport Hovav and Levin (1995b) and Talmy (1985), among others, argue that in French, the sense conveyed by the English Accomplishment uses of verbs of manner of motion cannot be expressed by the addition of a goal phrase to a verb of manner of motion, and that such meanings can only be expressed periphrastically, as in (11) and (12) (taken from Rappaport Hovav and Levin (1995b:10)).

(11)   a. Blériot flew across the Channel.
       b. Blériot traversa la Manche en avion.
          'Blériot crossed the Channel by plane.'

(12)   a. An old woman hobbled in from the back.
      b. Une vieille femme arriva en boîtant de l'arrière-boutique.
      'An old woman arrived limping from the back-store.'

According to them, these examples illustrate that in French, the manner of motion is typically expressed in a subordinate clause or adverbial phrase, and the goal of motion is expressed through the use of the appropriate verb of directed motion as the main verb. They thus conclude that English manner of motion constants can be associated with both Activity and Accomplishment lexical semantic templates, while French allows such constants to be associated only with Activity templates.

However, the examples in (10) do have an Accomplishment reading. This is because when the Object of the preposition is interpreted as a barrier, *à travers* is equivalent to English *through*, indicating movement 'into at one side or point and out at another, and especially the opposite side' (*Webster*), that is, it has a clear PATH (change of location) meaning. We claim that the preposition itself contributes the Accomplishment interpretation, by expressing the BECOME predicate in the Accomplishment template. Prepositions like *dans* 'in', *sous* 'under' and *sur* 'on', on the other hand, only have location meanings, and therefore cannot express the BECOME predicate.

However, if the Object of the preposition *à travers* is not interpretable as a barrier, then the Accomplishment reading is anomalous (13).

(13)   a.#L'enfant a couru à travers la pièce.
       'The child ran across the room.'

     b.#La souris a dansé à travers la pièce.
       'The mouse danced across the room.'

We have shown that given the appropriate types of prepositions (i.e. those with inherent PATH readings), some manner of motion verbs in French do behave like their English counterparts. The examples considered by previous authors (11–12) are simply not the relevant cases.

Bouchard (1995:191) makes the same point, using the examples in (14–15). In French the non-PATH reading is preferred when manner of motion verbs combine with neutral prepositional phrases (see (14a)) unlike their English counterparts (14b). But the same French verbs are good under a PATH reading when combined with directional prepositional phrases (15a), just like their English equivalents (15b):

(14)   a. Marie a flotté sous le pont.   (non-PATH only)
      b. Mary floated under the bridge.   (ambiguous)

(15) a. Ophélie a flotté vers/jusqu'à Hamlet.   (PATH only)
      b. Ophelia floated toward/up to Hamlet.   (PATH only)

This reinforces our point that the PATH prepositions contribute an Accomplishment reading for manner of motion verbs.

To summarize, Accomplishment readings in French are not the result of template augmentation from an Activity. Either the PATH preposition or the verb has to encode the PATH meaning, and this is what expresses the BECOME predicate in the Accomplishment template.

3   Resultatives

In the discussion of why French has only non-path meanings for manner of motion verbs occurring with prepositions like *sous* 'under' and *dans* 'in', we did not base our analysis on the idea that while English prepositions like *under* optionally encode path, the French ones do not. Instead, we argued for an explanation based on the lack of template augmentation for French verbs. We will show here that the facts from resultative constructions further support our analysis, but remain unexplained if we assume an analysis based on preposition ambiguity, since resultative constructions do not involve prepositions.

We have already shown that PATH prepositions can properly identify the subevent of BECOME AT LOCATION. Here, we look at the resultative construction as another instance of template augmentation. Resultative constructions are analyzed as Accomplishments with a complex event structure (see Dowty 1979, Pustejovsky 1992, Rappaport Hovav and Levin 1995b, Van Valin 1993). The resultative template is composed of a basic Activity template (as in (16)) that is augmented to give an Accomplishment template with a resultant state predicate (17):

(16) [x ACT]

(17) [[x ACT] CAUSE [y BECOME STATE]]

Following Levin and Rappaport Hovav (1995), we assume that the expression of a verb's arguments does not change with the addition of a resultative phrasal category. So each resultative construction must simultaneously meet two requirements on argument expression: (i) the verb's arguments must be expressed according to the lexical specifications of the verb and in accordance with the general linking rules; (ii) the NP denoting the entity that changes state is semantically unrestricted[3] (see Bresnan and Zaenen (1990)).

Resultative constructions involving Activity verbs are found in English, but are unavailable in French. We argue that French has no

---

[3] The "unrestricted" feature allows Objects of (active) transitive verbs, and Subjects of passive and unaccusative verbs to be arguments of the resultative predicate.

resultatives because it does not allow an extension of an Activity verb to one of causative change of state, while English does. We will show why an alternative account in terms of syntactic restrictions is implausible.

A regular resultative construction such as (18) is impossible in French (see (19)).

(18)   Pat wiped the table clean.

(19)   *Claude a essuyé la table propre.
       'Claude wiped the table clean.'

We claim that (19) is ungrammatical because French cannot augment the Activity template to an Accomplishment, as in (20).

(20)   [[x ACT$_{<WIPE>}$ y] CAUSE [y BECOME < CLEAN >]]

In order to express the result that the table becomes clean from wiping, French uses subordinate clause structures:[4]

(21)   a.   Dominique a essuyé la table ce qui l'a rendue propre.
            'Dominique wiped the table which caused it to be clean.'
       b.   La table est devenue propre suite à son essuyage par Alex.
            'The table became clean following its wiping by Alex.'

In (21a), the causation event—wiping 'caused' the table to become clean—is subordinated, and is expressed by the verb *rendre* 'render' (in the sense of 'cause to become'). In (21b), the wiping event is subordinated, and the change of state—'becoming clean'—is overtly expressed by the verb *devenir* 'become'. So French does not allow a resultative construction of the type in (18), where an Activity verb extends its meaning to include a meaning of causative change of state.

One hypothesis to account for the absence of resultative constructions could be that French has the same result state template as English, but it disallows predication (by some predicate other than the main verb) in general, and thus has no syntactic means of expressing the English equivalent of a resultative construction. This hypothesis is untenable, however, for the following reasons.

One, French allows *depictive* predication, as the examples in (22) show.

(22)   a.   Camille est arrivée fatiguée.
            'Camille arrived tired.' (i.e., Camille was tired when she arrived.)
       d.   L'ours a mangé le gruau chaud.
            'The bear ate the oatmeal hot.'

---

[4] These sentences are awkward translations of the English resultatives in the first place.

Two, verbs that inherently denote causative changes of state can take resultant predicates. A construction syntactically similar to (18) is possible with a verb like *rendre* 'render':

(23)   Claude a rendu les enfants heureux/célèbres.
       'Claude has made the children happy/famous.'

(Adapted from *The Oxford-Hachette French Dictionary*)

Rendre is the lexicalization of the semantic predicates ACT, CAUSE and BECOME. So it is a verb that is associated only to the Accomplishment template. The STATE predicate, on the other hand, has to be overtly instantiated by a primitive constant such as the adjective *lugubre* 'gloomy'.

Other verbs with inherent causation include *changer* 'change', *métamorphoser* 'metamorphose', *transformer* 'transform', and they also allow resultant predication.

(24)   a.   La sorcière a changé le prince en crapaud.
            'The witch turned the prince into a toad.'
       b.   Zeus métamorphosa Niobé en rocher.
            'Zeus metamorphosed Niobe into a rock.' (*Hachette*)
       c.   Claude a transformé le garage en bureau.
            'Claude transformed/converted the garage into an office.'

What the causative examples show is that French allows an Accomplishment template with resultant state predicates when the verb itself incorporates the semantic primitives CAUSE and BECOME. The adjective merely identifies the predicate STATE. We argue that resultative constructions are not allowed in French because they involve the extension of an Activity verb to one of causative change of state (incorporating CAUSE BECOME). English, on the other hand, allows this extension of meaning.

We have seen that in cases where there is no template augmentation, and no extension of verb meaning in French (e.g., in depictive predication), predication works. We would also expect predicate modification, which does not involve an extension of verb meaning, to be possible in French, just like in English. This is indeed the case. In examples (25) and (26), verbs like *break* and *casser* are Accomplishment verbs with the representation given in (27). In these examples, the prepositional phrases merely modify the broken state of the Object.

(25)   a. Pat broke the mirror into a million pieces.
       b. Pat folded the scarf in four.

(26)   a. Claude a cassé la branche en trois morceaux.
          'Claude broke the branch into three pieces.'

b. Claude a plié le mouchoir en deux/en carré.
'Claude folded the handkerchief in two/into a square.'

(27) [[x ACT] CAUSE [BECOME [y < BROKEN >]]]

4 Conclusion

To conclude, we have argued that the difference between English and French resides in the possibility of extending Activity templates to Accomplishments. From the evidence provided by verbs participating in locative and resultative predications, we have shown that French only allows Accomplishment readings where either the verb or the location predicate inherently encode the BECOME predicate in the Accomplishment template. On the other hand, English allows an Activity verb to extend its meaning to incorporate the BECOME predicate in the Accomplishment reading.

Acknowledgements

We thank Raymond de Vré, Louise Lavoie, and Marc Therrien for language consultation. We are grateful to Joan Bresnan, Eve Clark, Martina Faller, Brett Kessler, Paul Kiparsky, Scott Schwenter, Peter Sells, and Henriëtte de Swart for help, comments, and discussion.

References

Bouchard, Denis. 1995. *The Semantics of Syntax: A minimalist approach to grammar.* Chicago: University of Chicago Press.

Bresnan, Joan, and Annie Zaenen. 1990. Deep unaccusativity in LFG. In *Grammatical Relations: A cross-theoretical perspective,* ed. Katarzyna Dziwirek, Patrick Farrell, and Errapel Mejías-Bikandi. 45–57. Stanford: CSLI.

Carter, Richard J. 1988. Compositionality and polysemy. In *On linking: Papers by Richard Carter,* ed. Beth Levin and Carol Tenny. 167–204. Cambridge: Center for Cognitive Science, MIT.

Dowty, David. 1979. *Word meaning and Montague grammar.* Dordrecht: Reidel.

Goldberg, Adele E. 1995. *Constructions: A Construction Grammar approach to argument structure.* Chicago: University of Chicago Press.

Hoekstra, T. 1992. Aspect and theta theory. In *Thematic structure: Its role in grammar,* ed. I.M. Roca. 145–174. Berlin: Foris.

Hoekstra, Teun. 1984. *Transitivity.* Dordrecht: Foris.

Jackendoff, Ray. 1990. *Semantic Structure.* Cambridge, MA: MIT Press.

Levin, Beth, and Malka Rappaport Hovav. 1992. The lexical semantics of verbs of motion: The perspective from unaccusativity. In *Thematic structure: Its role in grammar*, ed. I.M. Roca. 247–269. Berlin: Foris.

Levin, Beth, and Malka Rappaport Hovav. 1995. *Unaccusativity: At the syntax-lexical semantics interface*. Cambridge, MA: MIT Press.

Pinker, Steven. 1989. *Learnability and cognition*. Cambridge, MA: MIT Press.

Pustejovsky, James. 1992. The syntax of event structure. In *Lexical and conceptual semantics*, ed. Beth Levin and Steven Pinker. Cambridge, Mass.: Blackwell.

Rappaport Hovav, Malka, and Beth Levin. 1995a. The elasticity of verb meaning. Paper presented at the DLG workshop on argument structure, Goettingen, Germany, Winter 1995.

Rappaport Hovav, Malka, and Beth Levin. 1995b. Morphology and lexical semantics. To appear in *Handbook of Morphology*, ed. Arnold Zwicky and Andrew Spencer. Oxford: Blackwell.

Rappaport Hovav, Malka, and Beth Levin. 1996. Building Verb Meanings. ms., Bar Ilan University and Northwestern University.

Slobin, Dan I. 1996. Two Ways to Travel: Verbs of Motion in English and Spanish. In *Grammatical Constructions: Their Form and Meaning*, ed. Masayoshi Shibatani and Sandra A. Thompson. Oxford: Clarendon Press.

Slobin, Dan I., and Nini Hoiting. 1994. Reference to movement in spoken and signed languages: typological considerations. *Proceedings of BLS 20* 487–505.

Talmy, Leonard. 1985. Lexicalisation patterns: Semantic structure in lexical forms. In *Language typology and syntactic description, Vol. 3: Grammatical categories and the lexicon*, ed. T. Schopen. 57–149. Cambridge: Cambridge University Press.

Talmy, Leonard. 1991. Path to realization: A typology of event conflation. *Proceedings of the Annual Meeting of the Berkeley Linguistic Society* 7:480–519.

Van Valin, Robert D. Jr. 1990. Semantic parameters of split intransitivity. *Language* 66:221–260.

Van Valin, Robert D. Jr. 1993. A synopsis of Role and Reference Grammar. In *Advances in Role and Reference Grammar*, ed. Robert D. Jr. Van Valin. 1–164. Amsterdam: John Benjamins.

Vendler, Zeno. 1957. Verbs and times. *Philosophical Review* 56:143–160.

Verkuyl, Henk. 1972. *On the compositional nature of the aspects*. Dordrecht: Reidel.

Verkuyl, Henk. 1993. *A theory of aspectuality.* Cambridge: Cambridge University Press.

Semantic Principles of Predication

ADELE E. GOLDBERG

University of California, San Diego

1 Introduction

This paper addresses the question of what types of events can be construed together to form a single semantic predication.[1] By a "single semantic predication," I intend a unitary grammatical expression of an action, state or combination thereof applied to a single argument. Three different cases are discussed: subevents evoked by a single verb, events evoked by the combination of a verb's lexical semantics and the semantics of a clause-level construction, and finally, the events designated by conjuncts in principled violations of the coordinate structure constraint. It is argued that each of these three types of predications shows a strikingly similar set of possible relations and thus leads us toward a general theory of cognitively plausible predication structures.

2 Individual Lexical Items

One proposal for a constraint on the possible semantics of verbs comes from Croft (to appear:20), who proposes that "a possible verb must have a continuous segment of the causal chain in the event ICM as its profile and as its base." That is, verbs are claimed to only evoke (and designate) two subevents if the two subevents are directly causally related.

In order to explore this claim, we need to address two definitional issues. First is the question of what should count as distinct subevents within a

---

[1] I would like to thank Michael Israel, Bill Morris, Mark Turner, an anonymous reviewer for this volume, and the audience at CSDL II for helpful comments on this topic.

lexical item's designation, and second is the issue of what should count as a causal relationship.[2]

It is not always obvious what should count as a distinct subevent in a lexical item's designation. For example, do we construe *saute* as designating two events "heat with a small amount of fat" and "stir" or only one? How do we decide? We cannot use the fact that a word can be paraphrased with a single verb as the criterion without begging the question: can a single verb designate two causally unrelated events?

It is likewise not clear when we construe a causal relationship to exist. For example, does being genetically predisposed for some disease cause the disease if not everyone who has the predisposition ends up with the disease?

These issues have been debated for centuries, and the lack of concensous casts some doubt on the idea that there exist necessary and sufficient conditions for deciding either of these two questions. Given present day theories of categorization, it is in fact not clear that we should expect such necessary and sufficient conditions in this domain (Croft 1991; Espenson 1991). In any case, I do not attempt to fully resolve these questions here, but I think some progress can be made on the present topic by considering cases that are rather clearcut.

For present purposes I will assume conservatively, that a verb is construed to involve two subevents if and only if there are two independently describable aspects of what is designated by the verb that do not entirely overlap in their temporal dimension:

> Two events e_1 and e_2 are distinct subevents of an event E designated by a verb V, iff $E \rightarrow e_1$ & e_2, and e1 is not completely within the temporal extent of e_2.

According to this definition, *saute* is construed as only designating one event since the two aspects of heating and stirring overlap temporally such that the stirring is completely within the temporal duration of the heating. That is, while it is certainly possible to continue stirring after the heating is finished, such continued stirring is not implied by the sauteing event.

On the question of causality, I will consider any event that is sufficient to lead to a new state or event to be a cause. That is, if an event, e_1 is sufficient to lead to a second event or state, e_2, then I will assume that e_1 causes e_2. I will not consider necessary conditions causal unless they are also sufficient. According to this definition, being predisposed for some disease does not strictly speaking cause the disease since, while it may turn out to be a necessary condition, it is by hypothesis, not a sufficient condition.

Verbs which designate both an activity and the endstate of that activity–

---

[2]Here an below I am referring to what are construed to be two events and what is construed to be a causal relation, not the more philosphical and probably unanswerable question of what an event or a causal relation really is in the world.

Dowty's (1979) *accomplishments*–can be classified as having two subevents that are causally related. The activity and the resulting state are considered two distinct subevents because the resulting state does not completely overlap temporally with the activity. Examples include *strangle*, "to squeeze someone's neck until death" and *fill* "to infuse until full." This analysis of accomplishments and achievements is in accord with longstanding and widespread assumptions about this type of predicate (see e.g. Gruber 1965; McCawley 1968; Dowty 1979; Pustejovsky 1991; Grimshaw & Vikner 1993; Hovav & Levin 1996.) The two subevents are related causally because the activity is sufficient to bring about the change of state.

Lexical accomplishment verbs clearly follow the generalization that individual lexical items evoke causally linked subevents. However, a close look at certain lexical items suggests that the generalization does not always hold.

2.1 Preconditions in a Semantic Frame

Consider the verb *appeal* as in:

(1)   The lawyer appealed the case.

This verb presupposes the existence of a previous complex event involving a trial which resulted in a guilty verdict, and asserts a subsequent act of filing legal papers for the purpose of a retrial. The two subevents are not causally related: one does not cause the other, nor vice versa.

The verb *appeal* evokes a complex frame in the sense of Fillmore (1975, 1982, 1985) or idealized cognitive model (ICM) in the sense of Lakoff (1987). A verbal frame is an idealized cognitive model based on the recurrence of one or more events or states in human experience. We have as part of our world knowledge the understanding that trials which result in guilty verdicts may be retried; *appeal* gives a name to this complex frame of experience, foregrounding or asserting the filing of legal papers. Other examples can be found as well. Two general classes of such verbs include verbs that are prefixed with *pre-*, and those that are prefixed with *re-*. For example, *preview* designates an event of viewing while presupposing another subsequent public event of viewing. The first viewing event does not cause and is not caused by the later viewing event. *Reconsider* designates an act of considering, while presupposing a previous act of considering. *Reattach* presupposes both a previous state of attachment, and an intermediate event of detachment. The final change of state involving becoming attached is asserted. Table 1 summarizes the events evoked by these verbs:

	Asserted	Presupposed Event
appeal	to file for retrial	after court case was lost
preview	to view	before a subsequent (public) viewing
reconsider	to consider	after previous act of considering
reattach	to attach	after initial attachment, detachment

Table 1. Verbs that evoke complex frames

These verbs assert one subevent and presuppose another, without a causal relation between the two. Instead, we can view the presupposed subevent as a *precondition* of the asserted event.

2.2 Negation of an aspect of a frame

Other lexical items designate the denial of an implication in an idealized cognitive model. For example the verb *stiff*, as in *to stiff a waiter* means "to fail to tip after eating a meal at a restaurant." The ICM of eating at a restaurant implies that a tip is left at the end of the meal, but this verb serves to contradict that implication. There are two distinct subevents involved: a presupposed event of eating a meal at a restaurant, and an asserted event involving the diners failing to leave a tip. Again the two events are not causally related: the eating of the meal does not cause and is not caused by the failure to tip. Another example is *betray* which evokes the semantic frame of individuals being in a state of sharing a trusting relationship, when at some point an individual acts in an unexpected and hurtful way. In these cases, the verbs designate the denial of an aspect of an idealized cognitive model. In the case of *stiff* the restaurant ICM is evoked; in the case of *betray* an ICM involving how people are expected to act in a trusting relationship is evoked. Other examples like these cases include:

	Asserted	Presupposed Precondition
stiff	to fail to tip	after eating at a restaurant
betray	to fail or desert someone	after having the person's trust
renege	to change one's mind	after promising to do something
miscarry	to spontaneously abort	after becoming pregnant

Table 2. Verbs that specify the failure to satisfy an ICM

2.3 Summary

To summarize, as observed by Croft, many verbs designate causally linked subevents (*strangle, fill,* etc). Tables 1 and 2, however, provide examples that do not involve a causal sequence of subevents. Table 1 consists of cases in which the verb involves a sequence of subevents in an idealized cognitive model (e.g., *appeal, preview, reconsider, reattach*). In these cases, one subevent acts as a precondition for another asserted subevent. Table 2 provides examples in which the scenerio designated by the verb designates the violation of some part of an idealized cognitive model (*stiff, betray, renege, miscarry*).

The question may arise as to what types of subevents are not possible aspects of a single verb's designation. Croft (1991) offers the example of "spinning and getting hot" as an impossible meaning for a verb. Of course such a meaning is only impossible if there is no semantic frame that relates these two events. If we imagine some kind of superstitious ritual in which a ball is spun rapidly on a turn table in an oven until the ball bursts (the time until bursting taken to indicate, for example, the length of a pregnancy), then it is not hard to imagine giving a name to this process, e.g. *The guru hotspun the ball*. What are not allowed to become subevents within a single word's designation are two or more subevents that are not related by a semantic frame. The frame can relate the two events by a causal connection, by a simple juxtaposition found with some regularity, or by serving as a counterfactual for what is asserted by the verb.

In the following section, a second case is examined; this case involves a slightly more elaborate instance of predication than that of the individual verb in isolation. In particular, the combination of the event designated by the verb and that designated by the construction is considered.

3   Predications designated by Verb and Construction

There is a growing consensus among many researchers that it is important to distinguish a verb's inherent or "core" lexical semantics from the semantics associated with the grammatical structures in which the verb can occur (Goldberg 1992a, 1992b, 1995, 1997; Pinker 1994; Fauconnier & Turner 1994, 1996; Mandelblit 1995; Fillmore & Kay 1995; Hovav & Levin, 1996). The way I have discussed this idea is that the simple sentence types are directly correlated with semantic structures. For example, in English we find the following correspondences:[3]

Ditransitive:	Subj V Obj1 Obj2	X CAUSES Y to RECEIVE Z
Caused-Motion:	Subj V Obj Obl	X CAUSES to MOVE Z
Resultative:	Subj V Obj Pred	X CAUSES Y to BECOME Z
Transitive:	Subj V Obj	X ACTS ON Y;
		X EXPERIENCES Y

Table 3.

---

[3] The form of constructions is defined in terms of grammatical relations in order to abstract over the linear order of constituents. For example, I assume the same ditransitive construction is involved when it is questioned, e.g. *What did Pat give Chris?* or clefted, e.g. *It was a book that Pat gave Chris.* I should also note that the constructional semantics given in Table 3 is somewhat oversimplified, since one formal pattern is typically polysemous and occasionally ambiguous (See Goldberg 1995 for discussion).

See Goldberg (1995) for motivation for this distinction between lexical and constructional meaning. If we assume this distinction for a moment, it makes sense to ask whether the range of possible semantic relationships between the event designated by the verb and the event designated by the construction display similar characteristics to those we saw for subevents within a single lexical item's designation.

It is clear that the most common case is one in which the verb and the construction do not designate two separate events. Rather the verb serves to lexically code or elaborate the event that the construction designates. For example, if we assume that the ditransitive construction has roughly the meaning of transfer, "X CAUSES Y to RECEIVE Z" then it is clear that the verb *give* lexically codes this meaning. The verbs *hand* and *mail* lexically elaborate, or further specify, this meaning. More interestingly for the present purposes are cases wherein the verb does not itself lexically designate the meaning associated with the construction, in which case we have two distinguishable events.[4]

3.1 Causal Relations

Talmy (1985) has noted that a common pattern in English, Chinese, and Dutch is that the verb can code the means of achieving the act designated by the construction. This is the case in each of the following examples:

(2)   a. Amy kicked Paul the ball.
      b. Elena sneezed the foam off the cappuccino. (Ahrens 1995)
      c. Ken wrote his way to fame and fortune.

Kicking is the means of achieving transfer; sneezing is the means of achieving caused-motion; and writing is the means of achieving metaphorical motion.

Pinker (1989) discusses the following example from Talmy (1985):

(3)   The bottle floated into the cave.

He notes that this sentence is not felicitous in the situation in which the bottle is carried into the cave in a bowl of water. It is only acceptable in the case that the floating is the means of the bottle moving into the cave.

Croft (1991) similarly observes the difference in the following two examples:

(4)   a. The boat sailed into the cave
      b. *The boat burned into the cave.

---

[4]I do not rely in this case on the before mentioned criterion for determining distinct events. In particular, the events may be temporally coextensive in some cases. It is clear we have distinguishable events if we assume one is designated by the verb and another by the construction.

He notes that (5a) is acceptable because sailing is the means by which the the boat moves into the cave; (5b) is not acceptable because the burning is not the means of effecting motion.[5]

There are other ways that verbs' designations may be causally related to the meanings of constructions: the verb may code an instrument or the result as well as the means.

(5)   a. Arther wristed the ball over the net.
        (the wrist is the instrument of the caused motion)
      b. The train screeched into the station.
        (the sound is the result of the motion)

Therefore, as we saw was the case with lexical accomplishment verbs, it is possible to combine two subevents into a single predication if a causal relation holds between the two subevents.

In addition, there are certain cases, some of which were previously mentioned in Goldberg (1995), that involve relationships other than causally related ones. The cases discussed in sections 3.2 and 3.3 are strikingly parallel to the types of non-causal relationships we saw for individual verbs in sections 2.1 and 2.2, respectively.

3.2   Precondition in Semantic Frame

If we assume that the ditransitive construction has roughly the meaning of transfer, i.e., "X CAUSES Y to RECEIVE Z" (e.g., Goldberg 1992b), then we find that this construction allows the verb to designate a precondition of transfer, namely, the creation or preparation of the transferred entity. For example:

(6)   Dave baked Elena a cake.

Here the preparation of the cake is a precondition for Dave's transferring the cake to Elena. Transferring something from an agent to a recipient is associated with a certain frame of semantic knowledge. In particular, we know that what is transferred from one person to another is often prepared for that purpose. The preparation or creation of the transferred entity can thus be viewed as a salient action within our frame semantic knowledge of transferring.

Interestingly, for many speakers, the verb does not designate a precondition as readily in other English constructions. For example, for a theme to move in a direction requires the precondition that the theme be free of physical restraints. In the following construction which designates caused motion, the verb designates the precondition of removing constraints that

---

[5]These cases were what led Croft to propose that lexical items only designate causally linked events. However these cases are treated here as combinations of verb and constructional meaning.

Example 5b is acceptable on the interpretation that the boat's image became engraved on the cave by burning. This interpretation is predicted to be acceptable since the burning is in that case the cause of the boat's image being on the cave.

will enable motion. However, judgments on the following examples vary, with speakers ranging from finding them fully acceptable to clearly unacceptable:

(7) a. % The warden freed the prisoner into the city.
     b. % Pat unleashed the dog into the yard.

The reason that the precondition of preparation in the scene of transfer may be more available than the precondition that restraints be removed in the scene of caused motion may be simply that preparation preceding transfer may be a more frequent occurrence in our experience than removal of restraints enabling motion. In transferring something from one person to another it often happens that the transferred goods have to be prepared or created for the purpose. On the other hand, it is generally not necessary to remove any restraints before causing an entity to move: most entities that might move are relatively unrestrained.

3.3 Negation of an aspect of a frame

In certain cases, the verb may specify that the scene designated by the central sense of the construction does not hold. For example, again assuming the ditransitive construction designates roughly "X CAUSES Y to RECEIVE Z," the verbs in the following serve to deny that entailment:

(8) a. Pat denied Chris a popsicle.
     b. Pat refused Chris a kiss.

This is also possible in the caused-motion construction, the basic sense of the construction being "X CAUSES Y to MOVE Z." Example (10) entails that Pat caused Chris not to move into the room, thereby negating the entailment of motion associated with the construction.

(9) Pat locked Chris out of the room.

A parallel possibility exists with the transitive construction. If we take the relevant constructional sense to be "X ACTS ON Y", the following verbs serve to negate the meaning of the construction:

(10) a. Pat ignored Chris.
      b. Adam resisted the marshmellows.

3.4 Co-occurring activity

Finally, there exists a case which involves a relation between events that does not parallel the cases we saw for lexical items. The *way* construction for some speakers allows the verb to designate a a co-occurring activity that is not related to the action designated by the construction in any of the above-mentioned ways (see Levin & Rapoport 1988, Jackendoff 1990, Goldberg 1995 for discussion of this construction). For example,

(11) (%) "He seemed to be **whistling** his way along." (Oxford University Press Corpus)

Interestingly, this case is less than fully robust and is not possible for all speakers. Still, it should be noted that a subset of speakers who accept (12) find the same relation possible with the intransitive motion construction:

(12)   %He whistled out of the room.

However, notice a co-occurring activity is not generally possible wth all constructions. For example, I have found no speakers who accept the following expressions involving the resultative (14) or ditransitive (15) constructions:

(13)   *She whistled the metal flat.
       (to mean, she caused the metal to become flat while whistling)

(14)   *She whistled him a box.
       (to mean, she gave him a box while whistling.

4   Syntactically Complex but Semantically Unitary Predications

It turns out that there is another type of predication that is semantically unitary although syntactically complex: the case of certain syntactic conjunctions that form single predications. That is, as Ross (1967) noted, there exist coordinate structures that do not obey the Coordinate Structure Constraint (see also Goldsmith 1985; Lakoff 1986; Culicover & Jackendoff 1995). For example,

(15)   What did you go to the store and buy?

Notice that there is nothing "extracted" from the first conjunct, *go to the store*, although there is something extracted from the second conjunct, *buy [ ]*. As Lakoff, Deane, and Culicover & Jackendoff have noted, there is a sense in which the conjuncts form a semantically unitary predication although they are syntactically complex.

Interestingly, Lakoff describes three distinct cases in which such violations of the coordinate structure constraint are possible. Examples of each of the three are described below.

4.1   Causal Relations

There exist violations of the coordinate structure constraint that involve conjuncts which are causally related. For example:

(16)   a. Who did he go berserk and start shooting at? (Deane 1991:24)
       b. That's the stuff that the guys in the Caucasus drink and live to
          be a hundred. (Lakoff 1986)

See also Culicover and Jackendoff (1995). These are cases which Lakoff refers to as Type III. These cases are analogous to the accomplishment verbs such as *strangle, fill,* etc. as well as to the cases in which the verb designates a causal aspect of the frame designated by the construction as discussed in section 3.1.

4.2 Preconditions in a semantic frame

Consider the following violations of the coordinate structure constraint:

(17)   a. Who did he grab his pen and write to?
       b. Who did he pick up the phone and call?
       c. Who did he open his arms wide and hug? (Deane 1991:23)

Lakoff describes this type of exception as involving a natural sequence of events. For example, picking up a pen and writing a letter constitutes a sequence of events in the certain semantic frame of knowledge. What is intriguing is that this case is analogous to the lexical examples in Table 1 (e.g. *appeal, preview, reattach*) and the constructional cases involving verbs of creation in the ditransitive construction (*Pat baked him a cake*). Recall that the previous examples also involved a series of events linked by an Idealized Cognitive Model. In these cases as in the lexical and constructional cases, one subevent is a precondition for a distinct asserted event. As Deane (1991) points out, the first conjunct in each of the examples in (20) designates a "preparatory action" or a precondition. For example in (20a), going to the store is a precondition for buying something in the ICM of shopping; in (20b), taking a pen is a precondition for writing a letter; in (20c), opening one's arms wide is a precondition for hugging.[6]

4.3 The denial of an implication of a frame

Another type of violation of the coordinate structure constraint involves examples such as the following:

(18)   a. How much can you drink and still stay sober?
       b. How small a meal can you eat and feel satisfied?

These are Lakoff's Type II cases, and they involve the negation of a final aspect of an idealized cognitive model. That is, we have frame semantic knowledge that tells us that drinking causes us to get drunk; drinking and staying sober violates this implication. Similarly, we know we may not feel satisfied if we don't eat enough food; the suggestion that a small meal be eaten and be satsifying negates the implication of our frame semantic knowledge.

These cases are analagous to the lexical examples in Table 2 (*stiff, betray, dissemble, renege, miscarry*), and the constructional examples 9-11 (e.g., *She denied him a popsicle*). In all of these cases, certain events are presupposed while the denial of an aspect of the ICM is asserted.

---

[6] These cases are not uniformly necessary preconditions, of course, since it is possible to buy things by telephone or mail, and it is possible to write letters on the computer or by dictation. However, these are preconditions in an Idealized Cognitive Model of how shopping or letter-writing are often done.

4.4 Discussion

We have seen that the semantic generalizations about semantically complex lexical items, the generalizations about the range of relations between verb and construction, and the generalizations about which kinds of coordinate structures can violate the coordinate structure constraint show striking parallels. All three cases all the following three possibilities: 1) a causally related sequence of events, 2) a sequence of events which constitute an ICM in which one or more events are backgrounded or presupposed, or 3) a sequence of events in which one aspect of an ICM is negated.

The parallel between the lexical facts, the facts relating verb and construction, and the facts about the types of violations of the coordinate structure constraint is not accidental. Lakoff states the explanation of what types of phrases can be involved in coordinate structure violations in terms of a Predication Condition: the coordinated structure must be construable as predicating something of the isolated element (the filler) (see also Deane 1991, Kluender 1992). Thus the three generalizations are mutually reinforcing and serve to help form an empirical foundation for what types of scenarios can count as legitimate predications.

5 Other places to look

Other domains in which to look for a similar pattern include serial verbs and other complex predicates. An initial look indicates that a similar pattern can be found. Focusing on related issues in Alamblak, Bruce (1988) observes:

> "Serialization of roots in a verb stem is restricted to sequences of events which are commonly associated culturally or for which there is a cultural basis or pragmatic reason for their close association."

This quote indicates the necessity of a semantic frame in the sense discussed above. Bruce also specifically mentions a causal relation as a prototypical subtype of serial verb, a relation that is common in serial verbs cross linguistically.

Finally, while serial verbs are often largly inseparable, negative morphemes typically can intervene between individual verbs. This fact indicates that the negation of an aspect of a frame is a possibility for single predications designated by serial verbs as we saw was the case for the other unitary predications already discussed.

6 Conclusion

This paper has explored the question of what constitutes the range of legitimate semantic predications. In particular, we have considered three types of predications:

a. Subevents evoked by a single verb,

b. Events evoked by combination of verb and constructional semantics,

c. Events designated by conjuncts which violate the coordinate structure constraint

All three cases have been found to involve strikingly similar possibilities:

1. a causally related sequence of events,

2. a sequence of events constituting an ICM (one or more events may be presupposed),

3. a sequence of events in which one aspect of an ICM is negated

One interpretation of the findings presented here goes beyond the linguistic generalization to provide a more general foundation for what kinds of subevents can be united semantically to be construed as a single complex event.

7 References

Ahrens, Kathleen. 1995. The Mental Representation of Verbs. University of California, San Diego dissertation.

Bruce, Les. 1988. Serialization: From Syntax to Lexicon. *Studies in Language* 21-1. 19-49.

Clark, Eve V. and Herb H. Clark. 1979. When nouns surface as verbs. *Language*.

Croft, William. 1991. *Syntactic Categories and Grammatical Relations.* Chicago: University of Chicago Press.

Croft, William. to appear. Event Structure in Argument Linking. In *Projecting from the Lexicon* (eds) Miriam Butt and Wilhelm Gender. CSLI Publications.

Culicover, Peter and Ray Jackendoff. 1995. Semantic Subordination Despite Syntactic Coordination. Ms. Ohio State University and Brandeis University.

Deane, Paul. 1991. Limits to Attention: A Cognitive Theory of Island Phenomena. *Cognitive Linguistics* Vol 2-1.

Dowty, David 1979. *Word Meaning and Montague Grammar.* Dordrecht: Reidel.

Espenson, Jane. 1991. Metaphors of Causation. Ms. UC Berkeley.

Fauconnier, Gilles and Mark Turner. 1994. Conceptual Projection and Middle Spaces. UCSD Cognitive Science Report 9401.

Fauconnier, Gilles and Mark Turner. 1996. Blending as a Central Process in Grammar. In A. Goldberg (ed) *Conceptual Structure, Discourse and Language.* Stanford, CA: CSLI Publications.

Fillmore, Charles. 1975. An Alternative to Checklist Theories of Meaning. *BLS 1.*

Fillmore, Charles J. 1982. Frame Semantics. *Linguistics in the Morning Calm*, 111-138. Seoul: Hanshin.

Fillmore, Charles J. 1985. Frames and the Semantics of Understanding. *Quaderni di Semantica 6 2.* 222-53.

Fillmore, Charles J and Paul Kay. 1995. Construction Grammar. Manuscript. UC Berkeley.

Goldberg, Adele E. 1992a. Argument Structure Constructions. University of California, Berkeley dissertation.

Goldberg, Adele E. 1992b. The Inherent Semantics of Argument Structure: The Case of the English Ditransitive Construction. *Cognitive Linguistics.*

Goldberg, Adele E. 1995. *Constructions: A Construction Grammar Approach to Argument Structure.* Chicago: University of Chicago Press.

Goldberg, Adele E. 1997. Relationships between Verb and Construction. In Marjolijn Verspoor and Eve Sweetser (eds) *Lexicon and Grammar in Cognitive Linguistics.* New York: John Benjamins.

Goldsmith, John. 1985. A Principled Exception to the Coordinate Structure Constraint. *CSL 21 Part 1* Chicago: Chicago Linguistic Society.

Grimshaw, Jane and Sten Vikner. 1993. Obligatory Adjuncts and the Structure of Events. In *Knowledge and Language* Eric Reuland and Werner Abraham (eds). Kluwer Academic Publishers.

Gruber, Jeffrey. 1965. *Studies in Lexical Relations.* MIT dissertation.

Hovav, Malka Rappaport and Beth Levin. 1996. Building Verb Meanings. Ms. Bar Ilan University and Northwestern University.

Kluender, Robert. 1992. Deriving Island Constraints from Principles of Predication. In *of Island Constraints: Theory, Acquisition and Processing.* Helen Goodluck and Michael Rochemont (eds) Kluwer Acadmeic Press: Dordrecht.

Jackendoff, Ray. 1990. *Semantic Structures.* Cambridge, Mass: MIT Press.

Lakoff, George. 1986. Frame Semantic Control of the Coordinate Structure Constraint. *Parasession on Pragmatics and Grammatical Theory CLS 22.*

Lakoff, George. 1987. *Women, Fire and Dangerous Things.* Chicago: University of Chicago Press.

Levin, Beth and Rapoport. 1988. Lexical Subordination. *CLS 24.*

Levin, Beth and Malka Rappaport Hovav. 1990a. The Lexical Semantics of Verbs of Motion: The Perspective from Unaccusativity. In I.M. Roca (ed), *Thematic Structure: Its Role in Grammar.* Berlin: Mouton de Gruyter.

Mandelblit, Nili. 1995. Blends in Hebrew Causatives. Ms. UCSD Cognitive Science department.

McCawley, James D. 1968. The role of semantics in grammar. In Bach and Harms (eds) *Universals in Linguistic Theory.* New York, NY: Holt, Reinhart and Winston. 124-169.

Pustejovsky, James. 1991. The Syntax of Event Structure. *Cognition* 41: 47-81.

Pinker, Steven. 1994. How Could a Child Use Verb Syntax to Learn Verb Semantics? in L. Gleitman and Barbara Landau (eds) *The Acquisition of the Lexicon.* Cambridge, Mass.: MIT Press. 377-410.

Pinker, Steven. 1989. *Learnability and Cognition: the acquisition of argument structure.* Cambridge, Mass: MIT Press.

Ross, John Robert. 1967. Constraints on Variables in Syntax. MIT dissertation. Published as John R. Ross. 1986. *Infinite Syntax.* Norwood, NJ: Ablex.

Talmy, Leonard. 1985. Lexicalization Patterns: Semantic Structure in Lexical Forms. in T. Shopen (ed), *Language Typology and Syntactic Description*, vol 3: *Grammatical Categories and the Lexicon.* Cambridge: Cambridge University Press. 57-149.

Psycholinguistic Studies of Entrenchment

CATHERINE L. HARRIS

Boston University

1. Introduction

Intuitively, an entrenched expression is one familiar to speakers from frequent use. Langacker (1987) and other cognitive linguists have observed that linguistic structures fall along a continuous scale of entrenchment in cognitive organization. Every use of a structure is thought to increase its degree of entrenchment.

> An event type has unit status when it is sufficiently well entrenched that it is easily evoked as an integrated whole, i.e., when it constitutes an established routine (Langacker 1987, p.100).

If language structures are cognitive structures and are stored in memory, then psycholinguistic techniques can be used to investigate them. However, there is no established tradition in psycholinguistics of studying how humans process units larger than single words but smaller than sentences (see review in Tanenhaus 1988). (An exception is the recently burgeoning work on idioms, as in Cacciari & Tabossi 1993, Everaert et al. 1995.) My own view is that there is considerable storage of common word combinations and other entrenched items (Harris 1994b). An initial step towards validating this view is to show that mental structures representing units larger than words are activated when reading entrenched expressions. Two types of entrenched

55

constructions are investigated in this paper: multi-word idioms (*Great minds think alike, Til the cows come home*) and common word combinations (*last chance, faced with, good job*).

My question about idioms is whether an "idiom-level" of representation exists. For common word combinations (which I will call collocations) my question is whether collocation-level representations exist. An intuitive explanation of "idiom-level representation" is a cognitive structure which bundles together the information activated when an idiom is processed. The idea of a unified structure which bundles together relevant information comes from laboratory experiments on processing of letters, words and non-word letter strings. Under conditions of brief exposure duration and masking, subjects are faster and more accurate when processing words than when processing non-word letter strings. This was called the word superiority effect. Carr (1986) has summarized psycholinguistic explanations of the WSE as follows:

> "Words benefit from higher-order, unitized codes that bundle all the available stimulus information together in a form that is safe from visual masking and memorable for long enough to support all of the decision and response selection processes required by the task (Carr 1986).

The laboratory findings thus support the introspection that words (compared to word fragments and random letter strings) have a cohesive, unitized feel. Given that speakers recognize the cohesiveness of idioms and common word combinations, psycholinguistic tasks may reveal evidence for the existence of unitized structures supporting these constructions.

2. Does Exposure to One Part of an Idiom Activate the Whole Idiom?

A common experience is anticipating the completion of an idiom after hearing an initial word or two. This suggests that the first part of an idiom may be able to activate a representation of the whole idiom. A helpful architecture for such mutual activation is suggested by McClelland & Rumelhart's (1981) interactive activation model of word recognition (shown in Figure 1a). In this model, visual input activates letter-detectors, which in turn feed activation to word-level representations. Letter-detectors for letters which are not in a given word have inhibitory connections to the word-level representation for that word (dotted lines in Figure 1a). This architecture allows **pattern completion**: obstructed letters (as in a word partially obscured by an ink spot) are "filled in" because the perceived letters are sufficient to partially activate the word. Partial activation then starts a positive feedback loop, which culminates in recognition of the word.

Extrapolating this architecture to idioms, we can conceptualize each word in a multi-word idiom as feeding a unitized representation, which top-down activates its component words (Figure 1b). Idiom-completion happens when the first word or two activates the idiom level, which then top-down activates all words in the idiom, including the ending.

A prediction of this architecture is that one part of an idiom will prime another part. For example, *compare apples* may prime *oranges* because both are part of the idiom *comparing apples to oranges*. In the next section, I discuss the semantic priming task used to test this prediction.

2.1 Semantic Priming

Much research has shown that recognition of a word (called the target) is facilitated when it is immediately preceded by a related word (called the prime). A common method for measuring speed of word recognition is the lexical decision task, which requires subjects to decide if a string of letters is a word or a non-word. Semantic priming is measured by the difference between the reaction time to targets preceded by related primes relative to unrelated primes.

One of the mechanisms responsible for priming is thought to be **spreading activation** (see review in Neely 1991). The idea behind spreading activation is that words are connected in an associative network. Words which often occur together or are semantically related have the strongest connections to each other. The presentation of the prime word causes activation to spread along these connections. When the activation reaches the target, the recognition threshold of the target is decreased, facilitating later recognition of that word.

A second influence on priming is thought to be **semantic integration.** Processing of a target word is facilitated when it is conceptually cohesive with preceding material, possibly because people automatically try to

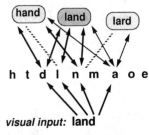

visual input: **land**

Figure 1a: McClelland & Rumelhart's (1981) IAM. Detectors for words are activated when letters are detected which are consistent with those words.

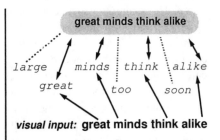

visual input: **great minds think alike**

Figure 1b: If idioms and phrases have a unitized storage, then each word in the visual input activates (and may be activated by) the phrases and idioms it is a member of.

Figure 2a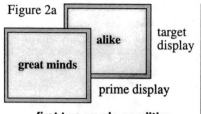

target display

prime display

first two words condition

Figure 2b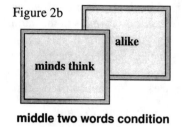

middle two words condition

semantically integrate words with their context. When a prime and target are unrelated, integration fails, leading to lack of a priming effect.

If we obtain the empirical result that the phrase *great minds* facilitates *alike*, either spreading activation or semantic integration may be responsible. Although both of these imply that knowledge of the idiom is influencing performance on the lexical decision task, evidence for spreading activation is stronger evidence for unitized storage of idiom parts. Spreading activation is thought to be a property of words' associative networks, while semantic integration is something that may take place outside of the lexicon.

To separately examine the possible effects of both spreading activation and semantic integration, my task varies whether the priming phrase is contiguous with the target or non-contiguous. In all trials, the target is the final word of a four-word idiom.

Figure 2a shows the condition where the prime is the **first two words** of the idiom. The presented material, *great minds -> alike* lacks semantic cohesion, since it violates both knowledge of the idiom and syntactic rules. Figure 2b shows the condition where the prime is the **middle two words** of the idiom. This expression also fails to completely match the idiom, but has considerable cohesion because there is no gap, and the three words can be assimilated to a noun-verb-noun syntactic schema. Because this sequence can be matched to a syntactic schema, the words can probably be semantically integrated. However, the gap produced by the "first two words" condition makes it likely that semantic integration will fail.

If semantic integration is the only cause of priming, then we expect significant priming when the prime is the middle two words, and no priming when the prime and target are separated by a gap, as is the case when the first two words are the prime. If words in an idiom activate other words in the idiom, then we expect significant priming in both conditions.

In general, the more tightly associated are two structures, the more they facilitate each other (but see Hodgson 1991 for a dissenting view). The explanation is that words spread activation to their associates as a function of their similarity or tightness of connection. To determine if parts of an idiom activate each other in proportion to their associativity, I normed a set of idioms for how strongly the first two or middle two words activated the idioms.

2.2 Method

Materials. The lack of previous priming studies with idioms means that one can only speculate about how the amount of priming obtained from words in idioms may compare to the priming obtained using standard associated materials. For this reason, in addition to 42 idioms, I used 90 prime-target pairs adapted from Chiarello et al (1990). Because the idiom items contained two-word primes, two-word primes were also constructed for the non-idiom conditions. The non-idiom conditions were either associatively related but not semantically similar (*baby cradle -> bottle*), semantically similar but not associated (*ear foot -> mouth*), or both associated and similar (*doctor nurse -> surgeon*). Because the task was lexical decision, an additional 90 word pairs were selected and paired with non-words; in half of these the two prime words were unrelated.

I constructed a paper-and-pencil word-association questionnaire containing the first two words or the middle two-words of each idiom, followed by a blank space. Questionnaire respondents were asked to write down the first word or phrase that came to mind for each item. The idiom items were randomly intermixed with the other stimulus items, meaning that only 42 out of 222 items (19%) were words taken from idioms, a percentage comparable to that of the priming experiment. A low percentage of idioms would hopefully prevent subjects from adopting an "idiom set" (actively trying to find an idiom completion).

Idiom items were scored for whether or not respondents wrote down any part of the idiom completion. The results revealed that for 30 of the idiom items, the first two words were more likely to result in an idiom completion than the middle two words, while for 12 of the idioms, the middle two words were more likely to bring to mind the idiom (see Examples in Table 1).

Experimental procedure. Research participants saw each target word in one of four priming conditions: first two words of idiom, middle two words of idioms, unrelated prime words, and a neutral prime (the words *something, blank* or *ready*). For the non-idiom materials (the semantically and associatively related items), there were only three prime conditions (related, unrelated, and neutral). The prime was presented for 250 msec in the center of a computer monitor, followed by the target which remained in view until a response key was pressed.

2.3 Results

Degree of priming for each target word was calculated by subtracting the

Table 1: Examples of how frequently phrases elicited target idiom

		Shown on Questionnaire	
Type of Idiom		First two words	Middle words
First two words best at eliciting idiom	Nothing ventured nothing gained	63	55
	Long time no see	42	11
	Breathing down my neck	55	21
	Cry your eyes out	63	0
Middle two words best at eliciting idiom	Little red riding hood	21	88
	Much ado about nothing	47	55
	Let sleeping dogs lie	27	50
	Let them eat cake	7	16

related condition from the unrelated conditions. Because the neutral condition and the unrelated conditions didn't differ from each other, these were pooled. Figure 3 compares the magnitude of priming for the idiom condition and the standard priming conditions. Priming was significantly greater than zero in all conditions. The magnitude of priming for the idioms was comparable to that for the three types of non-idiom materials. Average facilitation in milliseconds for each type of prime-target pair was: similar 57, associated 42, both 65, idiom 44.

Figure 3 shows facilitation plotted separately for the 30 idioms for which the first two words best activated the idiom in the word-association questionnaire, and the 12 idioms for which the middle two words were the best triggers of the idiom. Facilitation was greater when the prime was the middle two words, even for those idioms which were elicited best by the first two words in the paper-and-pencil task.

Correlations were calculated between the percent of subjects who identified the idiom in the word association questionnaire and the idiom's amount of priming. This correlation was significant when the prime was the middle two words ($r=0.37$, $p < .05$) but not when the prime was the first two words ($r=0.11$, n.s.).

2.4 Discussion

Phrases which are part of idioms prime the final word in the idiom. The amount of priming is comparable to priming found from materials commonly studied by psycholinguists, namely, semantically and associatively related words.

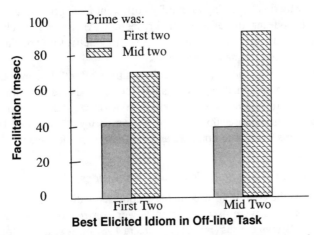

Figure 3. The middle two words of an idiom more strongly primed the final word, even for idioms in which the first two words more strongly elicited the idiom in the word-association questionnaire.

The priming data suggests that both spreading activation and semantic integration processes are at work. The finding of significant priming even when prime and target were separated by a gap suggests that the first two words of the idiom activate the entire idiom, which then activates all of its components, including the final word in the idiom, the target word. The finding of greater priming when the prime was the middle two words suggests that semantic integration was a factor in addition to spreading activation.

The large priming obtained when the middle two words were the prime is surprising when we consider that many of the middle two words contained a function word, and thus conveyed minimal information. (Consider: *compare apples to oranges, left holding the bag, beggars can't be choosers, all hot and bothered, live and let live, get off my back.*) Although in many cases the middle two words aren't obviously associated with the fourth word, they do always form a syntactically and semantically contiguous unit with it. The large amount of priming may thus stem from the facilitatory effect of sequential cohesiveness.

How frequently two words elicited their idiom in the word association questionnaire did not predict amount of priming, except when the middle two words were the prime, and even here the correlation was only modest in size ($r=0.37$). This suggests that the priming task and the off-line word association task are mediated by different processing factors. Intuitively, the off-line task seems to measure how easily a phrase brings to mind an idiom.

How and why this "bringing to mind" is different from priming is an important question deserving of additional research. All we can conclude right now is that sequential contiguity and spreading activation appear to separately contribute to semantic priming.

How general is the sequential cohesiveness effect? Is contiguity only important for entrenched expressions like idioms, or is the semantic priming task sensitive to sequential cohesiveness in novel word combinations? The next experiment explores this question by comparing the amount of priming for idiom parts to common phrases and non-common but syntactically cohesive phrases.

2.5 Priming in Sequentially Contiguous Expressions

Table 2 lists the conditions used in the second semantic priming experiment. The same idioms were used, but primes were restricted to the middle two words. The Brown corpus (Francis & Kucera 1982) was searched for phrases of length three which ended with each idiom's final word. If a phrase occurred several times in the corpus, it was called a "common saying." If it occurred only once, it was called a "grammatically legal" expression. In addition to the idiom, common saying, and grammatically legal conditions, a one-word prime condition was also included, although it was preceded by xxxxxx instead of a word. The unrelated condition (used to calculate degree of facilitation) was a no-prime condition. Here the target was preceded by a single xxxxxx.

Results. The greatest amount of priming was obtained for the idioms, especially the two-prime condition (Figure 4). When only one idiom prime word was used, facilitation was halved, although it was still significantly greater than zero. Two-word primes in the grammatically legal and common-saying conditions also led to significant facilitation, but did not differ from each other or the one-word idiom prime condition.

Table 2: Sequentially Contiguous Expressions

	Target	Idiom prime	Control prime	1-word prime
16 idioms matched to common sayings	nothing home alike	ado about cows come mind think	agree to comforts of even look	xxx to xxx of xxx look
16 idioms matched to grammatically legal expressions	young lie	good die sleeping dogs	prepare their that's a	xxx their xxx a
39 common sayings matched to legal expressions	queen image	like a in his	know a near his	xxx a xxx his

This result indicates that semantic priming is sensitive to sequential cohesiveness for sequences of three words. This holds true for both common sayings and grammatically legal expressions. One might have expected more priming for common sayings than for phrases which are merely grammatically legal. Failure to find this is consistent with the explanation that the priming effects for common sayings is exclusively a sequential cohesiveness effect, rather than priming derived from spreading activation between components of the common saying.

The case of grammatically legal expressions is important since it rules out an expectancy explanation (Neely 1991). Primes such as *know a* and *near the* do not seem plausible candidates for generating *queen* and *image*. Facilitation for these targets can not be attributed to expectancy, and should thus be explained as arising from the subjects' perception of cohesiveness. (See Goodman, McClelland & Gibbs 1981 for other work on priming of syntactically legal expressions.)

2.6 Discussion: Simultaneous Activation of Idiom and Syntactic Schemas?

The two experiments showed semantic priming to be sensitive to both entrenchment and sequential cohesiveness. Sensitivity to entrenchment was demonstrated with idioms, which are by definition entrenched units. Further-

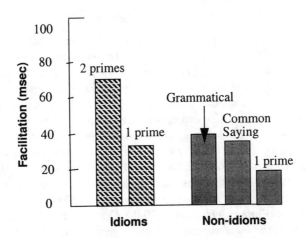

Figure 4. Experiment 2. Amount of priming for idioms and other sequentially cohesive expressions. All showed significant facilitation except the 1-prime non-idiom. T-tests between conditions revealed significant differences between 3 groups:
Idioms 2 primes >
(Idioms 1 prime, Grammatical, Common Saying) >
1prime.

more, priming was highest when entrenchment and cohesiveness were both present, as observed in the larger facilitation obtained when the prime and target created a continuous sequence (*minds think-> alike*).

In Experiment 2, facilitation was obtained for a target when it was the third word of a syntactically legal three-word combination. To explain this "syntactic priming" we can propose that syntactic schemas are activated. For *know a -> queen*, a schema such as verb+NP might be activated. Activating such a schema could correspond to the intuitive feeling that *know a queen* "makes sense."

The sequential cohesiveness effect for the idioms could come about because *minds think -> alike* activates the verb+NP schema at the same time that it activates an idiom-level representation. Failure to activate a syntactic schema, as happens with *great minds->alike,* reduces facilitation. But because the idiom-level representation is still activated, facilitation is only reduced, not eliminated.

The hypothesis that idiom-level representations are activated simultaneously with syntactic schemas is a new hypothesis which needs to be either validated or replaced by future research.

In the next section I turn to a different psycholinguistic task for investigating entrenchment: recognizing letters in words.

3. Do Common Word Combinations Have Unit Status?

Linguistic evidence on word-use suggests that the mental lexicon is more than a set of single words plus listed exceptions (Langacker 1987; Fillmore 1988; Goldberg 1995). Langacker (1987) has advocated a structure containing two types of regularities: overtly occurring expressions (single words and multi-word phrases such as *lose sight, never mind*), and generalizations over overtly occurring expressions. The source of these regularities is the corpus of phrases speakers encounter in daily life. For example, the set of word pairs *lose sight, lose touch, lose track,* and *lose count* may give rise to a generalization such as *lose*+NP. These local generalizations may also support more abstract generalizations, such as verb+noun, which in turn support basic word-order rules, as suggested by Langacker (1987) and by some connectionist work (Elman 1993; Harris 1994b). Generalizations at the level of phrases, such as the *let alone* construction, have been discussed extensively by Fillmore et al. (1988) and Goldberg (1995), in work broadly compatible with the approach advocated here.

According to this view, lexical structures form a continuum, from word combinations which have literally fossilized into single units (*goldfish, nightclub, sandbar*) to those that both exist as independent units and yet have bonds, varying in tightness, with the words with which they frequently co-occur. The *lose* examples given above illustrate this: *lose* can appear in many relatively unconstrained contexts, but also appears in the more formulaic contexts *lose sight, lose track and lose touch.*

A lexicon of variable-sized units fits easily into a connectionist framework. A key idea of connectionism is that the entities available to conscious reflection, and which appear to have causal force in human cognition, are emergent from an underlying microstructure (Smolensky 1988). According to this view, the units of lexical representation are not part of a fixed architecture, but emerge through extracting co-occurrence regularities. One implication of this idea is that unit-status, and the size of units, may be a matter of degree (Harris 1994b).

One candidate method for studying entrenchment of common word combinations is the semantic priming task discussed above. For example, if *last chance* has unit status, then the prime word *last* should semantically prime *chance.* Experiment 2 above in fact already showed this. The last two words of many of the idioms have some degree of entrenchment even separated from the first two words. For example, in the idiom *til the cows come home, come home* has at least some degree of entrenchment (a check of the Brown Corpus shows that this two-word sequence occurred four times). The one-prime idiom condition (in which just the third word of each idiom was used to prime the fourth) yielded 36 msec of priming. Other experimenters have also obtained semantic priming for entrenched pairs (Hodgson 1991).

The semantic priming task is useful for establishing that associations exist between prime words and target words, and it can also show the relative strength of the association. But it doesn't conclusively show that the prime and target are mentally represented as a unit. Associated words like *cradle* and *baby* show reliable priming, but no one would claim that priming of these words means they are stored as a unit. To show that *next step* and *head start* activate "collocation-level representations" I employed the same task used to establish unitized structures for words: the letter detection task.

3.1 The Letter Detection Task

The letter detection task is illustrated in Figure 5. After a brief display of a pair of words, the display is masked and two letter choices appear above the masked stimulus. Subjects are instructed to choose the letter which had appeared in the probed position. This task was originally used by Reicher (1969) and others (see review in Carr 1986) to examine the word superiority effect (WSE). The WSE is the finding (mentioned earlier) that processing of letters in words is superior to processing of letters in non-words. If collocation-level representations exist, then processing letters in collocations should be superior to processing letters in random word pairs. Three experiments using this technique are described below (a full report of this work can be found in Harris 1996).

Table 3 contains sample stimuli from the first experiment. Familiar word pairs (called simply collocations here) were compiled from searching the Brown corpus for word pairs that frequently occurred next to each other and were judged to form a familiar unit by native speakers. The comparison conditions were non-collocations (randomly conjoined word pairs) and "collocation neighbors" (a word pair identical to the collocation except for one letter change). The stimuli were yoked such that the critical letter appeared in the same word in different conditions (each subject saw only one version of the target word in each condition). The results of this experiment were that letter detection was better in the collocation than in the collocation neighbor and non-collocation.

Twenty years of research on context effects in perception have left still unresolved the question of how context benefits perception. One view is that context provides an alternative source of information to the perceiver (Jacobs & Grainger 1994). One name for this view is "sophisticated guessing" (Johnston 1978) because perceivers can use the alternative source to constrain guesses about the stimulus. Sophisticated guessing would explain the advantage of *tax bill* over *tax deep* as follows: The perceiver didn't see the *x* in *tax bill,* but saw enough of the context to guess that the stimulus was *tax bill.* The *x* can then be read-out of this reconstruction. The collocation-level

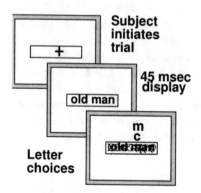

Figure 5. Letter detection task. Subjects' job is to choose whether **m** or **c** appeared in the position indicated by the choices. The typical finding is that letters are easier to detect when they appear in familiar contexts.

Table 3: Collocation Stimuli

Single Word	Collocation	Collocation-Neighbor	Non-Collocation	Letter Choices
ta<u>x</u>	ta<u>x</u> bill	ta<u>x</u> bell	ta<u>x</u> deep	x g
<u>n</u>ight	<u>n</u>ight club	<u>n</u>ight clue	<u>n</u>ight wall	n e
p<u>o</u>int	focal p<u>o</u>int	vocal p<u>o</u>int	cargo p<u>o</u>int	o a
wo<u>r</u>ld	free wo<u>r</u>ld	tree wo<u>r</u>ld	open wo<u>r</u>ld	r u

of information thus provides an alternative to the letter-level of information, and can supplement that level if it is missed due to noise arising from brief presentation and masking.

3.2 Testing Sophisticated Guessing

If the "sophisticated guessing" account is correct, then letter-detection accuracy will decrease if more than one collocation can be generated out of the letter's context, such as the *plaid sk/hirt*. If the letter in the probed position is missed, the subject will still have to guess between *skirt* and *shirt*.

A letter detection experiment was run using 50 morphologically related pairs (*lose sight/lost sight,* and *blue eyes/blue eyed*) and 39 "accidental neighbors", such as *bog down/bow down*. The experiment used the procedure outlined in Figure 5.

Superiority of detection of words in collocations over non-collocations was found to be equally as strong when only one letter choice created a collocation, and when both letter choices created a collocation. This argues against a sophisticated guessing explanation, and supports the position that words in collocations benefit from top-down activation from collocation-level representations.

3.3 Are Collocations Activated in Response to Partial Input?

To test if collocation-level representations are activated before words are recognized, I used stimuli in which the incorrect letter choice created a collocation. These are called 'trick' items because similarity to a collocation can trick subjects into choosing the incorrect letter choice. For example, the trick items corresponding to the collocations in Table 4 are *tag bill, eight club, focal paint, free would.* Lowered performance on the trick items is a measure of how much of the collocation advantage is attributable to collocation-level constraints.

The results showed that accuracy was drastically impaired in the 'trick' conditions (65% correct compared to 90% in the collocation condition). This indicates that the trick item is being misread as its collocation neighbor (*free would* being misread as *free world*). Theorists have explained word misreadings as happening because a number of word-representations are activated during the initial stages of word recognition, and the incorrect word 'wins' the competition to pass critical threshold first (Jacobs & Grainger 1994). Since misreadings of collocations happen relatively easily, we can infer that collocation-level representations are activated when reading word pairs.

In a subsequent experiment, trick items were labeled "semantically congruent" if they could be assimilated to an adjective noun schema. Examples include *first kid*, the trick version of *first aid*, or *blond type*, the trick version of *blood type*. Trick items were labeled "anomalous" if they could not be assimilated to a syntactically legal schema (*held start*, the trick version of *head start*), or which violated semantic constraints (*low coat*, the trick version of *low cost*). Experimental results showed that letter detection was less impaired in congruent than in semantically anomalous trick items. I interpret this to mean that two unitized structures were activated during recognition: the collocation-level structures (which supported the incorrect letter choice), and abstract adjective-noun structures, which weakly supported the correct letter choice. The pattern of data is thus consistent with a view of the lexicon as containing both word pairs and schematizations over word pairs.

4. Conclusions

Speakers recognize idioms and common word combinations as familiar. Does this feeling of familiarity derive from the existence of "idiom level" and "collocation level" data structures? This question was investigated using techniques originally developed to study the mental representation of words.

A semantic priming task showed that the last word of a four-word idiom is processed more quickly when it is followed by either the first two words or the middle two words of the idiom, suggesting that idiom-level representations exist. To explain the sequential cohesiveness effect (more facilitation when prime and target didn't leave a gap), I suggested that the idiom components also activate syntactic representations. This activation succeeds when there is no gap, as with *minds think -> alike*, but fails when there is a gap (*great minds -> alike*). A second experiment supported this interpretation by showing that semantic priming is sensitive to the cohesiveness of novel but syntactically coherent phrases.

The experiments on entrenched word pairs used a different task (letter detection) but warrant similar conclusions: common word pairs activate unitized representations for the word pair, as well as schematic representations consistent with the word-pairs' syntactic structure. Both sets of studies thus found evidence that two types of structures are activated when reading phrases: (1) entrenched structures specific to those phrases, and (2) structures sensitive to sequential cohesion between the words in the phrases (which could be schemas for syntactic regularities). These results resemble what is known to happen in connectionist models, as when a network activates both specific and abstract context-dependent representations (Harris 1994a).

The idea that phrases are stored units strikes non-linguists as common-sense, but there has been considerable resistance to this view in past decades (Jackendoff 1995). The mechanics of a lexicon containing variably-sized phrases remain to be worked out. However, it is worth holding firmly in mind the benefits of starting along this path. If phrases can be the unit of lexical access, the question of how polysemous words are interpreted in context becomes easier, since many polysemous words may be stored with both their contexts and the unique meaning for that context. This means that on hearing an expression like *cut down*, listeners don't have to compute a meaning based on the intersection of a set of meanings for *cut* and the set of meanings for *down*. Instead, the conventional meaning for *cut down*, **reduce**, is immediately available. Child language acquisition may proceed simultaneously from learning how to combine single words into larger units, and from initially storing multi-word utterance, and then extracting the parts via distributional analysis (Bates, Bretherton & Snyder 1988). Low-frequency words may be protected from loss by being tightly bound to conventional contexts of use, as in the phrases *paragon of virtue, groveled at his/her feet*. Multiword units provide language that is "ready to speak," thus facilitating fluency. Lexical access problems in some forms of brain damage may result not so much from loss of stored meanings, but from problems activating a sufficiently rich context to make individual words accessible. Foreign language learners may have reduced fluency in their second language because they have stored a smaller corpus of phrases. Machine translation systems can reap the translation benefits of multi-word units by taking advantage of computers' large storage capacities and high search speed. Last but not least, many mysteries of the role of context in word recognition may be seen in a new light as researchers become more adept at separating out the contributing roles of congruent but novel context and congruent stored context.

5. References

Bates, E., Bretherton, I., & Snyder, L. 1988. *From first words to grammar: Individual differences and dissociable mechanisms.* Cambridge: Cambridge University Press.

Carr, T.H. 1986. Perceiving visual language. In K.R. Boff et al., eds., *Handbook of perception and human performance.* New York: Wiley.

Chiarello, C., Burgess, C., Richards, L., & Pollock, A. 1990. Semantic and associative priming in the cerebral hemispheres: Some words do, some words don't ... sometimes, some places. *Brain and Language, 38,* 75-104.

Elman, J.L. 1993. Learning and development in neural networks: The importance of starting small. In C. Umilta and M.Moscovitch, eds., *Attention and performance XV: Conscious and nonconscious information processing.* Hillsdale, NJ: Erlbaum.

Fillmore, C. J., Kay, P, & O'Conner M. C. 1988. Regularity and idiomaticity in grammar: The case of Let alone. *Language, 64,* 501-538.

Francis, W. N. & Kucera, H. 1982. *Frequency analysis of English usage: lexicon and grammar.* Boston: Houghton Mifflin.

Goldberg, A.E. 1995. *Constructions: a construction grammar approach to argument structure*. Chicago: University of Chicago Press.

Goodman, E,O., McClelland, J.L., & Gibbs, R.W. 1981. The role of syntactic context in word recognition. *Memory and Cognition, 9,* 580-586

Harris, C.L. 1994a. Backpropagation representations for the rule-analogy continuum. In J. Barnden, & K. Holyoak, (Eds.), *Analogical Connections.* Ablex.

Harris, C.L. 1994b. Coarse coding and the lexicon. In C. Fuchs and B. Victorri, Eds. *Continuity in linguistic semantics.* Amsterdam: John Benjamins.

Harris, C.L. 1996. Recognizing common word combinations: Towards a lexicon of variable-sized units. Manuscript under review.

Hodgson, J.M. 1991. Informational constraints on pre-lexical priming. *Language and Cognitive Processes, 6,* 169-205.

Jacobs, A.M., & Grainger, J. 1994. Models of visual word recognition -- sampling the state of the art. *Journal of Experimental Psychology: Human Perception and Performance, 20,* 1311-1334.

Jackendoff, R. 1995 The boundaries of the lexicon. In M. Everaert, E. Schenk, and R. Schreuder (Eds.), *Idioms: Structural and psychological perspectives.* Hillsdale, NJ: Lawrence Erlbaum.

Johnston, J.C. 1978. A test of the sophisticated guessing theory of word perception. *Cognitive Psychology, 10,* 123-153.

Langacker, R. W. 1987. *Foundations of cognitive grammar, Vol. I: Theoretical prerequisites.* Stanford, CA.: Stanford University Press.

Lund, K., & Burgess, C. 1996. Hyper-space analogue to language. *Behavior Research, Instruments, & Computers.*

McClelland, J.L. & Rumelhart, D.E. 1981. An interactive activation model of context effects in letter perception: Part 1. An account of basic findings. *Psychological Review, 88,* 375-407.

Neely, J.H. 1991. Semantic priming effects in visual word recognition: A selective review of current findings and theories. In D. Besner & G.W. Humphreys, eds., *Basic processes in reading: visual word recognition.* Hillsdale, NJ: Erlbaum.

Reicher, G.M. 1969. Perceptual recognition as a function of meaningfulness of stimulus material. *Journal of Experimental Psychology 81:*274-280.

Smolensky, P. 1988. On the proper treatment of connectionism. *Behavior and Brain Sciences 11:*1-74.

Tanenhaus, M.K. 1988. Psycholinguistics: an overview. In F.J. Newmeyer, ed., *Linguistics: The Cambridge Survey.* Cambridge University Press.

On Subjectification and Grammaticization

Ronald W. Langacker
University of California, San Diego

1. Introduction

In previous works (Langacker 1985; 1990; 1991), I have argued that **subjectivity** is an important dimension of construal, that **subjectification** is one kind of semantic change, and that subjectification is a factor in certain instances of **grammaticization**. My purpose here is to refine my previous characterization of subjectification, and to indicate in finer-grained detail how it contributes to two typical properties of highly-grammaticized forms: their **transparency** (in the sense of Langacker 1995b) and the extent of their **conceptual overlap** with co-occurring elements (Langacker 1992a; 1992b; 1995a).

2. Basic Notions of Cognitive Grammar

Conceptual structure involves a **subject** and an **object** of conception. The subject is an implicit locus of consciousness ("perspective point") which apprehends the object and—if it is *only* the subject—is not itself apprehended. The subject's activity determines the nature of the conceptual experience but does not per se figure in its "content". To the extent that an entity functions as the *subject* (or the *object*) *of conception*, it is said to be **subjectively** (or **objectively**) **construed**. It is construed with maximal **subjectivity** when it remains "offstage" and implicit, inhering in the very process of conception without being its target. It is construed

71

with maximal **objectivity** when it is put "onstage" as an explicit *focus of attention*.

The full range of conceptual content an expression evokes as the basis for its meaning is called its **overall scope**. Within this, there is a limited range—called the **immediate scope**—describable as the *general locus of attention* (the "onstage region"). An expression's **profile** (i.e. the entity it designates, its conceptual referent) is the *specific focus of attention* within the immediate scope. As seen for *elbow* in Figure 1, profiling is indicated notationally by heavy lines.

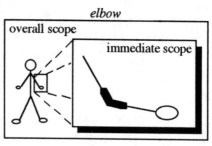

Figure 1

Either a **thing** or a **relationship** can be profiled. An expression's grammatical class is determined by the nature of its profile (Langacker 1987a; 1987b). Thus *elbow* is a noun because it profiles a thing, whereas *admire* is a verb because it profiles a particular kind of relationship (a **process**, i.e. a relationship whose temporal evolution is scanned sequentially). Observe the heavy dashed arrow in Figure 2 (a dashed arrow indicates a mental or experiential relation).

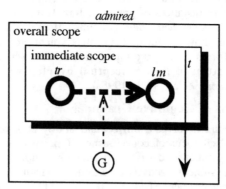

Figure 2

The conception of a relationship presupposes that of its participants, which are accorded varying degrees of *focal prominence*. The *primary* focal participant is termed the **trajector** (*tr*). When there is a *secondary* focal participant, it is called a **landmark** (*lm*). A noun phrase which specifies the trajector or the landmark of a relational expression thereby constitutes its grammatical subject or object, respectively.

The **ground** (G) comprises the speech event, its participants, and its immediate circumstances. Its primary elements are thus the speaker and the addressee, who function as conceptualizers, or *subjects of conception*, with respect to the meanings of linguistic expressions; this is indicated by the vertical dashed arrow in Figure 2. A noun phrase or a finite clause incorporates **grounding**: a grammaticized specification of how the profiled thing or process relates to the ground. The nominal grounding elements of English include demonstratives, articles, and certain quantifiers. The clausal grounding elements are tense and the modals. A crucial property of these elements—one that accounts for their special grammatical behavior (Langacker 1985; 1990)—is that they profile the *grounded entity*, not the *ground* or the *grounding relationship*. Thus, as seen in Figure 2, the grounded verb *admired* has the same profile as the verb stem *admire*: both the ground and the grounding relationship (wherein the conceptualizers "look back" in time to the profiled process) are offstage and subjectively construed.

3. Subjectification

I previously characterized **subjectification** as the *realignment* of some relationship from the **objective axis** to the **subjective axis**. That is, some relational component, given as Y in Figure 3, which originally holds between onstage elements that are objectively construed is replaced by an analogous relationship, Y', which holds between the onstage situation and some facet of the ground. Since Y' and G are offstage and subjectively construed, Y has undergone subjectification. Observe that this per se has no effect on the status of participants as trajector and landmark, but only on

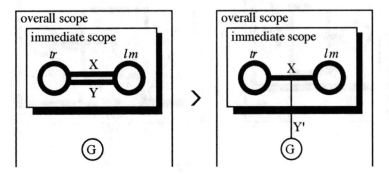

Figure 3

which facets of the original objective relationship involving them remain onstage and in profile.

For example, subjectification relates the two senses of *across* illustrated in (1):

(1)   a.   A giant chicken strode angrily across the street.

       b.   There was a KFC outlet right across the street.

Observe that in (1a) the trajector of *across* (the chicken) moves through space and successively occupies all the points along a path traversing its landmark (the street). In (1b), on the other hand, the trajector occupies only a single position vis-à-vis the landmark, the same one it occupies at the end of the path in (1a). There is still a sense of motion, however. Although the trajector is static, the conceptualizer traces a *mental* path—analogous to the physical path in (1a)—in order to specify the trajector's location in relation to the landmark, as reckoned with respect to some reference point (R).

In short, *objective* motion by the onstage *subject* is replaced by *subjective* motion on the part of the offstage *conceptualizer* (a facet of the ground). The change is sketched in Figure 4, where the solid arrow indicates spatial motion, and the dashed arrow represents the analogous mental scanning. This reorientation has no effect on the choice of trajector and landmark (onstage focal participants), but only on the trajector's role in the profiled relationship: instead of successively occupying every position along the spatial path, it occupies only a single position. Nonetheless, the profiled relation still serves to specify the trajector's location.

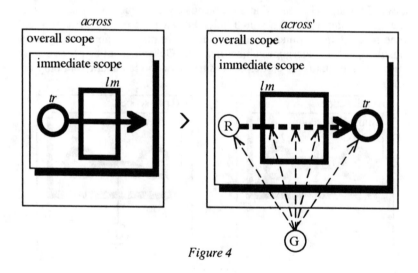

Figure 4

I have no doubt that subjectification does figure in these and other instances of semantic change and grammaticization. Only its proper characterization is at issue here. Various people, including Verhagen (1995), have suggested that the subjective component Y' is present all along, that it is *immanent* in Y, and that subjectification is consequently not a *reorientation* from the objective to the subjective axis, but merely a *loss* of the objective facets of Y, leaving its subjective basis, Y', behind. In other words, subjectification would amount to a kind of semantic "bleaching".

I believe these suggestions are correct. For example, in conceiving of the subject following the objective spatial path in Figure 4, the conceptualizer necessarily scans mentally along the same path as an inherent aspect of tracking the subject's motion. It is not that this is added to the conceptualization of the derived sense of *across*, but rather that it stands alone and is consequently more visible once the objective motion is stripped away. Hence:

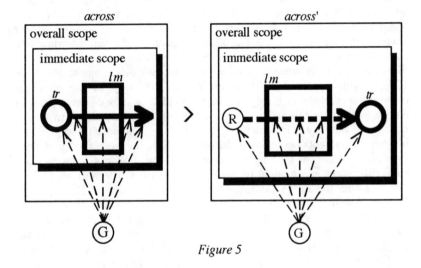

Figure 5

A revised characterization of **subjectification** can now be offered: An *objective* relationship fades away, leaving behind a *subjective* relationship that was originally *immanent* in it (i.e. inherent in its conceptualization). This is sketched in Figure 6, where Y' does not replace Y, but rather becomes apparent when Y is no longer present to provide it with an objective basis.

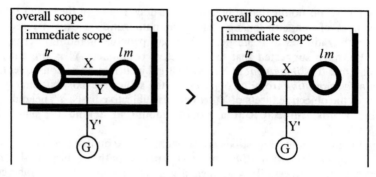

Figure 6

This revised characterization makes it easier to conceive of subjectification as being a *gradual* process. With the scheme in Figure 3, it is hard to conceive of there being any intermediate stages, but in Figure 6 one can easily imagine a gradual diminution in salience of the objective component Y. I doubt however that it simply undergoes a continuous linear decrease in salience; we can reasonably expect identifiable intermediate stages representing coherent and potentially stable values. A number of these may coexist as alternative values at a particular diachronic stage (Heine 1992), with a gradual shift in preference resulting in the eventual disappearance of the original value and the predominance of newer ones. I envisage the evolutionary process as involving small shifts in focus, changes in status (e.g. from actual to potential, or from specific to generic), obligatory elements becoming contingent, and the eventual fading of non-focal, non-actual, or contingent elements. In other words, I am viewing subjectification as a gradual process of **progressive attenuation**.

Consider the shift relating the two senses of *across* in (1), as seen in Figures 4 and 5. Sometimes called the *endpoint focus image-schema transformation* (e.g. Lakoff 1987: 440-441), it is in my terms a restriction in *profiling* analogous to that involved in deriving a stative-adjectival participle (e.g. *broken*) from a verb (*break*). That is, the derived sense profiles a single-configuration relationship equivalent to the last in an ordered series of relational configurations profiled in the original meaning. Now, it would seem that the transition from one to the other would have to be discrete—the trajector either traverses all the locations constituting the spatial path, or occupies only the final location, but there is no intermediate sense in which, say, it traverses only a portion of the path.

However, further data reveals that spatial motion does not so much disappear as undergo a change in status. Consider the uses of *across* in (2):

(2)   a.   The child hurried across the busy street.

b.   The child is safely across the street.

c.   You need to send a letter? There's a mailbox across the street.

d.   A number of shops are conveniently located just across the street.

e.   Last night there was an altercation right across the street.

Although spatial movement is profiled only in the first example, it figures in the most likely interpretation of all but the last, as respectively described in (3):

(3)   a.   profiled objective movement by subject

b.   static location resulting from unprofiled, past, actual movement of subject

c.   static location as goal of unprofiled, envisaged, future movement of addressee

d.   static location as goal of potential movement by a generalized or generic individual

e.   static location, no physical movement implied

Thus (2b) invokes previous movement by the subject as a necessary part of its overall scope, whereas (2c), in accordance with standard conventions for giving instructions, involves potential movement by the addressee. In (2d) the movement is construed in generalized or generic fashion, making it more contingent and more diffuse. Only in (2e) can one plausibly argue that the conception of physical movement is absent altogether.

We can thus observe a series of stages leading from the full-path objective motion sense of (1a) to the static location sense of (1b). The steps involve such factors as loss of profiling (a kind of attentional focus), changes in who does the moving (the grammatical subject, the addressee, or some generalized or unspecified individual), and shifts in its status (actual, potential, generic, or absent). These can all be regarded as cases of bleaching or attenuation, in that the mover and movement are rendered progressively less prominent: they begin as onstage foci of attention, but each step diminishes their salience, until any notion of physical movement has faded away entirely. What remains is something which has been there all along, namely subjective motion by the conceptualizer, who mentally traces along a path in order to specify the subject's location.

I believe this general sort of development to be quite common in grammaticization. Two other cases will now be examined in fair detail: *going to* > *gonna*, and the evolution of the English modals.

4. *Going To* > *Gonna*

It is well known that verbs meaning 'go' often grammaticize into markers of futurity. This is commonly analyzed in terms of metaphorical transfer from the spatial to the temporal domain (e.g. in Sweetser 1988), and space-to-time metaphor was incorporated as one component of my own account based on subjectification (1985; 1986; 1990). However, the revised formulation of subjectification now leads me to suggest that metaphor does not figure in the grammaticization of 'go' to a future marker, or at least that it has a different and lesser role than previously thought.

A sentence like (4a) is ambiguous. It can indicate either actual movement through space by the subject, with the intent of initiating an action at the endpoint of the spatial path, or else the futurity of the infinitival event, with no implication of spatial motion. Based on the characterizations in (4b) and (4c), I originally attributed this contrast to the combination of subjectification and metaphor: the former replaces objective movement by the subject with subjective movement by the conceptualizer, and the latter transposes it from space to time.

(4)   a.   Sam is going to mail the letter.

       b.   physical, objective movement through space by the subject

       c.   subjective movement through time by the conceptualizer

The two senses of *going to* are sketched in Figure 7. In the physical movement sense, the trajector—through time (t)—follows a spatial path, at the end of which he intends to initiate some activity. (Represented by a solid arrow, this activity functions as a relational landmark, and is specified overtly by the infinitival complement, just as the subject noun phrase specifies the trajector.) In the future sense, the conceptualizer traces a mental path through time (as indicated by the heavy-line dashed arrow), situating the infinitival process downstream in time relative to some reference point. The trajector (primary focal participant) no longer moves through space; its activity is now confined to its role within the landmark process. Thus, in the original account, I described the objective spatial movement as being reoriented to the subjective axis and shifted to the temporal domain, producing subjective motion through time on the part of the conceptualizer.

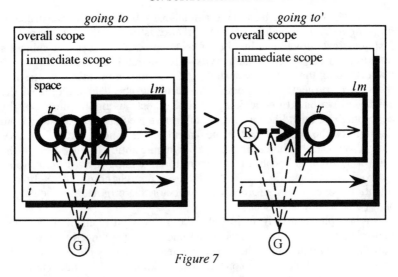

Figure 7

It should be evident, however, that the conceptualizer's subjective movement through time was there all along. As shown in Figure 7, the same temporal scanning that is characteristic of the future sense—being used to situate the envisaged process downstream in time—is also immanent in the physical motion sense: in conceiving of the trajector following a spatial path through time, the conceptualizer is necessarily scanning through time subjectively. It is not a matter of metaphorical projection from the spatial to the temporal domain. Rather, as objective spatial movement fades from the picture, the subjective temporal movement inherent in its conception is left behind and becomes more evident in its absence.

It seems unlikely, though, that the objective spatial movement disappears in a single step. We ought to explore the possibility of a finer-grained account involving progressive attenuation, analogous to the one proposed for *across* in (2)-(3). There are in fact a number of readily discernible stages in the progression from spatial movement to simple futurity, all of them common in contemporary speech. Examples are given in (5). (Whether they represent an actual diachronic sequence will of course have to be determined by appropriate historical investigation.)

(5)   a.   He was going to mail the letter but never reached the post office.

        b.   He was going to mail the letter but never got around to it.

        c.   If he's not careful he's going to tumble over the railing.

        d.   Something bad is going to happen—I just know it.

        e.   It's going to be summer before long.

It is not just the verb *go* that grammaticizes, but the entire construction *be going to V*. In a sentence like (5a), that construction involves more than just physical movement by the subject: it also conveys the subject's intention to engage in some activity (the landmark process in Figure 7) upon reaching the end of the spatial path. Having an intention implies that the subject projects a temporal path, scanning ahead to the time of the envisaged action. In conceiving of the subject having an intention, the conceptualizer must likewise trace a subjective mental path extending from the time of the profiled spatial movement to the time of the action. We must also recall that intention is a force-dynamic notion (Talmy 1985)—the subject's intention constitutes a mental force tending toward the action's realization. Hence the conceptualizer, in apprehending the subject's intention, conceives of a force-dynamic vector that originates in the subject and is directed toward that end.

When physical movement fades from the picture, all of these other factors may persevere. Thus a sentence like (5b) need not involve movement but does imply the subject's intention to carry out the infinitival process. The subject is still conceived as looking ahead in time and as the origin of a force-dynamic vector tending toward realization of the envisaged event. From there, the other uses arise via progressive attenuation of the subject's role. In (5c), the subject no longer *intends* to carry out the infinitival process but is nonetheless attributed a certain amount of *responsibility* in this regard. While there is still a force-dynamic vector tending toward the event's realization, it does not originate in the subject *qua* intentional agent. Rather, something in the subject's sphere of influence—in this case the subject's activity or inattentiveness—is construed as being its source. Moreover, the conceptualizer (though not the subject) continues to trace a subjective mental path from the time of the current activity to that of the envisaged event.

The other examples show further attenuation of the subject's role. In (5d), the subject per se has no responsibility in regard to potential realization of the future event—in fact, the subject (*something bad*) is indistinguishable from that event (*happen*) and does not yet exist. Here the source of the force-dynamic vector tending toward its realization is maximally diffuse. From a global assessment of present circumstances, the conceptualizer apprehends an ill-defined force projected as bringing about the event's occurrence. The subjective apprehension of this force has of course been there all along; the example differs from previous ones merely in the absence of any specific objective element to identify as its origin. Naturally, the endpoint of this progression is the total disappearance of the force-dynamic component along both the objective and subjective axes. Sentences like (5e) exemplify (or at least approximate) this stage, where nothing remains onstage except an event downstream in time from a reference point. This is the configuration shown on the right in Figure 7.

The conceptualizer apprehends the profiled relationship by subjectively scanning through time (just as he does through space with *across*).

We see, then, that the temporal value of *gonna* emerges as primary by virtue of other components of meaning being successively eliminated. Note in particular that, as we go through the examples in (5), the subject's role is progressively diminished. There is no change of subject: the subject of *be going to* is at every stage the same as the trajector of the landmark process. What happens is that its additional roles—with respect to motion, intention, and responsibility—are successively stripped away, until none are left. Cases like (5c) represent a transition, the last stage where the subject per se projects a temporal or force-dynamic path. In the phases exemplified by (5d) and (5e), the subject's objective role is wholly confined to its participation in the landmark process specified by the infinitival clause. This does not however prevent it from being the subject of *gonna*, granted cognitive grammar's characterization of grammatical relations (Langacker 1991: 7.3). The subject of *gonna* is simply the noun phrase which specifies its *trajector*, in turn defined as its *primary focal participant*. It is not required that the trajector have any specific semantic role, nor even that it be most directly involved in the profiled relationship.

When the subject's role is wholly confined to its participation in the landmark process, as in (5d) and (5e), the result is a kind of **transparency**: anything eligible to be the subject of the infinitival complement is also eligible to be the subject of the main clause predicate (*be gonna*). This phenomenon is well known in the generative tradition, where it has normally been handled by positing a rule of Subject-to-Subject Raising (e.g. Postal 1974). I have shown (1995b) that no such rule is necessary in cognitive grammar. It is evident in Figure 7 that the trajector of the landmark process and the trajector of the profiled temporal relationship are one and the same. Thus both are specified when the main clause subject elaborates the schematic trajector of *be gonna*. We have seen, moreover, that subjectification leaves the trajector with no objective role beyond its participation in the landmark process. Since nothing in the profiled relationship imposes any restrictions on what that trajector can be, all restrictions on its choice are determined by the infinitival complement.

By comparing the two diagrams in Figure 7, we can also see how grammaticization of this sort leads to greater conceptual overlap with co-occurring elements. Here the co-occurring element is the infinitival clause. At every stage there is overlap in the sense that the main clause and the infinitival clause have the same trajector. In (5a), however, that trajector (the subject) carries out overt physical activity above and beyond the process specified by the infinitival complement. This additional activity is in fact focused as the process profiled by the sentence as a whole. In the later stages this activity is eliminated. All which then remains—outside the scope of the infinitival complement—is subjective scanning through time by the conceptualizer; nothing is left onstage except a certain expanse of time and a tacit temporal reference point. This approximates the limiting case of overlap, where the content evoked by the grammaticized expression is wholly subsumed by co-occurring elements. In such cases (e.g. with the auxiliary verb *do*—see Langacker 1987a: 9.2.2) the grammatical element's meaning is merely a schematic characterization of what it combines with.

A true tense marker, i.e. a grounding element as previously described, comes even closer to the limiting case. English *be going to* remains periphrastic, with *be* still the "main verb" in the sense that the process it profiles (the continuation through time of the relationship of futurity) is the one grounded by tense and modality. Most likely it will continue to grammaticize and eventually evolve into a true future tense marker serving a grounding function. This will come about when the temporal reference point R is obligatorily equated with G, offstage and subjectively construed, with the consequence that the temporal path it anchors is also construed subjectively. Since profiling requires objective construal as a matter of definition, all that will then remain onstage and in profile is the process whose temporal location is being specified. That schematic process (originally the landmark of the profiled temporal relationship) is identified with the specific process profiled by the verb or clause the new tense marker combines with. This grounding element has no onstage content that is not fully subsumed by the elaborating structure (cf. Figure 2).

Observe that the story just told does not involve metaphor. In particular, it is not being claimed for sentences like (5b)-(5e) that the subject is moving metaphorically through time, by analogy to spatial motion. Only the conceptualizer is said to be tracing a temporal path, and the conceptualizer is not onstage as a target of metaphorical construal. I would not however rule out the possibility that metaphor does figure in the initial step, i.e. the transition between examples like (5a) and (5b). That is, a sentence like (5a) may have invoked the source domain of spatial motion toward a destination for purposes of apprehending the target domain of making progress toward realizing an objective (cf. *He's well on his way to deciding whether to resign*). With the eventual fading of this metaphor (the loss of any idea of spatial movement), the *be going to* construction would be left as a means of indicating future intention, as in (5b). If metaphor did in fact have such a role, it is nonetheless true that the notion of future intention was not added to sentences like (5a) via metaphorical extension but was present from the outset.

5. English Modals

The modals are known to have evolved from verbs with meanings like 'want', 'know how to', 'have the strength to', etc. Such verbs have two crucial properties both reflected in grammaticized modals: they are *force-dynamic* (Sweetser 1982; Talmy 1985), and the target of the force—the action described by the verbs' complements—remains *potential* rather than being actual. Thus, as shown in Figure 8, the situation profiled by the original main-clause verbs involves some kind of **potency** tending in one way or another toward realization of an action, which constitutes the landmark of the profiled relationship. The potency is represented by a double arrow, dashed to indicate that it is not necessarily unleashed in real action. Observe that the source of this force-dynamic vector is also the actor of the target event.

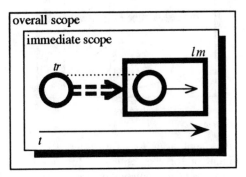

Figure 8

I can only describe the grammaticization of the modals collectively and in coarse-grained terms. One overall development is a decrease in the specificity of the source of potency. Originally it was the same individual as the actor in the target event. At the stage when we can properly speak of modals, the source is more diffuse, in the sense of being unspecified or even in the sense of not being localizable at all. A detailed description of the evolution of modals would presumably uncover numerous overlapping stages of this progressive attenuation (cf. Aguirre and Goossens 1977).

A second development, responsible for modals becoming grounding elements in English, is subjectification of the modal force. No longer onstage, the source of the potency is identified with either the ground itself of some facet of the ground's immediate circumstances, namely current reality (r) as assessed by the speaker, as seen in Figure 9. Like its source, the potency is thus offstage and subjectively construed, so it cannot be profiled. Left onstage as the profiled entity is the process (originally the relational landmark) serving as target of the force-dynamic vector. That process, which the modal itself represents only schematically, is identified with the specific process profiled by the grounded verb. The trajectors of the modal and of its complement are thus the same, just as they were at the original main-verb stage. As in previous examples, what changes is the extent of the trajector's role beyond its role in the complement process. In the 'ability' sense of *can* (e.g. *He can do 100 pushups*) we find the last vestige of the trajector being the source of potency as well.

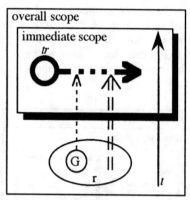

Figure 9

A modal is thus analogous to a future tense marker, except for its additional component of force or potency. In the case of a root modal interpretation, the *source* of this potency is often the speaker, but it can also be another individual evident from the context, or even some generalized locus of authority:

(6)   a.   You may not go out tonight—I forbid it!

        b.   You must do your homework—your teacher demands it.

        c.   Passengers should confirm their reservations two days in advance.

        d.   You must not covet your neighbor's wife.

(This is of course analogous to the progressive diffusion of responsibility noted for *gonna*.) Likewise, the *target* of the potency is often the subject, or else the addressee, but it can also be another individual, or even left completely unspecified:

(7)   a.   Sean can leave now.

        b.   This work must be done by tomorrow—you had better get busy.

        c.   This work must be done by tomorrow—you had better tell Harry.

        d.   There may not be any beer served at the party.

        e.   ??It must rain tonight!

Modals are for the most part transparent, since the subject is not the source of the potency (except for certain uses of *can*) and not necessarily its target. Because the subject need not be capable of exerting, perceiving, or responding to such force, constraints on its choice are wholly determined by its role in the grounded process. Of course, a root modal interpretation may still be problematic, as in (7e), owing to the pragmatic infelicity of raining being imposed as an obligation. Such expressions can however be salvaged by imagining an appropriate context. Thus (7e) would be felicitous if uttered by the supreme god in a pantheon to the subordinate god in charge of rain.

Since the deontic notions of obligation, permission, desire, and ability imply at least some localization of either the source or the target of potency, the complete absence of localization is concomitant with—and perhaps responsible for—the distinction between root and epistemic modals. The latter are maximally diffuse in regard to the source and the target of potency, hence fully transparent:

(8) a. It may very well rain tonight.

  b. There could be massive starvation in the next century.

  c. Tabs will most likely be kept on all prominent dissidents.

I have previously described the potency of epistemic modals as inhering in the **evolutionary momentum** of reality itself, as assessed by the speaker: given how reality has been evolving up through the present, what is the likelihood of it continuing to evolve in such a way as to "reach" the target process? I contrasted this to Sweetser's notion (1982; 1990) of the speaker being construed metaphorically as the target of force in the domain of reasoning. If her account is taken at face value, we would expect the speaker to be put onstage as a focused object of conception. In fact, however, the speaker is not even mentioned and is evidently construed subjectively. Unlike Sweetser's, the analysis I proposed directly accommodates the surface grammar of modal sentences.

The two analyses are nonetheless very much alike in spirit, and the revised account of subjectification presented here brings them even closer together. As a first step toward making the subjectification of modals conform to the revised model, let me restate the characterization of epistemic modals to emphasize the speaker's role as conceptualizer. To say that the speaker assesses the evolutionary momentum of reality and its likelihood of reaching the target process is basically equivalent to saying that this conceptualizer carries out a *mental extrapolation* of ongoing reality, projecting into the future. We can plausibly describe the speaker as sensing the degree of force impelling this mental extrapolation in the envisaged direction, or the degree of resistance encountered in projecting it through to the target. In this way we portray the force dynamics as being inherent not in reality but in the conceptualizer's mental experience, hence subjectively construed in a narrow sense.

If the revised view of subjectification is correct, this force-dynamic experience ought to be inherent in the conception of the main verbs from which the modals evolve, as depicted in Figure 8. I have no proof that this is so, but I consider it to be both reasonable and helpful in thinking about the semantics of such elements. For instance, 'want' is a force-dynamic notion, in which the subject experiences an impulsion or attraction toward a future event. I find it attractive to speculate that, in conceptualizing the subject having such an experience, the speaker must to some degree vicariously have a comparable experience. This raises the general and critical issue of the extent to which recognizing other viewpoints involves mentally adopting those viewpoints in some attenuated way. At the very least, the conception of other minds and their experience must be parasitic on or derivative of the conceptualizer's own experience.

More obviously, perhaps, conceiving of someone having the strength or ability to do something involves imagining the person engaging in the activity. This requires a mental extrapolation, since these notions do not pertain to any actual occurrence of the action. Hence the conceptualizer implicitly assesses the degree of mental effort involved in making this extrapolation. For what it is worth, in conceptualizing (9a) I almost tangibly feel the mental resistance that has to be overcome in imagining the subject standing up, as signaled by *barely*. Especially suggestive is an ambiguity exhibited by the force-dynamic adverb *easily*. In (9b), it may be indeterminate whether (or to what extent) *easily* pertains to the force-dynamic experience of the subject, in carrying out the act of lifting, or to that of the conceptualizer, in imagining its possibility. I propose that the conceptualizer has this experience in conceiving of the subject having it, and that the "epistemic" sense of *easily* emerges to the extent that the notion of the subject having it fades away.

(9)   a.   He barely has the strength to stand up.

        b.   She is easily able to lift it.

There is independent support for localizing the force dynamics of modals in the speaker's mental extrapolation. This account extends straightforwardly to an important use of modals, namely to specify the likelihood of a *present* situation obtaining (rather than a future one occurring):

(10)   a.   He must be satisfied (or he would have complained).

       b.   She should be home by now (so we can phone her).

       c.   Larry may be angry at me (he hasn't said a word all evening).

Here it is evident that the force-dynamic value of the modals does not pertain to the evolution of reality per se—whether the situation obtains or not has already been determined at the level of reality. It pertains instead to evolution of the *knowledge* of reality: what kind of momentum or resistance the speaker encounters in mentally projecting currently accepted reality to encompass the situation. I am suggesting that this force-dynamic experience, inherent in the conceptualizer's mental extrapolation (hence subjectively construed), is equally characteristic of both the present- and the future-oriented modal uses. In either case the conceptualizer is doing the extrapolation, and having the force-dynamic experience. All that differs is whether the conceptualizer's expanding conception of reality is coming to encompass future events (where the outcome has not yet been determined objectively) or facets of the present (already determined) that are not yet known. These extrapolations are experientially quite comparable despite their different objective status.

6. Conclusion

I will not offer any sweeping theoretical conclusions. For one thing, I have no doubt grossly oversimplified some complex historical developments. Moreover, I have only been examining certain kinds of semantic change and one basic type of grammaticization. I believe grammaticization to be complex and multifaceted, so that no simple formulation, nor the postulation of any single mechanism, can do justice to it. My basic, limited conclusion is that subjectification—characterized as the laying bare of subjective factors immanent in more objective conceptions—does play a significant role in semantic change and grammaticization. This is ultimately a kind of loss, or "bleaching", since what remains was there all along, and not everything remains.

I believe this conception to be compatible with previous statements by others which have emphasized semantic gain, as a corrective to the natural tendency to think of grammaticization as *solely* a matter of loss:

> ... Semantic change in the early stages of grammaticalization does not necessarily involve bleaching: on the contrary, it usually involves specification achieved through inferencing ... of two kinds, metaphor and metonymy ... (Traugott 1988: 413-414)

> ... There is a sense in which grammaticalization involves loss of meaning, and another sense in which it does not ... When an image-schematic structure is abstracted from a lexical meaning ... there is a potential loss of meaning. The image schema does not have the richness of the lexical meaning in the source domain ... But if the abstracted schema is transferred ... to some particular target domain, then the meaning of the target domain is *added* to the meaning of the word: thus an instance of *go* which has lost the sense of physical motion has gained the sense of futurity, intention, or prediction. (Sweetser 1988: 400)

As noted earlier, the story I have told has not been centered on metaphor (nor metonymy). Metaphor is certainly more significant than I have made it out to be, probably even for the phenomena considered, yet it is interesting to see how much of a plausible and interesting nature emerges even without it. My position is compatible with Traugott's because her comment pertains to "the early stages of grammaticalization", whereas I have been more interested in the later stages, where objective elements are progressively stripped away, to the point where little if anything is left behind onstage.

If there is disagreement with Sweetser, it is not severe. Her comments may also be taken as applying to the earlier stages of grammaticization, and I suggested the possibility of metaphor figuring in the first step in grammaticizing *be going to*. I claim, however, that even the spatial movement sense of *be going to* subsumes the notions of futurity, intention, and prediction, both objectively and subjectively. These are not gained via metaphorical extension, as is evident once it is recognized that the entire construction *be going to* undergoes grammaticization, not just *go*. In later stages I do not regard the subject as moving metaphorically through time— it is rather the conceptualizer who moves through time, subjectively, to locate a process in which the subject has a role. Yet the conceptualizer's subjective motion was there all along, the later stages of grammaticization being primarily a matter of its objective support progressively fading from the picture.

I would however agree with a further comment:

> Grammaticalization may be seen as laying bare the deeper structural characteristics of earlier lexical meanings of morphemes. (Sweetser 1988: 401)

Subjectification is the "laying bare" of conceptual operations which are immanent in the original lexical meanings and in that sense constitute their "deepest" properties. Givón deserves to be cited as well for an early formulation of the same basic insight:

> ...The internal semantic structure of verbs turns out to be the very embryo of our tense system. (Givón 1973: 921)

These two quotations point to the essential dialectic of an optimal research strategy. On the one hand, recurring paths of grammaticization offer an important source of evidence concerning the meanings of the elements that undergo it. At the same time, grammaticization cannot be properly described or understood unless the semantic structure of these elements is elucidated in considerable detail. Both facets of the enterprise need to be pursued, each informing the other.

References

Aguirre, Manuel, and Louis Goossens. 1977. Dynamic Synchrony: An Illustration from the English Modals. *Antwerp Papers in Linguistics* 11.

Givón, Talmy. 1973. The Time-Axis Phenomenon. *Language* 49:890-925.

Heine, Bernd. 1992. Grammaticalization Chains. *Studies in Language* 16:335-368.

Lakoff, George. 1987. *Women, Fire, and Dangerous Things: What Categories Reveal About the Mind.* Chicago and London: University of Chicago Press.

Langacker, Ronald W. 1985. Observations and Speculations on Subjectivity, in John Haiman (ed.), *Iconicity in Syntax*, 109-150. Amsterdam and Philadelphia: John Benjamins. Typological Studies in Language 6.

-----. 1986. Abstract Motion. *Proceedings of the Annual Meeting of the Berkeley Linguistics Society* 12:455-471.

-----. 1987a. *Foundations of Cognitive Grammar*, vol. 1, *Theoretical Prerequisites.* Stanford: Stanford University Press.

-----. 1987b. Nouns and Verbs. *Language* 63:53-94.

-----. 1990. Subjectification. *Cognitive Linguistics* 1:5-38.

-----. 1991. *Foundations of Cognitive Grammar*, vol. 2, *Descriptive Application.* Stanford: Stanford University Press.

-----. 1992a. Prepositions as Grammatical(izing) Elements. *Leuvense Bijdragen* 81:287-309.

-----. 1992b. The Symbolic Nature of Cognitive Grammar: The Meaning of *of* and of *of*-Periphrasis, in Martin Pütz (ed.), *Thirty Years of Linguistic Evolution: Studies in Honour of René Dirven on the Occasion of his Sixtieth Birthday*, 483-502. Philadelphia and Amsterdam: John Benjamins.

-----. 1995a. A Note on the Spanish Personal "a", in Peggy Hashemipour, Ricardo Maldonado, and Margaret van Naerssen (eds.), *Studies in Language Learning and Spanish Linguistics in Honor of Tracy D. Terrell*, 431-441. New York: McGraw-Hill.

-----. 1995b. Raising and Transparency. *Language* 71:1-62.

Postal, Paul M. 1974. *On Raising: One Rule of English Grammar and Its Theoretical Implications.* Cambridge, Mass. and London: MIT Press. Current Studies in Linguistics 5.

Sweetser, Eve E. 1982. Root and Epistemic Modals: Causality in Two Worlds. *Proceedings of the Annual Meeting of the Berkeley Linguistics Society* 8:484-507.

-----. 1988. Grammaticalization and Semantic Bleaching. *Proceedings of the Annual Meeting of the Berkeley Linguistics Society* 14:389-405.

-----. 1990. *From Etymology to Pragmatics: Metaphorical and Cultural Aspects of Semantic Structure.* Cambridge: Cambridge University Press. Cambridge Studies in Linguistics 54.

Talmy, Leonard. 1985. Force Dynamics in Language and Thought, in William H. Eilfort, Paul D. Kroeber, and Karen L. Peterson (eds.), *Papers from the Parasession on Causatives and Agentivity*, 293-337. Chicago: Chicago Linguistic Society.

Traugott, Elizabeth. 1988. Pragmatic Strengthening and Grammaticalization. *Proceedings of the Annual Meeting of the Berkeley Linguistics Society* 14:406-416.

Verhagen, Arie. 1995. Subjectification, Syntax, and Communication, in Dieter Stein and Susan Wright (eds.), *Subjectivity and Subjectivisation: Linguistic Perspectives*, 103-128. Cambridge: Cambridge University Press.

Part II

Discourse

Three Grammaticalization Paths for the Development of Person Verbal Agreement in Hebrew

MIRA ARIEL

Tel-Aviv University

"The changes of tomorrow are the consequences of our acts of communication today. A theory of language change is thus at one and the same time a theory of the functions and principles of communication" (Keller 1994: 14). This has in fact been the research agenda for some functional discourse analysts (Hopper and Thompson 1980, Du Bois 1987b, inter alia). Macro-level structural linguistic change, argues Keller, is the **unintended** result of multiple, micro-level, natural and motivated individual actions. But since there is no "great planning" involved, one cannot fully predict linguistic change. Moreover, since language change is brought about by individual speakers, they only have their individual local goals in mind. Thus, no teleological change is assumed for the creation of new (communicative) functions (see also Hopper and Traugott 1993, Bybee, Perkins and Pagliuca 1994), and the (historical) end result need not even be directly motivated by the individual synchronic actions adopted. In fact, linguistic change is not at all guaranteed to end up being functional, except that if it turns out to be dysfunctional it will probably disappear through lack of use.

If change is caused by multiple, **locally** motivated factors, it is not surprising that the same linguistic phenomenon may undergo different changes in different languages, and even within the same language. However, linguistic change can still be argued to follow the same natural, possibly universal, synchronic principles which govern successful communication. The different actual processes (leading to potentially different historical changes) can be argued to result from the specific implementations, which depend on highly local, even ad hoc circumstances. I propose to exemplify these assumptions with the three different person verbal inflectional paradigms in Hebrew.

1. The Three Inflectional Paradigms of Hebrew

Table (1) presents the past tense inflectional paradigm for the regular verb 'count' in the 'Kal' paradigm:

Person	'Count'		Person Marker
1st	safar	+	ti
2nd f/m	safar	+	t/ta
3rd m/f	saf(a)r(a)	+	Ø
1st pl	safar	+	nu
2nd pl f/m	s(a)far	+	ten/tem
3rd pl f/m	safru	+	Ø

Table 1: Hebrew past verbal person inflections

This basic person agreement paradigm in Hebrew is the universally unmarked pattern whereby 1st and 2nd persons are overtly marked on the verb, and 3rd person is Ø marked (see Moscati et al 1969, Benveniste 1971, Givón 1976, Bybee 1985, Haiman 1985, Mithun 1986b, 1988, 1989, 1991, Du Bois 1987a, Huehnergard 1987, Helmbrecht 1995 for arguments and/or findings corroborating this claim). This pattern holds for past and future tenses of all the 7 verbal paradigms in Hebrew. Present tense verbs inflect for number and gender, but not person.

But Hebrew (especially archaic/formal Hebrew) has two other, marginal inflectional paradigms, which pattern differently.[1] First, these paradigms are exceptional in that they show person

---

1. Thus, Harel 1992 (Hebrew telephone conversations) contains only one such form (*yeshno* 'exist-3rd-m-sg'), out of 810 verbs. The more formal style of the written *Noga* magazine (short stories and interviews) contains 7 *eyneni/eyni* 'I am not/don't' and 1 *eynxem* 'you-pl-m are not/don't' (8 out of 500 verbal forms). The Hebrew translation of Chomsky's *Language and mind* contains 4 *svurani* and 1 *xoshvani*, both 'I think'.

agreement in present tense. Second, the inflected forms here are not always obligatory, as the above forms are. In fact, most of them cannot cooccur with overt subjects. They mostly exist as alternatives for the (more) analytic forms, which do not inflect for person. Third and foremost, in these verbal paradigms, 1st and 2nd persons do not cluster together in being both overtly marked on the verb as opposed to no marking for 3rd person.

The first exceptional pattern concerns very few cognition verbs (e.g., 'think', 'be afraid', 'remember'), which inflect only for 1st sg. person. Since this pattern is based on present tense forms, which distinguish for gender, this paradigm is unique in having distinct forms for feminine and masculine in first person:

(1) a. Xoshevet/xoshva[2]   ani   -->   xoshvat+ni
         Think-fem   I
     b. Xoshev   ani   -->   xoshva+ni
         Think-msc   I

The second exceptional paradigm is restricted to particles turned into verbs: *yesh* 'there is', *eyn* 'there isn't', *hinne* 'here/behold', *harey* 'hereby/behold'. The pattern here shows person agreement for **all** persons (but there are some differences between these particle-turned verbs -- see below):[3]

---

[2] I thank Randall Garr for drawing my attention to the possibility of deriving the feminine forms from the pattern of *xoshva*.

[3] In modern Hebrew almost all speakers have reduced the geminate *nn* to a single *n*. Also an epenthetic *e* is inserted whenever the person marker begins with *n* (1st persons).

Person	Particle			Person Marker
1st	hinne -->	hinn	+	ni
2nd f/m	hinne -->	hinn	+	ax/xa
3rd f	hinne -->	hinn	+	a / hinne+hi
3rd m	hinne -->	hinn	+	o / hinne+hu
1st pl	hinne -->	hinn	+	nu
2nd pl f/m	hinne -->	hinn	+	xen/xem
3rd pl f/m	hinne -->	hinn	+	an/am

Table 2: The inflectional paradigm for *hinne* 'here/behold'[4]

Why did Hebrew develop 3 different inflectional paradigms, one restricted to 1st person sg., another restricted to/overtly marking only 1st and 2nd persons, and one inflecting for all three persons? I would like to argue that all three historical paths involved here are well-motivated, and the reason that different, potentially conflicting, functional motivations applied in the three cases is that other, independently motivated factors are involved in each case (see Du Bois 1985).

2.1 Marking Predicates: Particle-Turned Verbs

Frequent forms are usually the least marked, often even Ø marked (Greenberg 1966, Bybee 1985, 1994, Croft 1990, inter alia). Indeed, most typologists are in agreement that the prototypical verbal person agreement pattern, whereby 3rd person is Ø marked/reduced and 1st/2nd persons are overtly (more) marked, stems from the fact that 3rd person verbal forms are more frequent than 1st/2nd person verbs (see Greenberg 1966, Kuryłowicz 1968, Givón 1976, Moravcsik 1978, 1987, Tiersma 1982, Bybee 1985, 1988, Lapointe 1987 Croft 1990, Mathews 1991, Hopper and Traugott 1993).

1st person verbal forms are usually thought to be less frequent than 3rd person verbal forms, but significantly more frequent than 2nd person verbal forms (see the statistics for Spanish, as quoted by Bybee 1985, and a few of the texts in Ariel to appear). In some contexts, however, it is 1st person which is the most frequent verbal form (see Tiersma 1982), and/or the less marked (see Helmbrecht 1995). Hence, typological markedness predicts that whereas mostly 3rd person verbal forms should be least marked, sometimes 1st, rather than 3rd person may be coded by the least marked form. Indeed, for

---

[4] I do not here list forms which are marginal even for these forms, such as *hinneha* for 3rd person fem. sg.

the Hebrew verbs here concerned, when there are markedness differences between the forms, it is 1st, or 3rd, or 1st and 3rd person verbal forms which are least marked. As expected, 2nd person verbal forms are never the most popular forms. Whereas 3rd person forms are more frequently used for *eyn* 'is not'+inflection, 1st person is more frequently used for *hinne* 'here is'+inflection. The data for *yesh* 'there is'+inflection indicates that even in the Bible, it was quite a rare inflection. In fact, in modern Hebrew, only 3rd person *yesh*+inflection forms occur (the Biblical data in Table 3 comes from Mandelkern 1937, the *Old Testament* concordance; The Mishnaic data comes from Kasowsky 1955, the Mishnaic concordance):[5]

	Hinne+	Eyn+	Yesh+	harey+	Total
1	**183=75.6%**	12=12.2%	Ø	**159=100%**	354=69.7%
2	18=7.4%	20=20.4%	5=55.5%	Ø	43=8.5%
3	41=16.9%	**66=67.3%**	4=44.4%	Ø	111=21.8%
T	242=99.9%	98=99.9%	9=99.9%	159=100%	508=100%

Table 3: The distribution of *hinne* 'here-be', *eyn* 'there-be-not' and *yesh* 'there-be' in the Bible and *harey* 'hereby' in the Mishna according to person

When we analyze the **forms** at hand, we see that there is a clear difference between 1st/3rd persons and 2nd persons. 1st person and most of the 3rd person agreement markers derive from independent pronouns, the agreement markers clearly being the reduced counterparts of the independent pronouns: Compare *ani* with +*ni* (1st sg), *hi/hu* with +*hi/hu* (3rd sg fem./msc.), *anu* with *nu* (1st pl.), *hen/hem* with *an/am* (3rd pl fem./msc.). Second person independent pronouns have a *t* consonant in Hebrew (*at, ata, aten, atem* -- 'you-sg,fem/sg,msc/pl,fem/pl,msc'), but the inflectional markers are of the *x* series (most probably from a cislocative origin), as is the norm for nominal declensions. In fact, an alternative 3rd person sg. marker for the first three roots above (*a/o*, 'fem/msc') is also patterned according to the nominal paradigm (a few particle verbs, such as *eyn* 'there isn't' have alternative verbal and nominal declensions).

I believe that the inflectional paradigms of these particle verbs are best accounted for by typological markedness and its adjunct assumption in explaining verbal marking, namely, predicate marking. Note that one cannot argue that 3rd person verbal forms are the most frequent, and hence least marked, without first motivating a distinction on verbs according to person.

---

[5] The Mishna is the edited version of oral Jewish laws (200 a.d).

After all, why make a distinction between verbs at all? A reasonable motivation for marking verbs is that such a marking signals a function-argument relation between the subject and its predicate, the verb.[6] Whereas this may not actually be necessary for verbs (see Du Bois 1987b), it does seem useful when the predicates involved are not at all verbs originally, as is the case with the particles under discussion ('hereby', etc.). The main function of agreement in this exceptional inflectional paradigm, I maintain, is to mark that a predicate has been formed out of the particle.

Now, if these particles are to be analyzed as predicates/ verbs, they require some special verbal marking, since they do not conform to any of the verbal paradigms, which all Hebrew verbs must conform to. This marking is required regardless of the person the verb relates to. Indeed, this is what we find here. All persons are overtly marked on the verb, and there is no Ø marking (if a verb is to be formed at all). Moreover, whereas independent nominative pronouns are a good source for deriving person agreement markers, they are by no means the only reasonable source for turning a particle into a verb. Hence the variation in the inflectional paradigm of particles between the regular verbal pattern (agreement derives from independent nominative pronouns) and the nominal pattern (agreement derives from cislocatives or from more drastically reduced, possibly nonnominative pronouns, e.g., *ani* -> *i* for 1st person sg. -- *ni* in the regular paradigm, *hu* -> *o* for 3rd person msc. sg., Ø in the regular paradigm).

Last, note that whereas the common overtly inflected verbal forms (1st/2nd person in past/future tenses) quite freely allow Ø subjects (because this agreement is a development of the clearly referential independent pronouns), the 3rd person inflected forms here concerned (e.g., *hinna/o*, *yeshna/o*, *ey(ne)na/o*) do not allow Ø subjects. In other words, they are not taken as containing a referential expression. These features, which distinguish the particle-verb inflectional paradigm from the basic verbal paradigm, all stem from the function agreement serves in this case. Whereas the basic agreement markers serve a referential function (at least initially), I propose that the function which brought about the creation of these agreement markers is predicate creation. Then, once the particle-verb is formed, frequency

---

[6] An alternative hypothesis is that agreement arises in left and right dislocated sentences, in which case the origin of agreement in pronouns is accounted for. However, it is not clear why it is mostly 1st/2nd person verbs that are inflected for person, when dislocated NPs are for the most part 3rd person. See Ariel to appear on this issue.

considerations may dictate that highly frequent verbal forms be less formally marked than infrequent ones. This accounts for the relative markedness of 2nd person forms.

2.2 Frequency-Driven Morphologization: Cognition Verbs and the Gaps in the Inflectional Paradigms of Particle Verbs

A different mechanism is responsible for the second exceptional inflectional paradigm, as well as for some pardigmatic gaps in the particle-verb inflections above. Recall that a few cognition verbs inflect only for 1st sg. person in present tense, which is remarkable for present tense verbs, since they do not inflect for person at all. Now, unlike the particle-verbs, where some marking may have actually been sought for in order to convert the particles into verbs, cognition verbs, like all other present tense verbs, are recognized as such without the person agreement, because they are lexically marked as verbs.[7]

But then, fusion often occurs mainly due to the frequent adjacency of two forms (Givón 1971, Bybee 1985, Bybee et al 1990, Croft 1990, Keller 1994). No wonder inflection did not necessarily develop for all persons, but rather for the one person which most commonly cooccurs with cognition verbs, namely 1st person sg.[8] A 1st versus 2nd/3rd person split is to be expected when verbs of perception and emotion are concerned according to Tiersma 1982. Helmbrecht 1995 proceeded to exemplify such systems in many Caucasian and Indian languages, offering various hierarchies of tenses (future versus present), modes (irrealis versus realis) etc., where a 1st versus 2nd/3rd person split is expected, because the 1st person is a self-conscious person. Indeed, see Thompson and Mulac 1991a,b for a high cooccurrence rate of 1st person pronouns with *think* and *guess* in English, Weber and Bentivoglio 1991 for the same in Venezuelan spoken Spanish, Bybee et al 1994 for the high cooccurrences of *I* with *shall* and *will*, originally verbs of obligation and desire, and Tao 1996 for a high frequency of 1st person pronouns with

---

[7] Historically, so-called present tense is a nominal form, and hence the inflection for number and gender only. But by Mishnaic times such participles are routinely used as verbs.

[8] Interestingly enough, Aramaic, from which Late Mishnaic Hebrew borrowed this grammatical option, is less restrictive, although it is not fully productive there either (see Nöldeke 1904, Segal 1958, Kadari 1971 and Tal 1974).

cognition and speech act verbs in Chinese).[9] Japanese and Hua show a similar pattern, in that they lack (direct) forms for expressing 'you/ s/he want(s)' (Wierzbicka 1987: 15). So the special Hebrew agreement pattern above no doubt results from the fact that it is mostly 1st sg. person pronouns which cooccur with such verbs of cognition. The fusion of the verbal form with a reduced 1st person pronoun then results from the very frequent adjacent cooccurrence of these two (in a VS order).[10] Indeed, Mishnaic Hebrew, where this inflection first appears, mostly placed pronouns following such verbal forms (Weiss 1867), thus explaining the suffixing agreement system.

The inconsistency between the person frequencies of the different particle verbs (see Table 3 above) can also be motivated when we take into consideration the plausibility of their use with each person. In this respect, these particle verbs differ from each other quite drastically. Whereas they all form part of very formal Hebrew, *yesh* 'there is'+3rd person inflections can also be used colloquially. *Yesh*+1st/2nd persons are quite unacceptable in all registers. *Eyn* 'there isn't'+ inflections is unrestricted re person. *Harey* 'behold' is mostly restricted to 1st person in the Mishna, but it does occur with a 3rd person inflection in Modern Hebrew (see Ariel 1985: 297). It never even developed for 2nd person. *Hinne* 'here'-inflected forms are today distinctly rarer than the other particle verbs.

The nonoccurrence of 1st and 2nd person *yesh* 'exist/is nearby located' forms (even in the Bible) stems from the plausible assumption that the speaker and addressee are assumed to exist/be present, so there is no need to predicate their 'being here' in present tense (the 5 occurrences of 2nd person

---

[9] For example, Thompson and Mulac 1991b find that 83% of the subjects of epistemic main verbs taking complements are *I* and 5% are *you*. All other subjects constitute only 12%. Weber and Bentivoglio show that 79% of the subjects of 'believe' and 'think' are 1st person (7% are 2nd person, and 14% are 3rd person). In a small sample where I checked singular forms only (Lotan 1990: 1-4), 1st persons constitute 63% of the subjects of cognition verbs, although they only constitute 32.5% of the subjects of action verbs. 3rd persons, on the other hand, constitute 50% of the subjects of action verbs, but only 11.1% of cognition verb subjects.

[10] *Kimduma+ni* 'it-seems-to-me', however, is probably created by analogy to the cognition verbs mentioned above, because its pre-inflectional source would have been *kimdume alay*, where 1st person is an indirect object.

yesh in the Bible have a different meaning).[11] The high frequency of the 1st person sg. *hinneni* in the Bible and of *hareyni*, mainly in the Mishna, but also (infrequently) in modern Hebrew (both 'here+1st'), stems from their usage as performative markers ('hereby'), which are common with 1st person, since speech act verbs naturally take 1st person subjects (see Tao 1996 again).

As argued by Bybee 1985, mere high frequencies of adjacency do not guarantee fusion. Some semantic cohesion is often required for fusion to take place. Indeed, it is mostly cognition verbs used epistemically which allow this special inflection (see Thompson and Mulac 1991a,b). *Xosheshani* is acceptable, but *poxdani is not, even though both mean 'I'm afraid-msc'. Only the former is an epistemic marker. Moreover, when the literal meaning is intended, as in 'I'm afraid of the lion', the special inflected form may not be used, even with the "legitimate" *xoshesh*, and speakers must use the uninflected verb accompanied by an overt pronoun. The same semantic constraint applies to the inflectional paradigms of particle verbs (2.1). An examination of the cooccurrence of 3rd person independent personal and demonstrative pronouns with *harey* 'hereby' in the Mishna reveals that these two cooccur with *harey* significantly more often than 1st person pronoun or agreement (the two 3rd person pronouns are, however, often hyphenated to *harey* in the Mishna). Table 4 lists independent as well as agreement person markers cooccurring with *harey* in the Mishna (data again based on Kasowski 1955):

1st	2nd	3rd Pers	3rd Demons	Total
172=16.7%	19=1.8%	413=40.1%	427=41.4%	1031=100%

Table 4: *Harey* frequency of cooccurrence with various pronouns

Yet, it is 1st, rather than 3rd person personal or demonstrative pronouns which had fused with *harey* by Mishnaic times. This can be motivated by noting that 3rd person inflected *harey* forms are often no more than the combination of their parts. 1st person *harey* forms create a semantic concept of performativity.

---

[11] A rare modern spoken example I overheard was:

E.L:	ata	**yeshnexa**	maxar?
	You	are-located-here	tomorrow?
E.S:	ken,	ani	**yeshneni**.
	Yes,	I	am-located-here.

Note that both speakers did not use the normative forms, but rather, created new forms, on analogy with the *eyn* paradigm. In fact, they both laughed, as they felt the strangeness of the forms.

No wonder 1st person inflected *harey* grammaticalized earlier than 3rd person (as is attested to by the non-occurrence of the latter in the Mishna), despite the former's relative lower frequency. Thus, frequency-driven **semantically coherent** morphologization processes can motivate the creation of 1st but not 2nd/3rd person agreement for cognition verbs, they can motivate the nonoccurrence of 1st/2nd person *yesh* 'exist here' forms and the earlier creation of 1st person *harey* and *hinne* 'here, behold' forms for expressing performativity.

2.3 Accessibility Theory: The Prototypical Inflectional Pattern

In Ariel (to appear) I argue that a third type of process is responsible for the predominant verbal agreement pattern, whereby 1st and 2nd persons are overtly marked on the verb, whereas 3rd persons are not overtly marked. I have argued that straight frequency-driven morphologization or typological markedness cannot be assumed to solely account for this pattern. First, regarding typological marking, which relies on frequency, natural data do not consistently reveal a 3rd person verbal predominance. This is especially true in conversational data, the source most reliable for detecting linguistic change (see Greenberg 1966, Croft 1990, Milroy 1992). Thus, in Lotan 1990 (Hebrew face to face conversations), there are no significant differences in the frequency of 1st, 2nd and 3rd person verbs:

1st person	2nd person	3rd person	Total
47=32.4%	45=31.0%	53=36.5%	145=99.9%

Table 5: Verb frequency according to person in Lotan 1990

Children's face to face conversations I analyzed (children's age 5:7-7:5, Feb. 1996) show 1st person to be the most frequent, followed by 3rd person (Only future tense verbs are here considered):

1st person	2nd person	3rd person	Total
51=56.7%	11=12.2%	28=31.1%	90=100%

Table 6: Verb frequency according to person in children's Hebrew conversations

Finally, in Harel 1992 (long telephone conversations between acquaintances) 1st person verbal forms are the most frequent ones, followed by 2nd person verbs. 3rd person verbs are least frequent:

1st person	2nd person	3rd person	Total
370=45.7%	255=31.5%	185=22.8%	810=100%

Table 7: Verb frequency according to person in Harel 1992

I have further argued that a frequency-driven morphologization process, strictly applied, cannot explain this pattern either. If it is pronouns adjacent to verbs which reduce and fuse with them, thus becoming agreement markers, we should consider the relative frequencies of 1st, 2nd and 3rd person subject pronouns. Now, since 3rd person references are frequently made using lexical NPs, whereas 1st and 2nd person references are made by pronouns in an overwhelming majority of the cases, it might be assumed that 1st/2nd person pronouns occur adjacent to their verbs much more often than 3rd person pronouns. While this is true in **some** texts for **some** 3rd person pronouns (feminine forms mainly), it is not invariably so. Consider the frequencies of Ø's and overt personal pronouns (these would have been the source for creating agreement in a non-Ø-subject language -- see Ariel to appear) in Harel 1992 and in Levy 1995 (a Hebrew narrative). Table 8 presents the frequency of the various persons according to the gender and number of the subject as well, for each of the Hebrew agreement markers show a direct affinity with the corresponding independent pronoun (in other words, fem. and/or pl. forms are not derived from the corresponding msc./sg. forms by adding some fem. and/or pl. morpheme):

Levy 1995		Harel 1992	
	Least frequent		
Y-fm-sg/Y-fm-pl/Y-ms-pl	0	**Y-fm-sg/Y-fm-pl/**They-fm	0
She/They-fm	2	She	9
Y-ms-sg/**They-ms**	11	Y-pl-ms	21
I	15	We	26
We	24	**They-ms**	27
He	45	**He**	67
		Y-ms-sg	234
		I	341
	Most frequent		

Table 8 : Frequency of Ø/pronouns in Levy 1995 and Harel 1992 Persons in bold= "improper" place in the frequency hierarchy.

Given the frequency-driven morphologization model, according to Levy 1995, agreement should have developed for 3rd person sg. ms. primarily (which it does not), for 1st person sg. and pl. (which it does), and possibly also for 2nd person sg. ms. (it does) and 3rd person pl. ms. (it does not). It should certainly have not developed for 2nd person fm. (sg. or pl.) and 2nd person ms. pl. (but of course it does). Similar problems are posed by Harel 1992 (see Table 8).

I have therefore proposed that it is the prototypical difference between 1st/2nd referents and 3rd person referents, which is responsible for the different agreement patterns for 1st/2nd versus 3rd person verbs. To see the working of this mechanism we need to look at the correlation between referring expressions and the mental representations (or referents) they are used to retrieve. In effect in line with Sanford and Garrod 1981, Givón 1983 and Chafe 1987 (inter alia), I have proposed (Ariel 1985, 1990, 1991) that referring expressions are accessibility markers. They each encode the degree of accessibility with which the mental representation intended as referent is entertained by the addressee (as assessed by the speaker). Other things being equal, (the mental representations of) the speaker and the addressee are much more accessible than that of (the mental representation of) an entity which is neither the speaker nor the addressee (3rd person).

Accessibility theory claims that there is a coding principle whereby the more accessible the mental representation intended, the more reduced (and the less informative and more general/ambiguous) the referring expression is. Indeed, pronouns are routinely reduced when they refer to highly accessible entities. In (2), after the speaker has referred to the press as *they* many times, he utters the following (see Ariel 1990 for sources and analysis):

(2)   i ...   **h**[=hem]+   mociim   et   ze   kaxa...
             They   publish   acc.   this   like-this...
      ii   aval **hem**   madgishim... **h**   notnim kama...
             But   they   emphasize... they   give   some...
      iii od   davar she+   **hem**   asu...
             Another thing that   they   did...

Note that the speaker consistently switches to a full pronoun whenever he judges that the addressee may have considered a change of topic, due to the break markers ('but', 'another thing...'). In (3) the speaker starts by referring to the established discourse topic (Cameron) by a pronoun, whereas the non discourse topic is referred to by a lower accessibility marker, a name (Nubar). However, when Nubar becomes highly accessible, the coding difference is maintained by using a pronoun for the less accessible antecedent and a reduced pronoun for the more accessible discourse topic:

(3)   Preceding discourse -- translated: Cameron$_i$... HE$_i$... he$_i$ talked to
            Nubar$_j$... Nubar$_j$ said... Nubar$_j$ was still...
      h$_i$ [=hu]   pashut   diber   ito$_j$,...   **hu$_j$** xashav...
      He   simply   talked   with-him   He   thought...

(4) shows the same point with respect to the use of an overt pronoun versus Ø
subject for a 1st person referent. Note that (a) and (b) below form a minimal
pair, where the local sentence topic preceding the crucial last reference to the
speaker is 'the mother'. But an overt pronoun is used only in (b). The reason
is that the high accessibility of the speaker-narrator is reduced because of the
reference to the mother's death, which constitutes a major break in the story
line, unlike the reference to the mother not knowing about the rape:

(4)   a.   ze   haya   davar shel ma bexax   bishvil yalda
            It   was   nothing   for   (a) girl
            o   isha   le+heanes. ani acmi neenasti,
            or   (a) woman to get raped. I   myself was
                   kshe+Ø   hayiti bat-shtem-esre. **ima** af paam
            raped, when [I] was   twelve-ys.-old. **Mama**   never
                   lo yada, u- Ø   meolam lo siparti le-ish.
            knew, and [I]   never told   (to) anybody.
            (*Noga* 1985).

       b.   Hu   pashut   himshix   le-nasot   le-alec   oti la-
            He   just   kept   trying   to make   me to
            cet ito,   ve-lifamim, mi-tox hergel,
            go-out with-him,   and sometimes, out of habit,
            ani   xoshevet, Ø halaxti ito.   gufi
            I   guess,   [I] went with-him.   My-body
            asa   ma she+shulam she-Ø-yaase.   ve-
            did   what (that it) was-being-paid to do.   And
            ima meta.   ve-**ani** haragti et   buba (Same).
            Mother died.   And **I** killed acc.   Bubba.

Now, when we compare the usage of those markers which were prone to have
undergone reduction originally (current Hebrew Øs and pronouns), we see a
clear distinction between the 3 persons. Whereas 1st/2nd person references are
consistently made by using these very high accessibility markers, 3rd person
references are often made by low accessibility markers (lexical NPs) rather

than pronouns or Øs:

	1st	2nd	3rd
Harel:	367=99.2%	255=100%	93=50.3%
Levy:	39=100%	11=100%	55=25.7%

Table 9: Pronoun/Ø in Harel 1992 and Levy 1995

Even the one repeated discourse topic in Levy 1995 was not consistently referred to by Øs or pronouns. A lexical NP was used in almost half of the cases (45.6%). According to accessibility theory, verbal agreement is a marker of a very high degree of accessibility. It is, moreover, a grammaticalized accessibility marker. Hence, it requires that the mental representations commonly retrieved by it are **consistently** highly accessible. The lower proportions of highly accessible referents for 3rd persons vs. 1st/2nd persons, I claim, motivates the creation of agreement for 1st/2nd persons, but not 3rd persons. 1st/2nd person referents are consistently highly accessible, whereas 3rd person referents are only inconsistently so.

3. Accessibility, Frequency-Driven Morphologization and Typological Markedness

Accessibility theory, frequency-driven morphologization and typological markedness are in principle compatible with each other. They may even converge on producing the same effects, since they complement each other. Note that whereas typological markedness considers the markedness and frequency of **verbal** forms, accessibility theory considers the markedness and frequency of **referential** forms, and frequency-driven morphologization considers the same for **pronoun-verb** cooccurrences. The crucial difference between the latter two is that frequency-driven morphologization relies on **absolute** numbers for person frequencies, whereas accessibility theory relies on **proportional** numbers. I calculate the **intra-person** percentages of reduced pronouns (the source for agreement) and then compare these percentages across the three persons. Hence, even if 3rd person references turn out to be the most frequent, the proportion in which they are made by using reduced pronouns is still lower than that of the possibly less frequent 1st/2nd person reduced pronouns (see Ariel to appear for a more extensive discussion).

It seems that all three processes are at work, but in different verbal paradigms: Typological marking in many of the high Hebrew particle-verb formations (2.1); absolute-number-frequency morphologization in high Hebrew cognition verb inflection (2.2); and accessibility-related processes in the basic prevalent verbal inflectional pattern, where pronouns are reduced to agreement markers (2.3).

Note, however, that there are potential conflicts between the three theories. Consider again cognition verbs. If these are predominantly used with 1st person sg. subjects, then typological markedness predicts incorrectly that 1st person verbs should be Ø or least marked, and 2nd/3rd person verbal forms be marked. In other words, we expect the opposite pattern: Verbs should inflect for 2nd/3rd and not 1st person. Accessibility theory incorrectly predicts that agreement should develop for both 1st and 2nd persons, since these are the more salient persons (although arguably 1st person is more so, especially given that the verb is a cognition verb). Frequency-driven morphologization, on the other hand, correctly predicts that only 1st person inflection develops, due to the high frequency of the cooccurrence of 1st person pronouns with cognition verbs. Similarly, for the particle-verbs, typological markedness correctly predicts Ø marking for the most frequent person of each of the verbs (see the discussion above), but frequency-driven morphologization predicts incorrectly that precisely the frequent verbal forms are the ones that should develop overt agreement marking (for the relevant persons). Accessibility theory predicts incorrectly 1st/2nd person overt versus 3rd person Ø marking.

In addition, although we explained the non-development of certain cognition verbs and certain particle-verbs with specific persons -- 3rd person *harey* 'hereby' -- by reference to Bybee's 1985 semantic constraint on fusing elements, 3rd person pronouns are nowadays attachable to one specific type of *harey* (Dominance *harey*). This *harey* signals the beginning of a dominant clause (see Kouzar 1980, Ariel 1988). There is thus no inherent connection between this *harey* and the following subject pronoun. This development, which goes against Bybee's 1985 semantic restriction on fusing elements, seems to have taken place simply because of the high frequency with which this *harey* and 3rd person pronouns cooccur adjacently (both this *harey* and grammatical subjects are sentence-initial in Hebrew). Such a change testifies to the working of automatic processes due to mere high frequencies, disregarding the coherence restriction. In fact, the very creation of verbal person agreement is somewhat surprising, as Bybee notes, since agreeing verbs conflate two categories (initially, at least): noun+verb, which do not necessarily create a complete new category. There are, then, conflicting motivations in language change (see Du Bois 1985).

I cannot at this stage offer anything near a full-fledged explanation for the resolutions of these conflicts. The objective of this paper is more to point to a research question than to solve it. In order to understand how these apparent conflicting forces work, I think we should follow Keller 1994 in assuming that speakers act with small-scale synchronic functional goals in mind, and Du Bois 1985 in noting that competing motivations have predictable and far from arbitrary linguistic implications. Croft's 1990: 158/9 point about no marking versus Ø marking is also highly relevant here: "if a grammatical semantic category is very infrequent, it simply will not be expressed as a distinct grammatical category in many languages". Perhaps this can motivate the nondevelopment of 2nd/3rd person inflection for cognition verbs, as well as 2nd person *harey* 'behold' and 1st/2nd person *yesh* 'be-here'. The necessity for marking verbs as such (the particle-verbs) motivates inflection for all 3 persons. This in turn paves the way for frequency considerations to operate, encouraging less marking for the most frequent verbal forms, rather than for accessibility theory to apply (since ALL persons need to be marked). Thus, highly local circumstances determine which of the functionally motivated, potentially conflicting mechanisms should apply in each case. I therefore conclude that a language can have three very different inflectional paradigms, yet each of them is functionally well motivated, where functionally motivated is understood in a non-teleological manner, as representing micro-level synchronic tendencies, which when cumulative, are recognized as a structural, macro-level historical change. In this respect, my conclusion is very similar to that of Du Bois 1987b re split ergative systems.

References

Ariel, Mira 1985. *Givenness Marking*. Doctoral dissertation, Tel-Aviv University.

___ 1988. Retrieving propositions from context. *Journal of Pragmatics* 12: 5/6. 567-600.

___ 1990. *Accessing NP Antecedents*. London: Routledge.

___ 1991. The function of accessibility in a theory of grammar. *Journal of Pragmatics* 16:4. 141-161.

___ to appear. The development of person agreement markers: From pronouns to higher accessibility markers. In Michael Barlow and Suzanne Kemmer eds. *Usage-Based Models of Language*.

Barlow, Michael and Charles A Ferguson eds., 1987. *Agreement in Natural Language*. Stanford: CSLI.

Benveniste, Emile 1971. *Problems in General Linguistics*. Coral Gables, Fa: University of Miami Press.

Bybee, Joan L. 1985. *Morphology*. Amsterdam: John Benjamins.

___ 1988. Morphology as lexical organization. In Hammond and Noonan eds.

119-41.

___ 1994. The grammaticalization of zero: Asymmetries in tense and aspect systems. In William Pagliuca ed. *Perspectives on Grammaticalization*. Amsterdam: John Benjamins. 235-54.

___, William Pagliuca and Revere Perkins 1990. On the asymmetries in the affixation of grammatical material. In William Croft, Keith Denning and Suzanne Kemmer eds. *Studies in Typology and Diachrony*. Amsterdam: John Benjamins. 1-42.

___, Revere Perkins and William Pagliuca 1994. *The Evolution of Grammar*. Chicago: The University of Chicago Press.

Chafe, Wallace L 1987. Cognitive constraints on information flow. In Russel Tomlin ed. *Coherence and grounding in discourse*. Amsterdam: John Benjamins. 21-51.

Croft, William 1990. *Typology and Universals*. Cambridge: Cambridge University Press.

Du Bois, John W 1985. Competing motivations. In Haiman, John ed. *Iconicity in syntax*. Amsterdam: John Benjamins. 343-65.

--- 1987a. Absolutive zero: Paradigm adaptivity in Sacapultec Maya. *Lingua* 71: 1-4. *Special Issue: Studies in Ergativity*. R.M.W Dixon ed. 203-22.

___ 1987b. The discourse basis of ergativity. *Language* 63:4. 805-55.

Givón, Talmy 1971. Historical syntax and synchronic morphology. *CLS* 7. 394-415.

-- 1976. Topic, pronoun, and grammatical agreement. In Li, Charles N ed. *Subject and Topic*. New-York: Academic press.ed. 149-88.

1983. ed. *Topic Continuity in Discourse: A quantitative Cross-Language Study*. Amsterdam: John Benjamins.

Greenberg Joseph H. 1966. *Language Universals, with Special Reference to Feature Hierarchies* (Janua Linguarum series minor 59). The Hague: Mouton.

Haiman, John 1985. *Natural Syntax*. Cambridge: Cambridge University Press.

Hammond, Michael and Michael Noonan 1988. eds. *Theoretical Morphology*. San Diego: Academic Press.

Helmbrecht, Johannes 1995. The typology of 1st person marking and its cognitive background. Unpublished ms.

Hopper, Paul J and Sandra A Thompson 1980. Transitivity in grammar and discourse. *Language* 56: 4. 251-99.

Hopper, Paul J and Elizabeth Closs Traugott 1993. *Grammaticalization*. Cambridge: Cambridge university press.

Huehnergard, John 1987. "Stative", predicative form, pseudo-verb. *Journal of Near Eastern studies* 47: 3. 215-32.

Kadari, Menachem Zvi 1971. *The grammar of the Aramaic language of the Zohar*. Jerusalem: Kiryat Sefer (in Hebrew).

Kasowsky, Chaim Yehoshua 1955. *Otsar leshon ha-Mishna, sefer ha-chatimot*. Jerusalem: Massada.

Keller, Rudi 1994. *On language change*. London: Routledge.

Kouzar, Ron 1980. On the linguistic marker *harey*. *Machbarot* 1: 50. (In Hebrew).

Kuryłowicz, Jerzy 1968. The notion of morpho(pho)neme. In Winfred P Lehmann and Yakov Malkiel eds. *Directions for Historical Linguistics*. Austin: University of Texas press. 65-81.

Lapointe, Steven G. 1987. Toward a unified theory of agreement. In Barlow and Ferguson eds. 67-87.

Mandelkern, Solomon. 1937. *Veteris Testamenti Concordantiae Hebraicae Atque Chaldaicae*. No place name: Shocken.

Mathews, P H 1991. *Morphology*. Cambridge: Cambridge university press.

Milroy, James 1992. *Linguistic Variation and Change*. Oxford: Blackwell.

Mithun, Marianne 1986b. When zero isn't there. *BLS* 12. 195-211.

_____ 1988. Lexical categories and the evolution of number marking. In Hammond and Noonan eds. 211-34.

_____ 1989. Historical linguistics and linguistic theory: Reducing the arbitrary and constraining explanation. *BLS* 15. 391-488.

_____ 1991. The development of bound pronominal paradigms. In Winfred P Lehmann and Helen-Jo Jakusz Hewitt eds. *Language Typology 1988*. Amsterdam: John Benjamins.

Moravcsik, Edith A 1978. Agreement. In Joseph H Greenberg ed. *Universals of Human Language*. Stanford: Stanford university Press. Vol. 4. 331-374.

_____ 1987. Agreement and markedness. In Barlow and Ferguson eds. 89-106.

Moscati, Sabatino, Anton Spitaler, Edward Ullendorff and Wolfram von Soden 1969. *An Introduction to the Comparative Grammar of the Semitic Languages*. Wiesbaden: Otto Harrassowitz.

Nöldeke, Theodor 1904/1970: 45. *Compendious Syriac grammar*. Translated into English by James A Crichton. London: Williams & Norgate. Repreinted in Israel 1970.

Sanford, Anthony J and Simon C Garrod 1981. *Understanding Written Languages*. Chichseter: John Wiley and sons.

Segal, M H 1927. *A grammar of Mishnaic Hebrew*. Oxford: The Clarendon Press.

Tal (Rosenthal) Avraham 1974. *Leshon ha-Targum li-Nviim rishonnim u-maamada bi-chlal nivei ha-Aramit*. Tel-Aviv: Tel-Aviv University Press.

Tao, Hongyin 1996. *Prosody, discourse and grammar*. Amsterdam: John

Benjamins.

Thompson, Sandra A and Anthony Mulac 1991a. The discourse conditions for the use of the complementizer *that* in conversational English. *Journal of Pragmatics* 15. 237-51.

___ 1991b. A quantitative perspective on the grammaticization of epistemic parentheticals in English. In Traugott, Elizabeth Closs and Bernd Heine eds. *Approaches to grammaticalization*. Amsterdam: John Benjamins. Vol II. 313-29.

Tiersma, Peter Meijes 1982. Local and general markedness. *Language* 58: 4. 832-49.

Weber, Elizabeth G and Paola Bentivoglio 1991. Verbs of cognition in spoken Spanish: A discourse profile. In Suzanne Fleischman and Linda R Waugh eds., *Discourse Pragmatics and the Verb: The Evidence from Romance*. London: Routledge. 194-213.

Weiss, Meir 1867. *Mishpat leshon ha-Mishna*. Vienna.

Wierzbicka, Anna 1987. *English speech act verbs*. Sydney: Academic press.

Prototype Theory and Covert Gender in Turkish[*]

FRIEDERIKE BRAUN
University of Kiel, Germany

1. Introduction

Although gender is a social category of prime importance in Turkey, there is no grammatical gender distinction in the Turkish language. This discrepancy has struck many observers, some of them even going so far as interpreting the genderless language structure as the heritage of an egalitarian (pre-Islamic) past[1]. This paper describes ongoing empirical research on the supposed gender neutrality of Turkish. The main hypothesis under investigation is that the lack of grammatical gender does not imply a gender-neutral semantics. The results of this research will be discussed in the light of prototype theory and its linguistic adaptations.

---

[*] I would like to take this opportunity to thank all those colleagues who made suggestions on an earlier version of this paper. Special thanks go to my colleague and friend Geoffrey Haig for accompanying me in the various stages of my research with competent and constructive assistance as well as for tidying up my English.

[1] E.g. the former prime minister Bülent Ecevit in a speech he held in 1989 (Ecevit 1991).

2. Turkish as a genderless language

Turkish is a language without grammatical gender. It does, however, have some lexical gender distinctions, such as *anne/baba* 'mother/father', *kız/oğlan* 'girl/boy', *hanım/bey* 'lady/sir' - we would of course assume this to be a feature of all natural languages. But the majority of terms for person reference can refer to males as well as females, e.g. *komşu* 'female neighbor/male neighbor', *öğrenci* 'female student/male student'. In this respect Turkish resembles English. Unlike English, however, a gender distinction is lacking in the pronominal system: *o* 'she/he', *ev-i* 'her house/his house'.

In Turkish texts gender frequently remains unmarked. Even across lengthy stretches of discourse the gender of the characters need not receive any explicit expression. To give just one example, in the book *Kadının adı yok* (by Duygu Asena, İstanbul: Milliyet. 1994), a doctor (*bir doktor*) is introduced into the narrative on page 71 and is a topic of the following one and a half pages. But the doctor's gender is never revealed.

From a formal point of view, Turkish is undoubtedly gender-neutral. However, closer inspection of both written and spoken texts provides evidence that terms for person reference do in fact contain a gender bias. For example, when female reference is intended, there is a pronounced tendency to use an additional lexical gender marker such as *kız* 'girl' or *kadın* 'woman', giving rise to forms such as *kız atlet* 'girl athlete' and *kadın polis* 'woman police'. To express male reference, however, the terms *atlet* or *polis* alone are sufficient.

To tackle the putative gender bias of Turkish words systematically, a series of investigations was conducted which proceeded from the initial assumption that gender semantics in Turkish is largely determined by the gender belief system anchored in the socio-cultural environment of the speakers.

3. Covert gender in Turkish - empirical evidence

The pilot study was conducted at Hacettepe University in Ankara in February 1995 with 130 students (78 females, 52 males) participating as subjects.[2] The subjects were students from several different classes at five different departments. The questionnaires were distributed in the classes by the respective teachers. The questionnaires contained standardized instructions to minimize interviewer bias.

---

[2] 106 of the subjects came from the West of Turkey, 16 from the East (8 gave no information). 117 had spent most of their lives in an urban environment, 9 in a rural one (4 gave no information). These features show no notable effects on the subjects' responses. Neither did age, which ranged from 17 to 35 years (with an average of 21,6).

As a cover story, subjects were told that the research was aimed at investigating Turkish forms of address. The questionnaire contained a list of person categories, such as *sekreter* 'secretary', *kuyumcu* 'goldsmith, jeweler'. The subjects were asked to write down the terms of address most widely used for these types of persons. Many Turkish terms of address express the gender of the addressee, e.g. *hanımefendi* 'lady', *beyefendi* 'sir', *teyze* 'aunt', *amca* 'uncle'. Therefore the subjects' responses - the address terms they chose for a given person category - ususally showed which gender they had associated with the stimulus term. Notice that the instructions did not contain any explicit mention of the real intentions of the investigation.

One group of stimulus terms involved activities which represent typically male domains. The results for this group are as follows:

Table 1: male domain

term	male interpret.	female interpret.	female & male	gender not determinable
polis 'police, officer'	98%	0%	1%	1%
işportacı 'street vendor'	94%	0%	1%	6%
kuyumcu 'goldsmith, jeweler'	93%	0%	2%	5%
taksi şoförü 'taxi driver'	82%	0%	1%	17%
postacı 'mail man/ woman'	76%	0%	1%	23%
memur here: 'bank employee'	69%	10%	20%	1%

In all of these occupations males outnumber females by far. The statistical difference is somewhat less pronounced in the case of bank employees, which is reflected in the data. Moreover many of these occupations are male ones not only in a quantitative sense. They also imply activities which are considered not suitable for women: exposing oneself in public (street vendors, mail man/woman), being in close contact with members of the opposite sex (taxi drivers) or exerting power (police).

A second group of stimulus-terms involved activities from predominantly female domains:

Table 2: female domain

term	female interpret.	male interpret.	female & male	gender not determinable
temizlikçi 'cleaning person'	96%	1%	0%	4%
sekreter 'secretary'	94%	0%	5%	1%
tezgâhtar 'salesperson'	65%	9%	14%	12%
misafir 'visitor'	46%	19%	11%	24%

These results are also well in accord with the socio-cultural background. Cleaner (in a private household) and secretary are typically female occupations; there is also quite a number of women who work as salespersons in a shop (i.e., out of the public and more protected than a street vendor). It may be less obvious why 'visitor' should have a female bias - if a slight one, but it must be kept in mind that visiting each other at home is rather a female activity in Turkey. Men frequently meet their friends in cafés or restaurants.

The first two tables confirm what we would have expected. The results in the next table are, however, contrary to such common-sense assumptions.

Table 3: supposedly neutral domain

term	male interpret.	female interpret.	female & male	gender not determinable
köylü 'villager'	72%	5%	20%	3%
kişi 'person'	68%	8%	21%	3%
birisi 'someone'	68%	5%	28%	0%
yolcu 'passenger'	66%	6%	24%	4%

We find that all of these terms display a male bias. But why should a 'person' or 'someone' be more often thought of as male rather than female? Why should 'villagers' be seen as predominantly male, when most of the persons living in villages are women (a consequence of men's migration to the cities in search of work)? Obviously we cannot resort to the statistical distribution of men and women here.[3] This kind of male bias may be a consequence of the male dominance in almost all of the subsystems of Turkish society (economy, labor market, politics, law, religion). Men are at the same time the leading figures and also the privileged group in these subsystems. In addition males are more visible in many areas of everyday life in Turkey. Often there are more men than women to be seen in public places, in cafés, and restaurants. Traditional restaurants have an extra-room for women and families, called *aile salonu* 'family room', a phenomenon, which we can take as a symbol for women's place in society, for the *aile salonu* usually lies at the periphery of the building: in the back, upstairs or downstairs. Just as the *aile salonu* is marked as something special and peripheral, women come to be seen as special and peripheral members of society, which is reflected in the male bias of terms like *kişi* 'person'.

To sum up, the results show that Turkish terms for person reference have a significant gender bias, what I will term a 'covert gender'. This covert gender corresponds to the socio-cultural roles of and beliefs about women and men.[4]

A second study, which was carried out with 386 subjects (239 females, 147 males) in Ankara in October 1995, was designed to determine the impact of context infomation on the covert gender in person categories. This study had a 3 X 3 factorial design: The three terms *sekreter* 'secretary' (covert gender female), *kuyumcu* 'jeweler' (covert gender male), and *kişi* 'person' (not gender-specific in its lexical meaning, though male-biased) were presented in three different contexts - household activities (cooking), sports (soccer), watching television. These activities had been determined in a pretest as representing a female, male and neutral domain respectively. The results, which I can only sum up here, show that the context does affect the covert gender of the terms. In the case of *kuyumcu* 'jeweler', covert gender (male) is stable and varies only in intensity: *kuyumcu* is given 93% male interpretations in the male context, 83% in the neutral context and 70% in the female context. *Sekreter* 'secretary' is more sensitive to context effects, but its covert gender (female) is not completely reversed. The 90% female interpretations in the female context go down to 79% in the neutral and 47% in the male context. But still female interpretation is the most

---

[3] Because of the design of the investigation (address terms) it was not possible to present these terms without any context. Thus *birisi*, e.g., was presented as 'someone who is waiting in the bus queue'. I have not seen any significant differences in the numbers of women and the numbers of men waiting for buses in big Turkish cities, but an effect of context information cannot be excluded with absolute certainty. The results of the second study, however, confirm the male bias of 'neutral' terms as a robust effect.

[4] There were also effects of subject sex with some terms, especially those with a less pronounced gender bias (e.g. *köylü*, *misafir*): subjects tended to imagine a person of their own sex more readily.

frequent one. *Kişi* 'person' as the most vague of the terms is heavily affected by the context and changes its covert gender completely. Thus *kişi* is 75% female in the female context and 98% male in the male context. But interestingly enough *kişi* retains its male bias in the gender-neutral context (64% male interpretations).

We can conclude then that the covert gender of Turkish terms for person reference is a kind of default value, i.e., that interpretation which predominates when the context does not provide any further or any contradictory clues. But it can be so pronounced as to override context effects (cf. *kuyumcu*), in which case it may be one the way to become included into the term's lexical meaning.

4. Turkish person categories as prototype categories

As we have seen, person categories in Turkish have a covert gender, although gender is not a grammatical category in the language. But gender is not a **defining** feature for membership in person categories, usually it is only a **characteristic** feature.[5] Thus we can refer to a female as *kuyumcu* 'jeweler', e.g., although the covert gender of *kuyumcu* is clearly male. Turkish person categories are gendered in the sense that people expect exemplars of a category to have one gender rather than the other, if no information to the contrary is given.

With these characteristics person categories in Turkish seem to be an almost ideal case for prototype theory: According to prototype theory as developed by Eleanor Rosch and others category membership is not determined by necessary and sufficient features. Category membership is gradual rather than absolute so that there are central and peripheral members. The best example for the category is its 'prototype'.[6] The prototype functions as a default interpretation of the category term (Kleiber 1993: 81f). Although the peripheral members are less representative for the category as a whole, they are not excluded from it (just like a female jeweler is not excluded from the category *kuyumcu*).

Prototype theory thus provides an excellent descriptive framework for the structure of person categories in Turkish. But can it also explain or predict the gender of the prototype in a given person category? The data show that an explanation must be sought in the respective roles of women and men and in the gender stereotypes in Turkey. Prototype theory,

---

[5] Although I use the terms *defining* and *characteristic* features, this is not intended as support for the position of Smith/Shoben/Rips as summarized in Hampton (1995). I just want to point out that if the person categories in question should have defining features, gender is not one of them.

[6] Differences in typicality do not necessarily imply that category membership is **not** an all-or nothing matter (Lakoff 1987: 44f). Nevertheless, it seems clear that categories must have some kind of internal structure and it is in this sense that I use the term 'gradual membership'.

however, emphasizes structural aspects as the determining factor for prototypicality: the more attributes a category member has in common with other members of the category and the fewer attributes in common with members of contrasting categories, the more prototypical it is (Rosch 1977: 35).[7] It is doubtful whether this can serve as an explanation for the covert gender in Turkish person categories, which is but one of the attributes of the prototype. Certainly the prototype of *kuyumcu* 'jeweler' shares the attribute 'male' with many members of its category. But it also shares this attribute with many, if not most, contrasting categories, i.e. other occupational terms such as 'carpenter' or 'bus driver'. Moreover it is difficult to see how this explanation would apply to categories like *birisi* 'someone' or *köylü* 'villager' where maleness obviously is not an attribute shared by the majority of the category members.

There are a few allusions to cultural factors in Rosch's publications. She points out repeatedly that prototypes reflect the cooccurrence of attributes (attribute clusters) in the environment, which is of course, ultimately determined by culture (Rosch 1977: 28, 39). The attributes of 'selling gold' and 'being male' certainly cluster together in the Turkish environment. Rosch also refers to a possible effect of item frequency (Rosch et al. 1976: 501), which might explain the male prototype of *kuyumcu* 'jeweler', because male *kuyumcu*s are more frequent than female ones. But again, the male prototypes of 'person' or 'villager' cannot be accounted for in this way.

Apart from such scant reference to socio-cultural environment, prototype theory is just not concerned with the question of how and to what extent culture, society and categorizing are interrelated. Sociolinguists will find it baffling that such obvious correlations could have been neglected. But this negligence becomes understandable when we think of the kind of categories investigated by Rosch and her colleagues. They are categories like color, dot patterns, vehicles or birds, all categories for which socio-cultural aspects play a less conspicuous role (cf. Dahlgren 1985a: 109f for the differences between these and social categories).

What remains a gap in prototype theory proper has been tackled within the linguistic adaptation of the theory. The works of Dahlgren (1978, 1985a,b) are - to my knowledge - the ones which are the most directly concerned with applying the prototype approach to person categories. In her investigations Dahlgren provides empirical evidence that person categories[8] as well have a prototype structure, with family resemblance as an important factor (cf. Dahlgren 1985b). The attributes of these categories include social function, place in a social hierarchy, personality traits and cultural stereotypes. Such attributes can be part of a 'belief system which constitutes a social theory' (Dahlgren 1978: 67). Dahlgren assumes a high degree of

---

[7] This hypothesis is investigated in Rosch/Mervis (1975).

[8] Dahlgren calls them 'social categories' or 'social rank terms'.

interaction between society and language, which is confirmed by her research into the semantic history of English social rank terms. As the extension of a term determines its meaning, social conditions within the language community find their way into the semantics of a term (Dahlgren 1978). Dahlgren's work is an important step forward in applying prototype theory to social categories and in examining the interrelations of language and society/culture within this framework. But even her approach is not elaborated enough to provide an explanation for the Turkish data. Can the male bias of *birisi* 'someone' be traced back to extension? What kind of social theory is the basis for attributes of person categories and, above all, how does this social theory permeate into linguistic concepts?

A promising approach to this question might be the theory of 'Idealized Cognitive Models' as formulated by Lakoff (1982a,b; 1987) with reference to Fillmore. According to Lakoff ICMs are ideal models of reality which consist of oversimplifications, metaphors and folk theories of experience. They form a level of their own and it is to this level that word meanings relate. The meaning of the word *bachelor*, e.g., derives from cultural conceptions of marriage, of a marriageable age etc. But as the ICM 'says nothing about the existence of priests, 'long-term unmarried couplings', homosexuality, etc.' (Lakoff 1982b: 165), there are exemplars in the world which do not correspond to the ICM and therefore become peripheral members of the category (e.g., the Pope). Those exemplars which fit ICMs best are the prototypes. Without discussing the theory of ICMs in detail I would just like to make the following point: While ICMs seem a promising approach for the Turkish data (they could even handle the male bias of *birisi* 'someone'), they leave us with a number of questions.[9] How can ICMs be determined? How do we know what exactly is part of an ICM and what isn't? What scope do ICMs have - could an ICM consist of a complete folk theory of gender or should we think of terms for person reference as relating to several different ICMs?

To sum up, I agree with linguists like Dahlgren, Lakoff and others that socio-cultural factors have an important impact on language, hence on linguistic categories. But just how such factors are transferred into linguistic categories has not yet been adequately explained.

5. Conclusion

There has been a considerable amount of research on the semantics of gender in languages like English (e.g. MacKay 1983, MacKay/Fulkerson 1979, Martyna 1978, Janicki/Jaworski 1990), yet virtually no research has been conducted on languages which lack a grammatical gender distinction

---

[9] For a critique of ICMs see Konerding (1993: 61ff).

completely.[10] This study is one step towards filling this gap. Although the findings of my investigations still raise a number of questions, they also give us some empirical answers. It can now be stated that a genderless structure may co-exist with a covert gender in the semantics of person categories and that Ecevit and others were wrong in interpreting the lack of grammatical gender as a semantic 'equality of the sexes'.

References

Dahlgren, Kathleen. 1978. The nature of linguistic stereotypes, in D. Farkas et al., ed., *Papers from the parasession on the lexicon, Chicago Linguistic Society, April 14-15, 1978*. Chicago: Chicago Linguistic Society. 58-70.

Dahlgren, Kathleen. 1985a. Social terms and social reality. *Folia Linguistica Historica* 6:1. 107-125.

Dahlgren, Kathleen. 1985b. The cognitive structure of social categories. *Cognitive Science* 9:3. 379-398.

Ecevit, Bülent. 1991. Çağdaşlaşma ve demokratikleşme sürecinde kadın. in N. Arat, ed., *Kadınlar ve siyasal yaşam. Eşit hak - eşit katılım*. İstanbul: Cem. 153-173.

Engelberg, Mila. 1992. Maskuliini, feminiini, virkamies? *Naistutkimus - Kvinnoforskning* 4. 39-50.

Hampton, James A. 1995. Testing the prototype theory of concepts. *Journal of Memory and Language* 34. 686-708.

Janicki, Karol and Adam Jaworski. 1990. Against extensive sound symbolism: another short argument for prototype linguistics. in J. Fisiak, ed., *Further insights into contrastive analysis*. Amsterdam/Philadelphia: Benjamins. 55-65.

Kleiber, Georges. 1993. *Prototypensemantik. Eine Einführung*. Tübingen: Narr.

Konerding, Klaus-Peter. 1993. *Frames und lexikalisches Bedeutungswissen. Untersuchungen zur linguistischen Grundlegung einer Frametheorie und zu ihrer Anwendung in der Lexikographie*. Tübingen: Niemeyer.

Lakoff, George. 1982a. *Categories and cognitive models. = L.A.U.T*. Series A. No. 96. University at Trier.

Lakoff, George. 1982b. Categories: An essay in cognitive linguistics. in Linguistic Society of Korea, ed., *Linguistics in the Morning Calm. Selected Papers from SICOL - 1981*. Seoul: Hanshin. 139-193.

Lakoff, George. 1987. *Women, fire and dangerous things. What categories reveal about the mind*. Chicago/London: Univ. of Chicago Press.

MacKay, Donald G. 1983. Prescriptive grammar and the pronoun problem. in B. Thorne et al., eds., *Language, gender and society*. Cambridge: Newbury House. 38-53.

MacKay, Donald G. and David C. Fulkerson. 1979. On the comprehension and production of pronouns. *Journal of Verbal Learning and Verbal Behavior* 18. 661-673.

---

[10] Engelberg (1993) reports an investigation about the male bias in certain terms for person reference in Finnish.

Martyna, Wendy. 1978. What does 'he' mean? Use of the generic masculine. *Journal of Communication* 28. 131-138.

Rosch, Eleanor. 1977. Human categorization. in N. Warren, ed., *Advances in cross-cultural psychology*. Vol. 1. London et al.: Academic Press. 1-49.

Rosch, Eleanor and Carolyn B. Mervis. 1975. Family resemblances: Studies in the internal structure of categories. *Cognitive Psychology* 7. 573-605.

Rosch, Eleanor, Card Simpson and R. Scott Miller. 1976. Structural bases of typicality effects. *Journal of Experimental Psychology: Human Perception and Performance* 2:4. 491-502.

The Pragmatics of Precision: Geometric and Non-Geometric Periphrastic Progressives in Modern English

ROBERT S. KIRSNER AND WILLEM A. VAN DER KLOOT

University of California, Los Angeles and Rijksuniversiteit Leiden, the Netherlands

1. Introduction

In their discussion of the development of the English progressive form *be + -ing*, Bybee, Perkins and Pagliuca argue that the construction derives historically from a locative expression; i.e., an expression which specifies the place where the grammatical subject may be found. First they cite a remark by Dwight Bolinger indicating that the *be + -ing* form may be used in response to a 'location inquiry.' The question *Where's Lou?* can be answered with *He's taking a bath* or *He's having a nap*, which — they suggest —communicates even more information than bona fide locative expressions such as *He's in the bathroom* or *He's in bed*. The subject is somehow 'situated in the activity' and the activity has a typical place in which it is carried out. In consequence, *He's taking a bath* communicates not only where the subject is (as *He's in the bathroom* would) but also what he is doing there.

The authors then go on to say the following (1994:1335):

Even though the English Progressive has advanced considerably from its origins and is used in a wider range of contexts than progressives in other languages (Comrie 1976:33; Dahl 1985:90), it still conveys much more than simple aspectual meaning. What it conveys seems to be directly derivable from a locative source, from a meaning 'the subject is in the midst of doing something'... The implication of the subject being located in the midst of this activity is that the subject is actively involved, probably originally as the agent in the activity, but perhaps later extended to predicates in which the subject is an experiencer...

It is this paragraph which serves as the point of departure for the present paper. While the line of thought it presents is suggestive, there are gaps in the argumentation. Although placing the subject in the middle of an activity does indeed obscure the activity's initial and final phases, which is consistent with a progressive interpretation (cf. Langacker (1991:201)), it remains unclear exactly WHY location of a subject in the middle of an activity should suggest AGENCY on the part of the subject. What semantic and/or pragmatic mechanism would bring this about? Furthermore, no empirical evidence is offered from any language (including Modern English) that locative or locative-like constructions do in fact exhibit any tendency towards favoring agentive subjects.

Accordingly, the present paper has a double purpose: First, we outline a discourse pragmatic mechanism which can explain why a locative-like construction would be associated with and come to favor agentive interpretation. Second, we provide intersubjective evidence —based on two quantitative studies of the Modern English progressive paraphrases *in the middle of -ing, in the midst of -ing,* and *in the process of -ing* — that the locative-like constructions do indeed favor agentive interpretation of their subjects.[1]

---

[1] This study was originally inspired by the observation that the Modern Dutch 'progressive' construction with *aan het* is much more restricted to agentive grammatical subjects than is English *be + -ing.* A Dutch 'progressive' sentence such as *Jan is dat boek aan het lezen,* literally 'John is that book on the reading,' can paraphrase the unmarked (non-'progressive') active sentence *Jan leest dat boek* 'John reads/is reading that book,' but corresponding to the simple passive sentence *Dat boek wordt door Jan gelezen* 'That book is/is being read by John' there is no 'progressive' such as **Dat boek is door Jan aan het gelezen worden* or **Dat boek is door Jan gelezen aan het worden.* Elsewhere, *aan* occurs as an unambiguous locative: cf. *aan wal* 'on shore, ' *aan tafel* 'at table.' For further discussion, see Kirsner (1996:165-167).

2. On the Semantics of *middle, midst,* and *process*

In addition to the traditional progressive, as in *Sue was writing the letter when the phone rang*, native speakers of English have various means of communicating progressive messages. We shall here consider three: *Sue was in the middle of writing the letter ..*, *Sue was in the midst of writing the letter...*, and *Sue was in the process of writing the letter ...* The constructions with *middle* and *midst* clearly contrast with the one containing *process* in explicitly communicating locative or geometric information. When one uses *process* to refer to an event, all one claims is that the event in question involves a change, development, or progression of some kind and that one is focussing on a period past the most initial stage in this progression. When, in contrast, one presses lexical items like *middle* or *midst* into service as aspectuals, one claims that part of their original locative or geometric meaning will be relevant to the way in which the event is to be conceptualized.

Both *middle* and *midst* communicate that the entity in question, their trajector, is in the more central, less peripheral part of the landmark. In both there is a sense of complete enclosure or containment: cf. *The house stood in the middle/midst of a forest (*, with its Eastern wall right at the forest's edge).* They differ in that whereas *middle* communicates the exact geometric center of an enclosure, *midst* communicates a vaguer kind of containment, often requiring contact (as *middle* does not) with a containing medium. Compare *The space ship was floating in the middle/*midst of a huge hollow sphere; The bullet went right through the middle/*midst of Clyde's forehead; Bill was standing in the middle/midst of a crowd of well-wishers* (both O.K.) but *Bill was standing in the precise middle/*midst of the crowd.*

When *middle* and *midst* are applied to events, which occupy stretches of time, what we may call this image of CONTAINMENT IN THE CENTER is mapped onto the single (linear) dimension of the event, which can be viewed as an instance of the PATH schema (cf. Johnson (1987:26) on CONTAINMENT and (1987:112-114) on PATH). Accordingly, even though *in the middle of -ing, in the midst of -ing,* and *in the process of -ing* all refer to a temporal region after the event has started and before it has ended, the geometric paraphrases *middle* and *midst* are much more precise or specific than the non-geometric *process*. They contrast with it in profiling a more specific central region, roughly midway between the event's inception and its end. This difference in precision can be demonstrated in various ways. For example, the intensifier *very* (as in *standing on the very edge of the windowsill*) can be used far more easily with *middle* or *midst* than with *process*: Compare *Sue was in the very middle /midst /?process of mailing out her résumés when the phone rang and she was offered the new position.* Note also that *process* implies far less than *middle* or *midst* that the event has progressed beyond minimal beginning stages. When in 1996 a shower at the UCLA Rehabilitation Center went unfixed for several months, patrons were confronted every day with a sign reading (in part) *THIS SHOWER IS IN THE PROCESS OF BEING REPAIRED BY FACILITIES* ... During that period, no workmen and no tools were ever in evidence (as would have been more strongly implied by *middle* or *midst*).[2]

3. A Hypothesis Based on the Precision Strategy

We suggest that a driving mechanism behind the original association in earlier English of *be* + *-ing* with the agentive interpretation of the subject NP (discussed by Bybee et. al. 1994) is the Precision Strategy (see below). We also suggest that, in Modern English, this strategy motivates the different ways in which the progressive periphrases with *middle*, *midst*, and *process* will be exploited by native speakers. It will be clear that when speakers choose *in the middle/ midst/ process of -ing* rather than *be* + *-ing*, they are providing more specific information about, a richer conceptualization of the event, than the progressive form does. (This is why, in some cases, simple replacement will not work: cf. *Your jacket is (*in the middle/ midst/ process of) hanging in the front closet.*) In other words, compared to *be* + *-ing*, the constructions with *middle*, *midst*, and *process* are relatively precise (with *middle* and *midst*, in turn, being more precise than *process*). It is equally clear that, in earlier English, progressive *be* + *-ing* was the more precise, marked form, conveying more explicit, more specific information than the unmarked simple verb.[3]

The Precision Strategy to which we wish to appeal may now be stated as follows: MORE INFORMATION AND MORE PRECISE INFORMATION IS PROVIDED FOR THOSE PARTS OF MESSAGES IN WHICH THE SPEAKER HAS GREATER INTEREST.[4]

---

[2] Section 6, below, gives empirical evidence supporting the hypothesized difference in precision between *middle* and *midst*, on the one hand, and *process* on the other.

[3] Jespersen (1964:263) states that in earlier English *What do you read, my Lord?* could communicate the same message as *What are you reading, my Lord*. That is, the non-progressive simple verb form *read* behaved the same way the 'unmarked' simple verb form of Modern Dutch does today; cf. footnote 1, above.

[4] This principle was first presented in Diver 1987 and has been elaborated in Reid 1991. In his discussion of the use of the Greek dual in the *Iliad*, Diver shows that when two things are being referred to (and hence the speaker can employ EITHER the (specific) dual form OR the non-specific plural form), the dual is used more often when the two things in question belong to a central character (such as Odysseus)

In the present context, the operative question then becomes: What will the human speakers of a language find interesting, hence 'worth' the extra investment in precision? The answer we suggest is: by and large agentlike entities, particularly humans.[5]

Accordingly, our hypothesis may be stated as follows: THE GEOMETRIC PROGRESSIVE PARAPHRASES *be in the middle of -ing* AND *be in the midst of -ing*, GIVING MORE INFORMATION THAN THE NON-GEOMETRIC PARAPHRASE *be in the process of -ing*, WOULD TEND TO BE USED FOR THOSE REFERENTS OF SUBJECT NPs WHICH ARE 'WORTH' THE EXTRA-PRECISION OF INFORMATION: ACTIVE PARTICIPANTS, PARTICULARLY HUMANS.

4. The Questionnaire Experiment

A questionnaire experiment provides the first evidence we present for our hypothesis. On the basis of the preceding section, we would expect native speakers of English to find sentences with HUMAN SUBJECTS acceptable with BOTH non-geometric AND geometric paraphrases (and of course acceptable with the regular progressive construction *be + -ing*). Given the greater specificity of *be in the middle/midst of -ing,* these two constructions might be judged as less usual with animates than the plain *be + -ing* form would be, but nonetheless they should be fully acceptable. The same holds for the non-geometric *be in the process of -ing* construction. One might expect *be in the process of -ing* to be somewhat more usual than *be in the middle/midst of -ing,* and less usual than *be-ing,* but still, all forms should be judged acceptable, i.e. 'normal' English.

With sentences containing NON-HUMAN subjects, however, it is a different story. Here we would expect sentences with *be + -ing* to be acceptable, sentences with *be in the process of -ing* to be worse, perhaps bordering on the unacceptable, and sentences with *be in the middle/midst of -ing* to be definitely unacceptable.

---

rather than a peripheral character. Reid shows for English that cognitively salient animals (which his questionnaire respondents had actually seen, such as *deer*) were more often marked with *-s* in the plural than less 'important' animals, which no one had ever seen (such as *bison*). For further comments on precision, see Diver (1995: 86-92).

[5] Linguistic evidence for this proposition is, of course, considerable: cf. the widespread presence of special marked passive constructions in the world's languages, whose function is to background or demote the (normally highly topical) human agent. For non-linguistic evidence, see now Verfaillie and Daems 1996.

4.1 Method

Twenty-six volunteers, all native speakers of English, were asked to rank on a nine-point scale (1 = MOST STRANGE; 9 = MOST NORMAL) how acceptable each of 50 sentences sounded. The test sentences contained the single verb *irradiate*, either a human or an inanimate logical subject (*The doctor/ The X-ray machine*), and either a human or inanimate logical object (*the patient/ the test-tube*). Sentences were presented in three voices — active, full passive (i.e., with an agentive *by*-phrase), and truncated passive (without an agentive *by*-phrase) — and in five aspects — *be + -ing, be in the process of -ing, be in the middle of -ing, be in the midst of -ing,* and *be through -ing.*[6] Sentences ended with the clause *when a nurse barged in.* Half the answer sheets presented the sentences in one random order; the other half in the reverse, mirror-image order.

4.2 Results

To indicate the 'flavor' of the results, we list five test sentences with their average scores: *The doctor was irradiating the patient when a nurse barged in* (8.11 on a scale of 9), *The patient was in the process of being irradiated by the doctor when a nurse barged in* (6.72), *The test-tube was in the process of being irradiated when a nurse barged in* (6.00), *The patient was in the middle of being irradiated by the X-ray machine when a nurse barged in* (4.50), *The X-ray machine was in the midst of irradiating the test-tube when a nurse barged in* (3.22).

Technically, the questionnaire experiment formed an incomplete four-factor within-subjects design. The design was incomplete because

---

[6] Although *be through-ing* signals 'terminative' rather than 'progressive' aspect, sentences with *be through-ing* were included in the questionnaire to provide a further test of the Precision Mechanism hypothesis. *Through*'s geometric meaning, which we may gloss approximately as PATHWAY TRAVERSING BOUNDARY FORMED BY LANDMARK, suggests less precision than either *middle* or *midst* (where the trajector is entirely enclosed by a boundary) but more precision than the non-geometric *process*. Accordingly, we would expect it to be intermediate in acceptability between *process* and *middle/midst*. Certainly the terminative *be through-ing* construction (with originally locative *through*, as in *through the forest*) shows similar restrictions to the progressives: Compare *The children were through rolling down the hill, The children were in the middle of rolling down the hill* with both *?The rocks were through rolling down the hill* and *?The rocks were in the middle of rolling down the hill*. Though we cannot discuss *be through -ing* in any depth in the present paper, we include data on it in the figures for the sake of completeness.

sentences with the truncated passive construction contained no *by*-phrase and, hence, no logical subject. To render the data more tractable, the original variables were redefined to yield new variables which would all combine with each other without any gaps. The aspect variable, ASPECT, was left untouched, but voice, logical subject, and logical object were combined into two new factors: GRSUB (grammatical subject) and VOICEP2 (voice plus a second — oblique —participant, if any). GRSUB (animate or inanimate) was set equal to the logical subject in the active sentences and to the logical object in the passive sentences. VOICEP2 contained five categories (active voice with animate object, active voice with inanimate object, full passive with animate logical subject, full passive with inanimate logical subject, and truncated passive). This resulted in a design with grammatical subject (GRSUB), voice (as VOICEP2) and ASPECT as the three within-subject factors.

Table 1, on the following page , summarizes the results of the analysis of variance. All main effects, as well as the two-way interaction effects of VOICEP2 were significant at the .05 level or below. The two-way interaction of GRSUB and ASPECT, and the three-way interaction of GRSUB, ASPECT, and VOICEP2 did not reach statistical significance. The omega squared statistic (ω^2) reveals that the statistically significant main effects and the interactions with VOICEP2 explained from approximately 1% to 8% of the variance (cf. Dodd and Schultz 1973).[7]

Summarizing the main effects, we note that with respect to the variable GRSUB, human grammatical subjects were significantly more acceptable than inanimate grammatical subjects. With respect to ASPECT, post-hoc statistical tests revealed that the acceptability scores formed the scale *be + - ing* (most acceptable) > *be in the process of -ing* > *be in the middle of -ing, be in the midst of -ing,* and *be through -ing* (all three equally worse than the construction with *process,* but without significant differences between them). Finally, with respect to VOICEP2 (i.e., voice plus second participant, if any), post-hoc statistical tests revealed that all active sentences, all truncated passives, and full passives with a *by*-phrase containing a human NP were judged to be more normal than full passives with an inanimate *by*-phrase. [8]

---

[7] Accordingly, the magnitude of the effects and interactions are appropriately characterized as 'medium' and 'small' rather than 'large'; cf. Keppel (1982:92).

[8] We will take up this finding below, in our discussion of the data for voice diagrammed in Figures 2 and 3.

Table 1

Analysis of variance of the questionnaire data.

Effect	F value	Significance[9]	ω^2
GRSUB	$F(1,25)$ = 41.83	p<.001	7.9%
ASPECT	$F(4,100)$ = 19.08	p<.001	4.2%
VOICEP2	$F(4,100)$ = 5.52	p<.050	1.2%
GRSUB*VOICEP2	$F(4,100)$ = 7.27	p<.025	0.8%
ASPECT*VOICEP2	$F(16,400)$ = 2.99	p<.010[10]	1.1%

Figure 1, on the following page, shows the combined impact of the main effect for grammatical subject and the main effect for aspect (averaged over voice; i.e., over the one type of active and two types of passive sentences). Observe that the only sentences which are judged clearly unacceptable (below 5 on the 9-point scale) are those containing both non-human subjects and geometric progressive paraphrases. These results are consistent with the Precision Strategy hypothesis. [11]

---

[9] Geisser-Greenhouse conservative F-tests: cf. Keppel (1982:470).

[10] After correction with Geisser-Greenhouse Epsilon (.455).

[11] A further comment about *be through -ing* and its relationship to *be in the midst/middle of -ing* : While there are no statistically significant differences between the means of the judgements for *midst, middle,* and *through,* 'terminative' *through* appears — as predicted — to score higher than *midst* and *middle* with both human and inanimate grammatical subjects. For the sentences with human subjects, the mean judgements are 6.22 for *through,* 6.05 for *midst,* and 5.81 for *middle* (all significantly lower than 6.65 for *process*). For the sentences with inanimate subjects, the respective means are 4.69 , 4.20 , and 4.31 (all significantly lower than 5.07 for *process*). Thus, as suggested in footnote 6, the less precise geometric paraphrase *through* ranks intermediate between *process* and the more precise geometric progressives *midst* and *middle.*

Figure 1

Mean scale values for 'Normal versus Strange' for all sentences, broken down by type of grammatical subject NP and aspect.

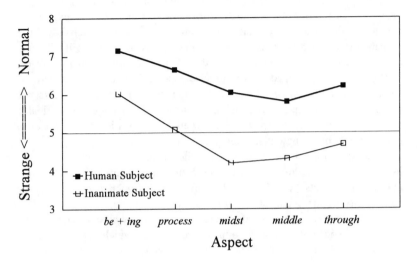

At this point it may be useful to clear up a potential misunderstanding. We have argued that the reason why a sentence like *The X-ray machine was in the midst of irradiating the patient when a nurse barged in* is judged as strange is that there is a pragmatic clash between (i) the precision of detail provided by *in the middle of-ing* and (ii) the 'non-focusworthiness' of the inanimate referent of *X-ray machine* (compared to the inherent 'focusworthiness' of the human referent of *doctor*). Now it could be claimed that what the experimental subjects reacted to was not any pragmatic clash AS SUCH but rather (i) the relative frequencies of human and inanimate subjects in discourse and (ii) the relative frequencies of the aspectuals *be + -ing*, *in the process of -ing*, etc. In other words, one could argue that Figure 1 shows only that less frequent kinds of sentences will be judged as 'less normal' than frequent ones. Given, first, that sentences with inanimate subjects tend to be less frequent in normal discourse than sentences with human subjects and, second, that sentences with 'marked' phrasal aspectuals such as *in the middle, midst* and *process of-ing* require much more special contexts than *be + -ing*, one could argue that Figure 1 shows 'nothing more' than the addition of two effects, each explicable from discourse frequency alone, and that this has nothing to do with the Precision Strategy.

We would disagree. Differences in discourse frequency do not exist in a void. They are not given in advance but are PART OF THE VERY DATA TO BE

EXPLAINED. Even if our experimental subjects were reacting solely to differences in discourse frequency and not DIRECTLY to a pragmatic clash between aspect and grammatical subject (as we have suggested above), one must still ask WHY the less frequent constructions are in fact less frequent. In brief, we argue that the pragmatic considerations in section 3 explain the frequency differences. Typically the (human) speakers of English will find humans more worthy of attention than non-humans and hence will talk about them more often and over longer stretches of discourse. And usually one deploys more specialized, more precise aspectual meanings (such as that signaled by *in the midst of -ing*) only when they are strictly necessary in discourse; for example, when the event in question shows a great deal of development or 'internal structure,' or when the speaker is relating the event in question to other, potentially competing events.[12]

Certainly one observation which argues against any SIMPLE 'discourse frequency' interpretation of our data is that the acceptability of sentences with inanimate subjects can be greatly improved by increasing the internal complexity of the event, cf. *The breadmaking machine is in the middle of making a loaf of rye.*[13] One can also increase acceptability by characterizing the referent of the inanimate subject noun-phrase in a way which suggests that it is capable of performing an intricate activity, as in *The new, fully-automated, computer-driven X-ray machine was in the midst of irradiating the patient when a nurse barged in.* Here, one might argue that by so doing, by making the inanimate entity more 'potent' and hence more inherently 'interesting', one makes it more similar to human referents which humans tend to find focus-worthy by default. In any case, whether the acceptability judgements reflect the pragmatic clashes DIRECTLY (as we have suggested) or are (partially) MEDIATED by a frequency effect (as might well be suggested by the downward slopes of the curves for the sentences with human subjects) is — at this point —not crucial. We would maintain that it is ultimately the interaction of the meanings of the 'progressive paraphrases' with pragmatic factors which motivate the acceptability judgements. In other words, it is the semantic and pragmatic factors which must be at the end of any explanatory chain, not the

---

[12] See section 6, below, for discussion of the use of *in the middle/midst of -ing* to indicate that an INTERRUPTION has occurred in the first event.

[13] We owe this example to Rick Grush of Washington University, St. Louis.

frequencies as such.[14]

Figure 2, below, presents the results for sentences with human grammatical subjects in greater detail.

Figure 2

Mean scale values for sentences with human grammatical subject NPs, broken down by voice and aspect.

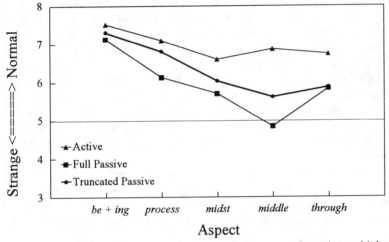

Note that active sentences ranked better than truncated passives which, in turn, ranked better than full passives. We suggest these data are the result of two factors. First, human NPs are most congruent as the grammatical subjects of active sentences, where the construction itself characterizes the grammatical subject as agentive (or at least MORE agentive than the object NP). Second, the lower ranking of the full passives relative to the truncated passives reflects a conflict between two opposing forces. On the one hand, full passives explicitly characterize the human logical object as the focal point of interest by making it the grammatical subject. On the other hand, in these very same full passive sentences the more natural topic, the logical agent, is explicitly mentioned in

---

[14] We thank an anonymous referee for stimulating discussion of this point. We would point out that our position, in which the discourse frequencies themselves must be explained, has many precedents in the linguistic literature. Consider Du Bois' classic 1987 paper on the discourse basis of ergativity. Du Bois did not content himself with merely observing hitherto unnoticed statistical trends in discourse and suggesting that these 'account for' the rise of certain grammatical constructions. Much of his paper concerns the multiple EXPLANATIONS for the observed frequencies in terms of such cognitive and pragmatic concepts as 'information packaging'.

a *by*-phrase. There is thus a pragmatic clash between the attention demanded by the grammatical subject and the attention normally demanded by the logical agent of the action. In comparison to the full passive, the truncated passive (without the *by*-phrase) elegantly solves the problem by eliminating any competitor for the attention being focussed on the grammatical subject.[15]

Scrutiny of Figure 2 reveals that the drop in acceptability judgements falls far less precipitously (as one proceeds from *process* to *midst* and *middle*) for the active sentences than for either type of passive. This is as it should be, for both passives characterize their grammatical subjects as non-agentlike, which — according to our hypothesis —conflicts pragmatically with the detail provided by the geometric progressive periphrases. If one averages the scores for *middle* and *midst,* one obtains 6.74 for active sentences, 5.83 for truncated passives, and 5.28 for full passives. The scores for *process* are 7.10 for active sentences, 6.81 for truncated passives, and 6.14 for full passives. Accordingly as one goes from *process* to *middle/midst,* the scores drop by only 0.4 scale points for active sentences compared to a full 1.0 scale points for truncated passives, and 0.9 scale points for full passives. These results accord with our prediction that the geometric paraphrases will favor agentlike grammatical subjects.

Note further that post-hoc statistical tests show that, of all the aspectual forms, *middle* and *through* were judged as significantly MORE normal in the active sentences than in the passive ones.(There were no differences for *be + - ing, process,* or *midst.*) Although it would have been more pleasing if the data

---

[15] Here a comment is in order about our earlier observation that (averaged over ASPECT) full passives with INANIMATE *by*-phrases were judged as significantly less acceptable than all other sentence types (i.e., full passives with human *by*-phrases, truncated passives, and actives). Examination of the data for the variable VOICEP2 shows that judgements for passive sentences with human grammatical subjects run entirely parallel to those for the less acceptable passives with inanimate grammatical subjects. In BOTH curves, the truncated passives rank as most normal, the full passives with human *by*-phrases rank worse, and the full passives with inanimate *by*-phrases rank as the least normal. The reason why the passives with inanimate *by*-phrases rank worst is that they have 'two strikes against them.' Presumably the purpose of the English passive is to background an agent in order to foreground an object. The 'first strike' is that full passives explicitly mention the agent, which conflicts at least somewhat with the backgrounding. The 'second strike' is that the agent they do mention — an inanimate entity — is less easily construed as naturally agentlike, hence less easily construed than a human being is as meriting the very backgrounding which an explicitly passive construction provides. Of all the choices facing the experimental subjects, the full passives with inanimate *by*-phrases were thus the most pragmatically self-contradictory.

for *midst* had paralleled those for *middle* and *through*, these findings do accord with our prediction that the geometric paraphrases will favor agentive interpretation of the subject noun-phrase more than non-geometric *process* will. Had there been a significant difference in acceptability between active and passives for the sentences with *process* and NOT for the sentences with *midst* or *middle* (or *through*), our hypothesis would have been refuted.

Figure 3, below, diagrams the effects for sentences with inanimate grammatical subjects.

Figure 3

Mean scale values for sentences with inanimate grammatical subject NPs, broken down by voice and aspect

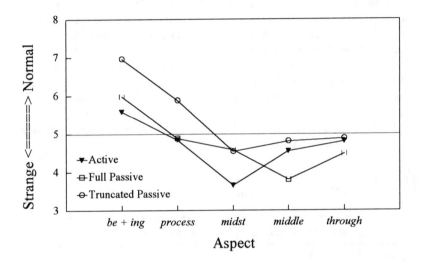

Note first that, in comparison to the lines in Figure 2 above, all scores are displaced downwards — a difference which is statistically significant, as was already pointed out. The observation that truncated passives tend to be judged as more normal than full passives is explained by the same two factors outlined previously. The fact that HERE active sentences (with inanimate grammatical subjects) score significantly LESS NORMAL than passives (with inanimate grammatical subjects) is explained by the fact that inanimate entities, tending to be NON-agentlike, would clash with the agentive role thrust upon them by an active sentence, but would not clash with the explicit patient role given them in a passive sentence. However, as soon as one moves from *process* to *middle/midst*, even these passive sentences dip below the midpoint score of 5, which accords with our prediction.

5. Observations on Agency from Corpora

A further test of the hypothesis that *in the middle/midst of -ing* will favor human and agentive subjects more than *in the process of -ing* is provided by textual data. Since subject NPs in passive constructions are (by virtue of the construction) explicitly non-agentive, they should be — by and large —less compatible with and hence less frequent with *middle* and *midst* than with *process*. This is not to say that such combinations would be 'ungrammatical', but rather that there would be less occasion for speakers to focus in such great detail on participants which normally do not merit such attention.

Because *in the middle/midst of -ing* (as a consequence of their specific, precise meanings) are extremely infrequent in normal texts, it was decided to do computer searches of large electronic data bases. Two pilot searches were carried out with the Cobuild Direct Mail Service Corpus at the University of Birmingham. The first search, on one 20-million word sample, yielded 12 instances of *middle*, all active, 6 instances of *midst*, all active, and 78 instances of *process* (67 active, 11 passive). The second search, on a DIFFERENT 20 million word sample, yielded 10 cases of *middle*, all active, 5 cases of *midst*, all active, and 64 cases of *process* (57 active, 7 passive). We summarize in Table 2, below. A Fisher's exact test (one tail) indicates that this skewing (in the predicted direction) is significant at the .02 level; i.e, it could occur by chance less than one time out of 50.

Table 2

Data from two Cobuild Direct Mail searches (40 million words).

	in the middle/midst of -ing	in the process of -ing
Active	33 (100.0%)	124 (87.3%)
Passive	0 (0.0%)	18 (12.7%)
TOTAL	33 (100.0%)	142 (100.0%)

A subsequent full-scale search was carried out on the entire 200-million word Cobuild Bank of English corpus.[16] The results are given in Table 3, following.

---

[16] The figures in Table 3, below, constitute all the cases found of *be in the middle/midst of -ing* and a representative sample of the more numerous *be in the process of -ing*. We coded all examples of *in the process of -ing* in half of the 16

Combining the corresponding figures for *middle* and *midst* and comparing them with the corresponding figures for *process*, we calculate the odds ratio to be $(88/516) \div (3/152) = 8.64$. Passives are thus nearly nine times as likely to occur with *process* than with *middle/midst*.

Table 3
Data from search in the 200 million-word Cobuild Bank of English.

	Geometric		Non-Geometric
	middle	*midst*	*process*
Active	100 (98.0%)	52 (98.1%)	516 (85.4%)
Passive	2 (2.0%)	1 (1.9%)	88 (14.6%)
TOTAL	102 (100.0%)	53 (100.0%)	604 (100.0%)

Examples of sentences in the corpus include *I was in the middle of filming the TV series, THEM AND US, but the BBC halted production and paid for me to see a Harley Street specialist* (Today), *Congress is in the midst of rewriting the nation's banking laws* (NPR), *I'm in the middle of being booked for speeding* (Australian news), and *This ideology, which came to the fore under Ronald Reagan and Margaret Thatcher, is now in the process of being discredited.* (Independent).

6. Observations on Precision from Corpora

One can obtain further evidence for the hypothesized greater PRECISION of *middle* and *midst* in contrast to *process* by examining the relative frequency of cases in which there is an explicit indication (from either lexical items or the general context) that the event in question has been interrupted. The rationale is as follows: Unlike *process*, which indicates only that some event involving a progression or development is underway, both *middle* and *midst* claim (by virtue of their geometric meaning) that this event is roughly halfway between initiation and completion. One reason why it might be communicatively relevant to explicitly state that the action is at this particular point is if

---

subcorpora and roughly half of the examples in each of the eight remaining subcorpora.

completion is not attained; i.e., if the event is broken off halfway. [17] A case in point is the very first example cited at the conclusion of section 5 above, *I was in the middle of filming the TV series,...but the BBC halted production...*[18] Accordingly, we predict that there would be more explicit contextual or lexical indications of pausing, stopping, or interrupting with *middle* and *midst* than with *process*.

A first test of this prediction is provided by the Cobuild Direct data used earlier to produce Table 2. The results are shown in Table 4, below. The skewing shown — in which 30% of the instances of *middle/midst* occurred with a contextual indication of interruption versus 0% of the instances of *process* —is significant at the .001 level (Fisher's exact test).

The data from the full-scale search in the 200 million word Bank of English yield analogous distributions, as is shown in Table 5, immediately following Table 4. The odds ratio in Table 5 of $(8/147) \div (3/601) = 10.9$ indicates that with the geometric paraphrases *middle/midst*, indications of interruption occur nearly eleven times as frequently as with the non-geometric paraphrase *process*.

Table 4

Data from two Cobuild Direct Mail searches (40 million words).

	middle/midst	*process*
Interruption	10 (30%)	0 (0%)
None	23 (70%)	142 (100%)
TOTAL	33 (100%)	142 (100%)

---

[17] Note that it is more normal to say something like *I was in the middle of phoning the Chancellor when I began to have second thoughts about the matter and hung up* than to say *I was in the middle of phoning the Chancellor when I began to gain confidence that I was entirely correct to do so, and stayed on the line.*

[18] Recall that information about interruptions was not provided by the questionnaire experiment, since there all test sentences mentioned an interruption (the nurse walking in).

Table 5

Data from search in the 200 million word Cobuild Bank of English

	middle/ midst	*process*
Interruption	8 (5.2%)	3 (0.5%)
None	147 (94.8%)	601 (99.5%)
TOTAL	155 (100.0%)	604 (100.0%)

7. Conclusions

We have presented experimental and correlational evidence that the geometric periphrastic progressive forms *in the middle/midst* of *-ing* contrast with the NON-geometric periphrastic form *in the process of -ing* in more strongly favoring subject NPs with 'topic-worthy' referents: human beings, especially agents. We have also shown, with correlational evidence, that *middle* and *midst* are more likely to be used than *process* if there are explicit lexical or contextual cues that the event in question has been interrupted or stalled.

These results are what one would expect from the hypothesis that *middle* and *midst* give MORE PRECISE INFORMATION about the contour of the event in question than does *process*. The observations on agency make sense if one assumes that (i) human speakers tend to provide more information and more precise information about the things which interest them most, and that (ii) human speakers tend to be more interested in humans than non-humans and in agents than non-agents. The data on interruptions make sense insofar as the extra PRECISION of *middle* or *midst* is likely to be brought into play in actual communication only when it is relevant; e.g., when — in a minority of cases, as it turns out — something intervenes to stop the event prematurely.

We shall conclude by suggesting that the Precision Strategy outlined here fills an important gap in Bybee, Perkins, and Pagliuca's argumentation (1994). The REASON the locative ancestor of *be + -ing* could suggest agency might well be that this construction simply provided more information than the 'simple' verb form, information which speakers would not usually squander on 'uninteresting' entities.[19]

---

[19] Kirsner's work was supported in part by grant 2964 from the Academic Senate of the University of California, Los Angeles and by Bezoekersbeurs [Visitor's Fellowship] B 33-215 from the Nederlandse Organisatie voor Wetenschappelijk

References

Bybee, Joan, Revere Perkins, and William Pagliuca. 1994. *The Evolution of Grammar: Tense, Aspect, and Modality in the Languages of the World.* Chicago: The University of Chicago Press.

Diver, William. 1987. The Dual. *Columbia University Working Papers in Linguistics* 8:100-114.

Diver, William. 1995. Theory, in E. Contini-Morava and B. Sussman Goldberg, eds. *Meaning as Explanation: Advances in Linguistic Sign Theory.* Berlin - New York: Mouton de Gruyter.

Dodd, David.H. and Roger. F. Schultz Jr. 1973. Computational Procedures for Estimating Magnitude of Effect for Some Analysis of Variance Designs. *Psychological Bulletin,* 79:391-395.

Du Bois, John W. 1987. The Discourse Basis of Ergativity. *Language* 63.4: 805-855.

Jespersen, Otto 1964. *Essentials of English Grammar.* Alabama: University of Alabama Press.

Johnson, Mark. 1987. *The Body in the Mind: The Bodily Basis of Meaning, Imagination, and Reason.* Chicago. The University of Chicago Press.

Keppel, Geoffrey. 1982. *Design and Analysis: A Researcher's Handbook.* Second Edition. Englewood Cliffs, N. J.: Prentice Hall.

Kirsner, Robert S. 1996. Determinism versus Contingency and Synchrony versus Diachrony: Explaining 'Holes' in Dutch Grammatical Patterns, in W. Z. Shetter and I. Van der Cruysse, eds. *Contemporary Explorations in the Culture of the Low Countries.* Lanham - New York - London: University Press of America.

Langacker, Ronald W. 1991. *Foundations of Cognitive Grammar II: Descriptive Application.* Stanford, CA: Stanford University Press.

Reid, Wallis. 1991. *Verb and Noun Number in English: A Functional Explanation.* London and New York: Longman.

Verfaillie, Karl and Anja Daems. 1996. The Priority of the Agent in Visual Event Perception: On the Cognitive Basis of Grammatical Agent- Patient Asymmetries. *Cognitive Linguistics* 7.2:131-147.

Onderzoek [Dutch Organization for Scientific Research]. He would like to thank Jeremy Clear for making the Cobuild Bank of English material available and Marianne Celce-Murcia of the UCLA Department of TESL and Applied Linguistics for originally drawing his attention to it.

Conceptual Dependency and the Clausal Structure of Discourse

JOOST SCHILPEROORD AND ARIE VERHAGEN
Utrecht Institute of Linguistics OTS

1. Introduction

One prominent goal of discourse analysis is to uncover the conceptual structures denoted by a discourse. For many studies of discourse structure (Polanyi 1988, Mann & Thompson 1988, Sanders & Van Wijk 1996), analytical practice includes a characterization of the coherence structure of discourse, that is, the way in which the basic discourse units are connected to each other.[1] The notion *coherence structure* refers to connectedness of discourse that sets it apart from random sets of sentences. If discourse analysis is employed as a method for investigating cognitive processes in

---

[1] In this paper, we will confine ourselves to the analysis of monological, written discourse, i.e. *texts*.

reading and producing discourse, the coherence structure may reveal significant insights in the way people maintain or build a cognitive representation of texts (Van der Pool 1995, Sanders, Janssen, van der Pool, Schilperoord & van Wijk 1996, Sanders & Schilperoord *to appear*, Schilperoord 1996). However, a prerequisite for the analysis of discourse coherence is that the basic elements, or *discourse segments*, between which coherence relations hold, are identified by the analyst. An important question, then, becomes how one should proceed in dividing discourse into discourse segments. If, for example, a *Claim-Argument* relation is said to hold between two segments A and B, such that A expresses a claim and B an argument favouring that claim, then prior to this analysis and according to some criterion, A and B must have been labelled as 'discourse segments'. Such a criterion should meet various conditions. Apart from being feasible, it should properly identify the basic building blocks constituting a discourse. In addition, the criterion should be unbiased towards the theory of coherence relations underlying the analysis of discourse structure. Mann & Thompson (1988) have been particularly explicit on this matter: '(...) the division of the text into units should be based on some theory-neutral classification.'

The importance of this demand can be put into perspective by considering one outstanding definition of a coherence relation as *an aspect of meaning of two or more discourse segments which cannot be described in terms of the meaning of the segments in isolation* (Sanders, Spooren & Noordman 1992). This definition first of all presupposes a possibility to identify the 'segments in isolation'. Moreover, its validity crucially hinges on the availability of a procedure which does not already include this 'aspect of meaning' that cannot be described in terms of the isolated segments. For this reason, Mann and Thompson (and also Sanders & Van Wijk 1996) propose to employ a criterion based on the syntactic properties of sentences (the so-called *clause criterion*, to be discussed in more detail later on). In brief, they propose treating *grammatical clauses* as the basic discourse segments. Since clauses can, at least in theory, be identified on the basis of their structural properties, this criterion avoids inclusion of the meaning of segments, and the meaning of the relations holding between them, in identifying discourse segments. Mann and Thompson themselves have acknowledged that the criterion cannot be applied in a simple and straightforward manner. However, the exceptions they have therefore introduced are not, as we shall see, fully adequate and they furthermore lack explanatory import. It is these two problems that we want to address simultaneously in this paper.

Our first objective in this paper is to argue that a purely syntactic criterion sometimes makes predictions as to the segmentation of discourse that are counter-intuitive, and that where is does make plausible predictions it fails to *account* for this plausibility. Subsequently, we will show that a procedure for properly segmenting discourse should take into account the *conceptual* relations between clauses. We therefore introduce a notion of *conceptual dependency* between clauses, and show that where it holds between two clauses, these clauses cannot enter into a discourse-level coherence relation with each other. We propose a procedure for segmentation that takes this very notion as its point of departure, and we will show that it results in the right kind of segmentation, where the strictly syntactic procedure fails to do so. Section 2 highlights Mann & Thompson's proposal, and demonstrates a number of problematic cases of segmentation. Section 3 introduces and exemplifies the notion of conceptual dependency. The procedure that is based upon this notion is exemplified for several types of clauses. Section 4 works out some consequences of our proposal by relating it to the notion of 'elaboration sites', introduced by Langacker (1987).

2. Formally determined discourse segments

The clause criterion as it is applied by Mann and Thompson and by Sanders & van Wijk can be summarized as follows (see 1).

(1)   i.   Each clause is a segment, and a clause is a structure headed by a finite of infinite verb
      ii.   Exceptions to i are:
            a. restrictive relative clauses
            b. clausal subjects
            c. clausal complements
      iii. In cases of contracted coordinate clauses, the second conjunct is a segment provided only one major constituent is contracted.[2]

Now, consider a sentence like (2).

(2)   Because John refuses to eat he is visibly getting thinner

---

[2]   We will ignore clause-complexes containing coordinate clauses in this paper.

There are two finite verbs, hence two clauses, in this sentence. The exceptions mentioned in rules ii and iii do not apply, so that the clause criterion splits the sentence into two segments: 'Because John refuses to eat' (= A) and 'he is visibly getting thinner'. The two segments in isolation can thus be identified as *John refuses to eat* and *he is visibly getting thinner*. The aspect of meaning that is not describable in terms of these segments is the causal relation between them, which, in the present case, is marked explicitly by the connector *because*. The coherence structure of (2) therefore is something like 'BECAUSE (segment a, segment b)'. The fact that *because* marks one segment as expressing a cause and the other as expressing a consequence cannot be derived from the meanings of segment a and b, for in isolation they simply designate two events. To sum up, for sentence (2) the clause criterion leads to a plausible analysis – the discourse segments are identified on the basis of their grammatical structure, and the coherence relation holding between them can be analyzed independently from the two segments. The causality relation is therefore situated on the level of *discourse*. Note that, in principle, it is not crucial for the causality relation to hold whether or not an explicit causality marker is present, or, if it is, what this marker is (cf. 'John refuses to eat; he is visibly getting thinner'). Sometimes the conjunction *and*, or punctuation, may suffice to allow the reader to construct the appropriate coherence relation between the two clauses/segments. In addition, the location of the coherence marker is of no relevance here either – compare for example 'John refuses to eat and *therefore* he is visibly getting thinner'.

However, there are some serious problems with the clause criterion. One of these shows up when we consider rule ii in (1). As this rule points out, several types of clauses are excluded from the set of possible discourse segments, namely *restrictive relative* clauses and *complement* clauses.[3] Granting for the moment the definition of coherence relations, this implies that such clauses *cannot* enter into a coherence relation with another clause in the discourse. Therefore, the connections they entertain with their respective matrix structures cannot be located on the level of discourse but have to be located on the level of grammatical structure. The clause criterion thus makes a distinction between two types of clauses in terms of their ability to enter into a coherence relation (cf. Mann & Thompson 1988:248; Sanders 1992:115). This distinction is quite fundamental, but

---

[3] We take clausal subjects to be a type of complement clauses (cf. below).

no motivation whatsoever is provided. Relative clauses and complement clauses are only listed as exceptions on rule i, without there being provided a proper (linguistic) justification for this exceptional status.

Another, related problem emerges in actual analytic practise. Consider (3), taken from a large corpus of Dutch formal judicial letters.[4]

(3)   **Daarbij komt // dat zijn vrouw ernstig gehandicapt is // en dat hij een gezin heeft te onderhouden.**

(Thereby comes // that his wife severely disabled is // and that he a family has to take care of.)

To this it can be added that his wife is severely disabled and that he has to take care of his family.

Sentence (3) presents a highly frequent sentence types in the corpus. Especially the specific argumentative use of the verb 'komen' in 'Daarbij komt' ('To this it can be added') is highly frequent in Dutch formal prose. As to its partitioning, (3) consists of a main clause *Daarbij komt*, and two coordinated complement clauses *dat zijn vrouw ernstig gehandicapt is* ('that his wife is severely disabled') and *dat hij een gezin heeft te onderhouden* ('that he has a family to take care of'). Slashes indicate the clausal make-up of (3).

How many discourse segments are there in (3)? According to the clause-criterion (3) expresses *one* 'idea unit' because, according to rule (1)ii, complement clauses are considered part of their matrix constituent (regardless of *how many* complement clauses are governed by the same matrix). However, intuition suggests that (3) contains *two* segments instead of one for it expresses the ideas that 'his wife is severely disabled' and 'he has a family to take care of'. Between these two ideas the logical relation of addition holds (expressed by the conjunction *en* (and)) so that the coherence structure is something like 'AND (segment 1, segment 2)'. Clearly, this altogether plausible segmenting is prohibited by the clause

---

[4] Much of the work reported here was motivated by the fact that we had to analyze the structure of formal judicial texts. Especially the division of these texts into discourse segments turned out to be problematic if the clause criterion was applied in the standard way (see Schilperoord 1996, 142ff.).

criterion. Consider another example, taken from the same corpus, containing a degree clause.

(4)   De situatie is echter in zoverre verschillend // dat in PLAATSNAAM reeds voor DATUM sprake was van accu-opslag (...)

(The situation is however to this extent different // that in PLACE already before DATE exists 'battery storage'.)

The situation differs to the extent that in PLACE battery storage had already existed before DATE.

Since the subordinate clause *dat in PLAATSNAAM reeds sprake was van accu-opslag* is neither a complement clause nor a relative clause, the clause criterion (1) evaluates (4) as containing *two* discourse segments, that is, the clause boundary corresponds to a boundary between two discourse segments. This analysis implies the existence of some coherence relation holding between the two clauses/segments. However, it's not easy to determine the nature of this relation. For instance, one cannot simply state this relation to be one of *specification*. To see the reason why, consider again the aforementioned definition of coherence relations. It explicitly preserves the meaning of the segments in isolation by defining coherence at a super segment-level. So, if the two clauses in (4) were two segments as well, then the following coherence relation can be deduced: SPECIFICATION (segment b, segment a). If this analysis were correct, then *omitting* segment b should only bear on the *coherence* relation between a and b, but *not* on the meaning of segment a. Omitting segment b would leave the meaning of segment b unspecified to be sure, but not entirely uncomprehensible. However, deleting the subordinate clause results in a segment that *cannot* be properly comprehended (and one that is in fact plainly ungrammatical), as is demonstrated by (4a).

(4)   a ?De situatie is echter in zoverre verschillend

The comprehensibility/grammaticality of sentence (4a) can only be saved by deleting the adverbial phrase *in zoverre* as well. Actually, the tight connection between such degree expressions and degree clauses is also evidenced by the fact that various degree adverbs project specific complementizers (see Jackendoff 1977:202ff.), as testified by sentences (5).

(5)   Hij is *te* dronken *om* te staan (*He is too drunk to stand up*)

Hij is rijk *genoeg om* een huis te kopen (*He is rich enough to buy a house*)

Hij is *dusdanig* groot *dat* dit pak hem niet past (*He is so big that this suit doesn't fit him*)

These observations suggest that the connection between the two clauses in (4) is not one to be located at the discourse level. Again, however, this is obscured by the clause-criterion.

A third example of a frequent sentence type raising segmentation problems is (6).

(6)   Te uwer informatie merk ik nog op dat cliënt voorziet dat het niet eenvoudig zal zijn om snel ander werk te vinden.

(For your information remark I also that client foresees that it not simple shall be to soon other work to find.)

For your information I should also like to add that my client foresees that it will not be simple to find another job in the short term.

Sentence (6) presents a case of deep embedding of the clause expressing the actual substance of the compound sentence. The clausal make-up of (6) is presented in (7).

(7)   Te uwer informatie merk ik nog op //

dat cliënt voorziet //

dat het niet eenvoudig zal zijn //

om snel ander werk te vinden.

Verbs participating in the first two clauses express statements of communicative intent (*opmerken*, 'inform'), and of belief (*voorzien*, 'foresee'). Such verbs typically require a complement clause for their conceptual completion, so here there are no problems in applying rule (1). Things are different, however, with the deepest embedded clause 'om snel ander werk te vinden'. As this clause seems to elaborate the adverbial element 'niet eenvoudig' ('not simple'), rule (1) draws a segmental boundary between the first three composite clauses and the fourth one. Again, intuition tells us such a decision is off the mark. Stated rather loosely, it seems that the first two clauses express some kind of *perspective* on the assertion expressed in the final clause, whereas the third clause *evaluates* that assertion. To put this in more appropriate theoretical terms, the first two clauses may be said to denote a number of connected *mental spaces* of which the content is ultimately designated by the final clause (see Fauconnier 1985, Sanders 1994). Therefore, an adequate procedure for classification should do justice to this kind of dependency and evaluate (6) to be *one* discourse segment.

We could, of course, proceed by presenting alternative types of compound sentences raising segmentation problems. However, we believe that the problematic cases discussed so far exemplify a more general problem with the clause criterion – the fact that it ignores the *conceptual* relations that may exist between different types of clauses. Whether or not a *syntactic* clause is a discourse segment as well crucially depends on how the information expressed by this clause relates conceptually to the information expressed by other clauses within the structure. We want to propose a method for segmenting which is based on a notion that we will refer to as *conceptual dependency*. In brief, one clause is conceptually dependent upon another clause, if its semantics cannot be conceptualized without essential reference to the conceptualization of another clause. If such an interdependency exists, we argue that the two clauses cannot enter into a coherence relation with each other. Moreover, as will be demonstrated, *conceptual dependency* not only preserves the segmentation decisions that follow from the original clause criterion, but additionally accounts for the rather arbitrarily listed exceptions concerning relative clauses and clausal complements.

3. Conceptual dependency

If defined at the proper level of abstraction, the problems encountered in the segmentation of sentences into component clauses that correspond to discourse segments can be solved as soon as we acknowledge the kind of conceptual dependency relations holding between clauses. This notion was already hinted at in the former section, here we will elaborate it in more detail. We shall do so by discussing a classic grammatical problem: the distinction between restrictive and non-restrictive relative clauses.

In Verhagen (1996), an analysis is presented of different types of relative clauses independently of the problem of discourse segmentation, which will allow us to make a first move towards a better understanding of the relationship between clause-status and segment-status. Consider example (8).

(8)   I liked the man who took that dog with him even more than the one who brought it in.

Here the conceptualization of (the intended referent of) *the man*, in this particular sentence, can be said to be **dependent** on the conceptualization of the relative clause. Without the latter information, the conceptualization of the object of "like even more" is incomplete. So what we can say is that a restrictive relative clause is one that the nominal head is conceptually dependent on. In contrast, consider the nominal head in (9):

(9)   They asked the vicar, who so far has refused to state his personal opinion, to act as an intermediary.

In this case, the conceptualization of the object of "ask" is not dependent on the information in the relative clause; so we may say that a relative clause is non-restrictive if its head is **not** conceptually dependent on the contents of the clause. Verhagen therefore suggested that the **interpretive** relations between both types of relative clauses and their matrix clauses are different. Following this suggestion, we can say the following:

-       A restrictive relative clause is a part of the conceptualization of a participant in the event denoted by the matrix clause, hence an integral part of the conceptualization of the matrix;
-       A non-restrictive relative clause is not an integral part of the conceptualized event of the matrix; it has a much more 'loose' conceptual connection to the matrix; for instance, Daalder (1989:202) calls the function of such clauses "adverbial-like" (we will get back to this parallel later).

Now it is only natural to say that a unit that is an integral part of the conceptualization of a clause cannot enter into a coherence relation with that clause on the level of discourse interpretation. Given that it is **conceptually** integrated into the higher clause, it is no longer available as a separate discourse segment, as it were. Now if the essence of a restrictive relative clause is that some part of the **matrix** is conceptually dependent on it, as we just suggested, we may formulate the following hypothesis on the relation between such conceptual dependency and the possibility of a status as a separate discourse segment:

> If a constituent of clause A is conceptually dependent on a clause B, B is an integral part of the conceptualization of A, and therefore not available as a separate discourse segment (cannot enter into a discourse coherence relation with A, or any other part of the discourse).

For the discourse analyst this means that a matrix element being conceptually dependent on a subordinate clause, makes it impossible to treat the left hand boundary of the subordinate clause involved as the beginning of a separate discourse segment.

Now that we have formulated the idea in this general way, how does it apply to the problematic cases that we introduced earlier? Take the frequent type (3), repeated here as (10).

(10)   Daarbij komt dat zijn vrouw ernstig gehandicapt is en dat hij een gezin heeft te onderhouden

In fact, the idea applies straightforwardly. The phrase *Daarbij komt (dat)* in itself is **necessarily** incomplete; speakers of the language can be said to **know** that it is incomplete as an element of use: for the phrase to make sense in actual usage, it is indeed dependent on the contents of the actual subordinate clause. So there can be no discourse segment starting at the first occurrence of *dat*. However, when we have reached the end of the first subordinate clause (...*is*), we have a situation where the conceptualization may be completed, so it is not dependent on what follows; hence we do not only have a new clause starting here, but also a new discourse segment. In this way, then, this string contains two discourse segments, which is precisely what we wanted: intuitively, there are **two** coordinated additional supporting arguments to what has already been stated before.

This is not to say that restrictive relative clauses and this type of complements (actually: a subject clause) are similar in **all** respects. In one sense, they are even in contrast: a restrictive relative does not constitute a discourse segment, whereas the subordinate clause in (10) actually provides the substance of the relevant discourse segment. However, this is

completely due to the difference between the conceptual roles of the
matrix constituents that the respective clauses are subordinated to. As we
said, in restrictive relatives, this phrase denotes a participant in the event
depicted by the matrix clause. The matrix phrase (in this case the entire
matrix clause) in (10) does not even relate to the content level of the
discourse, but rather to the speech act level.[5] That is, the element *Daarbij*
refers not to the contents of preceding discourse, but instead to the *act of*
uttering this information, argumentation, or whatever speech act the
speaker/writer performed with the previous discourse segment.
Consequently, the conceptual contents of the syntactic main clause in (11)
is (at least) one level 'higher' than the contents of the preceding main
clause; graphically:

(11)

speech act level:	....	Daarbij komt dat	en dat
content level:	preceding argumentation/ information	zijn vrouw ernstig gehandicapt is	hij een gezin heeft te onderhouden

By the same token, the contents of the two **subordinate** clauses with
Daarbij komt dat are conceptually on the same level, as the figure
indicates, as the **main** clause preceding them. In other words: If the
speech act part and the content part are distributed over a matrix and a
subordinate clause, these two parts do not constitute separate discourse
segments, but this does not make the subordinate clause less a subordinate
one (i.e. as long as the main clause is perceived as such), namely
subordinated to the explicit expression of the speech act level part. Thus
we want to claim that applying these independently motivated distinctions
to the problem at hand, allows one to say **at the same time** that the
contents of some subordinate clauses is in fact not subordinate (i.e. at the
content level in relation to other discourse segments), and is (i.e. to the
particular speech act in which it is being produced).

---

[5] Loosely speaking, our main point is that it relates to a higher level than the
content level. Perhaps we should just call it 'metalinguistic', but nothing in our
argument here hinges on the choice of terminology.

The situation of a restrictive relative clause may, in contrast, be depicted graphically as follows:

(12) *content level:*   I liked the man even more than the one who took that dog with him who brought it in

Here, the fact that there are syntactic subordinate clauses does not result in a difference of the level at which the conceptual contents is relevant, since the heads themselves are already functional at the content level. But this does not alter the fact that we are allowed to make the generalization proposed above: Whenever a subordinate clause provides information that (part of) the matrix is conceptually dependent on, this clause does not constitute a separate discourse segment.

Let us finally have a look at conceptual dependency relations in sentences containing a complex consisting of a degree expression and a degree clause. Consider (4) again, repeated here as (13).

(13)   De situatie is echter in zoverre verschillend dat in PLAATSNAAM reeds voor DATUM sprake was van accu-opslag (...)

The structural regularities in degree clauses captured in section 2 can be subsumed under the header of conceptual dependency. Consider the semantics of the *Deg*-phrase 'in zoverre'. This phrase evokes the idea of some kind of scale, of which the poles are defined by the adverbial phrasal head 'verschillend'. The scale thus ranges from 'completely identical' to 'completely different'. However, the Deg element not only evokes the scale, it also suggests a particular point on that scale. The tight structural connection it entertains with the degree clause can then be accounted for conceptually if it is acknowledged that the scale itself is 'calibrated', as it were, by the subordinate degree clause 'dat in PLAATSNAAM...'. And since one cannot conceptualize the scale without some means of calibration, there exists conceptual dependency between the two clauses. This rather complex semantic structure is captured schematically by diagram (14).

(14)   identical

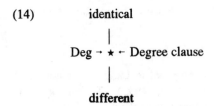

different

Together, **the conceptualization** has an argumentative stance. The dependent clause *justifies* the scale point indicated by the adverb 'verschillend', but it only does so because of the designated scale itself. The idea that a clause such as (15):

(15)   ?De situatie is in zoverre verschillend

is conceptually 'incomplete', so to speak, arises from the insertion of 'in zoverre'. For example, it is very well possible to state:

(16)   De situatie is verschillend / De situatie is anders

Hence, it can be concluded that a dependency relation holds between the dependent clause and the element 'in zoverre'.

Returning to our main theme now, we want to suggest the following extension of our proposal. As we have seen, a relative clause in itself allows for a two-way interpretation: It either is restrictive, thus not a separate discourse segment, or it is non-restrictive and has the status of a segment. However, other types of syntactically subordinate clauses do not allow such a choice, but have to be taken as either one type or another, independently of the context. Adverbial clauses, introduced by different kinds of conjunctions, never provide information that some matrix part is conceptually dependent on, thus they always constitute discourse segments. On the other hand, the (first) complement of a predicate (both in subject- and in object-functions), introduced by the non-specific complementizer *that*, always specifies information that the matrix is conceptually dependent on, and thus **never** constitutes a discourse segment. Then again, a second (third, etc.) complement added on to (by means of coordination) to the first one, does not necessarily provide information that the matrix is conceptually dependent upon, and thus may be a discourse segment on its own.[6]

4. E-sites

In the final section we want to link our proposal to Langacker's notion of 'elaboration-sites' (e-sites) (Langacker 1987, 1991). Throughout this paper we have been using the notion 'dependence' in a way that is not standard in general linguistic practice: Usually all syntactically subordinate constituents are considered 'dependent', while we have applied this notion to matrix phrases the conceptualization of which is, in some sense, not 'complete' without the embedded information. This actually runs parallel to Langacker's notion of conceptual dependence:

> D is conceptually dependent on A to the extent that A elaborates a salient substructure of D. (Langacker 1991:436)

In the case of relational predicates, this 'salient substructure' is a part of the predicate's representation, called an *elaboration site* or *e-site* (Langacker 1987:304); in non-relational predicates it is something constructed on a more ad hoc basis; we will suggest, however, that conceptual dependence is neutral as to the source of the relevant substructure.

An e-site of a particular structure is a more or less *fixed* schematic component of that structure which is subsequently elaborated by another structure. An *elaboration*, then, involves an instantiation of an e-site which is consistent with its schematic specification, but which is also 'more fully and precisely specified' (Langacker 1987:489). The relation between the two structures[7] can then be quasi-formalized as in (17) in which the subscript *De* denotes the e-site of D.

(17) $D (_{De} A)$

Although Langacker did not envisage the types of phrases and relations that we are concerned with, and, more specifically, although his proposal

---

[6] Note that we are only concerned here with the determination of segment-status, not with the place of a segment in the (hierarchical) text structure.

[7] Compare Langacker's treatment of *valence relations* (1987, 277ff.).

did not involve the problem of discourse segmentation, it is not difficult to extend it to those areas.

The characteristic function of complement clauses is precisely to elaborate a salient substructure of the main clause: the e-site of the main verb, i.e. a relational predicate. These substructures can be assumed to be 'salient' as they refer to prominent participants in the event denoted by the main clause. In terms of (17), these interrelations can be stated as follows (18).

(18) $(...V\ (_{Ve}--)_{comp.cl.}...)_{main\ cl.}$

Because complement clauses elaborate the e-site of the main clause verb, their conceptualizations are an integral part of the conceptualization of the main clause. Without these, the conceptualization of the main clause would be necessarily incomplete, which is the reason why in these cases main clauses are conceptually dependent upon subordinate clauses. It then follows from Sanders' (1992) definition of coherence relations that complement clauses cannot enter into a discourse relation with the main clause. After all, this definition *presupposes* the possibility of independent conceptualizations of the clauses/segments between which a coherence relation holds.

The difference between these types of clauses and restrictive relatives can be described, in a way we will now explain, in terms of a difference of entrenchment of the relationship between main clause elements and their respective e-sites. Typically, illocutionary verbs, verbs of belief and the argumentative use of the verb 'komen' in formal Dutch prose are strongly associated with a schematic e-site. One may say that structures such as $V\ (_{Ve}--)_{cc}$ are part of the speaker's knowledge of his language, or his *Mental Grammar*: knowing a verb such as *note* or *propose*, or a typical fixed phrase such as *Daarbij komt* (cf. "It should be added"), simply involves knowing that it requires complementation in one way or another as well. Thus the salience of these substructures (e-sites) is a matter of memory, not dependent on particular conditions of use.

In the case of nominals, which are not even relational predicates to begin with, things are different. What we have to be crucially aware of here is that when put to use, nominals are not so much used to evoke the concepts associated with them in memory, but to evoke, *via* these concepts so to speak, the conceptualization of a particular ('grounded') *instance* of that concept.[8] From a communicative point of view, it is thus pivotal that a speaker allows his interlocutor to establish 'mental contact' with that particular instance of a concept. In other words, the speaker must provide his interlocutor with means to get access to the intended noun referent (cf. Langacker 1990:321). The notion of *accessibility* of noun phrase referents is now well entrenched in the cognitive linguistic literature (see especially Ariel 1988, 1990). Languages contain rich systems of linguistic means to make intended nominal referents accessible for listeners, and to signal the current accessibility status of a nominal referent. For example, (unstressed) pronouns, or zero-anaphors ('handle with care') signal high accessibility of the nominal referent, whereas full-fledged NP's containing adjuncts usually signal low accessibility. In addition, determiners and quantifiers are used to code accessibility: The instantiation of a new referent within a discourse is typically established by using indefinite articles.

What we want to propose here is that restrictive relative clauses can be treated as a way for the speaker to signal the level of accessibility of a nominal referent. They literally *restrict* the selection of instances from a set denoted by a concept. That is, a restrictive relative clause does not elaborate an e-site that is given by linguistic knowledge, but it does elaborate a conceptual substructure of the intended nominal conceptualization. One might suggest that elaborating a conceptual substructure of an intended nominal conceptualization is thus conceptually parallel to the elaboration of an e-site of a relational predicate – only here it is one that is situationally evoked, determined by the accessibility of the intended discourse referent. Arguably, if the intended referent of a noun is relatively *new* in a discourse, or if it has to be reestablished, or if it is to be distinguished from referents competing for attention with the intended one, the function of restrictive relative clauses may be one of identifying its referential domain. In such cases the relative clause indeed does elaborate a situationally evoked salient substructure of the *intended conceptualization* of the main clause. This situation contrasts with the one where a noun is accompanied by a nonrestrictive relative clause. Consider the sentences in (20):

(20) a. I liked the man *who took that dog with him,....*

  b. I liked the man, *who took that dog with him,....*

---

[8] In principle, the distinction is relevant in the case of verbs as well, but it is not so crucial for the sense of conceptual dependence that we are concerned with here.

Langacker (1991:431) argues that the head noun elaborates a salient participant of the relative clause, and in that sense one might say that the relative clause is dependent on its head noun; this holds for both (20)a and b, as the trajector of the relative clause in each is only schematically indicated by the relative pronoun, indicating a participant elaborated as *the man* in the matrix clause. However, in sentence (20)a there is an additional dependency in that the denoted referent of the head noun is made accessible by the relative clause (see also Deane 1992:105, who describes this dependency in terms of 'referential dependency'). In other words, it is only by virtue of the information provided in the restrictive relative clause, that the intended referent of the noun-phrase can be established, or made accessible. It is in that sense, therefore, that we propose that the conceptualization of the noun phrase is dependent upon the restrictive relative clause. Once again, without the restrictive relative clause, the conceptualization of the head-noun by itself does not suffice. For that reason, the restrictive relative clause cannot be regarded as a distinct discourse segments. In (20)b, on the other hand, the relative clause only serves to modify, and not to *identify* the intended conceptualization of the noun phrase; in that case, the head noun does suffice for identification, and therefore the conceptualization is *not* dependent upon the relative clause. For that reason, non-restrictive relatives *are* distinct discourse segments that enter into a coherence relation with the main clause (a relation that can be, for instance, 'specification' or 'modification', and sometimes even concession; cf. Daalder 1989).

The difference between, on the one hand mental state verbs or illocutionary verbs, which contain an e-site to be elaborated by a complement clause, and nouns on the other, is thus a matter of degree of fixedness. Whereas the verbs mentioned here typically contain fixed e-sites of the structure $V_{(v_e--)_{cc}}$, the strength of the connection between a nominal concept and the elaboration of a substructure of that concept is much more loose, and dependent upon the current discourse situation. Once the referent of a noun phrase is established properly, the need to identify that referent vanishes, at least for some time during discourse processing. That is, if nouns refer to concepts already *given*, or inferrable from the previous discourse, relative clauses cannot be considered to elaborate a substructure of the nominal concept (and are therefore *non-restrictive*).

Now, let us have a look at clause complexes containing connecting elements, such as *because* or *while*. Such connectors are prototypical means for indicating relations between clauses on the discourse level. In Langacker's view, they even go so far as to *profile* the interclausal relationship (ibid, 426). *While,* for instance, results in temporal inclusion of the events denoted by two clauses. As this typically requires the contents of these clauses to be conceptualized independently, *while* defines clausal connections on the discourse level, which is perfectly in line with the definition of coherence relations. In Langacker's analysis, *while* contains *two* e-sites, called the trajector and the landmark respectively, which are elaborated by the two connected clauses (i.e. the main clause and the subordinate clause). It follows that a subordinate clause elaborates the e-site of a clause connector C, *not* of a clause participant, which is the very reason to consider these (adverbial) clauses as discourse segments. This is schematized in (21).

(21) $C ((_{Ce1}··)_{c1}, (_{Ce2}··)_{c2})$

The independent nature of the clauses 1 and 2 is accounted for by not letting one clause depend on the other one, whereas the autonomous status of the connector C is accounted for by not letting it participate within one of the connected clauses. In a sentence such as (22) (taken from Langacker 1991), the contents of the clauses can be conceptualized independently, but their respective contents are modified by 'placing' them together in some specific context.

(22)   While ((she was working in the garden)(Janet found a lizard))

Rather then going into the details with respect to the impact the contents of these clauses have upon each other (see Langacker 1991:425), we maintain that, generally speaking, these effects result from a specific discourse relation which is imposed, so to speak, on the structure as a whole. We emphasize this point because an adverbial clause might have the effect of conceptually modifying the contents of a main clause (which, then, would be a type of conceptual dependency). Therefore we conclude this paper by discussing examples such as (23), taken from Pander Maat (1994).

(23)   Je werkt tot de bel gaat (You work till the bell goes, *You must work till the bell rings*)

Pander Maat argues that (23) expresses *one* discourse segment, and not *two* as we would say, because the subordinate clause has the effect of *restricting* the meaning of the main clause (cf. Pander Maat 1994:33, see also Haliday 1987). Sentences such as (23) thus seem to run counter to the distinctions made here. So how are we deal with it?

We think we simply have to be explicit about the possible relations between conceptual (in)dependency of syntactically subordinate clauses and the elements introducing these clauses (phrases introducing the relevant clauses and the words in the 'complementizer'-position). In principle, we have three logically possible kinds of relations:

a)   if a clause C is introduced by element X, the matrix is always conceptually dependent on C (X marks C and its matrix as conceptually dependent);

b)   if a clause C is introduced by element X, the matrix is never conceptually dependent on C (X marks C and its matrix as conceptually independent);

c)   the matrix of a clause C introduced by X sometimes is conceptually dependent on C, and sometimes it is not (X in itself does not mark C and its matrix as conceptually dependent or independent).

Relative clauses are clearly of type c): the 'simple' fact that a clause is introduced by a relative pronoun is in itself insufficient to decide whether the head noun is conceptually dependent on the clause, or if the clause constitutes a separate discourse unit. In such cases, conceptual (in)dependency is purely a matter of the meaning of the entire structure.

The cases that constituted the problem that we started out with are of type a): Whenever we have a phrase like *Daar komt bij dat*, we know this to be conceptually dependent on the clause following it, so that the latter is not a separate discourse unit. In fact, we would ultimately like to explore the possibility that the conjunction *dat* ('that'), the marking typical of complement clauses, functions precisely as a lexical manifestation of a relation of conceptual dependency between clauses.

Adverbial clauses like (20), introduced by conjunctions such as *omdat* ('because'), *terwijl* ('while'), etcetera, are of type b): Whenever we encounter *because, while*, etc., we know that the clauses surrounding or following it are separate discourse units, and that its matrix is not conceptually dependent on these clauses.[9]

We would like to suggest now that a subordinate clause introduced by the preposition *tot* is of type c), just like a relative clause: being introduced by *tot* (like being introduced by a relative pronoun) is in itself a strict marking neither for conceptual dependency, nor for independence. In (21), the meaning of the entire structure apparently imposes a relation of conceptual dependency (the subordinate clause is taken as a restrictive modifier, in this case of the predicate), at least as a kind of default. Such relations in fact parallel the use of *tot* as a straightforward preposition with a nominal complement, as in *Je werkt tot zes uur*, 'You will work till six o'clock'. In other cases, however, *tot* introduces a non-restrictive clause; an example is (24):

(24)   Jan heeft aan het slothoofdstuk van zijn dissertatie zitten werken, tot(dat) de bel het diner aankondigde.

(John has on the final-chapter of his dissertation been working, until (that) the bell the dinner) announced

John has been working on the final chapter of his dissertation, until the bell announced dinner.

It may be the case that in such cases the more elaborate alternative *totdat* ('compound' of *tot* and the subordinating conjunction) is in fact preferred over the simple *tot* - something that would be expected from the point of view of iconicity. However, intuitions are subtle in this area, and we have not yet undertaken a further investigation of this suggestion. Be this as it may, one can in principle 'force' a non-restrictive interpretation on the *tot*-clause in (23) (indicated in writing by punctuation), without *tot* becoming impossible - indicating that *tot* in itself is compatible with both types of interpretations. In any case, this would mean that there is a class of

---

[9]   Note that this idea, if correct, might provide a basis for explaining the intuition that *dat* is semantically more 'empty' than other subordinating conjunctions. That is, we would still maintain that *dat* has a meaning, i.e. has a cognitive function to fulfill, but that its specific function is purely 'relational': an operation on the relation between the conceptual contents of two clauses (dependency), whereas *because*, *although*, etc. primarily denote a relation of a certain *kind* (causal, concessive, etc.), and as a consequence also indicate a relational operation (in this case: of conceptual *independence*). We hope to explore these ideas further in later work.

expressions introducing subordinate clauses, which does not determine the profile elaborated by the clause (specifically: *dat*), so that such a clause is always conceptually integrated into its matrix. On the other hand, there is a class of expressions which does determine the subordinate clause's profile; such clauses may or may not be conceptually integrated: certain elements necessarily mark their clauses as separate discourse units, while others (like *tot*) are indeterminate in this respect.

Our point of departure in this paper was Mann and Thompson's conviction that semantic factors should not interfere with the division of discourse into discourse units. We have attempted to argue that their formal criterion does not always arrive at a proper segmentation. Also, we have argued that problematic cases for a formal criterion always, in one way or another, involve conceptual dependency of clauses. By doing so, we have offered a semantic account for the list of exceptions on the formal clause criterion mentioned by Mann and Thompson. Restrictive relative clauses, and complement clauses cannot be distinct segments because they elaborate a salient substructure within their matrix. In addition, the notion of conceptual dependency has been extended to other types of clause-complexes, notably complexes involving degree-clauses. To conclude, although in its present form our proposal applies to a restricted set of 'problematic' clausal complexes, we claim that its implication exceeds this domain. Needless to say, however, more research will be necessary in order to arrive at a conceptually based, sound criterion for segmenting discourse. We maintain, however, to have made a case for such a conceptual approach to this problem by demonstrating that applying insights from cognitive linguistics is crucial to the very basis of discourse analysis: the identification of relevant discourse units.

Acknowledgements
We would like to express our gratitude to Henk Pander Maat, Ted Sanders, and an anonymous reviewer for their comments and advice.
Authors' address: Utrecht institute of Linguistics OTS, Trans 10, 3512 JK Utrecht, The Netherlands. Email: Joost.Schilperoord@let.ruu.nl, Arie.Verhagen@let.ruu.nl.

References

Ariel, M. 1988. Referring and accessibility. *Journal of Linguistics* 24, 65-87.

Ariel, M. 1990. *Accessing noun-phrase antecedents*. London: Routledge.

Daalder, S., 1989. Continuative Relative Clauses, in N. Reiter, ed., *Sprechen und hören. Akten des 23. Linguistischen Kolloquiums*. Tubingen: Niemeyer.

Deane, P.D., 1992. *Grammar in Mind and Brain. Explorations in Cognitive Syntax*. Berlin: Mouton de Gruyter.

Fauconnier, G., 1985. *Mental Spaces: Aspects of Meaning Construction in Natural Language*. Cambridge, Mass.: MIT Press.

Jackendoff, R., 1977. *X-bar syntax: a study of phrase structure*. Cambridge Mass.: MIT Press.

Langacker, R.W., 1987. *Foundations of Cognitive Grammar, Volume 1 Theoretical Prerequisites*. Stanford: Stanford University Press.

Langacker, R.W. 1990. *Concept, Image, and Symbol. The Cognitive Basis of Grammar*. Berlin: Mouton de Gruyter.

Langacker, R.W., 1991. *Foundations of Cognitive Grammar, Volume II Descriptive Application*. Stanford: Stanford University Press.

Mann, W.C. & S.A. Thompson, 1988. Rhetorical Structure Theory: toward a Functional Theory of Text Organization. *Text* 8, 243-281.

Pander Maat, H., 1994. *Tekstanalyse, een pragmatische benadering*. [Text analysis, a pragmatic approach.] Groningen: Martinus Nijhoff.

Polanyi, L., 1988. A formal model of the structure of discourse. *Journal of Pragmatics* 12, 601-138.

Pool, E. van der, 1995. *Writing as a conceptual process. A text-analytical study of developmental aspects*. Doctoral dissertation, University of Tilburg.

Sanders, J., 1994. *Perspective in Narrative Discourse*. Doctoral Dissertation, Tilburg University.

Sanders, T., 1992. *Discourse structure and coherence; Aspects of a cognitive theory of discourse representation*. Doctoral dissertation, University of Tilburg.

Sanders, T., W. Spooren & L. Noordman, 1992. Toward a taxonomy of coherence relations. *Discourse Processes* 15, 1-35.

Sanders, T., D. Janssen, E. van der Pool, J. Schilperoord & C. van Wijk, 1995. Hierarchical structures in writing products and writing processes, in G. Rijlaarsdam, H. van den Bergh & M. Couzijn, eds., *Theories, models and methodology. Current trends in research on writing*. Amsterdam: UvA-press.

Sanders, T. & C. van Wijk, 1996. PISA - A Procedure for Analyzing the Structure of Explanatory Texts. *Text* 16, 91-132.

Schilperoord, J., 1996. *It's about Time; Temporal Aspects of Cognitive Processes in Text Production*. Amsterdam: Rodopi.

Schilperoord, J. & T. Sanders, *Pauses, Cognitive Rhythms and Discourse Structure*, to appear.

Verhagen, A., 1996. Sequential Conceptualization and Linear Order, in E.H. Casad, ed., *Cognitive Linguistics in the Redwoods; the Expansion of a New Paradigm in Linguistics*. Berlin/New York: Mouton de Gruyter.

Part III

Metaphors

An AI System for Metaphorical Reasoning about Mental States in Discourse

JOHN A. BARNDEN

The University of Birmingham

1 Introduction

In real discourse, mental states and processes are often described metaphorically. This point has been substantially neglected in Artificial Intelligence research on mental states. The present paper is on an AI project that seeks to correct this neglect. A prototype system called "ATT-Meta" that reasons about mental states, including metaphorically described ones, has been implemented. (An early version is described in Barnden *et al.* 1994, and the general approach is discussed in Barnden *et al.* 1996). The system has built-in knowledge about specific conceptual metaphors of mind such as MIND AS PHYSICAL SPACE, and is not designed to deal with ones that are novel for it. However, the system does cater for novel ways in which the built-in metaphors can be manifested in sentences.

Although metaphors of mind are the only metaphors the system has been equipped with so far, its facilities for metaphor are not confined to, or specialized for, this special case. The system's approach to metaphor is founded on the view that it is unnecessary and (often) excessively difficult to make a decision about what the metaphorical meaning of a given metaphorical sentence is. It is enough for the understander to work out an appropriate literal meaning and to use it as a basis for ultimately generating contextually-relevant inferences about the tenor domain of the metaphor as used in the sentence.[1] % The approach places no constraints on the amount or type of reasoning that goes into the production of the inferences. Whether one chooses to regard some subset of the inferences as the meaning of the sentence is a matter of nomenclature with which the ATT-Meta approach is not concerned.

However, the approach does not preclude the possibility that in particular cases it may be relatively easy for the understander to compute something that can clearly be regarded as the metaphorical meaning of the sentence. The approach therefore does not go as far as Davidson (1979) does in claiming that metaphorical sentences only have literal meanings. That view has it that any metaphorical message conveyed to the understander is always a matter for pragmatics rather than for semantics. Thus, if Davidson's approach is semantically atheist when it comes to metaphor, ATT-Meta's is semantically agnostic.

2 Metaphors of Mind

The metaphors of mind that the ATT-Meta project has been most concerned with are MIND AS PHYSICAL SPACE, MIND PARTS AS PERSONS and IDEAS AS INTERNAL UTTERANCES. I will describe these briefly, and then make observations about some other important metaphors. I have discussed the metaphors more extensively elsewhere (Barnden 1992, Barnden et al. 1996, Barnden in press).

Under the metaphor of MIND AS PHYSICAL SPACE (which includes the special case of MIND AS CONTAINER), a person's mind is a physical region within which ideas, thinkings, hopings, etc. have locations and can change location. The metaphor is manifested in expressions such as 'he believed in the recesses of his mind that,' 'she pushed the idea into the back of her mind,' 'he didn't bring the ideas together in his mind' and 'the idea just popped into his mind.' It is common, though not universal, for MIND AS PHYSICAL SPACE manifestations

---

[1] If, for instance, MIND AS PHYSICAL SPACE is used in a sentence to help describe an agent's mental state, the "tenor" domain is the mind of that agent. The "vehicle" domain is the domain of physical space (and physical objects).

to involve IDEAS AS PHYSICAL OBJECTS as well. Entities in the mind can be viewed as many different sorts of physical object.

A paramount feature of the MIND AS PHYSICAL SPACE metaphor is that ideas that are not spatially "together" in the mind are likely not to interact inferentially. Thus, if an agent has not brought some ideas together, or they are in "different parts" of the agent's mind, the agent is not likely to have drawn conclusions from them. This is because the MIND AS PHYSICAL SPACE metaphor is based in part on a correspondence between mental interaction and physical interaction; and, in a folk view of the mundane world, physical things that are not spatially close together do not, normally, physically interact.

Another major aspect of the metaphor is that mental entities in particular subregions of the mind space, such as the front of the mind, play an active role in governing the person's further thoughts and actions, whereas those in other particular subregions, such as the back of the mind, do not (or only do so to a lesser extent).

The following three sentences manifest the metaphor of IDEAS AS INTERNAL UTTERANCES, as long as they are not describing out-loud speaking events:

(1) *Sally said to herself that Mike was untrustworthy.*

(2) *Sally told herself, 'Mike is untrustworthy.'*

(3) *Sally thought, 'Mike is untrustworthy.'*

The metaphor casts a thinking event as an event of "internal speech." Internal speech is not *literally* speech. Two of the above sentences use a speech verb, but it is not necessary that a speech verb be used at all for the metaphor to be manifested—see for instance the third sentence. Straightforward manifestations of IDEAS AS INTERNAL UTTERANCES appear to indicate conscious, occurrent thoughts that play a major, active role in the agent's inner and outer behavior. This is presumably because almost all real speech is consciously produced and, when interpreted at all, consciously interpreted — or, at least, that is how things are in a common-sense view of the world. It is the active role of internal speech that has been the main focus of attention in the development of ATT-Meta .

The following two sentences manifest the metaphor of MIND PARTS AS PERSONS:

(4) *One part of Mike knows that Sally has left for good.*

(5) *Part of Mike was insisting that Sally had left for good.*

Under the metaphor, which is related to a multiple-selves metaphor discussed by Lakoff (1993), a person's mind is viewed as having "parts" that are themselves people — or, at least, complete minds. These inner persons have their own thoughts, hopes, emotions, and so forth. The inner persons can communicate in ordinary language, as the word 'insisting' in (5) indicates. In sentences such as (4) and (5) there is no implication that the inner persons have any long-term existence or any special role in the mind: they can just be postulated by the speaker for the communication purposes of the moment. Different inner persons can have conflicting mental states, or a mental state held by one can fail to be held by another. This is the aspect of the metaphor that the ATT-Meta research has focused on.

As shown by (5), MIND PARTS AS PERSONS can be mixed with IDEAS AS INTERNAL UTTERANCES. This happens very frequently.

3 Other Metaphors and Connections between Metaphors

Many authors have commented on metaphors of mind, including Cooke & Bartha (1992), Jäkel (1993), Johnson (1987), Lakoff & Turner (1989) and Sweetser (1987). There are, of course, several extremely prevalent, general and well-known metaphors of mind other than those discussed above. Two of these we may call IDEAS AS EXTERNAL PHYSICAL OBJECTS and COGNIZING AS SEEING. The metaphor of IDEAS AS EXTERNAL PHYSICAL OBJECTS is manifested in sentences such as 'Mary grasped the idea' and 'The idea tugged at him.' Under COGNIZING AS SEEING, mental events, states and processes of various types are viewed as visual events, states and processes: consider for instance 'They looked at the question of ...' and 'Their vision of the problem was obscured.' These two metaphors and others are discussed in Barnden *et al.* (1996) and Barnden (in press). Also, an extensive databank of examples of metaphor of mind in real discourse can be found at web page http://www.cs.bham.ac.uk/ jab/ATT-Meta/Databank/.

The metaphors mentioned so far are not independent of each other. There are some taxonomic relationships between them, and metaphors are often smoothly combined in the same sentence. Notably, IDEAS AS INTERNAL UTTERANCES and MIND PARTS AS PERSONS are special cases of MIND AS PHYSICAL SPACE. Internal utterances are "internal" to the agent's mind, and inner persons inhabit the agent's mind. Nevertheless, the particular locations of the utterances or inner persons are typically not salient or significant. However, in MIND PARTS AS PERSONS there is an implicit positional factor of great significance: the inner persons are often taken to be in verbal communication with each other, so that presumably they are assumed to be in relatively close physical proximity.

As for combinations of metaphors, we have already seen that IDEAS AS PHYSICAL OBJECTS and MIND AS PHYSICAL SPACE are often combined, as are MIND PARTS AS PERSONS and IDEAS AS INTERNAL UTTERANCES. The latter mixing allows communication and other interaction between inner persons to take on the full complexity of real linguistic and social interaction. As one small illustration of the implications of this, consider (5) again. A person normally only insists that something, X, is the case when someone in the same conversation has objected to X. This is a common-sense observation about ordinary conversational interaction. Thus, in the example we can take it that some other inner person has probably objected to X. Thus, the agent is in a strongly conflicting state of mind.

The current ATT-Meta system has the beginnings of a capability for dealing with mixing of metaphors, but the project has not explored this potential to any great extent.

4   Some Consequences for Discourse Understanding

The ATT-Meta project has been directed at some important consequences of the metaphors of mind for the task of discourse understanding, and in particular for the task of establishing discourse coherence. Notice in particular the following aspects of the three main metaphors discussed above, namely MIND AS PHYSICAL SPACE, IDEAS AS INTERNAL UTTERANCES and MIND PARTS AS PERSONS. Under MIND AS PHYSICAL SPACE, physical separation between ideas usually implies lack of interaction. Under IDEAS AS INTERNAL UTTERANCES, internally-spoken thoughts are in a strong position to actively affect the person's behavior and further thoughts. Under MIND PARTS AS PERSONS, different inner persons can have different and even conflicting thoughts. Now suppose we are confronted with the following passage (or spoken discourse):

(6) *John had to see his boss at 10am. But he'd arranged to go for a run at the same time. He just hadn't brought the arrangements together in his mind.*

Clearly, the intended meaning is that John hadn't realized that his arrangements clashed. That John failed in this respect is an important inference for the understander to make, partly because it could help with the understanding of later parts of the discourse. Suppose, for instance, that the next sentence is *'He was always messing things up like this.'* To work out what the pronoun 'this' refers to, it is helpful for the understander to be able to find some messing-up in the prior discourse. The messing-up in question includes John's not noticing the arrangements-clash and thus causing problems for himself and possibly other people. (The mere failure to bring two ideas together is not in and of itself a messing-up.)

Importantly, the reasoning the understander must do is appreciably *uncertain* and *defeasible*. The fact that two physical objects are not close together does not definitely imply that they do not interact. It is just that they can be *presumed* not to interact pending further evidence to the contrary.

As for MIND PARTS AS PERSONS, the following passage has an effect analogous to that of (6):

(7) *One part of John believed that he should get the first prize. But another part of him thought he shouldn't get it.*

The two beliefs are held by different inner persons, so they presumably don't inferentially interact. The passage has a completely different effect from:

(8) *John believed that he should get the first prize. But he thought he shouldn't get it.*

This just sounds blatantly contradictory, presumably because when we hear that an agent has two related beliefs we assume he sees the connection—at least in the case of sufficiently simple beliefs about familiar, mundane subject-matters.

An important possibility under MIND PARTS AS PERSONS, that is not brought to the fore by MIND AS PHYSICAL SPACE in general, is that the agent can *notice* that some inner persons have conflicting beliefs. Indeed, part of the connotation of (7) appears to be that John feels conflict, rather than blithely going around his business with no awareness of any clash, which is what (6) suggests. Under MIND PARTS AS PERSONS, one can presume that there is a "central self," an inner person that has a distinguished role in the current society of inner persons. Just as a person can believe things about other people's mental states (through observing their communications and other behavior), so it is reasonable to suppose that the central self can have beliefs about the mental states of the other inner persons. This is especially so if the inner persons interact conversationally.

A passage that leads to diametrically opposite effects from (6) and (7) is:

(9) *John realized he had to see his boss immediately. But he thought, "I'm going on that run now." He put on his running gear and headed out.*

As a reasonable default, if an agent realizes something, P, then the belief-that-P plays a "central" and active role for the agent. The use of

IDEAS AS INTERNAL UTTERANCES in the second sentence of the passage renders the intention to go for a run also "central" and active. So, there is a very strong connotation that John went on his run in the full knowledge that he was flouting the obligation to see his boss.

Nevertheless, IDEAS AS INTERNAL UTTERANCES does allow a failure of realization in special situations. The internal utterance can be qualified in such a way as to render it relatively inactive, unimportant and unattended to. This happens, for instance, in

(10) *John wanted to go for a run. In a distant corner of his mind a voice murmured, "You ought to see your boss now." But he put on his running gear and headed out.*

The middle, metaphorical, sentence is similar to ones I have observed in real discourse.

5 Inferentialism and Semantic Agnosticism

Much work on the understanding of metaphorical language—within AI, philosophy, psychology and linguistics at any rate—considers an individual metaphorical sentence to have one or more determinable metaphorical meanings, as well as one or more usually-inappropriate literal meanings. A major exception is Davidson's view, already mentioned in the Introduction. The ATT-Meta position is that a metaphorical sentence *may* have some metaphorical meanings, but that that is just a special case arising in relatively simple manifestations of familiar metaphors. The important quality of a metaphorical sentence is the set of *inferences* it leads to; and in particular the set of inferences that help to tie the sentence to surrounding discourse and the world. In some cases, some of these inferences might be theoretically deemed to constitute the meaning of the sentence; but a theoretical move of this sort has little importance for the actual mechanisms of discourse understanding.

This focus on inferences as opposed to meanings needs much more discussion than is possible in the present paper, but it is important for understanding the ATT-Meta system. One motivation for it is the well-known, frequent difficulty of adequately paraphrasing metaphorical sentences in non-metaphorical terms. For the field of AI (and other process-oriented fields) the analogous difficulty is that of coming up with internal meaning-representation structures for metaphorical sentences, where those structures are not themselves metaphorical.

Consider (6) again. The important inferences from the last, metaphorical, sentence in this passage is that John's two arrangement-ideas didn't interact, and that he (therefore) didn't notice the clash. But what would the *meaning* of the metaphorical sentence be? What non-metaphorical account could we give of ideas being in different positions in a mind, so that they need to be "brought together" in order for inference to happen? This is not just a difficulty for the layperson: no scientist, linguist or philosopher knows enough about the mind to answer the question. Similar points can be made about, say, (5). What non-metaphorical account could one give of the notion of a "part" of the mind "insisting" something? And why should one bother? What's important in understanding the discourse is to notice that the agent is being portrayed as being in a conflicted state of mind, where the conflicting beliefs are individually strongly held. It does not really matter, either to speaker or listener, what objective, non-metaphorical reality underlies this state of affairs.

On the other hand, there is no reason to insist that metaphorical sentences *never* have determinate, metaphorical meanings specifiable in non-metaphorical terms. For instance, the sentence 'John gave Bill that idea' can, perhaps, be paraphrased non-metaphorically as something like 'John caused Bill to have that idea.'

6   What ATT-Meta Accomplishes

The implemented ATT-Meta system is aimed at the metaphor-based inferencing needed for understanding of passages such as (6,7,9). It is not a full understanding system: rather, the system is given specific sorts of reasoning goal that could plausibly arise in understanding such passages. For example, the goal could be that of inferring from (6) whether John realized he had an arrangements clash. The system as currently implemented does not take natural language input, and is therefore purely a reasoning system. The input to the system consists of formal representational expressions that couch the core of a literal meaning of small (two or three sentence) discourse chunks.[2] To be more specific, here is an example of the system's capabilities:-

INPUT — hand-coded, simplified internal representations of:

> Peter thought he had to see his doctor that day.
> He knew he had to meet his boss at the same time.
> But these ideas were separated from each other in his mind.

METAPHOR MANIFESTED (in third sentence):   *Mind As Physical Space.*

---

[2]However, a front-end for going from simplified English discourse to the internal formal representations has been partially implemented and works on a subclass of the sentences of interest.

A QUESTION FOR REASONING: *Did Peter believe that he had a meeting clash?*

SYSTEM'S ANSWER: *There is no reason to presume that Peter believed he had a meeting clash.*

SYSTEM'S EXPLANATION:[3] (a) Peter presumably did not draw the inference that there was a clash from his belief about the doctor meeting and his belief about the boss meeting. (b) He did not draw the inference because these believed propositions presumably did not inferentially interact. (c) This is because they presumably did not physically interact in Peter's mind. (d) This is because they were spatially separated from each other in Peter's mind.

Because of (a), ATT-Meta can come up with no line of evidence to support a presumption that Peter believed he had a clash.

ATT-Meta can deal with variants of the above example. For instance, if the last sentence of the INPUT were missing and not replaced by some other metaphorical statement, then ATT-Meta would answer that Peter presumably did believe that there was a meeting clash. This is because ATT-Meta assumes by default that people do make the inferences from their beliefs that ATT-Meta itself observes that it could draw. (See section 10.1.)

An important feature of ATT-Meta is that it engages in *uncertain, defeasible reasoning.* In practice, one can never be certain about what people believe or what they infer—irrespective of whether there is any metaphorical quality to the descriptions of mental states provided by a discourse. Additionally, when metaphors are involved, inferences based on them are uncertain and defeasible. To complicate the situation, other agents themselves reason uncertainly about the world and about each other.

Uncertainty and defeasibility are signaled in the above example of ATT-Meta's operation by the words "presume" in the ANSWER and "presumably" in the EXPLANATION. A hypothesis to which ATT-Meta attaches the 'presumably' tag is something that ATT-Meta thinks is probably the case, but the system would change its mind about it if sufficiently strong contrary evidence came along. We say that such evidence would *defeat* the hypothesis in question.

---

[3]The system's answer and explanation are actually formal expressions. English glosses are given here for the sake of readability.

7 Levels of Certainty in the System

The certainty tags that ATT-Meta has are *certainly-not, possibly, suggestedly, presumably* and *certainly*. These are in increasing order of strength. The first and last are self-explanatory. *Suggestedly* is attached to hypotheses for which there is *some positive evidence*, but not enough for ATT-Meta to take them as presumptions. ATT-Meta attaches *possibly* to any hypothesis for which it has no positive evidence and to which it does not attach *certainly-not*.

As ATT-Meta investigates a hypothesis, looking at different potential pieces of evidence for and against it, it incrementally develops an tag for it. A hypothesis starts off with *possibly*, and may (or may not) go through *suggestedly* and/or *presumably* before ending up with *certainly* if it ever does. And a hypothesis may get to *presumably* at some point, only to be downgraded to *suggestedly* or *certainly-not* later on.

ATT-Meta can end up with, say, *presumably* for H and *suggestedly* for not-H. This is not a contradiction. However, it cannot end up with *presumably* for both H and not-H. The system has a conflict-resolution mechanism that comes into play when there is strong evidence for H and not-H that tries to make both hypotheses have level '*presumably*.' The mechanism tries to find which body of evidence is to be preferred, using a specificity-based heuristic; accordingly, either H or not-H is downgraded to the *suggestedly* level. If the conflict-resolution mechanism cannot make a choice, both hypotheses are downgraded to the *suggestedly* level.

The certainty tags are used also within belief layers. So, for example, ATT-Meta can *presume* that Peter is *certain* that Mary believes P with strength *suggestedly*.

Rules have certainty tags attached to them. A rule tag serves as an upper bound on the certainty tag that the rule can return. For example, suppose ATT-Meta has the rule

> IF person X is at a meeting then X (presumably) believes with strength *certainly* that (s)he is at the meeting.

Even if ATT-Meta is certain that Peter is at a meeting, then in the absence of other relevant rules ATT-Meta merely *presumes* that Peter believes (with strength *certainly*) that he is at the meeting.

8 Metaphor-Imbued Representations

ATT-Meta's internal representations are predicate-logic expressions annotated with certainty tags. I will use a simplified representational format in this paper for brevity. Information about the actual representational scheme used is provided in Barnden *et al.* (1994). For a sentence such as *'The idea was in the recesses of Peter's mind'* ATT-Meta uses the following internal representation (in the simplified notation):

(11) `in(idea1, t0, recesses-of(mind-of(Peter))`

assuming that `idea1` is a constant denoting the idea in question and `t0` denotes the time interval in question. The expression has a *certainly* tag attached to it. (Currently, tags for representations of input sentences are always *certainly*.) Because the sentence manifests the MIND AS PHYSICAL SPACE metaphor, the system is also given the premise

(12) `is-physical-space(mind-of(Peter))`,

with a *certainly* tag attached to it.

A crucial feature of (11) is that the predicate symbol `in` and function symbol `recesses-of` are exactly those that would be used for describing real spatial relationships. Now, this would not amount to much if the symbols couched concepts that were so general that they encompassed both physical and mental in-ness and recess-ness. However, the symbols do not couch such general concepts. Their meaning for the system arises from their inclusion in a rich set of knowledge rules that are purely designed for the needs of spatial in-ness and recess-ness — irrespective of whether those rules give correct, useful or even interpretable results when used to describe minds or mental states as in (11) and (12). The rules in question are part of a knowledge base of rules about physical space, physical objects and their interactions.

Thus, it is legitimate to say that ATT-Meta's internal representations, such as (11), can be *metaphor-imbued*: they can involve the extension of (for example) physical terms to describe mental states, just as physical terms in natural language can be extended to describe mental states.

9   Conversion Rules and Within-Vehicle Reasoning

9.1   Conversion Rules

ATT-Meta's knowledge of a metaphor consists of a set of *conversion rules* for metaphors. These map information expressed in vehicle terms to information expressed in tenor terms, or vice versa. Here is an English paraphrase of a representative conversion rule for MIND AS PHYSICAL SPACE:

> *IF—under a metaphorical view of person X's mind as a physical space—the idea that P and the idea that Q are in person X's mind AND P and Q do not physically interact THEN (presumably) X does not draw inferences from P and Q.*

ATT-Meta also has a converse of this rule, a contrapositive of it, and a converse-contrapositive of it. For example, the converse infers lack of physical interaction from lack of inferential interaction. The contrapositive infers physical interaction from inferential interaction.

9.2 Within-Vehicle Reasoning

The conversion rules for metaphors are typically at the level of generality of the one shown just above, and directly refer only to limited aspects of the metaphor vehicles. For instance, there is no rule that says that

> *if ideas are far apart in someone's mind then they don't inferentially interact.*

Rather, ATT-Meta would infer, from the fact that the ideas are spatially far apart, that they presumably do not *physically* interact. It is crucial to realize that this step is *within the terms of the vehicle domain of the metaphor, i.e. the domain of physical space*, and is similar to an inference that could be made about ordinary physical objects that are far apart in space. Having inferred that the ideas presumably do not physically interact, ATT-Meta would *cross from the vehicle to the tenor* by using one the the conversion rules above, and infer that X presumably does not make inferences from the propositions in question.

Here we see a two-stage process: inference within the terms of the metaphor vehicle (the PHYSICAL SPACE domain), followed by a crossing-over to the tenor domain. Much more elaborate episodes of within-vehicle reasoning are possible prior to crossing over. In our example, the hypothesis that allows the crossing-over is that the ideas in question do not physically interact. Thus, *any* chain of reasoning that supports that hypothesis can be countenanced. This means that the input discourse can make arbitrarily complex, obscure and novel use of the metaphor, as long as the metaphorical statements in the discourse lead to the conclusion that the ideas do not physically interact.

The use of a non-certain qualifier such as *presumably* in the conversion rules is extremely important. It allows ATT-Meta's metaphor-based inferences to be blocked by other information. For instance, ATT-Meta may be certain that agent X does draw inferences from ideas P and Q even though other evidence suggests they P and Q not physically interact.

Within-vehicle reasoning must be "protected" or "cocooned" in a certain sense. For instance, the system may have rules that enable it to conclude that a mind is certainly *not* a physical space, contradicting a special premise such as (12). Informally, we can think of ATT-Meta's reasoning about Peter's mind-as-a-physical-space proceeding within a *metaphorical pretence cocoon* within which the system pretends that Peter's mind really is a physical space, his ideas really are physical objects, and so on. Metaphorical pretence is handled by ATT-Meta just as if it were ordinary pretending (as when a child pretends that he or she is a bird). And, pretending is handled in much the way that believing is. Just as ATT-Meta can handle agents having beliefs different from its own, it handle its own pretence as involving "beliefs" such as (12) different from its own real beliefs.

9.3 Semantic Agnosticism Again

In line with the semantic agnosticism discussed in section 5, ATT-Meta does not produce representations of metaphorical meanings of metaphorical sentences as a matter of course. A sentence such as 'John hadn't brought the ideas together in his mind' merely gets a literal meaning representation, as part of the "metaphorical pretence" that the sentence is to be taken literally. Within-vehicle inferences that the literal meaning representation leads to may connect up with conversion rules. The rules then produce inferences couched in the terms of the tenor rather than the vehicle.

In special cases, of course, it may happen that the literal meaning representation itself immediately links up with conversion rules. For example, given the conversion rule in section 9.1, a sentence explicitly saying that two ideas do not physically interact immediately enables the system to infer that the ideas do not inferentially interact. Whether this conclusion should be called (part of) the *meaning* of the sentence is a subsidiary matter for the purposes of the ATT-Meta project.

9.4 Non-Individuation of Metaphor

Although ATT-Meta needs to know that it is dealing with a metaphorical description of someone's mental states, it does not need to assume that the description uses just a single, clearly individuated metaphor. Rather, clues in the discourse are assumed to suggest various special cocoon premises (such as (12): 'John's mind is a physical space'); and the set of conversion rules that thereby become relevant need not be part of just one metaphor. For instance, if the discourse casts the agent's ideas as ANIMATE ENTITIES, then conversion rules both for this metaphor and for MIND AS PHYSICAL SPACE can be applied. As the ANIMATE ENTITIES metaphor is independent of MIND AS PHYSICAL SPACE, in that it could instead be used in conjunction with, for instance, the metaphor of ideas as EXTERNAL physical objects, this constitutes a mixing of metaphor.

9.5 Tenor-to-Vehicle Conversion

Conversions can proceed not only from vehicle to tenor but also in the opposite direction. Consider again the rule mentioned in section 9.1, now slightly re-expressed to bring out the role of pretence:

> IF—under a metaphorical pretence that person X's mind is a physical space—the idea that P and the idea that Q are in person X's mind AND P and Q do not physically interact THEN (presumably) X does not draw inferences from P and Q.

As I noted earlier, the system also has a contrapositive of this, *viz*.:

> IF—under a metaphorical pretence that person X's mind is a physical space—the idea that P and the idea that Q are in person X's mind AND X draws inferences from P and Q THEN (presumably) P and Q physically interact.

Therefore, in a discourse which paints ideas P and Q as being far apart from each other in X's mind, and yet indicates that X does draw inferences from P and Q, the system can infer that, despite the far-apartness, the ideas do physically interact within X's mind-space. This could have an important effect on further inferences within the terms of the vehicle (i.e., within the metaphorical pretence), and therefore on the understanding of the discourse as a whole.

10 Simulative Reasoning and Nesting of Reasoning

10.1 Simulative Reasoning

Putting metaphor aside, ATT-Meta's main tool for reasoning about mental states is *simulative reasoning*. This is a popular technique in AI and has been the subject of much debate in philosophy and psychology (Davies & Stone 1995, Carruthers & Smith 1996). Simulative reasoning about an agent consists of pretending temporarily to adopt some of the agent's mental states ("standing in the agent's shoes"), seeing where they lead to by means of one's own panoply of reasoning techniques, and then (defeasibly) ascribing the results to the agent. A particular scheme for simulative reasoning is described in Barnden *et al.* (1994), although the current implementation of ATT-Meta now uses a considerably changed algorithm.

An important feature of ATT-Meta is that simulative reasoning generally leads at most to *presumably*-tagged conclusions about the mental states of agents. For one thing, the reasoner doesn't know whether the agent really makes the inference steps alleged by the simulation. Additionally, those *presumably*-tagged conclusions can be defeated (or bolstered) by the results of metaphor-based reasoning about the agent, as we saw in the example in section 6. Often, the use of metaphor-based reasoning in ATT-Meta is to defeat a hypothesis that says that a given agent performs an alleged inference step.

ATT-Meta can nest simulative (and non-simulative) reasoning about mental states within a simulation, to get the effect of reasoning about agents' reasoning about agents' beliefs and reasoning, etc. We now go on to look at the three other nesting possibilities: metaphorical pretence within simulation, simulation within metaphorical pretence, and metaphorical pretence within metaphorical pretence.

10.2 Ascribing Metaphorical Reasoning to Agents

Because any of ATT-Meta's inference techniques can be used within the simulation of an agent, the system can ascribe metaphorical reasoning to agents themselves. This capability has barely been addressed in the metaphor field. However, it is important in the treatment of real discourse. For instance, quoted speech in newspaper articles often involves metaphor. An ATT-Meta-based approach to understanding such speech attributions would be to assume that the speaker is thinking in terms of the metaphors manifested in the utterance. Therefore, it is necessary to reason about the speaker's own metaphor-based reasoning. In this situation, we have a nesting of metaphorical reasoning within a simulation (of the speaker).

More broadly, if it is true that people actually reason metaphorically rather than just use metaphors in communication, then it is important to be able to reason about such reasoning.

10.3 Ascribing Reasoning to Metaphorical Agents

The dual of the nesting in the previous subsection is that simulative (and non-simulative) reasoning about mental states can be used within metaphorical pretences. Suppose for example that a passage describes an agent's mental states by means of the MIND PARTS AS PERSONS metaphor. Then, within the metaphorical pretence that there are some inner persons within the agent's mind-space, ATT-Meta can reason, simulatively and otherwise, about the mental states of the inner persons.

Equally, consider the case of an ordinary anthropomorphization, as in regarding a computer or a car as having mental states. Within the metaphorical pretence that the object is a person, ATT-Meta can reason about that "person's" mental states.

10.4   Chained Metaphor

The remaining type of nesting—of metaphorical reasoning within itself—is also of great interest, as it provides an account of chained metaphor. An illustration of chained metaphor, taken from real discourse, is for a thought to be viewed as a cloud, and for the cloud to be viewed as a person. This example, and the general issue, is discussed in Barnden *et al.* (1996). The treatment that would be used in the ATT-Meta framework is to have a metaphorical pretence for the cloud-as-person metaphor nested within the pretence for the thought-as-cloud metaphor. Since pretence is handled much as belief is, the nesting of pretences, and therefore chaining of metaphor, receives an algorithmic handling that is similar to the handling of belief nesting.

11   Comparison to Some Other Work on Metaphor

ATT-Meta's style of metaphorical reasoning resonates with other metaphor research in Cognitive Linguistics and Artificial Intelligence. Notably, the approach to metaphor that Lakoff and colleagues have put forward may involve within-vehicle reasoning. To take one case among many, when Lakoff & Turner (1989, p.62) discuss the metaphor LIFE AS JOURNEY they appear to be alluding to within-vehicle inferences. In the following comments, I will paraphrase part of their discussion. Consider the sentence

(S)   *Peter hit a roadblock in his life.*

A plausible inference the hearer can make is that Peter must deal with the roadblock somehow, for instance by moving round it or removing it. Unfortunately, Lakoff and Turner state this inference metaphorically (cf. "moving round" and "removing") and do not make clear (either in the cited source or elsewhere) whether

(a) the inference H that is generated in the hearer's mind is itself *metaphorical* (i.e., the hearer's mind contains an internal representation that is metaphorical and is analogous to some such sentence as "Peter must get round or move the roadblock")

or

(b) the inference H generated in the hearer's mind is in itself *non*-metaphorical, but we outside observers can choose, for purposes of theoretical discussion, to paraphrase it by some metaphorical sentence such as "Peter must get round or move the roadblock."

Possibility (a) would involve within-vehicle reasoning much like that in ATT-Meta: the hearer's reasoning to H would be based entirely on knowledge of real, physical roadblocks. (Of course, once the hearer has arrived at the metaphorical H, he or she may be in a position to create a non-metaphorical version of it as well.) Possibility (b) could proceed by converting the literal meaning of (S) into non-metaphorical terms and then deriving the non-metaphorical H, using inference patterns that are merely *analogous* to those used in the vehicle domain (the domain of real journeys). Possibility (a) would would seem to be more in keeping with Lakoff's overall thinking than (b) would be, and in particular with the principle that metaphor is a conceptual matter rather than a purely linguistic matter. Thus, there is no claim that within-vehicle reasoning appears only in ATT-Meta. Rather, ATT-Meta serves to provide a computationally specific, uncertain-reasoning framework within which to study within-vehicle reasoning.

ATT-Meta's approach to metaphor appears to be compatible with, and in some broad respects quite similar to, that of Grady (this volume). This is partly because ATT-Meta's conversion rules tend to be of a very general, basic nature (e.g., "if things in a mind don't physically interact then they don't inferentially interact"), rather than being closely tailored to dealing the full richness of metaphorical vehicles—for instance, conversion rules for MIND AS PHYSICAL SPACE are not concerned with the vast array of different specific types of physical object. A second and related similarity to Grady is the point about metaphor non-individuation made in section 9.4.

We turn now to AI research on metaphor. Most of it (e.g.: Fass 1991, Iverson & Helmreich 1992, Lytinen *et al.* 1992, Russell 1992, Veale & Keane 1992, Weiner 1984, Wilks 1978) has focused on deriving representations of the meanings of individual metaphorical expressions as essentially isolated items, rather than on drawing whatever inferences are appropriate for linking the expressions to their surrounding discourse context. (This linking is what ATT-Meta is oriented towards.) The main exception is the metaphor research of Hobbs (1990), which is within his more wide-ranging work on discourse coherence (Hobbs 1990, Hobbs *et al.* 1993). The work of Martin (1990) can also be viewed as dealing with the role of metaphor in discourse, albeit in a more restricted way. In addition, Carbonell (1982), Carbonell & Minton (1985), Indurkhya (1992), Russell (1992) and Weiner (1984) are sensitive, in varying degrees, to discourse issues concerning metaphor. However, with the exception of the work of Hobbs, the research mentioned does not integrate metaphor-based reasoning seamlessly into an implemented, general purpose reasoning framework. Both Hobbs' work and the ATT-Meta project do this, although Hobbs' framework differs greatly from the one used in ATT-Meta.

In case it might be thought that an AI metaphor project should not tackle discourse issues until the question of interpreting isolated metaphorical expressions has been sorted out, it should be borne in mind that the ATT-Meta approach avoids the claim that it is generally practical to derive the meaning of a metaphorical expression in the first place. (Recall section 5 on ATT-Meta's semantic agnosticism.) Instead, the focus is precisely on the web of inferences that can be drawn from metaphorical expressions. And a major guiding force for the inference-making is the need to link the expressions into the discourse as a whole.

Because of the concentration in AI on isolated metaphorical expressions rather than on discourse, terms such as "metaphorical reasoning" are usually taken by AI researchers to refer just to the transfer of information from vehicle to tenor, rather than allowing for extensive inference within the vehicle domain itself. The latter is the within-vehicle reasoning that is central to ATT-Meta. Nevertheless, some use of within-vehicle reasoning can be discerned in AI research. The main example is Hobbs' work on conventional metaphor, although he appears not to be as focused as the ATT-Meta project is on elucidating the benefits of within-vehicle reasoning. (See Barnden *et al.* 1996 for further discussion of the benefits.) Another example is that Martin's scheme for dealing with novel manifestations of its built-in metaphors can be viewed as involving a restricted form of within-vehicle reasoning. A further computational framework that involves some within-vehicle reasoning is the approach to metaphor-based reasoning proposed in Narayanan (1993). This approach does not embed metaphor-based reasoning in a general uncertain-reasoning framework as ATT-Meta does.

An important similarity to Martin's research, to some of Hobbs', and to that of Carbonell (1982), is the strong reliance on a built-in stock of metaphors. Much other AI work on metaphor has concentrated on processing metaphor from scratch, thus treating every metaphor as novel. However, there is nothing in ATT-Meta's approach that would preclude the introduction of a facility for dealing with novel metaphors. Presumably part of the facility would be an algorithm for inventing conversion rules as part of an analogy-discovery process.

The conversion rules in ATT-Meta are broadly similar to the conventional mappings between vehicle and tenor domains proposed by Lakoff, and also adopted in, for instance, Martin's (1990) and Hobbs' (1990) AI-oriented accounts of conventional metaphor. However, in contrast to Lakoff's and Martin's work, both the ATT-Meta project and Hobbs' provide a specific computational treatment of uncertainty of reasoning, and in particular of the uncertainty of mappings between vehicle and tenor. Also, a distinctive feature of ATT-Meta is that conversions proceed not only from vehicle to tenor but also in the opposite direction, as discussed in section 9.5.

12 Concerning the Psychology of Metaphor

Although ATT-Meta itself is not intended as a psychological model, some version of the approach could conceivably form the basis for such a model in the future. We should therefore look at an apparent tension between

(a) the fact that ATT-Meta is biased towards deriving inferences— and, possibly, metaphorical meanings—from *literal* meanings of metaphorical utterances

and

(b) the fact that some psychological experiments appear to suggest that people do *not* compute metaphorical meanings from literal ones, at least if the metaphorical sentences are in an appropriate context and use familiar metaphors. (See Gerrig 1989 for discussion.)

The experiments alluded to in (b) rest on showing that people take no longer to understand a metaphorical sentence (when the metaphor is familiar and the sentence is in a natural context) than to understand a literal sentence.

A possible resolution of this tension is that other experiments (Onishi and Murphy 1993) suggest that the metaphor-takes-no-longer result ceases to hold when metaphors are used "referentially" as opposed to "predicatively." An example of a referential use is 'The creampuff lost the round' where 'the creampuff' refers to some boxer. An example of a predicative use is 'The boxer is a creampuff.' The metaphorical utterances with which the ATT-Meta research is concerned are more like referential uses of metaphor than predicative uses, as can be seen from examples (1) to (5) in section 2.

13 Conclusion

ATT-Meta provides a framework within which to study complex, flexible metaphor-based reasoning processes in a detailed way. Although the work has focused on metaphor for mental states, there is nothing in the approach that is tailored to that special case. The approach achieves flexibility by using within-vehicle reasoning, and repudiating the assumption that metaphorical utterances should have metaphorical meanings computed for them, where it is the metaphorical meanings that are the bases for further inference. Rather, much inference is based on literal meanings of metaphorical utterances and proceeds within the pretence that the literal meanings are true.

The ATT-Meta research fully recognizes the uncertainty of metaphor-based reasoning. It allows the within-vehicle reasoning to be uncertain; it relies on uncertain conversion rules (for converting within-vehicle propositions to within-tenor propositions); and it allows the results of metaphorical reasoning to be defeated by other evidence.

As regards the application to mental states, ATT-Meta is the first system to use metaphor-based reasoning as a filter on reasoning about mental states, thereby bringing the mental states area of AI closer to dealing with realistic discourse. Also, by casting metaphorical reasoning as a type of pretence, it achieves a substantial conceptual union between metaphorical reasoning and simulative reasoning.

Acknowledgment

The work was supported in part by grants IRI-9101354 and CDA-8914670 from the National Science Foundation.

References

Barnden, J.A. (1992). Belief in metaphor: taking commonsense psychology seriously. *Computational Intelligence, 8* (3), pp.520–552.

Barnden, J.A. (in press). Consciousness and common-sense metaphors of mind. In S. O'Nuallain, P. McKevitt & E. MacAogain (Eds), *Reaching for Mind: Foundations of Cognitive Science.* John Benjamin.

Barnden, J.A., Helmreich, S., Iverson, E. & Stein, G.C. (1994). An integrated implementation of simulative, uncertain and metaphorical reasoning about mental states. In J. Doyle, E. Sandewall & P. Torasso (Eds), *Principles of Knowledge Representation and Reasoning: Proceedings of the Fourth International Conference,* pp.27–38. (Bonn, Germany, 24–27 May 1994.) San Mateo, CA: Morgan Kaufmann.

Barnden, J.A., Helmreich, S., Iverson, E. & Stein, G.C. (1996). Artificial intelligence and metaphors of mind: within-vehicle reasoning and its benefits. *Metaphor and Symbolic Activity, 11*(2), pp.101–123.

Carbonell, J.G. (1982). Metaphor: an inescapable phenomenon in natural-language comprehension. In W. Lehnert & M. Ringle (eds), *Strategies for natural language processing,* Hillsdale, N.J.: Lawrence Erlbaum.

Carbonell, J.G. & Minton, S. (1985). Metaphor and commonsense reasoning. In J.R. Hobbs & R.C. Moore (Eds), *Formal Theories of the Commonsense World*, pp.405–426. Norwood, NJ: Ablex.

Carruthers, P. & Smith, P.K. (Eds). (1996). *Theories of theories of mind.* Cambridge, UK: Cambridge University Press.

Cooke, N.J. & Bartha, M.C. (1992). An empirical investigation of psychological metaphor. *Metaphor and Symbolic Activity, 7* (3 & 4), pp.215–235.

Davidson, D. (1979). What metaphors mean. In S. Sacks (Ed.), *On Metaphor,* pp.29–45. Chicago: University of Chicago Press.

Davies, M & Stone, T. (Eds) (1995). *Mental simulation: evaluations and applications.* Oxford, U.K.: Blackwell.

Fass, D. (1991). met*: A method for discriminating metonymy and metaphor by computer. *Computational Linguistics, 17* (1), pp.49–90.

Gerrig, R.J. (1989). Empirical constraints on computational theories of metaphor: comments on Indurkhya. *Cognitive Science, 13* (2), pp.235–241.

Hobbs, J.R. (1990). *Literature and cognition.* CSLI Lecture Notes, No. 21, Center for the Study of Language and Information, Stanford University.

Hobbs, J.R., Stickel, M.E., Appelt, D.E. & Martin, P. (1993). Interpretation as abduction. *Artificial Intelligence, 63,* pp.69–142.

Indurkhya, B. (1992). *Metaphor and cognition: An interactionist approach.* Dordrecht: Kluwer.

Iverson, E. & Helmreich, S. (1992). Metallel: an integrated approach to non-literal phrase interpretation. *Computational Intelligence, 8* (3), pp.477–493.

Jäkel, O. (1993). The metaphorical concept of mind: mental activity is manipulation. Paper No. 333, General and Theoretical Papers, Series A, Linguistic Agency, University of Duisburg, D-4100 Duisburg, Germany.

Johnson, M. (1987). *The body in the mind.* Chicago: Chicago University Press.

Lakoff, G. (1993). How cognitive science changes philosophy II: the neurocognitive self. Presented at *16th International Wittgenstein Symp.,* Kirchberg am Wechsel, Austria, 15-22 August 1993.

Lakoff, G. & Turner, M. (1989). *More than cool reason: a field guide to poetic metaphor.* Chicago: University of Chicago Press.

Lytinen, S.L., Burridge, R.R. & Kirtner, J.D. (1992). The role of literal meaning in the comprehension of non-literal constructions. *Computational Intelligence, 8* (3), pp.416–432.

Martin, J.H. (1990). *A computational model of metaphor interpretation.* Academic Press.

Narayanan, S. (1993). Schema-based modeling of commonsense understanding of causal narratives. In *Procs. Workshop on Neural Architectures and Distributed AI: From Schema Assemblages to Neural Networks,* Center for Neural Engineering, University of Southern California, Los Angeles, CA, 19–20 October 1993.

Onishi, K.H. & Murphy, G.L. (1993). Metaphoric reference: when metaphors are not understood as easily as literal expressions. *Memory and Cognition, 21* (6), pp.763–772.

Russell, S.W. (1992). Metaphoric coherence: distinguishing verbal metaphor from "anomaly." *Computational Intelligence, 8* (3), pp.553–574.

Sweetser, E.E. (1990). *From etymology to pragmatics: metaphorical and cultural aspects of semantic structure.* Cambridge, U.K.: Cambridge University Press.

Veale, T. & Keane, M.T. (1992). Conceptual scaffolding: a spatially founded meaning representation for metaphor comprehension. *Computational Intelligence, 8* (3), pp.494–519.

Weiner, J. (1984). A knowledge representation approach to understanding metaphors. *Computational Linguistics, 10* (1), pp.1–14.

Wilks, Y. (1978). Making preferences more active. *Artificial Intelligence, 10,* pp.75-97.

Metaphoric Gestures and Some of Their Relations to Verbal Metaphoric Expressions

ALAN CIENKI

Emory University

1. Metaphor, Verbal Metaphoric Expressions, and Metaphoric Gestures[1]

Since Lakoff and Johnson (1980), a body of research has developed around the ways in which phenomena such as metaphor, metonymy, and mental spaces (Fauconnier 1985) play a major part in our ordinary conceptualization of the world. In this research, the term metaphor refers to "a cross-domain mapping [from a source domain onto a target domain] in the conceptual system" (Lakoff 1993a: 203), and is therefore sometimes referred to as "conceptual metaphor". The term "metaphoric expression" then applies to a surface realization of such a cross-domain mapping (*ibid.*). Our everyday behavior reflects our metaphorical understanding of experience (Lakoff 1993a: 204). While the behavior in which conceptual metaphors receive

---

[1] I would like to thank David McNeill and Adam Kendon for helpful discussions on the topic of this paper and their course on gesture at the 1995 Summer Linguistic Institute; McNeill and Karl-Erik McCullough for a helpful training workshop in gesture analysis; and Eve Sweetser for further helpful discussion about metaphoric gestures.

expression clearly includes language, it is not limited to spoken, signed, or written language. Recent research on the role of metaphor in domains that do not necessarily involve language bears this out, e.g., Lakoff (1993b) on metaphor in dreams, and Johnson (1987: chapter 4) and Hausman (1989) on metaphor in the visual arts (although the latter is not a direct application of conceptual metaphor theory).

Gesture is a fairly new domain for metaphor research. Metaphoric gestures were first discussed in Calbris's (1990) work on French gesture, and McNeill (1992) includes them as one of the four basic types in his classification of spontaneous gestures which includes *beats* (rhythmic, pulsing gestures which mark words or phrases as significant for their discourse/pragmatic content), *deictics* (gestures which point at concrete entities or at abstract spaces that the speaker "sets up"), *iconics* (depictive gestures which bear a close formal relationship to the semantic content of the accompanying speech), and *metaphorics* (whose pictorial content presents an abstract idea). These categories are not meant to be mutually exclusive; they can overlap to varying degrees (McNeill, personal communication), e.g., a metaphoric gesture can be deictic (pointing to something in abstract as if it were present in concrete space). Note that for the purposes of the present study, the criterion for establishing a gesture as (at least partially) metaphoric is that the gesture characterizes an abstract domain (here we will discuss mostly the domains of morality and time) in terms of the concrete (spatial form, location, and movement of the hands and forearms).

One goal of the present study is to further demonstrate the importance of gesture for metaphor research. In brief, gestures provide evidence of conceptual metaphors independent of verbal communication per se. As McNeill (1992) emphasizes, gesture, and specifically, spontaneous gesture accompanying speech, can show other aspects of how a speaker is formulating an idea for expression. It can reveal some of the processes involved in what Slobin (1987) has called "thinking for speaking", and what McNeill and Duncan (to appear) discuss as the "growth point" of an idea. The study of spontaneous gesture (as well as dreams, non-verbal arts and other cultural practices) is important for metaphor theory because it breaks the vicious cycle of saying that verbal metaphoric expressions are evidence of conceptual metaphors, and then saying that we know that because we see conceptual metaphors expressed in language.[2] Gesture, and other non-verbal means of expression, can serve as independent sources of evidence of the psychological reality of conceptual metaphors.

---

[2]Cf. Gibbs and Colston (1995: 354): "Psychologists often contend that cognitive linguistic research suffers from circular reasoning in that it starts with an analysis of language to infer something about the mind and body which in turn motivates different aspects of linguistic structure and behavior."

As we will see, metaphoric gestures do not simply reiterate accompanying verbal metaphoric expressions in manual form; in fact, they sometimes occur with non-metaphoric speech, and may even reveal conceptual metaphors which do not receive verbal expression. Even when the gesture is redundant of certain aspects of the verbal metaphoric expression, it normally reveals additional information about the form and the force-dynamic properties of the source domain.

2. Metaphoric Gestures and their Contexts

2.0 Source of the Data

The present study is part of a larger investigation examining U.S. American college students' metaphors for honesty and dishonesty in the context of taking exams. The study entails engaging pairs of undergraduate students at a mid-sized American university (Emory University) in conversation-interviews about American academic practices. The students are paid for their participation. Pairs who are friends or acquaintances are used to encourage natural spontaneous interaction between them. They are given several written questions and a hypothetical scenario to discuss with each other at their own pace. Among other things, the questions ask them to describe what it means to conduct oneself honestly during an exam, and how they would feel if they found out someone in a class they are in cheated on an exam and therefore received a better grade on it than they did. Their conversation is videotaped with their permission; I, as interviewer, remain off-camera until they complete their discussion, at which time I join them to ask some final questions based on the issues they have raised. The entire procedure usually lasts about 30-40 minutes and provides extended discourse with which to study (a) *where* verbal and gestural metaphoric expressions occur, (b) what the *relation* is between where the two occur, as well as (c) *patterns* of gestural use by a speaker over time, which is helpful for interpreting the meanings of gestures.

In the examples, each pair of students is indicated with a pair of letters: A and B, C and D, etc. The two students were seated at about a 120-150 degree angle. Relevant verbal metaphoric expressions will be marked in the transcribed examples in bold type. Self-interruptions and restarts will be indicated with a backslash (/). Speech co-occurring with the main stroke of each gesture will be shown within brackets ([ ]). Speech co-occurring with motion preparing a gesture, with the main stroke, and with a gesture held in place after the main stroke (the post-stroke hold), will all be underlined. The system for transcribing gestures is a simplified version of that in McNeill (1992), indicating the hand with which the gesture was made, the shape of the hand (first via a rough description, then in terms of American Sign Language hand shapes), orientation of the palm (away from body, toward a given direction [center, up, down, left, or right], or at an oblique angle and so marked with a combination [e.g., away from body/toward down]) and orientation of the fingers (direction in which the base segment of the four main fingers point), location of the gesture according to the chart in Figure 1, and motion. Motion involving change in any of the other parameters is described accordingly in terms of "from X to Y" (e.g., "orientation: palm from toward down to toward center").

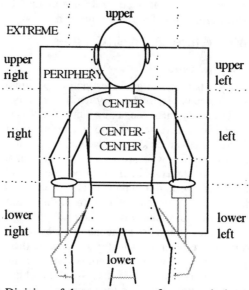

Figure 1: Division of the gesture space for transcription purposes (adapted from McNeill 1992: 378).

2.1 Metaphoric Gestures <u>with</u> Verbal Metaphoric Expressions

In some cases, metaphoric gestures express the same conceptual metaphors which are being revealed in speech. For example, there are a number of metaphors in American culture (which are clearly not exclusive to it) in which honesty, telling the truth, or being maximally informative are characterized as being (oriented) straight, e.g., *to be straight as an arrow* (honest), *straight talk* (telling the truth) (see Cienki, in preparation). In most cases, a correlate of the metaphoric straight nature of the target domain entity is that it is conceived of as having an absolute quality. In some cases, this aspect of the metaphor is reinforced with related metaphors concerning absolute qualities, as in example (1).

(1)   A: You can't really say that people that go to Harvard are like gonna be <u>[all]</u> **hundred percent** like **real straight** and aren't gonna look over y/ other people's papers...

Gesture 1:
hand: left
shape: relaxed flat open hand (loose 5)
orientation: palm toward center/toward down, fingers away from body
location: lower center
motion: small downward stroke (relaxed chop)

With a straight-hand gesture the speaker not only reinforces the absolute nature of the honest behavior which he doubts the students will conform to, he also anticipates the upcoming verbal expression "straight" by gesturing while uttering the other 'absolute' metaphoric expression ("all hundred percent"), thus integrating the concepts of 'absolute' and 'straight' via the gesture.

In example (2), speaker C is claiming that there is not a consensus nowadays in American culture as to what is moral, and both speakers are cynical about people's motives:

(2)   C: I think a lot of it's just based on a situational basis. It's a lot of
           like: who's looking, who's watching, what are the consequences,

        D: and what can I justify,

        C: and what can I get out of it, y'know? It's like [**balancing** all

                                                    r   *l*   *r*

        these things]......., and trying to figure out... how you can come

           *l*_____   *r l*

        out the best.

Gesture 2:
hand: both
shape: relaxed claw (loose bent 5)
orientation: palm towards up , fingers away from body
location: central
motion: hands and forearms (bending at elbow) alternately move up
        (remaining below shoulder height) and down (above waist height); "r"
        and "l"indicate when right and left hands each reach the upward peak of
        motion, with "l ___" indicating when the left hand was held upward for
        a period.

The metaphor invoked by the speaker, which involves "balancing" in the sense of "weighing", can be charactized as CONSIDERING THE IMPORTANCE OF DIFFERENT FACTORS IS WEIGHING DIFFERENT OBJECTS,[3] and entails a few others which are made more salient by the

---

[3]Obviously more than one example of a verbal metaphoric expression is needed in order to infer the existence of a conceptual metaphor. Though I am not

accompanying gesture, namely the metaphors (MOTIVATING/SITUATIONAL) FACTORS ARE OBJECTS, and IMPORTANCE IS WEIGHT. (See Johnson [1987: 87-96] on the importance of BALANCE as a source domain for many metaphors relating to psychological states, morality, and law, among other domains.) The cupped hands are turned upward in the gesture, as if holding a small object in each hand, the repeated up and down motion of the forearms -- with first one hand raised and the other lowered, then the reverse -- shows the weighing process, and the fact that the high and low points that each hand reaches in motion are about the same reveals the balancing of the different factors.

In (3) the event that occurred, *the exam passed*, is described using the common metaphor that AN EVENT IN TIME IS MOVEMENT THROUGH SPACE, or more generally, CHANGES ARE MOVEMENTS (Lakoff 1993a: 220). The gesture indicates the movement in physical form, manually, with a motion to the speaker's left side. We will return below to the possible significance of the *left* side in this context, and to gestures 3.2 and 3.3, in section 2.2.1 below.

(3)   E: Oh, are you saying like th/the e[xam] **passed** and this person has

gesture 3.1

to [make] up that exam or are you saying like [last] semester?

gesture 3.2   *gesture 3.3*

Gesture 3.1:
hand: left
shape: flat hand, fingers together, thumb apart (B-spread)
orientation: palm toward down, fingers away from body
location: left periphery to extreme left
motion: small vertical arc moving from left periphery   to the extreme left

We can therefore note that some of the same metaphors appear in gesture as appear in spoken language when thinking about and discussing abstract domains. The metaphoric gestures, however, can express spatial and force-dynamic information about the speaker's conceptualization of the given event or entity that are not necessarily expressed in speech.

It is also worth noting that different metaphors may be expressed in speech and gesture, with the two representing different aspects of a coherent metaphorical model. In (4) the speaker is discussing 1950's America as an example of "traditional morality", and she uses the basic opposition of light and dark to metaphorically represent the clearly defined categories of good and bad moral behavior within such a traditional system. She contrasts this

---

discussing them in detail here, I believe the metaphors mentioned are evident in other expressions in American English, e.g., *giving a lot of weight to a certain factor, you have to weigh what's important to you*, etc.

with the situation today in which moral categories are not as clearly defined (they're "gray").

(4)   C: Yeah, when I think of traditional morality I think of the 50's, when...everything had its place, and [everything] was **black and**

                    ^   ^

                gesture 4.1

white. Tra[ditional morality's] **black and white**. Today

        ^   ^   ^

              gesture 4.2

everything's [just **gray**].

              gesture 4.3

Gesture 4.1:
hand: two hands
shape: both open flat, fingers together, thumb apart (B-spread)
orientation: both – palm toward center, fingers away from body
location: lower periphery (legs are crossed, right over left; hands are resting on right thigh)
motion: left – held stationary; right – slight vertical arc toward right, touching leg at start and end points (marked with ^ under text in example)

Gesture 4.2:
hand: two hands
shape: both open flat, fingers together, thumb apart (B-spread); right hand flatter and more tense than in gesture 4.1
orientation: both – palm toward center, fingers away from body
location: lower periphery (legs are crossed, right over left; hands are resting on right thigh)
motion: left – held stationary; right – moves slightly toward right, touching leg (beats) at three points (marked with ^ under text in example)

Gestures 4.1 and 4.2 by speaker C reveal her spatial conceptualization of the verbal "color" metaphor: in 4.1 she marks the separate "moral spaces" of black and white; in 4.2 the tense, flat right hand chopping the space in front of her in two reveals a well-defined division (a straight line) between these two opposing "moral spaces". This contrasts with gesture 4.3.

Gesture 4.3:
hand: both
shape: loose open "claw", fingers loosely bent (relaxed bent 5)
orientation: both – palm toward center

left – fingers away from body
right – from away from body/toward up   to away from body
location: lower periphery; left hand rests on right leg, right wrist rests on
right leg
motion: left – held stationary;
right – hand pivots at wrist, tipping fanned-out fingers down such that
little finger rests on right leg

Speaker C refers to the lack of clearly defined moral categories with another "color" metaphorical expression, saying that neither good nor bad are clearly defined, but that rather the two are blended (into gray). Consonant with this, the co-occurring gesture, with the moving right hand, does not define a boundary, and in fact reflects a curve, a more vaguely defined form. In this way, the metaphors in speech and gesture draw on different source domains (those of color and spatial form), but in a coherent way.

2.2 Metaphoric Gestures <u>without</u> Corresponding Verbal Metaphoric Expressions

2.2.1 Expressions for Time

In a number of the interviews, speakers consistently gesture to the left and right spaces when making reference to the past and the future, respectively, whereas the opposite pattern was observed much more rarely. This use of space occurred in example (3) (repeated below), but not only when the speaker employed a simultaneous verbal metaphoric expression for TIME AS SPACE (*the exam passed*), but also when verbal reference to the past did not involve this metaphor (gesture 3.3 with the phrase "*last semester*").

(3)   E: Oh, are you saying like <u>th/the e[xam]</u> **passed** and <u>this person has</u>

gesture 3.1

<u>to [make] up that exam</u> <u>or are you saying like [last] semester?</u>

gesture 3.2   *gesture 3.3*

<u>Gesture 3.3:</u>
hand: left
shape: hand open, finger only loosely curved (slightly bent 5)
orientation: palm from toward down   to toward center/toward up;
fingers away from body
location: extreme left to slightly further left
motion: slight movement of hand to left, with palm turning from toward
center   to toward up

While gesture 3.2 relates to the past (to an exam that was taken in the past by one's classmates), its meaning is complicated by the fact that it refers to completing an action that one should have done in the past -- making up an exam, i.e., taking an exam that one should have taken already. Note that in gesture 3.2 the left hand (marked metaphorically in gesture 3.1 as the exam taken by others in the past) is held up and becomes a point of reference in gesture 3.2, in which the right hand (the person making up the exam) moves toward it (the person "goes back" to make up the test).

Gesture 3.2:
hand: two hands (simultaneous movement)
shape (left): from flat hand, fingers together, thumb apart (B-spread)
　　to relaxed open hand (slightly bent 5)
orientation (left): palm from toward down to toward center,
　　fingers from away from body　to away from body/toward up
location (left): extreme left
motion (left): turn at wrist, palm moving from toward down　to toward
　　center

shape (right): relaxed open hand (slightly bent 5)
orientation (right): palm toward center/toward down, fingers away from body
location (right): from center right　to center left
motion (right): movement to left with slight upward arc

In some cases, the speaker makes repeated reference to past and/or future time and, in the process, establishes reference to them with gestures to distinct spaces, often the left and right, respectively. In example (5), the students are discussing whether it is ethical to use a back-test, an old copy of a written test from when the same class was taught in the past, in order to prepare for an upcoming test. The majority of speaker D's gestures here were metaphoric/deictic (to abstract spaces). Rather than analyzing all of the gestures in this segment, only the metaphoric/deictic gestures will be marked, and only for the following features: two-handed gesture (2h), right-handed gesture (rh), a gesture pointing to the space to the speaker's right (R), left-handed gesture (lh), a gesture pointing to the space to the speaker's left (L), and a movement going from one space to the other (->).

(5)　C: I mean, I don't think that they're useful because I mean you can get a back-test and then the teacher can change the test. Y'know?

　　　D: Getting the back/ But, look,/ so it doesn't matter like if you get a back-test and if

　　　C: I'm just talking generally. I think that people don't, like...

　　　D: I'm just saying if you/ <u>do you think if you [stu]dy from uh, from</u>
　　　　　　　　　　　　　　　　　　　rh L

　　　　<u>a [back]-[test] as[sum]ing</u> that you um have <u>the [ques]tions to the</u>
　　　　rh L -> R　*rh R*　　　　　　　　　　　*2h L*　　　　*->*

　　　　[test] and [study] for this, and even though he [chang]es it, you
　　　　R　　　*L*　　　　　　　　　　　　　*rh R*

still [committed this], but the [test]-taking experience [was],

    2h center   *rh R*   *2h R*

whatever, the [nat]ural test-taking experience, you [come] in not

    2h R   *2h R*

knowing, [and] you're tak[ing] this test, but you have this [guilt]

    2h R   *2h R*   *2h L*

beforehand, [but it doesn't save...]

    2h L –> R

C: Why have guilt?

D: For [stud]ying the [back]-test that you [thought] was gonna [be]

    lh L   *lh L*   *lh L*   *lh stays L, rh R*

the test.

C: Right.

This excerpt provides an elaborate example of the consistent use of left and right spaces, witnessed in a number of the interviews as well as anecdotally, which can be described metaphorically as PAST IS TO THE LEFT and FUTURE IS TO THE RIGHT. Complementing this is another use of gesture, commonly found among American speakers of English, in which speakers indicate that the PRESENT IS CLOSE IN FRONT OF US. (Calbris [1990] discusses a similar metaphoric use of left and right spaces for French speakers, but she claims that for them the present is at one's feet.) Note that in almost all cases in (5) the metaphoric gestures do not co-occur with verbal metaphoric expressions, and in several cases the co-occurring words do not even relate directly to past or future time as much as they concern the simple sequence of events (e.g., "and study [L] for this", "the questions [L] to the test [R]"). In this segment, speaker D seemed to use these gestures on a more conscious level for reference to past and future times as he developed his point; whether used consciously or not, such gestures seem to reflect the speaker's framework for metaphorically conceiving of time in spatial terms.

Note, however, that this is not a metaphor that appears verbally in English, for example, *"I did X to the left of Y" is not used to mean "I did X before Y". The metaphorical time frame in which the future is in front of us and the past is in back is well documented among speakers of English (e.g., Clark 1973, Lakoff and Johnson 1980). This raises the issue that the primary means of expression for some metaphors in our culture is not verbal, but *non*-verbal, via gesture and other culture-specific conventions (viz. the left-to-right graphic depiction of a time line, the depiction of rules in symbolic logic [if --> then], as well as the depiction of an action chain in cognitive grammar diagrams). But why do we find this metaphor in gesture and not in speech? Calbris (1990: 87) attributes this to the fact that in our culture (French, American, and European in general), we write (manually) from left to right; to this could be added that we read (scanning visually) from left to right. Writing and reading provide the experiential basis for the left-to-right metaphorical time line which we see expressed manually in gesture. A way to test this would be to study metaphoric gestures for time among people who do not write from left to right. Informal questioning of native speakers of Hebrew provides tentative support in that several speakers indicated they would point with their right finger toward their right shoulder if discussing the past in contrast to future time. (Even if they are indicating the space behind them, it is interesting that they would point toward their *right* shoulder). This gestural reference to the future was not consistent, however, as they pointed either downward or toward the space out in front of them.[4]

2.2.2 Expressions for Truth and Honesty

Additional evidence of metaphoric expression in gesture without redundant, co-occuring verbal metaphoric expression can be seen in the following examples of the straight-hand gesture exemplifying TRUTH IS STRAIGHT. In examples (6) and (7) we see the same flat hand "chop" gesture discussed in section 2.1 above, but here it occurs unaccompanied by any verbal expression of the same metaphor.

(6)   G: Like dishonest suggests, like, um, not truthful, like, the [truth] is what, like,...

Gesture 6:
hand: left
shape: open flat hand (5 hand)
orientation: palm toward center, fingers from away from body/toward up to away from body
location: lower center to lower periphery
motion: hand moves down, forearm bending at elbow to just above left leg, then hand rests on leg (palm down)

As we see in (7), STRAIGHT serves not only as a source domain for TRUTH, but also for the closely related domain of HONESTY (i.e., AN HONEST PERSON IS/SPEAKS/ACTS STRAIGHT), especially with regard to a person who is thought of as one who usually tells the truth: "she's straight as an arrow", "he's a real straight shooter", etc.

---

[4]Dedre Gentner (personal communication) also suggested that the front-back time frame may be avoided in gesture so as to not to point at one's interlocutor or into his/her personal space when indicating the future, which could be socially awkward. By transforming the time line to the left-right axis, the speaker can remain within his/her conventional gesture space.

(7)   G: So like, you're asking the question, if/ can you say something is
            a certain honesty? Like, 'this is a very/ 'he's a [very] honest
            person'? Like, can you say that, or do you have to say he's a
            dishonest person because he's not completely honest?

Gesture 7:
hand: right
shape: flat hand, fingers close together but not touching, thumb slightly
    raised (between B-spread and 5 hand)
orientation: palm toward body/toward left;
    fingers from toward up/toward left/away from body to toward left/away
    from body
location: lower left periphery
motion: hand chops down quickly to just above left leg

2.2.3 Compositionality Possible with Metaphoric Gestures

As is clear from the way in which gestures have been described or coded for
the purposes of this study, gestures involve several spatial parameters which
are largely independent of each other: which hand is involved, the palm
orientation, finger orientation, hand shape, location in gesture space, and
motion or stability. As we have seen, gestures can have metaphorical
significance according to at least several of these parameters, e.g., shape
(straight versus bent) and location (left versus right gesture space). (It is
possible that each of these parameters may be capable of some degree of
metaphorical expression [cf. Webb 1996], but this issue will be left open
for the present.) In contrast to McNeill's (1992: 21) assertion that gestures
are noncombinatoric, the present data provide evidence that a given
combination of parameters (gestural forms) can sometimes express a
combination of metaphors (gestural significance). In example (8), speaker F
utilizes (at least) two different metaphorical frameworks which combine in a
coherent way. One is the left/right framework for past versus future time,
and the other involves elements of the up/down framework representing
things that are good versus bad. The speaker is discussing whether the
decision to act honestly or dishonestly in a given circumstance is clear or
not. Only selected gestures have been transcribed here.

(8)   F: Um, I think it's... it has more to do with the means than the
            ends. Um, if you're just looking at it as a pure activity -- um,
            either being honest or not honest -- if you/ if you try to avoid the
            end result and, say, OK: Does it matter in the long run? Just
            right now, do I do the right thing or do I do the wrong thing? --
            it's very clear cut. It's not a difficult decision if you look at it

that way. The problem comes in when you start analyzing what's [next], you know, what re[sult] will either of these have,

gesture 8.1   *gesture 8.2*

y'know, if y/ if you do th/ the [ho]nest [thing], will you maybe

gesture 8.3 a,   *b*

[get] the worse grade and, y'know, [have] trouble in the future, or

gesture 8.4   *gesture 8.5*

if you do the [dis]honest thing, [will] [you] get ahead?

gesture 8.6   *gesture 8.7 a, b*

Gesture 8.1 ("what's next"):
hand: right
shape: relaxed open flat hand (5 hand)
orientation: palm from away from body/toward up/toward center to toward up; fingers from away from body/toward up/toward right to away from body/toward right
location: extreme right
motion: slight raising of hand and movement toward right, with palm turning upward; tensing and flattening of hand

Gesture 8.2 ("what result"):
hand: right
shape: relaxed open flat hand (5 hand)
orientation: palm toward center; fingers from toward left to away from body
location: from center to extreme right
motion: hand moves to right, forearm bending out at elbow and wrist

Gesture 8.3 ("if you do the honest thing"):
hand: both
shape: relaxed open flat hand (5 hand)
orientation: both – palm toward down, left – moves to palm away from body; both – fingers away from body; left – fingers move to toward up
location: lower left periphery to left periphery
motion: both hands beat down together (a) (anticipated with a preparatory beat marked as ^); then move up (b), with left hand rising more

Gesture 8.4 ("will you maybe get the worse grade"):
hand: two hands
shape: both – relaxed open hand (between 5 and loose bent 5)
orientation: left palm – toward down;
     right palm – from toward down to toward center
     left fingers – toward center (i.e., pointing to the right);

right fingers – from away from body   to away from body/toward
down/toward right
location: left – lower center;
    right – from lower right periphery   to extreme lower right
motion: both hands move in parallel; right leg is crossed over left, left hand
    beats on right leg, right hand turns out to right, turning at elbow and
    wrist

Gesture 8.5 ("have trouble in the future"):
Similar to 8.4, but more exaggerated in that both hands make small vertical
arc, moving slightly to the right.

Gesture 8.6 ("if you do the dishonest thing"):
hand: both
shape: open flat hand (5 hand)
orientation: palms from toward center/toward down   to palm toward down,
    fingers from towards up/towards center/away from body   to toward
    center/away from body
location: lower periphery
motion: hands turn down at wrist, "pushing" down in front of speaker
    stopping just above crossed leg, as if throwing an object down

Gesture 8.7 ("will you get ahead?"):
hand: a – right; b – left
shape: slightly curved open relaxed hands (between 5 and bent-5)
orientation: right palm (a) – from down   to toward center/toward up;
    right fingers from away from body/toward center   to away from body
    toward up
    left palm (b) – from toward down   to toward up;
    left fingers from away from body toward center   to toward center (i.e.,
    toward the right)
location: right (a) – from lower periphery   to right extreme periphery
    left (b) – lower periphery
motion: a – right hand opens up toward right, forearm bending at elbow
    b – left hand flip over to palm-up position and rests on crossed right leg
    Right hand finally returns to rest position (palm down) on top of open
    left hand (palm up).

Note in particular the following series of gestures, reflecting the given
sequence of reasoning about actions (in the hypothetical present) and their
possible consequences (in the future):

gesture 8.3 (to the left and up) –> gestures 8.4 & 8.5 (to the right and down)
do the honest thing (= good)   –>   *will you get the worse grade and*
                                        have trouble in the future (= bad)

gesture 8.6 (central and down) –>   gesture 8.7 (to the right and up)
do the dishonest thing (= bad) –>   *will you get ahead* (= good)

Gesture 8.7 provides a particularly interesting case in that it may not only represent a combination of the metaphors FUTURE IS TO THE RIGHT (hand location to the right) and GOOD IS UP (hand is located up), but also, with its co-occurring question, the metaphor UNKNOWN IS UP (hand is raised and palm is pointed up). The verbal expression of this metaphor has been discussed as early as Lakoff and Johnson (1980: 20), and its gestural expression is familiar from the common gesture for *"I don't know"* of shrugging one's shoulders and holding one or both raised palms pointing up, fingers pointing away from the body. Thus three notions expressed by the question (the uncertain status [1] of a good thing [2] in the future [3]) are reflected in different (and sometimes overlapping) parameters of the gesture, which physically depict the source domains of UP and RIGHT.

3. Some Further Conclusions

Though this analysis merely skims the surface of this topic, we can already draw some preliminary conclusions about the relations between the verbal and gestural expression of metaphors.

Some criteria for determining the meanings of metaphoric gestures include (a) other uses of the same gesture by a given speaker, (b) the contrastive function of gestures (the fact that they often reflect an increase in communicative dynamism of an utterance, that is, they often co-occur with new information in the verbal utterance (McNeill 1992), and (c) coding by more than one native speaker of the language to ensure reliability. One of the drawbacks of the current study is that the gestures under discussion have not been coded by more than one person, and the interpretations have only been confirmed through informal viewings of the taped material by others.

Metaphoric gestures can add expressive import on their own in that they need not be accompanied by verbal metaphoric expressions. When they do occur in the same utterance with related verbal metaphoric expressions, the metaphoric gestures often precede/anticipate the verbal expressions (especially in pauses) to the point where they can relate a metaphor before it has appeared at all in speech.

Some topics to be explored in further work include what the expression of metaphors through speech and gesture can reveal about cultural models, specifically those of honesty and dishonesty in American academic culture, and what we can learn from comparison with data on the topic from another language and culture, namely from Russian.

References

Calbris, Geneviève. 1990. *The Semiotics of French Gestures*. Bloomington, IN: Indiana University Press.

Cienki, Alan. In preparation. "STRAIGHT: An Image Schema and its Metaphorical Extensions."

Clark, Herbert H. 1973. "Space, Time, Semantics, and the Child." In T.E. Moore, ed. *Cognitive Development and the Acquisition of Language.* New York: Academic Press. 27-64.

Fauconnier, Gilles. 1985. *Mental Spaces: Aspects of Meaning Construction in Natural Language.* Cambridge, MA: MIT Press.

Gibbs, Raymond W. and Herbert L. Colston. 1995. "The Cognitive Psychological Reality of Image Schemas and their Transformations." *Cognitive Linguistics* 6: 347-378.

Hausman, Carl R. 1989. *Metaphor and Art : Interactionism and Reference in the Verbal and Nonverbal Arts.* Cambridge: Cambridge University Press.

Johnson, Mark. 1993. *Moral Imagination: Implications of Cognitive Science for Ethics,* Chicago: University of Chicago Press.

Lakoff, George. 1993a. "The Contemporary Theory of Metaphor." In *Metaphor and Thought,* A. Ortony, ed. Cambridge: Cambridge University Press. Second edition, 202-251.

Lakoff, George. 1993b. "How Metaphor Structures Dreams: The Theory of Conceptual Metaphor Applied to Dream Analysis." *Dreaming* 3: 77-98.

Lakoff, George and Mark Johnson. 1980. *Metaphors We Live By.* Chicago: University of Chicago Press.

McNeill, David. 1992. *Hand and Mind: What Gestures Reveal about Thought.* Chicago: University of Chicago Press.

McNeill, David and Susan D. Duncan. To appear. "Toward a Model of the Growth Point."

Slobin, Dan. 1987. "Thinking for Speaking." *Proceedings of the Thirteenth Annual Meeting of the Berkeley Linguistics Society,* 435-445. Berkeley, CA: Berkeley Linguistics Society.

Talmy, Leonard. 1988. "Force Dynamics in Language and Cognition." *Cognitive Science* 12: 49-100.

Turner, Mark and Gilles Fauconnier. 1995. "Conceptual Integration and Formal Expression." *Metaphor and Symbolic Activity* 10: 183-204.

Webb, Rebecca A. 1996. "Linguistic Features of Metaphoric Gestures." Ph.D. dissertation, University of Rochester, NY.

The "Conduit Metaphor" Revisited: A Reassessment of Metaphors for Communication

JOE GRADY
University of California, Berkeley

1. Introduction: the "Conduit Metaphor"

The "conduit metaphor," a hypothesized cognitive association between communication and the process of sending and receiving packages, has played a central role in the development of Lakoff and associates' linguistic theory of conceptual metaphor. Lakoff and Johnson have referred to Reddy's (1979) original presentation of this metaphor as an inspiration for *Metaphors We Live By* (1980), the ground-breaking work in which they laid down many of the principles of current theory. In this book they used the conduit metaphor as a prominent example illustrating the characteristics of conceptual metaphor. Subsequently, the conduit metaphor has been treated as one of the clearest and best established conceptual metaphors—one which bears on the understanding of speech acts (Johnson, 1987), the psychological reality of metaphor (Gibbs, 1994), the motivation for grammatical constructions (Goldberg, 1995), the evolution of lexical meaning (Sweetser, 1990), and so forth.

A close examination of data associated with this complex metaphor, however, reveals that there are important aspects of the evidence which are unaccounted for by existing analyses. In this paper I will review the features of the conduit metaphor as described by Reddy and Lakoff & Johnson—descriptions which have served as premises for subsequent works referring to the conduit metaphor—and then show that a more refined analysis of the data offers us several important benefits:

- a clearer view of the relationship between this metaphor and other metaphors,

- an account of the types of motivation which give rise to the metaphorical conceptualizations involved, and

- an explanation for why certain elements of the source domain (the transfer of containers) are mapped onto the target domain (linguistic communication) and others are not.

More importantly, a reanalysis of the conduit metaphor data sheds light on the whole phenomenon of conceptual metaphor at a level not fully addressed in earlier accounts. As we sort out the specific conceptualizations that underlie the linguistic expressions, we arrive at a more detailed picture of how conceptual domains are related to one another, and what kinds of experiences motivate these relationships.

Reddy's account

Reddy's paper was built around comments written by instructors on students' essays. These examples focused on the degree to which students succeeded in communicating their ideas, and on the presence or absence of significant content in their prose. In Reddy's analysis, there were several metaphoric constants which characterized a great number of the examples. Chief among them were the following:

- Language functions like a conduit enabling the transfer of repertoire members [i.e., thoughts, feelings, meanings, ideas] from one individual to another.

- In writing and speech, people place their internal repertoire members [RMs] within the external signals.

- Signals convey or contain the RMs.

- In listening or reading, people find the RMs within the signals and take them into their heads.

Here are some representative examples from Reddy's paper, showing the breadth of the conceptual correspondences involved:

(1)   It is very difficult to *put* this concept *into* words.

(2)   Harry always *fills* his paragraphs with meaning.

(3)   His words *carry* little in the way of recognizable meaning.

(4)   The passage *conveys* a feeling of excitement.

(5)   John says he cannot *find* your idea anywhere *in* the passage.

(6)   I have to struggle to *get* any meaning at all *out of* the sentence.

(7)   You know very well that I *gave* you that idea.

(8)   Your real feelings are finally *getting through to* me.

(9)   The man's thought is *buried in* these terribly dense and difficult paragraphs.

It is easy to see from these examples how a view of metaphor could arise which is very different from the traditional view of metaphor as involving unique, creative, and non-standard uses of individual words or phrases[1]. The expressions here appear to arise from a common and systematic way of speaking about communication, and moreover to reflect a way of *thinking* about communication. In fact, one of Reddy's chief motivations for writing the paper was his concern that this pervasive view actually damages our communications and even our culture, since it places too much responsibility on the speaker/writer, and too little on the listener/reader, and leads to a dangerous passivity regarding the exchange of ideas.

Reddy also discusses a number of "minor" variants of the conduit metaphor—e.g., a version in which ideas are inserted into texts which may never be read or even seen, and where there is consequently no notion of transfer from one person to another.

Lakoff & Johnson's account

Following up on Reddy's (1979) article, and using their own conventions for presenting metaphoric *mappings*—i.e., systematic correspondences between different conceptual domains, such as linguistic communication and the transfer of containers—Lakoff & Johnson proposed the following breakdown of the conduit metaphor into a set of conventional correspondence pairs:

(10) a.   IDEAS/MEANINGS ARE OBJECTS

     b.   LINGUISTIC EXPRESSIONS ARE CONTAINERS

     c.   COMMUNICATION IS SENDING

In Lakoff and Johnson's formulation, "the speaker puts ideas (objects) into words (containers) and sends them (along a conduit) to a hearer who takes the idea/objects out of the word/containers" (p. 10). L&J's concise description captures the essence of Reddy's proposal. Reddy's minor variants fall out from the set of correspondences—e.g., expressions involving the insertion of ideas into texts are motivated by the first two correspondences above, without reference to the third.

Reddy's discussion and L&J's more formal analysis constitute the understanding of the conduit metaphor which subsequent works, including those mentioned above, have drawn from. In the next section we will see some ways in which this understanding is incomplete.

2. Problems of existing accounts

Existing analyses of the conduit metaphor are somewhat problematic both in their ability to account for linguistic data and with respect to broader issues of conceptual metaphor. These problems can be grouped into several specific areas[2].

---

[1]This view dates back to Aristotle's *Poetics*.

[2]In a talk presented at the 1995 ICLA in Albuquerque, Claudia Brugman raised a

Lack of experiential basis

The following citation from *Metaphors We Live By* reflects the centrality of experientialism within Lakoff & Johnson's view of metaphor: "We feel that no metaphor can ever be comprehended or even adequately represented independently of its experiential basis...." (p. 19). It is not a trivial matter, then, if we can find no plausible experience to point to as the motivation for a particular mapping. In the case of the conduit metaphor, such an experiential basis is hard to find.

The most obvious sort of experiential basis for a metaphor is a salient overlap in our experience of the two relevant domains. For example, the proposed motivation for MORE IS UP, a metaphor which maps verticality onto quantity, is our recurring experience of observing that as the quantity of physical objects or substances increases, the level—e.g., of a pile or of the water in a glass—rises (L&J 1980, p. 16). Expressions such as "murder is *on the rise*" are ultimately motivated by experiences like these.

While our experience with the postal system could be proposed as the motivation for the conduit metaphor, since this institution facilitates both communication and the transfer of objects in containers, this proposal is not very satisfying. One reason is that the containers we mail which would seem to be the basis for most conduit metaphor expressions—i.e., containers which are "filled," or "packed," and whose contents might be difficult to "find" or "extract," etc.—are packages containing objects other than letters. That is, there is a limited experiential overlap between linguistic communication and the kinds of interactions with packages referred to in conduit metaphor expressions.

A second reason why the postal proposal is unsatisfying is that the experience of communication is so basic and frequent that it is hard to imagine that our conception of it is substantially derived from an activity which is relatively minor in our experience. Certainly, the vast majority of our communication does not take place via the mails. Some cultures, of course, have (or had) no tradition of writing or mailing letters whatsoever; if evidence for metaphors like the conduit metaphor could be found in these cultures and languages, this would provide further support for the claim that there must be other types of experiences which motivate the conduit metaphor data. This empirical question has yet to be investigated.

A final question about the experiential basis of the conduit metaphor, and perhaps the most obvious one, concerns how conduits and containers relate to each other. If linguistic expressions are containers,

---

number of questions about the conduit metaphor. This paper focuses on issues not mentioned by Brugman, but does address several of her concerns, including the fact that some of the conduit metaphor examples seem to be explainable by reference to much more general metaphors. One of Brugman's interesting objections which will not be discussed here is that Reddy's data were drawn from a very atypical sample of text, and that it was therefore misleading to draw any conclusions about the pervasiveness and harmfulness of the metaphor in the culture at large.

then what is it that is being metaphorically understood as a conduit, and what is the experience which unites the two concepts.

"Gaps" in the data

An additional sort of problem with the existing analyses of the conduit metaphor concerns the failure of certain elements from the source domain of package transfer to have conventional meaning in the target domain of communication. If there is really a conventional understanding of communication which is based on the experience of inserting contents into packages and sending them to recipients then salient aspects of that experience should be represented in the mapping. Yet it appears that some very prominent aspects of that experience have no conventional counterparts in the domain of communication:

(11)   ? I *opened* your essay and found the contents to be very clear.

(12)   ? She *sealed* her ideas in a lovely poem.

(13)   ? *box, envelope, courier, parcel, freight, delivery*, etc.

Sentences (11) and (12) can be interpreted, but not in a way which is consistent with the basic mapping proposed, for instance, in (10). For example, sentence (11) makes sense only on the interpretation that the essay has been physically "opened" in some way, rather than metaphorically opened—e.g., it had been sealed in an envelope. Sentence (12) implies that the poet's ideas are in some way inaccessible, and not simply that she has included content in her poem which will later be perceived by her readers. With regard to the lexical items in (13), these standard, salient elements of the experience of transferring packages from one person to another have no conventional counterparts in the domain of linguistic communication, although it is possible to arrive at interpretations of them, of course, with a bit of imagination.

While each of these expressions may be understood, what is surprising, based on existing accounts of the metaphor, is that their interpretation should involve anything other than the straightforward operation of the conduit metaphor mapping. (Possible motivations for some of these interpretations, involving additional metaphoric structure beyond the conduit metaphor, will be discussed below.) If the conduit metaphor doesn't clearly license references to opening, sealing, packages of specific sorts, couriers, and so forth, then is it really based on our experience of sending objects in containers?

No account of relationships to "other" metaphors

A third sort of difficulty with current understandings of the conduit metaphor is that they do not explain how this metaphor is related to other metaphors which clearly involve some very similar conceptualizations. Consider the following examples:

(14)   Bach *packs* many ideas/moods/etc. *into* a piece of music.

(15)   The detective couldn't *get* much information *out of* the partial shoeprint.

(16)   Tree rings *contain* the story of the region.

(17)   It was years before the fossils *yielded* any valuable information.

Each of these examples illustrates the fact that conceptualizations which seem characteristic of the conduit metaphor, as it has been understood, may underlie expressions which do not refer to communication. For instance, a piece of music is not a linguistic expression, as in (10b), and yet it can metaphorically contain ideas and feelings. Moving even further from the target domain of the conduit metaphor are expressions like those in (15)-(17), where there are no linguistic expressions, and no conscious agents responsible for the information "content" of the given objects. Nonetheless, these objects *contain* information, and the expressions look very much like some of those listed by Reddy and subsequent researchers.

Another way of stating this observation is that it is unclear whether the conduit metaphor has been analyzed at an appropriate level of generality. Is it possible that the conduit metaphor is a subcase of a more general metaphorical mapping, or that it borrows from more than one such mapping? The reanalysis presented in the next section proposes an answer to this question, and also addresses the other types of problems discussed above.

3. Reanalysis

Grady, Taub, and Morgan (1996), argued for the decomposition of many complex metaphors into more basic, independently motivated metaphors ("primary" or "primitive" metaphors) which combine into complex (or "compound") metaphors. The motivations for such reanalyses of the data included problems with existing accounts such as those discussed in the previous section. The process of decomposition involves seeking metaphors which are very plausibly and directly motivated by experience. These primary metaphors are also characterized by very simple mappings—i.e., they map as few elements, properties, and relations as possible, while still referring to coherent (if schematic) scenes, and still comprising enough structure to account for certain linguistic expressions. A decomposition of the conduit metaphor in just this manner yields an analysis which avoids all the problems discussed in the previous section, and also suggests ways in which concepts relating to communication might ultimately be derived from more basic physical concepts[3].

In this section, a number of more basic metaphors are discussed, each of which accounts for some subset of the examples which have been attributed to the conduit metaphor. Many of these metaphors are consistent with one another, although they are independently motivated and map different pairs of concepts. These compatible metaphors may combine (or "unify," to borrow a term from syntactic theory) to yield

---

[3]Hints that such an approach might ultimately be needed can be found in Lakoff & Turner's (1989) discussion of different levels of metaphor (i.e., "generic-level" vs. more specific metaphors) and in Lakoff's discussions of metaphoric inheritance (e.g., 1993).

more specific conceptualizations of various aspects of linguistic communication, and other target domains.

CONSTITUENTS ARE CONTENTS

Consider the following examples, which seem characteristic of the conduit metaphor:

(18) a. This writer *crams* words *into* sentences which are desperately *packed and crowded.*

   b. She *packs* a tremendous number of ideas *into* each carefully worded statement.

These examples suggest that there is a conceptualization of the constituents of sentences (either on a formal or a propositional level) as though they were *contained within* those sentences. This sort of conceptualization is not limited to the domain of linguistic forms, however:

(19)   There is both cotton and polyester *in* that shirt.

(20)   This drink is *loaded* with vitamins.

(21)   The class is *full* of bright students.

(22)   Our agenda is *packed* with events.

(23)   There are seven days *in* a week.

Examples such as these show us that constituents of structures of all kinds—not only linguistic forms—are metaphorically seen as the contents of those structures. In none of these cases is actual physical containment the central concept being referred to by the spatial expressions. This is especially clear in (22)-(23) where there is no question at all of physical containers, spaces, or boundaries.

There are several related experiential bases for a metaphor like CONSTITUENTS ARE CONTENTS. One motivation has to do with basic perceptual factors: when we look at a physical object that has distinct parts—differentiated by shape, color, function, etc.—these parts all fall within a visual boundary which defines the limits of the object. In other words, the parts appear to be contained within the space occupied by the object as a whole. (See figure 1a.)

Additionally, we observe that when ingredients are added to something—e.g., cooking ingredients, pieces of a toy, thread that is woven into a textile, etc.—these constituent items are literally moved towards and then into the space occupied by the object that is being created. Even though an end product such as a meal is not literally a container, the constituents being added are understood as ending up *inside* the meal, in some sense. This situation is represented schematically in figure 1b.

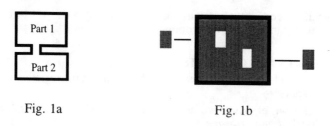

Fig. 1a   Fig. 1b

In order for these experiences to license the metaphor CONSTITUENTS ARE CONTENTS, we must also make the leap from physical constituents, as in (19)-(20), to abstract constituents. This leap is part of the very general mapping of physical structure onto abstract organization, which may be motivated by the fact that we often understand physical structure in terms of logical organization—e.g., in the case of functional part-whole structure—and may even be a consequence of neural architecture, if there are relationships between the neural structures that process our thinking about complex objects on these two levels. The motivations for a general metaphorical mapping between physical structure and abstract organization will not be discussed further here.

Given a metaphoric association between constituents and the contents of containers, sentences such as those in (18) can be explained without reference to a more specific "conduit metaphor" of communication, by the same principles that underlie examples (19)-(23). Words can be inserted into sentences, and ideas can be inserted into statements, simply by virtue of the fact that they are constituents of those structures. The quantity of constituents relative to the structure is interpreted as the quantity of contents relative to the size of a physical container—hence, *packed, crammed, empty*, etc.

A related concept which may not follow as automatically is the idea of sealing: virtually any container by definition allows contents to move in or out (at some point in time), but only certain types of containers—e.g., boxes and envelopes, as opposed to cups or bodily cavities, can be sealed. This fact may explain why *sealing* plays no conventional role in the conduit metaphor mapping.

ACHIEVING A PURPOSE IS ACQUIRING A DESIRED OBJECT

Example (6) above, repeated here as example (24), suggests that readers/listeners metaphorically remove (or attempt to remove) the RMs from a text as they read or hear it.

(24)   I have to struggle to *get* any meaning at all *out of* the sentence.

This conceptualization is not accounted for by the CONSTITUENTS ARE CONTENTS metaphor discussed in the previous section, since that mapping concerns the relationships between parts and wholes, and does not license a view of those wholes as receptacles or sources of independent objects. In other words, both the motivation and the mapping for CONSTITUENTS ARE CONTENTS suggest that structures are containers only with respect to the presence of their constituents—not that they are metaphorically equated with containers in all the various uses to which containers are put.

Instead, there is a metaphor (discussed in Lakoff 1993) which can account for aspects of this expression by principles much more general than the conduit metaphor, and without reference to communication in particular. Consider examples (25)-(28):

(25)   Talks have gone well, but I haven't *gotten* any promises *out of* him.

(26)   Success has *eluded* me.

(27)   I finally *got/found/landed* a good job.

(28)   It's *in the bag*.

In each of these cases, a goal is framed as a desired object. The metaphor ACHIEVING A PURPOSE IS ACQUIRING A DESIRED OBJECT pertains not just to communication, and to arriving at satisfying interpretations of linguistic forms, but to any attempt to achieve a purpose. This metaphor is motivated by the innumerable experiences we have in which our goal is literally to acquire some object[4]. In some of the cases under consideration, then, arriving at an interpretation is equated with *getting* an object, on principles much more general than the conduit metaphor.

Containers per se are not central to this mapping, though. Instead, the metaphor focuses on the desired object and the act of acquiring it. Containers may be relevant as a type of a barrier between us and objects we desire, as in (25), but they have no special status in the mapping. For this reason, we still have not explained why we so consistently see meaning as the contents of linguistic form, as in examples (1), (2), (5), (6), etc. After all, there are other kinds of barriers besides containers, and furthermore our conceptualization of linguistic "containers" often does not seem to focus on linguistic forms as barriers to understanding. In the next section we will examine further motivations for understanding meaning as the content of a linguistic form.

INFORMATION IS CONTENTS

We saw in a previous section that constituents of a whole may be understood as contents of that whole. For instance, individual ideas are contained within larger propositions and, on the level of form, words are contained in sentences. This mapping does not explain, however, why ideas are contained in words; i.e., it does not explain the asymmetry between form and meaning, given that both might be considered

---

[4]This mapping has been treated as part of the Event Structure Metaphor, e.g., in Lakoff 1993. The claim that this metaphor's psychological reality is dependent on a broad complex of other mappings is at odds with the types of analysis supported in this paper, but this issue will not be taken up further here.

"constituents" of linguistic structures. Meaning is commonly understood to reside within forms, but not vice versa.

Our explanation for this phenomenon should be able to account for examples (14)-(17), repeated here as (29)-(32), since they are so clearly parallel to conduit metaphor examples. Therefore we must find a mapping whose target domain is more general than the domain of linguistic communication. It is apparent from these examples that any physical configuration that allows us to deduce information (or other RMs) may be conceptualized as a container of that information:

(29)   Bach *packs* many ideas/moods/etc. *into* a piece of music.

(30)   The detective couldn't *get* much information *out of* the partial shoeprint.

(31)   Tree rings *contain* the story of the region.

(32)   It was years before the fossils *yielded* any valuable information.

(Note that this containment image is independent of any notion of an agent who might have inserted the contents into the container.)

We might try explaining these examples as instances of ACHIEVING PURPOSES IS ACQUIRING DESIRED OBJECTS, discussed above. In each example people are interested (perhaps) in retrieving the RMs encoded in the metaphorical container. Maybe any artifact or other object we use or interact with in trying to achieve a purpose is conceptualized as a container.

Unfortunately, this simple explanation does not withstand further examination. There are clear examples of purposes that can be conceived of as desired objects, but are not contained within the things that help us achieve them. For instance, a treaty isn't commonly understood as containing peace—although it can certainly be a tool for "bringing peace to a nation," and so forth. Weapons don't have control within them, though they allow people to "gain control."

In short, although ACHIEVING PURPOSES IS ACQUIRING DESIRED OBJECTS is relevant to some conduit metaphor examples, we still need further motivation for the containment image which applies so naturally to linguistic forms. In fact, there are several ways in which such a conceptualization could be motivated. Due to constraints of space, only a brief sketch of one very salient motivation will be offered here:

BECOMING ACCESSIBLE IS EMERGING: There are numerous linguistic examples which reflect a metaphoric association between perceptibility and location outside a container. The motivation for such a metaphor could not be more natural, of course, since perceptibility is literally correlated with location out in the open in so many cases. Examples include the following:

(33)   That sweater *brings out* the blue in your eyes.

(34)   Salt *brings out* the natural flavor of meat.

Since there is a strong literal association between perception and knowledge[5], this sort of mapping supports the framing of linguistic meaning as being contained within linguistic forms—the emergence of these contents corresponds to our successful interpretation of the forms. In sum, linguistic meaning is framed as something which can emerge from its container (linguistic form), become perceptible, and thus become known. The following examples are from Reddy:

(35) a. Closer reading *reveals* altogether uncharacteristic feelings *in* the story.

b. It's as if he wrote the sentences in such a way as to *seal up* the meaning in them.

c. John's analysis really *lays bare* the ideas in the chapter.

TRANSMISSION OF ENERGY IS TRANSFER

As we have seen, many conduit metaphor examples relate to the location of meaning within linguistic forms, to our ability to find and extract meaning, and so forth, but not to transfer. The concepts of transfer and containment seem to be independent in the data. For this reason, we need a separate account for those examples which refer explicitly to transfer, implying that meaning is a physical object that can be passed from one person to another. E.g.,

(36)   Your concepts *come across* beautifully.

One of the bases for this conceptualization is surely the fact that there is literal physical (though not necessarily direct) transfer involved in any communicative act: readers read actual books and papers which have come into their possession from some ultimate source; listeners interpret acoustic signals which arrive at their ears; Internet users have access to electric signals traveling through phone lines, and so forth. Meaning is metaphorically transferred while physical signals, notations, etc. are literally transferred. This framing of communication, by the way, explains the relevance of conduits in the earlier analyses, and demonstrates the independence of this view of communication from one involving containers and contents.

Claudia Brugman has noted (1995) that conduit metaphor examples like (36) seem to relate to a much more general mapping between results of actions, and transferred objects. Example (37), for instance, does not relate to linguistic communication, and (38) does not refer in any way to RMs or communication, but still frames an action as a metaphorical transfer.

(37)   This action should *send* the appropriate message *to* the Serbs.

(38)   He *gave me* a vicious kick[6].

---

[5]Of course, metaphors such as UNDERSTANDING IS SEEING are based on this sort of association, as well.

[6]It is not clear, by the way, that such examples could be considered instances of the object branch of the Event Structure metaphor as discussed in Lakoff (1993), since

Brugman refers to the target domain in such expressions as "transmission of energy,"[7] and suggests that the general mapping between transmission of energy and physical transfer may help motivate (some) conduit metaphor examples.

RMS ARE POSSESSIONS / LEARNING IS ACQUIRING

There is plenty of linguistic evidence demonstrating that ideas, thoughts, feelings, etc. can be metaphorically possessed:

(39)   This paper has *given* me new insights into equi.

(40)   I *have* a much better understanding of tax law now than I did before I took this course.

(41)   She *used* her knowledge of the terrain to help defeat the invaders.

These and similar examples may be motivated by our subjective experience of being able to examine, manipulate, and use the contents of our minds and our memories. In these respects the contents of mental processes seem very similar to physical possessions. If RMs are conceptualized as possessions then it follows that they can be acquired, given to us, etc.

4. Summary and Conclusion

The mappings discussed in the previous section are independent of one another, with respect to both their experiential bases and the particular linguistic expressions they license. Furthermore, nearly all of them apply to target domains much broader than linguistic communication. Since many of these mappings are mutually compatible, however, and since they all *may* apply to the target domain of linguistic communication, they form a relatively rich picture of this domain when taken together. In a sense this picture is like a patchwork or collage, with the pieces coming from very different sources. The various conceptualizations are not based on one unified scenario involving the transfer of containers from one person to another. This is why there are "gaps" in the metaphor if it is viewed as a single mapping from one domain to another. It is actually a collection of structures, each of which maps a different aspect of basic physical experience onto some aspect of the communicative process. Following is a brief summary of the aspects of communication which are mapped according to principles discussed above:

---

kicks, messages, and ideas are not attributes.

[7]This type of transfer could also be discussed in terms of "fictive motion," "subjective motion," etc. following Talmy and Langacker, respectively. I will not give arguments here regarding whether such conceptualizations should properly be called "metaphor," but I feel that there is a useful way of delineating metaphor which could include such cases.

- Large linguistic structures *contain* the smaller structures of which they are composed; writers/speakers *insert* these smaller structures (CONSTITUENTS ARE CONTENTS).
- Linguistic forms *contain* meaning (BECOMING ACCESSIBLE IS EMERGING).
- Meaning is *transferred* from one person to another via communication (TRANSMISSION OF ENERGY IS TRANSFER).
- Readers/listeners may *acquire* RMs by interacting with linguistic forms (ACHIEVING A PURPOSE IS ACQUIRING A DESIRED OBJECT, RMS ARE POSSESSIONS).

This outline explains the "failure" of certain elements of the experiential scenario of transferring containers to map onto linguistic communication. Only very specific elements of this scenario are actually mapped onto the target domain; the "scenario" itself is not the basis of the various independent conceptualizations. Notions such as the container's appearance, sealing the container, having it delivered by a third party, unwrapping or opening the container, and so forth, simply are not relevant elements of the various conventional mappings which underlie data like Reddy's and Lakoff and Johnson's. Less conventional expressions can be generated and interpreted based on additional metaphoric structure—e.g., *sealing* is licensed via further elaborations of BECOMING ACCESSIBLE IS EMERGING.

The advantages of the reanalysis offered here relate both to formal aspects of metaphor theory and to an account of the structure of our conceptual system and how it arises. The advantages internal to metaphor theory include more accurate prediction of data; more economical analyses of individual expressions (since they need not be accounted for by reference to large metaphorical complexes); a clearer account of the relationships between metaphors—complex metaphors may be related in that they share some more basic mapping; and additional support for the plausibility of experiential basis. More generally, this examination of the metaphoric associations relevant to communication provides important examples of the ways in which basic elements of our physical experience shape our conceptual structure, and thereby our language.

References

Brugman, C. 1995. Give and Take in conversation: a reinvestigation of the conduit metaphor. Talk presented at the 4th International Cognitive Linguistics Conference , Albuquerque.

Gibbs, Raymond W. Jr. 1994. *The Poetics of Mind: Figurative Thought, Language, and Understanding*. Cambridge: Cambridge University Press.

Grady, J. and S. Taub, P. Morgan. 1996. Primitive and Compound Metaphors, in A. Goldberg, ed., *Conceptual Structure, Discourse, and Language*. Stanford: CSLI.

Johnson, Mark. 1987. *The Body in the Mind*. Chicago: University of Chicago Press.

Lakoff, George and Mark Johnson. 1980. *Metaphors We Live By*. Chicago: University of Chicago Press.

Lakoff, George and Mark Turner. 1989. *More than Cool Reason: A Field Guide to Poetic Metaphor*. Chicago: University of Chicago Press.

Lakoff, George. 1993. The Contemporary Theory of Metaphor, in A. Ortony, ed., *Metaphor and Thought*, 2d ed. Cambridge: Cambridge University Press.

Mandler, J. 1992. How to build a baby, 2. *Psychological Review*, 99: 587-604.

Reddy, Michael. 1979. The Conduit Metaphor: a Case of Frame Conflict in our Language about Language, in A. Ortony, ed., *Metaphor and Thought*. Cambridge: Cambridge University Press.

Sweetser, Eve. 1990. *From etymology to pragmatics: metaphorical and cultural aspects of semantic structure*. Cambridge: Cambridge University Press.

Talmy, Leonard. 1983. How Language Structures Space, in H. Pick & L. Acredolo, eds., *Spatial Orientation: Theory, Research, and Application*. Plenum Press.

Turner, M. 1991. *Reading Minds*. Princeton: Princeton University Press.

Turner, Mark. 1987. *Death is the Mother of Beauty*. Chicago: University of Chicago Press.

Conceptual Metaphor in Mathematics

GEORGE LAKOFF AND RAFAEL NÚÑEZ

University of California, Berkeley

This is an essay within a new field of study — the cognitive science of mathematics. The contribution we seek ultimately to make is a new one: to characterize precisely what *mathematical ideas* are. You might think that this enterprise would leave mathematics as it exists alone and simply add to it an account of the conceptual nature of mathematical understanding. You could not be more wrong.

Studying the nature of mathematical ideas changes what we understand mathematics to be and it even changes the understanding of particular mathematical results. The reason is that a significant amount of 20th century mathematics rests on the assumption that mathematics is not about ideas, but rather about meaningless symbols and their model-theoretical interpretations. We call this 20th Century view *mind-free mathematics*, where the substance of mathematics is assumed to be independent of any human minds. Our enterprise is to bring embodied human minds, as they have come to be understood recently in cognitive science, back into mathematics, and to construct a precise *mind-based mathematics*. Mind-based mathematics is not just mind-free mathematics with some cognitive analysis added. Rather, the introduction of mind changes mathematics itself, not just mathematics education or the study of mathematical cognition.

Mind-free mathematics obscures the full beauty of mathematics. This essay is a first attempt to reveal that beauty through the characterization of a mind-based mathematics, and the changes made are in the service of revealing that beauty — and if possible, adding to it.

Our Goals

The enterprise of studying the mathematical conceptual system can be understood in at least three ways.

•As the empirical study of the unconscious conceptual system that constitutes mathematical thought.

•As the task of identifying and clearly describing the collection of ideas that constitutes what mathematics *is*.

•As a helpful task for mathematics education. If we are going to teach mathematical ideas, it is useful to know what ideas are to be taught and what the human conceptual system for those ideas is.

Much of the interest in mathematical conceptual systems has come from the third concern on the list — education — by means of studies of didactic processes, curricula, and pedagogical devices, but also by painstaking explorations of classroom realities, everyday mathematical thinking, informal and non-institutional teaching, and so on. We loudly applaud those educators who have been working to figure out the nature of mathematical understanding for the sake of teaching mathematics. Most of the contributions of this volume, are concerned with the third issue, and are good examples of this endeavor.

But the educational process as such is only a peripheral concern of ours here. We are mainly concerned with the first and second enterprises. We want to study the details of the conceptual system from which mathematics arises, and by which it is conceived and understood. Through that, we hope to describe what that mathematics is as a conceptual system. This entails a *new philosophy of mathematics, in which mathematics is product of the embodied human mind* — especially its imaginative capacities such as image-schemas and conceptual metaphors. Because we begin with results in cognitive science, and understand mathematics as product of embodied minds functioning in the world, we are neither platonists nor constructivists, neither objectivists nor subjectivists (see Lakoff, 1987; Núñez, 1995). Those a priori philosophical perspectives do not describe what mathematical ideas are and they simply cannot explain why mathematics has the structure it has nor how it can be learned anew by human bodies/brains generation after generation with an amazingly stable content.

We are aware that analyzing the conceptual structure of mathematics is a major enterprise, and we are at the very beginning of that enterprise. What we intend to do in the following pages is to give a general idea about the richness, complexity and beauty of the imaginative and embodied processes that make mathematics possible. In doing this, we want to sketch some elements we consider crucial in the study of the cognitive foundations of mathematics. We want to analyze a few interesting and important examples that show how mathematics is permanently created and sustained by imaginative resources such as conceptual metaphors, metonymies and blends, shared by those who practice, teach, and learn mathematics.

Fundamental Types Of Conceptual Metaphors In Mathematics

There is a branch of cognitive linguistics concerned with metaphor theory and we will be using the results of that discipline throughout. The major results are these:

•There is an extensive conventional system of conceptual metaphors in every human conceptual system.

•Metaphors are cross-domain conceptual "mappings". That is, they "project" the structure a "source domain" onto a "target domain." Such "projections" or "mappings" can be stated precisely.

•Metaphorical mappings are not arbitrary, but are motivated by our everyday experience — especially bodily experience.

•Metaphorical mappings are not isolated, but occur in complex systems and combine in complex ways.

•As with the rest of our conceptual systems, our system of conventional conceptual metaphors is effortless and below the level of conscious awareness.

•Metaphor does not reside in words; it is a matter of thought. Metaphorical linguistic expressions are surface manifestations of metaphorical thought.

•Unlike mathematical mappings, metaphorical "mappings" may "add" structure to a target domain.

•The inferential structure of the source domain is preserved in each mapping onto a target domain, except for those cases where target domain structure "overrides" the mappings (see Lakoff, 1993 for details).

•The image-schema structure of the source domain is preserved in the mappings.

•The evidence on which these general claims are based comes from eight sources: generalizations over polysemy, generalizations over inference patterns, extensions to novel cases, historical semantic change, psycholinguistic experiments, language acquisition, spontaneous gestures, and American sign language.

•Novel metaphors that we consciously concoct use the mechanisms of our everyday unconscious conventional metaphor system.

For basic references, see Lakoff and Johnson, 1980; and Lakoff, 1993.

The Literal Basis of Cognitive Arithmetic

It is well-known that human beings, as well as many other higher animals, have the capacity to instantaneously perceive quantities of objects. Human beings can accurately perceive and distinguish up to six objects at a glance. Some monkeys can do better — eight or more.

This capacity is technically called "subitizing" (from the Latin *subitare*, meaning to "arrive suddenly"). It is, of course, combined with other basic cognitive capacities such as the ability to form mental images, remember, form groupings, superimpose images, and so on. Such capacities have allowed human beings to create a literal, but primitive cognitive arithmetic. But it is metaphor that has allowed us to move beyond such a relatively primitive mathematical capacity to form an abstract mathematics of dizzying complexity.

Grounding Metaphors and Linking Metaphors

There are two fundamental types of metaphors used in forming mathematical ideas: *grounding metaphors* and *linking metaphors*. Grounding metaphors ground mathematical ideas in everyday experience. For example, they allow us to conceptualize arithmetic operations in terms of forming collections, constructing objects, or moving through space. Since metaphors preserve inference structure, such metaphors allow us to project inferences about collecting, constructing, and moving onto the abstract domain of arithmetic. Metaphorical projections preserve the structure of image-schemas — cognitive schemas for such things as containers (bounded regions in space), paths, entities, links, and so on. Consequently, grounding metaphors allow us to project precise yet abstract image-schema structure from everyday domains that we know and understand intimately to the domain of mathematics. And correspondingly, grounding metaphors project inferences about our everyday world that we implicitly understand as well as we understand anything onto the domain of mathematics. In short, our understanding of arithmetic rests on our intimate and precise understandings of domains like collecting, constructing objects, and moving.

While grounding metaphors allow us to ground our understanding of mathematics in familiar domains of experience, linking metaphors allow us to link one branch of mathematics to another. For example, when we metaphorically understand numbers as points on a line, we are linking arithmetic and geometry. Such metaphors allow us to project one field of mathematical knowledge onto another. In this case, we project our knowledge of geometry onto arithmetic in a precise way via metaphor. It is the conceptual metaphor that tells us exactly how our knowledge of geometry is to be projected onto arithmetic.

As we shall see below, both grounding and linking metaphors can be presupposed within definitions. We will call such cases "metaphorical definitions". When metaphors are given as definitions, we shall call such cases "definitional metaphors."

Let us now turn to the details. Here are some of our most basic grounding metaphors. The name of the metaphor is given at the top of the list, and each bullet demarcates a submapping.

Arithmetic is Object Collection

•Numbers Are Collections of physical objects of uniform size
•The Mathematical Agent Is a Collector of Objects
•Arithmetic Operations Are Acts of forming a collection of objects
•The result of an arithmetic operation Is A collection of objects
•The Unit (One) Is The Smallest collection

•The Size of the number Is The Physical size (volume) of the collection
•The Quantity measured by a number Is the Weight of the collection
•Equations Are Scales weighing collections that balance
•Addition Is Putting collections together with other collections to form larger collections
•Subtraction Is Taking smaller collections from larger collections to form other collections
•The number of times an action is performed Is the collection formed by adding a unit for each performance of the action
•Multiplication Is The Repeated addition of collections of the same size a given number of times
•Division Is The Repeated dividing up of a given collection into as many smaller collections of a given size as possible
•Zero Is An empty collection.

Arithmetic is Object Construction

•Numbers Are Physical Objects
•The Mathematical Agent Is a Constructor of Objects
•Arithmetic Operations Are Acts of object construction
•The result of an arithmetic operation Is A constructed object
•The Unit (One) Is the Smallest whole object
•The Size of the number Is the Size of the Object
•The measure of the size of a number Is The Collection of smallest whole objects needed to construct the object
•The Quantity measured by a number Is the Weight of the Object
•Equations Are Scales weighing objects that balance
•Addition Is Putting objects together with other objects to form larger objects
•Subtraction Is Taking smaller objects from larger objects to form other objects
•The number of times an action is performed Is the object formed by adding a unit for each performance of the action
•Multiplication Is The Repeated addition of objects of the same size a given number of times
•Division Is The Repeated Segmentation of a given object into as many objects of a given smaller size as possible.
•Zero Is The Absence of any object

These conceptual metaphors are not only used for conceptualizing arithmetic, but they also form the basis of the language we use for talking about arithmetic. Here are some linguistic examples of these conceptual metaphors. First, there is a group of cases which instantiate both the collection and objects construction metaphors. The reason that the examples fit both is that both metaphors are instances of a more general metaphor:

Numbers Are Physical Objects; Arithmetic Is Object Manipulation; Adding Is Putting Objects Together.

A trillion is a *big* number.

How many 5's are there *in* 20?

There are 4 5's *in* 23, and 3 *left over*.

Five from 12 *leaves* 7.

12 less 5 *leaves* 7.

How many times does 2 *go into* 10?

7 is too *big* to *go into* 10 more than once?

If 10 is on one side of the equation and 7 is on the other, what do you have to add to 7 to *balance* the equation?

There are of course linguistic examples that distinguish the Object Construction metaphor from the Object Collection metaphor.

Object construction:

If you put 2 and 2 together, it *makes* 4.

What is the *product* of 5 and 7?

2 is a small fraction of 248.

Object Collection:

How many *more* than 5 is 8?

8 is 3 *more* than 5.

Now let us turn to the Motion metaphor.

Arithmetic is Motion

•Numbers are Locations on a Path
•The Mathematical Agent Is a Traveler along that path
•Arithmetic Operations Are Acts of moving along the path
•The result of an arithmetic operation Is A location on the path
•Zero Is the Origin (starting point)
•The smallest whole number (One) Is A step forward from the origin
•The Size of the number Is The Length of the trajectory from the origin to the location
•The Quantity measured by a number is the Distance from the origin to the location
•Equations Are Routes to the same location

•Addition of a given quantity Is Taking steps a given distance to the right (or forward)

•Subtraction of a given quantity Is Taking steps a given distance to the left (or backward)

•The number of times an action is performed is the location reached by starting at the origin and taking one step for each performance of the action

•Multiplication Is The Repeated addition of quantities of the same size a given number of times

•Division Is The Repeated segmentation of a path of a given length into as many smaller paths of a given length as possible.

As in the above cases, this conceptual metaphor also provided language for talking about arithmetic.

How *close* are these two numbers?

37 is *far away from* 189,712.

4.9 is *almost* 5.

The result is *around* 40.

Count up to 20, without *skipping* any numbers.

Count *backwards* from 20.

Count *to* 100, *starting at* 20.

Name all the numbers *from* 2 *to* 10.

The linguistic examples are important here in a number of respects. First, they illustrate how the language of object manipulation and motion can be recruited in a systematic way to talk about arithmetic. The conceptual mappings characterize what is systematic about this use of language. Second, these usages of language provide evidence for the existence of the conceptual mappings — evidence that comes not only from the words, but also from what the words mean. The metaphors can be seen as stating generalizations not only over the use of the words, but also over the inferences patterns that these words supply from the source domains of object collection, object construction and motion, which are then used in reasoning about arithmetic.

Educational Extensions Of Natural Grounding Metaphors

In the Object Collection and Object Construction metaphors, zero is not the same kind of thing as a number. It represents the absence of attributes — the absence of a collection or constructed object. It is only in the Motion metaphor that zero is the same kind of thing as a number — it is a location in space. Because the Collection and Construction metaphors we use are so basic to the conception of number, we can see why it took so long for zero to be included and why there was so much resistance to calling zero a number.

It should be clear that the Collection and Construction metaphors also work just for the natural numbers. Multiplication by zero, for example, is not defined. Nor are negative numbers, rational numbers, and the reals. Many Math teachers attempt to use these metaphors to teach arithmetic — as they must, if students are to grasp the subject at all. But, unfortunately, such teachers often fail to grasp the limited role played by grounding metaphors, which arise quite naturally. Grounding metaphors are partial, limited only to the natural numbers and basic operations. They are the metaphors from which the most basic ideas of arithmetic arise. However, the arithmetic characterized by these metaphors has been greatly extended over the centuries through linking metaphors and metonymies, and there is no way to extend these metaphors in a consistent natural manner to cover all those extensions. But many teachers nonetheless concoct nonnatural novel and ad hoc extensions in attempt to take those metaphors beyond their natural domain.

Consider the example of negative numbers. The Object Construction and Object Collection metaphors do not give rise to simple natural extensions of the negative numbers. So some teachers extend the natural grounding metaphors in unnatural ways. For example, suppose we want to teach the equation using the object collection metaphor " $(-1) + (-2) = (-3)$ ". A teacher might introduce the ad hoc extension Negative Numbers Are Helium Balloons, and use it together with Quantity Is Weight and Equations Are Scales. Here helium balloons are seen as having negative weight, offsetting positive weight for the purpose of measuring weight on a scale. This ad hoc extension will work for this case, but not for multiplying by negative numbers. In addition, it must be used with care, because it has a very different cognitive status than the largely unconscious natural grounding metaphor. It cannot be added and held constant as one moves to multiplication by negative numbers.

Or take another ad hoc extension to the Object Collection metaphor: Negative Numbers are Objects Made of Anti-Matter. This is sometimes used to teach why " $3 + (-3) = 0$ ": 3 and -3 annihilate one another! Again, this can't be extended to teach multiplication by negative numbers. Moreover, the concept of anti-matter may be harder to teach than the concept of negative number by other means.

The easiest natural extension of one of the grounding metaphors to negative numbers is the Motion metaphor. If numbers are locations reached by walking in uniform steps in a given (positive direction from a source, and if zero is the source, then negative numbers are also locations, but locations reached by walking in the opposite direction. Thus, if positive numbers are to the right of the origin, negative numbers are locations to the left of the origin. Addition and subtraction of negative numbers can then be given by a relatively easy extension of the metaphor: when you encounter a negative number, turn around in place. Multiplication by a negative number is turning around and multiplying by a positive number.

But however straightforward these extensions are, they are still concocted novel extensions of the natural grounding metaphor, and so will seem a bit artificial because it is a bit artificial. Such metaphors are neither natural grounding metaphors, nor are they linking metaphors. They belong neither to the realm of the natural grounding of arithmetic, not to the linking of one branch to another, but rather to the domain of teaching by making up extensions of the natural grounding metaphors. As such they are neither part of the natural grounding of mathematical ideas nor the linking of one branch of mathematics to another. Hence, they stand outside of mathematics proper and are part of imaginative, and sometimes forced, methods of mathematical education. Since such purely educational metaphors, however useful for certain aspects of teaching, are not the subject matter of this paper, we will not discuss them further. (For an explicit statement of such educational metaphors, see Chiu, 1996). Instead we will proceed with our discussion of the natural grounding metaphors for basic mathematical ideas and the linking metaphors used to map one branch of mathematics onto another.

Metaphors For Set Theory

Set theory is grounded in two kinds of related experiences:

1. Grouping objects into conceptual containers

2. Comparing the number of objects in two groupings

The source domain of the metaphor uses a container-schema, which specifies a bounded region of space, with an interior, a boundary and an exterior. Container schemas may have a physical realization (a jar, a plot of ground marked off by a line, etc.), but, as used here, the boundary of the container is purely imaginative and need not be physically realized.

An image-schematic container consists of the boundary of the container schema plus the interior of that container schema. Objects within the boundary are *In* the container. When we conceptually group objects together we are superimposing a single container-schema on the objects so that the objects are conceptualized as being inside the boundary and overlapping with the interior of the schema.

Sets in mathematics are conceptualized as container-schemas, and the members of the sets are conceptualized as objects inside the container schema.

The Sets -As-Container-Schemas Metaphor

•A Set Is A Container-schema
•A Member of a set Is An Object in a container-schema
•A Subset of a set Is A Container-schema within a container-schema.

One of the properties of conceptual groupings is that the grouping is determined by the choice of the objects. A choice of different objects is a different grouping. Two choices of the same objects do not constitute different conceptual groupings. This property of objects conceptually grouped together by superimposition of a container-schema is an important property. This property is mapped by the Sets-As-Container-Schemas Metaphor into The Axiom of Extensionality in set theory, the axiom that states that a set is uniquely characterized by its members. In this case, an entailment of a grounding metaphor is an axiom — a self-evident truth that follows from the grounding metaphor. Not all axioms arise in this way. Some require additional metaphors.

Incidentally, this metaphor can be extended in a fairly obvious way to metaphorically define unions, intersections, and complements. But there are many aspects of naive set theory in mathematics that are not consequences of this metaphor and cannot be defined using it. Container-schemas are just cognitive mechanisms that impose conceptual groups. Though you can have sets of objects further grouped into subsets by additional container schemas inside an outer one, those internal container schemas are not themselves made objects by the Sets-As-Container-Schemas Metaphor, and since they are not objects, they cannot be members of the set.

However there is a metaphor that can turn such container schemas into objects, which would make it possible for them to be set members. This is not an ordinary grounding metaphor that naturally characterizes our nonmathematical understanding of a set. Instead it is a special metaphor for grounding the technical discipline of set theory.

The Sets Are Objects Metaphor

•Sets Are Objects

This extremely powerful metaphor, when combined with the Sets Are Container-Schemas Metaphor allows not just for subsets, but for sets to be *members* of other sets, since members are conceptualized as objects. But even though this metaphor allows sets to be members of other sets, combining this metaphor with the Sets Are Container-Schemas Metaphor will guarantee that it will still make no sense to conceptualize a set as being a member of itself. The reason is that container-schemas cannot be inside themselves by their very nature. Boundaries of containers cannot be parts of their own interiors. It therefore follows that, when The Sets Are Container-schemas Metaphor is being used to conceptualize sets, expressions like "sets that are members of themselves" and "sets that are not members of themselves" are nonsense and therefore cannot designate anything at all. Relative to this metaphor, the Russell's classical set-theoretical paradox concerning the set of all sets which are not members of themselves cannot arise. It arises only in a mind-free mathematics where set theory is developed axiomatically without an explicit characterization of ideas.

Consequences of Sets Are Objects

Once sets are conceptualized metaphorically as objects and not just cognitive container-schemas that accomplish grouping, then the submetaphor that Members of a Set Are Objects In a Container-Schema can apply and allow subsets of a set to be members of that set. And once a set is conceptualized as a container-object, it possible to conceptualize the empty set — the container-object containing no objects. Putting together the Sets Are Container-Schemas metaphor and the Sets Are Objects metaphor, we get new entailments. For example, it is entailed that every set now has a power set — the set of all its subsets. This is another fundamental axiom of set theory.

The Ordered Pair Metaphor

Once we conceptualize sets as objects and subsets as members, we can construct a metaphorical definition for ordered pairs. Intuitively, an ordered pair can be conceptualized nonmetaphorically as a subitized pair of elements (call it a PAIR-schema) structured by a PATH schema, where the source of the path is seen as the first member of the pair and the goal of the path is seen as the second member.

With the addition of the Sets Are Objects metaphor, we can conceptualize subsets of sets as members of sets. We can now use the idea of s subset that is also a member of set to conceptualize the concept of the ordered pair metaphorically in terms of sets.

•An ordered pair (a , b) Is The Set { a , { a , b } }

Using this metaphorical concept of an ordered pair, one can go on to metaphorically define relations, functions, and so on in terms of sets. One of the most interesting things that one can do with this metaphorical ordered pair definition is to metaphorically conceptualize the natural numbers in terms of sets that have other sets as members.

The Natural Numbers Are Sets Metaphor

•Zero Is The Empty Set, Ø
•A Natural Number Is The Set of its predecessors

Entailments:
•One Is The Set containing the empty set, {Ø}
•Two Is { Ø , {Ø} } (that is, {0,1})
•Three is { Ø , {Ø} , { Ø , {Ø} } } (that is, {0,1,2})

Here, zero has no members, one has one member, two has two members, etc. By virtue of this metaphor, every set containing three members is in 1-1 correspondence with the number three. Using these metapnors, one can metaphorically construct the natural numbers out of nothing but sets.

This is the basic metaphor linking set theory to arithmetic. It allows one to conceptualize one branch of mathematics, arithmetic, in terms of another branch, set theory. This metaphor projects all the truths of set theory onto arithmetic.

Same Size and More Than: The Everyday Common Sense Criteria

Our ordinary everyday conceptual system encodes the concepts Same Number and More Than. Among the criteria characterizing our ordinary everyday versions of these concepts are:

Same Number: Group A has the same number of elements as group B if, for every member of A, you can take away a member of B and at the end of the process there are no objects left in B.

More Than: Group B has more objects than group A if, for every member of A, you can take away a member of B and at the end of the process there will still be objects left in B.

It is important to contrast our everyday concept of Same Number with Georg Cantor's concept of Equipollence, that is, being able to be put in a 1-1 correspondence. For finite collections of objects, having the Same Number entails Equipollence. Two finite sets with the same number of objects can be put in a 1-to-1 correspondence. This does not mean that Same Number and Equipollence are the same idea. The ideas are different in a significant way, but they happen to have the same truth conditions for finite sets.

Compare the set of natural numbers and the set of even integers. As Cantor observed, they are equipollent. That is, they can be put into a 1-1 correspondence. Just multiply the natural numbers by two, and you will set up the 1-1 correspondence. Of course, these two sets do not have the same number of elements according to our everyday criterion. If you take the even numbers away from the natural numbers, there are still all the odd numbers left over. Therefore, according to our everyday concept of "more than" there are, of course, more natural numbers than even numbers. The concepts "same number" and "equipollence" are different concepts.

Our everyday concepts of "same number" and "more than" are, of course, linked to other everyday quantitative concepts, like "how many" or "as many as," "size" as well as to the concept "number" itself — the basic concept in arithmetic. In his investigations into the properties of infinite sets, Cantor and other mathematicians have used the concept of equipollence in place of our everyday concept of same number. In doing so, Cantor established a metaphor, which we can state as:

Cantor's Metaphor

•Equinumerosity Is Equipollence.

That is, our ordinary concept of having the same number of elements (equinumerosity) is metaphorically conceptualized, especially for infinite sets, in terms of the very different concept of being able to be put in a 1-1 correspondence.

But this has never been stated explicitly as a metaphor. As a result, it has produced confusion for generations of students. Consider a statement of the sort made by many mathematics teachers: Cantor proved that there are just as many even numbers as natural numbers. Given our ordinary concept of "just as many as," Cantor proved no such thing. He only proved that the sets were equipollent. But if you use Cantor's metaphor, then he did prove that, metaphorically, there are just as many even numbers as natural numbers.

The same comment holds for other proofs of Cantor's. Literally, there are more rational numbers than natural numbers, since if you take the natural numbers away from the rational numbers, there will be lots left over. But Cantor did prove that two sets are equipollent, and hence they metaphorically can be said (via Cantor's metaphor) to have the same number of elements.

The point of all this is that the conceptualization of arithmetic in terms of set theory is not literal truth. Numbers aren't literally sets. They don't have to be understood in terms of sets. But you can use the set-theoretical metaphor system for arithmetic if you want to study the consequences of those metaphors. It is literally false that there are the same number of natural numbers and rational numbers. But it is metaphorically true if you choose to use Cantor's metaphor and follow out its consequences.

The fact that the set-theoretical conceptualization of arithmetic is metaphorical does not mean that there is anything wrong with it. It just means that it does not provide literal, objective foundations for arithmetic.

Grounding Metaphors For Functions

Let us look next at the metaphors that ground our understanding of functions.

A Function Is A Machine

•The Domain of the function Is A Collection of acceptable input objects.
•The Range of the function Is A Collection of output objects.
•The Operation of the function Is The Making of a unique output object from each collection of input objects.

The notion of an algorithm is, of course, based on the machine metaphor. An algorithm, as a metaphorical machine *performs operations* sequentially on input objects to yield output objects. Since the machine is metaphorical and not real, the operations and objects are conceptual in nature, and they always apply perfectly in exactly the same way, since imperfections of physical objects are not mapped onto conceptual objects by the metaphor.

For arithmetic functions, this metaphor extends the grounding metaphor of Arithmetic As Object Construction. Here, the construction of output objects from input objects is done by a machine.

Here are some examples of expressions that make use of this metaphor.

Linguistic Examples:

Nonprime numbers are *made* up of primes.

Multiplication *makes* nonprime numbers out of collections of prime numbers.

The function $f(x) = x^2 + 5$ *takes* a number, *first squares* it *and then adds* 5, *to yield* a *new* number.

The function $f(x) = e^x$ *starts producing* huger and huger numbers as you put *in* moderately larger values of x.

A Function Is a Collection of Objects With Directional Links

•The Domain of the function Is A Collection of objects
•The Range of the function Is A Collection of objects
•The Function Is A Collection of Unique Paths from objects in the domain to objects in the range)
•The operation of the function Is the transportation of the domain object to the range object by an agent.
Metonymy: The function stands for the agent performing the function.

There are also common expressions in the English of mathematicians that use this metaphor. All of these cases use the metonymy in which the function stands for the agent performing the function. The function itself is seen as doing the carrying, sending, and projecting.

Linguistic Examples

$f(x) = x^2$ *takes/carries* 3 *into* 9

This function *projects* the integers *onto* the even numbers.

This function *sends* numbers *into* their inverses.

Given the metaphor that Ordered Pairs Are Sets, this grounding metaphor can be reformulated as a linking metaphor, characterizing functions metaphorically in terms of sets:

•A Function Is a Set of Ordered Pairs, in which the first member of the pair uniquely determines the second.

At this point, we are able to discuss one the central ideas in classical mathematics — the Cartesian Plane.

The Metaphorical Structure of The Cartesian Plane

Linking metaphors are commonly versions of grounding metaphors. For example, the fundamental metaphor linking set theory to arithmetic, Numbers Are Sets, is a technical version of the natural grounding metaphor Arithmetic is Object Collection. We can now turn to a second case in which there is a linking metaphor that is a technical version of a grounding metaphor. Corresponding to Arithmetic is Motion, with Numbers As Locations, there is a metaphor linking Arithmetic to Geometry, in which Numbers Are Points on a line.

The Arithmetic Is Geometry Metaphor

Assume a Euclidean plane, with all of the truths of Euclidean Geometry.
•Numbers Are Points on a line.
•Zero Is the Origin
•Quantities Are Distances (from the origin to a point).
•Greater than Is Above (for vertically oriented lines)
•Greater than Is To the right of (for horizontally oriented lines)

This metaphor maps all the truths of Euclidean Geometry onto Arithmetic! That is what makes this a metaphor that links the domains of Geometry and Arithmetic.

What is particularly interesting about this metaphor is that it is used to form a metaphoric blend, a composite of the source and target domains of the metaphor (Turner & Fauconnier, in press; Turner, in press), that is, a composite of numbers and points on a line known as the *number line*.

The Number Line Blend

A number line is a conceptual blend formed from the superimposition of the source domain (Geometry) of the Arithmetic as Geometry metaphor onto the target domain (Arithmetic). The entities in this blend are number-points — numbers that are metaphorically points.

The blend combines the truths of geometry with the truths of arithmetic, to yield new inferences about the target domain, arithmetic. Using the metaphorical concept of the number line, we can construct a much more complex metaphorical concept, the Cartesian Plane.

The Cartesian Plane

A metaphorical definition is a definition that presupposes one or more metaphors. All the definitions given below assume the Arithemtic Is Geometry metaphor. We will the double-bullet to mark metaphorical definitions.

••The x-axis Is a Number line.
••The y-axis Is a Number Line perpendicular to the x-axis.
••The intersection of the x- and y-axes Is An Origin for both axes.
••A coordinate point Is a point on an axis.
••The x-coordinate line Is the line parallel to the y-axis that crosses the x-axis at coordinate point x.
••The y-coordinate line Is the line parallel to the x-axis that crosses the y-axis at coordinate point y.
••A Cartesian coordinate system Is the collection of x- and y-coordinate lines.

The Cartesian Point Metaphor

Like any other plane in Euclidean geometry, the Cartesian plane is a collection of points. But in the Cartesian plane, a point in the plane is conceptualized in one of two ways, either (1) as an intersection of an x- and a y- coordinate, or (2) as an ordered pair of numbers on the x- and y-axes, respectively. Each of these conceptions is metaphorical Points don't have to be conceptualized as intersections of line, nor as ordered pairs of other points. But these alternate conceptualizations are inherent to an understanding of what the Cartesian Plane is.

•The Points are Intersections Metaphor: A Point in the Cartesian Plane Is The Intersection of an x-coordinate line and a y-coordinate line.
•The Point-for-Coordinate-Line Metonymy: A coordinate point P can Stand For the coordinate line L that intercepts an axis at point P.

By forming the composition of the Points Are Intersections Metaphor and the Point-For-Coordinate-Line Metonymy, we arrive at:

•The Cartesian Point Metaphor: Each Point in the Cartesian Plane Is an ordered pair of points (x,y) on the x- and y-axes.

The Cartesian Point Metaphor allows us to define a Cartesian Graph.

••A Cartesian Graph Is A Collection of points in the Cartesian plane.

This metaphorical definition allows us to conceptualize equations with two variables. (It presupposes the use of a very important metaphor that we are not going to discuss here: Variables Are Numbers. This metaphor lies at the base of the conceptualization of elementary algebra. The combination of this metaphor with the Arithmetic Is Geometry metaphor lies at the base of Analytic Geometry.)

••An equation with two variables Is A Cartesian Graph

Thus, we have the familiar examples:

$y = ax + b$ Is a line.

$x^2 + y^2 = r^2$ Is a circle of radius r with a center at the origin.

It is important to realize that these are metaphorical conceptualizations of equations, not the equations themselves.

Cartesian Functions

The Cartesian Plane is, as we have seen, a blend of arithmetic and geometry in which arithmetical is conceptualized in terms of geometry through the concept of the number line. The Cartesian Point metaphor conceptualized points in the plane as ordered pairs of number-points on the x- and y- number lines. This allows to define a Cartesian function using the metaphor discussed above, that a function is a set of ordered pairs. In this case, because we have a blend of numbers and points, a Cartesian Function maps two things at once. It maps points onto points and numbers onto numbers. The point-to-point mappings are constrained by geometry, while the number-to-number mappings are constrained by arithmetic.

••A Cartesian Function: A Cartesian function Is A Collection of points in the Cartesian plane, where each two points in the collection have different x-coordinates.

Since each point in the Cartesian Plane is metaphorically an ordered pair of points on the x- and y-axes respectively, Cartesian Functions can be conceptualized in terms of set theory as sets of ordered pairs, which are in turn metaphorically conceptualized as sets with a certain structure (as described above).

The Arithmetic of Functions Metaphor

Literally, functions are not numbers. Addition and multiplication tables do not include functions. But when we conceptualize functions as ordered pairs of points in the Cartesian Plane, we can create an extremely useful metaphor. The operations of arithmetic can be metaphorically extended from numbers to functions, so that functions can be metaphorically added, subtracted, multiplied and divided in a way that is consistent with arithmetic. Here is the metaphor:

•An arithmetic operation on functions Is That operation on the y-values at each point x of the functions.

To see how this works, consider addition.

Let $f = \{(x,y)\}$, that is, a set of pairs of values taken from the x- and y-axes respectively.

Let $g = \{(x,y')\}$, where x and y' are also values taken from the x- and y-axes respectively.

Consider only x-values in the intersection of the domains of the functions.

By the expression, "$f + g$" we mean "$\{(x,y)\} + \{(x,y')\}$". To understand what *that* means, we need a metaphor — a special case of the Arithmetic of Functions metaphor, restricted to addition. The special case of that metaphor is :

• $\{(x,y)\} + \{(x,y')\}$ Is $\{(x,y+y')\}$

Or, if you prefer English:

•The sum of two functions Is The sum of the y-values at each point x of the functions.

We write this as the familiar: $(f+g)(x) = f(x) + g(x)$. But notice that the "$=$" is a metaphorical $=$ and the "$+$" on the left is a metaphorical $+$.

The same applies for the rest of the arithmetic functions.

• $\{(x,y)\} - \{(x,y')\}$ Is $\{(x, y - y')\}$

• $\{(x,y)\} \cdot \{(x,y')\}$ Is $\{(x, y \cdot y')\}$

• $\{(x,y)\} \div \{(x,y')\}$ Is $\{(x, y \div y')\}$ (where $y' \neq 0$)

The following are therefore all metaphoric:

• $(f+g)(x)$ Is $f(x) + g(x)$

• $(f-g)(x)$ Is $f(x) - g(x)$

• $(f \cdot g)(x)$ Is $f(x) \cdot g(x)$

• $(f \div g)(x)$ Is $f(x) \div g(x)$, where $g(x) \neq 0$

In the Cartesian Plane, simple arithmetic functions of one variable can be conceptualized metaphorically as curves. The Arithmetization of Functions metaphor allows us to conceptualize what it means to add, subtract, multiply and divide such curves. This is a central idea in classical mathematics.

Conclusion

Our purpose here has been to provide a sense of our enterprise. We have shown that conceptual metaphor plays two crucial roles within mathematics: grounding our mathematical understanding in everyday bodily experience and linking branches of mathematics to one another.

We believe that mathematics is about mathematical ideas, not just about mind-free formalisms and set-theoretical models. There is no branch of mathematics that studies human ideas. The nature of ideas in human conceptual systems is studied empirically within cognitive science, especially cognitive semantics. Thus the study of mathematical ideas naturally falls to those of us in the field of cognitive semantics.

The content of mathematics does not exist without mathematical ideas, including metaphorical mathematics ideas. What this means is that the foundations of mathematics lies outside of mathematics proper, in cognitive sceince and in cognitive semantics, where actual and possible human concepts are studied.

The Platonic view of mathematics as existing in some objective, but ideal Platonic realm must therefore be false. Ideas, including mathematical ideas, are embodied. There are no bodies in the ideal Platonic mathematical realm, and without them, there are no mathematical ideas. Without mathematical ideas, there is no mathematics

References

Chiu, M. 1996. *Building Mathematical Understanding During Collaboration.* University of California at Berkeley Dissertation.

Davis, P.J. and Hersh, R. 1981. *The Mathematical Experience.* Boston: Birkhäuser.

Gibbs, R. 1994. *The poetics of mind: Figurative thought, language, and understanding.* Cambridge: Cambridge University Press.

Hersh, R. 1986. Some Proposals for Reviving the Philosophy of Mathematics. In T. Tymoczco (ed.), *New Directions in the Philosophy of Mathematics* (pp. 9-28). Boston: Birkhäuser.

Johnson, M. 1987. *The body in the mind: The bodily basis of meaning, reason and imagination.* Chicago: University of Chicago Press.

Lakoff, G. 1987. *Women, fire, and dangerous things: What categories reveal about the mind.* Chicago and London: University of Chicago Press.

Lakoff, G. 1993. The contemporary theory of metaphor. In A. Ortony (ed.), *Metaphor and thought,* 2nd ed., (pp. 202-51). Cambridge: Cambridge University Press.

Lakoff, G., and M. Johnson. 1980. *Metaphors we live by.* Chicago and London: University of Chicago Press.

Núñez, R.E. 1995. What Brain for God's-eye? Biological Naturalism, Ontological Objectivism, and Searle. *Journal of Consciousness Studies,* 2(2), 149-66.

Turner, M. 1996. *The Literary Mind.* Oxford: University Press.

Turner, M. and Fauconnier, G. Conceptual Integration and Formal Expression, Forthcoming *Journal of Metaphor and Symbol.*

The Relation between Grammaticalization and Event Structure Metaphor: Evidence from Uighur Auxiliation[1]

SARAH TAUB
University of California, Berkeley

1. Introduction

This paper addresses the remarkable similarity between two types of semantic shifts: those caused by EVENT STRUCTURE *metaphors*, or ESMs (Lakoff 1992), and those caused by *auxiliation*. ESMs are conventionally-established conceptual metaphors whose target domain is the structure of events: causation, temporal and aspectual structure, roles and numbers of participants, and so on. Auxiliation is a process by which open-class lexical items turn into grammatical elements that add information to a main verb; again, the types of information include causation, temporal and aspectual structure, roles and numbers of participants, and the like.

The two processes are parallel in several ways. Both produce

---

[1]This paper is a condensed version of Taub (1995). Thanks to Anwar Yussuf and the Berkeley Metaphor Group, including Barbara Dancygier, Jiansheng Guo, Joseph Grady, Christopher Johnson, George Lakoff, Kevin Moore, Pamela Morgan, Masaharu Oishi, Jeong-Woon Park, Eve Sweetser, and Lionel Wee, for data and discussions.

expressions which describe the structure of events, and both do this by profiling the "generic," event-level semantic structure implicit in any open-class noun or verb. (For an example of the event-level structure of open-class verbs, compare *hit* and *beat*: the first is inherently punctual, while the second denotes a repetitive action; cf. Talmy 1987.) One finding presented here is that these processes also draw on the same conceptual source domains for the lexical items they transform: as we shall see, the majority of auxiliaries and ESM expressions come from domains of bodily experiences: motion through space, object-manipulation, and physical sensation. The next sections will illustrate these generalizations with examples from Uighur, a Turkic language from Xinjiang Province of China.

Given these striking parallels, it is natural to ask how auxiliation and ESMs are related: for example, should we deduce that ESMs motivate the auxiliation process? I will argue that there are enough differences between the two processes that we should consider them to be different; however, both processes are most likely motivated by the same features of human experience: situations where two types of phenomena are consistently correlated.

2. ESM and Auxiliation in Uighur

Uighur is a good language for comparing ESMs and auxiliation, for it is rich in both processes. The following examples will briefly establish the two major Uighur ESMs, both of which use expressions from body-experience domains. The first, STATES ARE LOCATIONS, maps *being at a location* onto *being in a state*, *motion* onto *change*, and *caused motion* onto *caused change*.

(1)　STATES ARE LOCATIONS

　　a. men qayğu ičide.

　　　　I　　grief　interior-ITS-LOC

　　　　Literally: "I'm in grief." Metaphorically: "I am grieving."

　　b. xïjiliq　　　　ičide　　　　　　qaldi.

　　　　uneasy-NOM interior-ITS-LOC stay.behind-PAST-3rd

　　　　Literally: "He/she ended up in a bad situation."

　　　　Metaphorically: "His/her current situation is bad."

　　c.　men buniŋ　　höddisitin　　　čiqip kiteleymen.

　　　　I　　this-OF problem-ITS-FROM exit-P go-POT-AOR-1stSG

　　　　Literally: "I can get out of this problem."

　　　　Metaphorically: "I can make it so I don't have a problem anymore."

In (1a), a state, *grief*, is described as if it were a place that one could be at or inside. In (1b) and (1c), problems or bad situations are described as places one can enter or leave, and changes in circumstances are described as movements. Note that presence at a location really *is* a kind of state, and movement from place to place really *is* a change of state; as claimed above, this ESM profiles the event-level structure inherent in the understanding of movement through space.

The second ESM considered here is STATES ARE OBJECTS, where *possessing an object* is used to describe *being in a state*, *giving an object* maps onto *causing a change of state*, and *receiving an object* maps onto *changing state due to a cause*.

(2)   STATES ARE OBJECTS

   a. ğelve baš-ağiriqi biridu.
      noise head-pain give-AOR-3rd
      Literally: "The noise is giving me a headache."
      Metaphorically: "The noise is causing my head to hurt."

   b. ğelvedin   bešim   ağurup ketti,
      noise-FROM head-MY hurt-P   go-PAST-3rd
      amma muzik baš-ağiriqimni   aldi.
      but   music head-pain-MY-ACC get-PAST-3rd
      Literally: "My head started to hurt from the noise, but music took away my headache."
      Metaphorically. "My head started to hurt because of the noise, but music caused my headache to end."

   c. lağmen   temini   muštin   aldi.
      (noodle dish) flavor-ITS-ACC spice-FROM get-PAST-3rd
      Literally: "The lağmen got its flavor from the spice."
      Metaphorically: "The spice caused the flavor of the lağmen."

In (2a) and (2b), a headache is seen as an object that can be given or taken away, while in (2c), a flavor is an object that is received from its cause. Once again, having an object really *is* a kind of state, and to give a person an object really *is* to cause a change in that person's state; this ESM, like the other, profiles the event-level structure inherent in these expressions.

Turning to Uighur auxiliation, we find that about 15 Uighur verbs can take on an auxiliary meaning when they occur at the end of a verb series. These are listed in Table 1, and representative examples will be presented in the next section (see Taub 1995 for a full discussion). On scanning the list of verbs, one can see that most of the auxiliaries come from the source domains of movement in space and object-manipulation, and that verbs with similar primary meanings sometimes develop similar auxiliary meanings (e.g., /tur/, /oltur/, /yat/; /baq/, /kör/) and sometimes do not (e.g., /sal/, /qoy/; /ket/, /ket/ + /bar/).

Table 1: Uighur Auxiliaries (as final verb in a series).

VERB	PRIMARY MEANING	AUXILIARY MEANING
Object-manipulation:		
al	get	V affecting oneself
ber	give	V for someone
et	create	V despite misgivings
qoy	put	V a little bit, V for an ulterior motive
sal	insert	V accidentally
Motion in space:		
ket	go	unexpectedly V, V from loss of control
ket + bar	go + reach	be in the process of V-ing for some time
oltur	sit	only V, always V
qal	stay behind	unexpectedly V
tur	stand	continue V-ing over time
yat	lie	do only V, through laziness
yür	move, walk	continue V-ing over time
Sensory perception:		
kör	examine	(deeply) try V-ing
baq	look (at)	(superficially) try V-ing
toy	be full	V one's fill, V enough
Abstract:		
bol	become (ready)	finish V-ing

---

3. Comparing Selected Uighur Auxiliaries with Uighur ESMs

Since ESM expressions and auxiliaries have similar initial and final meanings, it is easy to compare their meaning-shifts. Let us go through a few case studies. We will start with auxiliaries whose shifts seem identical to the ESMs' and proceed to more idiosyncratic cases.

The verb /tur/ `stand', indicating continuing location, becomes an auxiliary signalling repetition or continuation of a state or action; (3a) below gives the main-verb sense; (3b) gives the auxiliary-verb use, and (4) restates the generalization.

(3) a. nimišqa   derexniŋ üstüde   **tur**up bu
    what?-work-TO tree-OF   top-3possd-AT stand-P this
    čaataqni   kisisen?
    branch-OBJ cut-NONPAST-2SG?
    "Why are you cutting this branch while standing atop the tree?"

    b. u   uxlap   **tur**di.
    that.one sleep-P stand-PAST-3rd
    "He/she kept sleeping."

(4)   Main-verb /tur/: to be located at a given place over time, to stay at
    a place; for humans, to stand in that place.
    BECOMES
    Auxiliary-verb /tur/: (for a given state, activity, or action) to
    continue or repeat over time.

Note how the generic structure of /tur/, a locative and a stative, is
profiled here. This shift is the same as the EVENT STRUCTURE mapping
exemplified in (1), where *being at a location* is mapped to *being in a
state*.

Another verb of continuing location, /yat/ `lie', follows the same
general pattern as /tur/, though it is less fully grammaticalized (e.g., it
cannot take inanimate subjects). (5a) demonstrates /yat/'s main-verb use,
(5b) gives an example as an auxiliary indicating continual, exclusive
action, and (6) summarizes the meaning-shift.

(5)   a. "men ˀjennet-ke čiigen   oxšaymen!'
    "I   'heaven-TO enter-PPL look.like-NONPAST-1SG'
    dep **yat**qantim,"   dep   javap biriptu.
    say-P lie-PPL-PAST-1SG" say-P answer give-P-3rd.
    "I thought, 'I seem to have gone to heaven!' as I lay there,"
    he answered.

    b. u   qelemlerni tepip **yat**ti.
    that.one pen-PL-ACC find-p lie-PAST-3rd
    "All he/she did was find pens."

(6)   Main-verb /yat/: to be located at a given place over time; for
    humans, to lie in that place (i.e., remain prone, a posture involving
    no effort).
    BECOMES
    Auxiliary-verb /yat/: (for a given state, activity, or action) to occur
    to the exclusion of other states, activities, or actions, because of
    laziness.

Here we have another locative that becomes a continuative marker, just as with /tur/ and with the ESM STATES ARE LOCATIONS. But /yat/ carries along information from certain specific contexts: a person who continually lies around is doing nothing else and can be considered lazy. This information is retained even when the specific information about prone posture is stripped away.

Now let us turn to /ber/ `give', a verb of object-manipulation, which becomes an auxiliary denoting an action or state undergone for someone's benefit. (7a) gives the main-verb meaning, (7b) shows the auxiliary use, and (8) summarizes the shift.

(7)   a. sen   maŋa   qazandɨn   tört-bešni
          you.SG.polite me-TO pot-FROM   four-five-ACC
          berdiŋ.
          give-PAST-2ndSG.polite
          "You gave me four or five pots."

       b. büvek anasɨğa   uxlap berdi.
          baby mother-its-TO sleep-P give-PAST-3rd
          "The baby slept for its mother."

(8)   Main-verb /ber/: to cause a change in someone's state, usually
       to his or her benefit, by giving him or her an object.
          BECOMES
       Auxiliary-verb /ber/: to cause a change in someone's state, to
       his or her benefit, by performing or undergoing a given
       state, activity, or action that affects that person.

Note how /ber/, which we might gloss as *causing a change by giving*, exhibits much the same shift as in (2) above, the STATES ARE OBJECTS ESM. But it brings along an additional sense, based on the prototypical "giving" situation, that the "giver" is helping the affected party. This is not mapped in the corresponding ESM, as (2a-b) above show: the noise, in causing a headache, is in no way benefitting the headache's "recipient."

The most idiosyncratic auxiliaries are /qoy/ `put' and /sal/ `insert'. In ESMs, we find that related words from the source domain are given correspondingly related meanings in the target domain. For example, when *give* means *cause a state*, *take* means *end the state* (cf. (2b) above). This is sometimes true for auxiliaries (cf. /tur/, /oltur/, /yat/, /qal/) but not always. Here two closely related words, /qoy/ and /sal/, grammaticalize to rather unrelated meanings: *with ulterior motive* and *accidentally*. Examples (9-11) below show the verbs' primary and auxiliary meanings, and their semantic shifts.

As the main verb, /qoy/ can be used for putting something anywhere, but /sal/ requires the location to be inside some container.

(9) a. men gošni   qazanga **saldïm**   / **qoy**dïm.
     I   meat-ACC pot-TO insert-PAST-1stSG / put-PAST-1stSG
     "I put the meat in the pot."

     b. men gošni   taxsïǧa ***saldïm**   / **qoy**dïm.
     I   meat-ACC plate-TO *insert-PAST-1stSG / put-PAST-1stSG
     "I put the meat on the plate."

Auxiliary /sal/ indicates that the main verb's event happened by accident; in English, one might say that the event was "stuck in." (10a-b) give /sal/'s auxiliary use and summarize the meaning-shift.

(10) a. men külüp   **saldïm**.
     I   laugh-P insert-PAST-1stSG
     "I laughed accidentally."

     b. Main-verb /sal/: to place an object into a container.
     BECOMES
     Auxiliary-verb /sal/: (for a given state, activity, or action) to occur accidentally.

Auxiliary /qoy/'s meaning varies depending on the subject's animacy and the telicity of the main verb (Taub 1995). In the prototypical case, with animate subject and non-telic verb, it means that the subject had some unusual motive for doing the event in question, and did it as little as possible while still getting the desired results. (11a-b) give a representative example of the auxiliary use and summarize the shift.

(11) a. u   uxlap   **qoy**di.
     that.one sleep-P put-PAST-3rd
     "He/she made him/herself nap (so as to be rested later)."

     b. Main-verb /qoy/: to cause an object to be located somewhere (perhaps temporarily, perhaps effortfully).
     BECOMES
     Auxiliary-verb /qoy/: (for a given state, activity, or action) to occur enough to satisfy an ulterior motive, to occur a little bit.

The shifts in (10b) and (11b) profile generic-level structure in the verbs in ways similar to the STATES ARE OBJECTS ESM: *manipulators* still become *agents*, *objects* are still *states*. But much information specific to idiosyncratic uses of each verb is brought along. It is as if /sal/ grammaticalized in those contexts where something was "put in" unexpectedly, and only in those contexts; and as if /qoy/ grammaticalized in only those situations where the "putting" was effortful and for a particular, time-limited purpose. The broad, general ESM STATES ARE OBJECTS, though in many ways consistent with the shifts in /qoy/ and /sal/, cannot itself motivate the precise, divergent meanings that they have taken on; only the particularities of the verbs' uses and histories can do that. This fits well with the current theory that words grammaticalize in very particular contexts.

4. Differences as well as parallels

We have seen how auxiliation and ESM in Uighur both start with expressions from physical-experience domains and both map them onto the structure of events in ways that make sense based on the generic-level structure of the words' original meanings. For these reasons, the meaning-shifts can often look identical. But are they the "same" process? For example, should we say that the conventional ESMs of a language motivate its auxiliation processes?

There are also significant differences between Uighur ESMs and auxiliation. As we have seen above, ESMs involve analogous uses of words with similar meanings, while auxiliation often does not; in ESMs, flocks of words travel across a well-established conceptual "bridge", while in auxiliation, each word seems to find its own way along a path heavily influenced by particular contexts in which it is used.

The event-structure expressions that ESMs and auxiliaries create differ subtly as well. Auxiliaries become part of the language's grammar, and get used indiscriminately with all kinds of verbs -- statives, activity verbs, action verbs -- regardless of whether their original structure was stative or telic. We see this in the English auxiliaries in (12) as well as with the Uighur auxiliary /tur/ in (13).

(12)   a. He *kept* running. He *kept* painting pictures. He *kept* sleeping.

     b. He *went on* running. He *went on* painting pictures. He *went on* sleeping.

     c. I'm *gonna* rest now. I'm *gonna* write a letter. I'm *gonna* play basketball tomorrow.

Though /tur/ originated as a stative, it can now denote the continuation or repetition of any state or action.

(13)   a. /tur/ = > continuing state
        buran-čapqun bulup   **tur**di
        storm   become-P stand-PAST-3rd
        "The storm has been around for a while."

       b. /tur/ = > continuing activity
        men uni   aŋlap   **tur**dum.
        I   that.one-ACC listen-P stand-PAST-3rd
        "I kept listening to him."

       c. /tur/ = > continuing repetition of action
        u   qelemlerni   tepip **tur**di.
        that.one pen-PL-ACC find-P stand-PAST-3rd
        "He/she kept finding pens."

ESMs, on the other hand, limit their expressions to uses that really fit the generic-level structure of the source expression. For example, in STATES ARE LOCATIONS, *staying at a location* maps to *continuation of a state*, not *continuation of an activity*, ruling out (14b).

(14)   a. She stayed upset for a long time.

       b. *She stayed finding pens for a long time.

Similarly, STATES ARE OBJECTS treats *possessing an object* only as *being in a state*, not *acting* or *changing state*, and so (15b) is questionable.

(15)   a. The noise gave him a headache.

       b. *The tragedy gave him a change of mind.

The evidence above shows that Uighur's auxiliaries and conventional ESMs are different enough that they cannot be explained by one or two specific conceptual shift patterns. That is, for example, the exact conceptual mapping that motivates STATES ARE OBJECTS expressions cannot explain all the details of /ber/, /qoy/, and /sal/. Though auxiliaries and ESM expressions both profile the generic-level semantic structure, they each seem to have arisen in their own ways.

5. Uighur is typical

Though space does not permit us to make an explicit comparison between auxiliaries and ESMs in other languages, there is a fair amount of evidence that the Uighur situation is typical.

The Berkeley Metaphor Group has begun to look for ESMs crosslinguistically. All the languages that have been considered, including English, Irish, Japanese, Korean, Malay, Mandarin, Polish, and Wolof, turn out to have productive metaphors mapping body experiences onto the structure of events. A few representative examples follow.

Polish maps *states* as *locations* and *change* as *motion*, as in (16) below.

(16) a. jesteśmy w rozpaczy.
        we-are in despair
        Literally: "We're in despair."
        Metaphorically: "We are despairing."

     b. wkroczyliśmy w nowy etap.
        we-stepped in new stage
        Literally: "We stepped into a new stage."
        Metaphorically: "A new stage has begun for us."

Japanese has a similar mapping, exemplified in (17).

(17) atarishii jidai ni hairu.
     new age to enter
     Literally: "Enter a new age."
     Metaphorically: "A new age begins."

The Irish example in (18) treats *change* as *motion*, and *means of change* as *paths*.

(18) ní maith liom na bóithre atá faoi.
     not good with-me the roads REL-are under-him
     Literally: "I don't like the roads that are under him."
     Metaphorically: "I don't like his manner of doing things."

Finally, the Malay proverb in (19) treats *change* or *action* as *motion*, and the proverb in (20) treats *giving a good object* as *causing good for a person* and *giving a bad object* as *causing bad things for a person*.

(19) awak meng-amil pengayoh, saya suday sampai sa-berang.
     you MEN-take paddle, I already arrive other.side
     Literally: "While you are getting hold of your paddle, I have already gotten across the stream."
     Metaphorically: "While you dawdle, I have already achieved my goal."

(20) di-lempar bunga, di-balas lempar tahi.
     DI-throw flower, DI-return throw filth
     Literally: "Throw a flower to someone, and s/he throws back filth."
     Metaphorically: "Treat someone well, and s/he treats you badly."
        (i.e., to be betrayed or tricked)

For a survey of auxiliation, we may turn to Heine et. al. (1993), an encyclopedia of documented instances of grammaticalization (with emphasis on African languages). To get a sense of which conceptual domains are used most often as sources for grammatical morphemes, I grouped grammaticalizing verbs into a number of different classes -- physical, mental, emotional, social, and abstract -- and various subgroups within these. For example, a verb meaning *go* would be classified *physical/motion*, and *say* would be *social/speech*.

Table 2: Major groupings of grammaticalizing verbs' domains.

abstract:	113 verbs
emotional:	13 verbs
mental:	15 verbs
physical:	328 verbs
social:	33 verbs

Table 3: Breakdown of physical-domain verbs.

development:	2 verbs
endurance:	4 verbs
food:	2 verbs
location:	41 verbs
motion:	157 verbs
objects in motion:	7 verbs
object-manipulation:	76 verbs
possessions:	12 verbs
sleep:	3 verbs
taste:	1 verb
touch:	1 verb
vision:	13 verbs
misc. actions:	9 verbs

The book contained 503 different grammaticalizations of verbs[2]. 328, or 65%, of these verbs originally came from physical domains, and of these physical verbs, 293, or 89%, came from the domains of spatial location and motion and object-manipulation. The full breakdown of verb groupings and physical-domain subtypes is given in Tables 2 and 3 above.

It is reasonable to surmise from this suggestive data that across languages, domains of body experiences, and in particular motion and

----

[2]A few of these verbs became prepositions, not auxiliaries; I believe that my generalization is unaffected by this.

object-manipulation, are the prime sources for event structure specifiers such as auxiliaries and ESMs.

6. Experiential Correlations Lead to Meaning-Shifts

It seems clear that ESMs and auxiliation produce expressions that have significantly different properties. Yet it is equally clear that both involve a similar profiling of generic-level structure in body-experience vocabulary. What could cause these differences and similarities? For an answer, let us look at the probable causes of both processes: correlations of phenomena in our everyday experiences.

There is a large body of work showing that auxiliaries arise gradually, through "contextual reinterpretation" (e.g., Traugott 1982, Heine et. al. 1991, Bybee et. al. 1994): when an expression is used in a context where two interpretations are possible, instead of the usual interpretation, a listener can decide that the expression has a less-likely meaning which the context supports. Over time, the expression will come to be used in contexts where only the second interpretation is possible, thus completing the process of semantic shift. (21a-d) below trace this process for the English *go*-future.

(21) a. I'm *going to* the store. (strong spatial, weak intention/futurity)

   b. I'm *going to* work. (weak spatial, strong intention/futurity)

   c. I'm *going to* (= > *gonna*) write a book. (intention/futurity only)

   d. It's *going to* (= > *gonna*) rain today. (futurity only)

Most theories about how metaphors arise invoke the idea of an *experiential basis* for cross-domain mappings: that is, when common experiences instantiate two conceptual domains at the same time, we learn correlations between the conceptual domains that we later establish as metaphorical mappings. For example, Lakoff & Johnson 1980 give as a basis for MORE IS UP our experience that more of a substance usually makes a taller heap. [See C. Johnson (in press) for a reworking of this account.]

Though grammaticalization works on individual words in specific contexts and metaphor links entire conceptual domains, the same experiential correlations can foster both processes. For our purposes, we can see that *any* specific event is necessarily correlated with "event structure" (agency, causation, aspect), and thus a potential source context for both ESMs and auxiliation. Indeed, contextual reinterpretations in such contexts will necessarily resemble ESMs derived from those contexts, because the processes will use the same correlations.

Note that contextual reinterpretation can be considered a metaphorical process in that we can set up a structure-preserving mapping from the original meaning to the new meaning; such a mapping also lays out exactly how the two interpretations are correlated in the source situation. For the *go*-future shift in (21), *current location* maps to and is correlated with *current time and situation, movement to new location over time* maps to *transition to new situation over time*, and *new location* maps to *future time and situation.* Such mappings will always be possible when the reinterpretation profiles an expression's event-level structure. As we have seen, they resemble but do not always match the language's conventionalized ESMs, which implies that they are not motivated by the conventional ESMs.

It is not surprising that a large proportion of ESM expressions and auxiliaries come from domains of body movements and sensations, given that our earliest experiences involve these domains. These particular types of events may be the child's first introduction to events in general; it seems entirely reasonable that when seeking to describe or understand causation, a child would draw on salient examples such as caused motion or caused possession.

This study of ESM and auxiliation has shown that both processes profile the inherent event-level structure of lexical items, both are motivated by experiential correlations, both draw primarily on body-experience domains, and both can be diagrammed as structure-preserving mappings. But their meaning shifts have significant differences: auxiliaries preserve more of the idiosyncrasies of the source situation, and modify any verb, regardless of whether it matches the auxiliary's original event-level structure. I conclude that the conventional ESMs of a language do not motivate its auxiliaries; rather, both types of shifts arise independently from the effects of experiential correlations on our minds and languages.

References

Bybee, Joan, Revere Perkins, & William Pagliuca. 1994. *The Evolution of Grammar: Tense, Aspect, and Modality in the Languages of the World.* Chicago: University of Chicago Press.

Chung, Yoon-Suk. 1992. On Verb Concatenation in Uyghur. Ms., U.C. Berkeley.

Heine, Bernd, Ulrike Claudi, and Friederike Hünnemeyer. 1991. *Grammaticalization: A Conceptual Framework.* Chicago: University of Chicago Press.

Heine, Bernd, Tom Güldemann, Christa Kilian-Hatz, Donald A. Lessau, Heinz Roberg, Mathias Schladt, and Thomas Stolz. 1993. *Conceptual Shift: a*

Lexicon of Grammaticalization Processes in African Languages. Cologne: Afrikanistische Arbeitspapiere.

Johnson, Christopher. In press. Learnability and the Acquisition of Multiple Senses: SOURCE Reconsidered. BLS 22.

Lakoff, George. 1992. The Contemporary Theory of Metaphor, in Andrew Ortony, ed., *Metaphor and Thought*, 2nd ed. Cambridge: Cambridge University Press.

Lakoff, George, Jane Espenson, and Alan Schwartz. 1991. Master Metaphor List, 2nd ed. Ms., U.C. Berkeley.

Langacker, Ronald W. 1987. *Foundations of Cognitive Grammar, Vol. I: Theoretical Prerequisites.* Stanford, CA: Stanford University Press.

Sweetser, Eve. 1990. *From Etymology to Pragmatics: Metaphorical and Cultural Aspects of Semantic Structure.* Cambridge: Cambridge University Press.

Talmy, Leonard. 1987. The Relation of Grammar to Cognition, in B. Rudzka-Ostyn, ed., *Topics in Cognitive Linguistics.* Amsterdam: John Benjamins Publishing Company.

Taub, Sarah. 1995. Meaning Shifts in Uighur Auxiliary Verbs: A Study of Grammaticalization in Progress. Ms., U.C. Berkeley.

Traugott, Elizabeth Closs. 1982. From Propositional to Textual and Expressive Meanings: Some Semantic-Pragmatic Effects of Grammaticalization, in W. Lehmann and Y. Malkiel, eds., *Perspectives on Historical Linguistics.* Amsterdam: John Benjamins Publishing Company.

Part IV

Mental Spaces

Sequencing Mental Spaces in an ASL Narrative[*]

Boris Fridman-Mintz and Scott K. Liddell
Universidad de Colima and Gallaudet University

1. Introduction

Speakers of any language will gesture toward real things in their physical environment as they talk about them. In fact, it would be quite unusual to ask someone to pick up a nearby book without making a gesture of some sort toward the book. In doing so, the speaker is gesturing toward some physically present entity, while speaking about it. Speakers of a sign language have the same option. A signer could hold up a book with one hand, direct eye gaze toward it, and sign LOUSY with the other hand. In addition, signers have an option not available in vocally produced discourse. Pronouns, determiners and a large number of verbs can be directed toward real things that are physically present. Liddell (1994) argues that directing such a sign toward a physically present entity should be analyzed as a mixture of linguistic elements, which account for the invariant aspects of the sign, and a pointing gesture.[1] This is based on a

---

[*] We are grateful to Robert Johnson and the anonymous reviewers for this chapter for their comments on an earlier version of this chapter.
[1] It has been assumed from the early days of ASL research that signs could be entirely decomposed into purely linguistic elements, including elements which directed the movement and placement of signs which use space (Fischer 1975, Kegl 1985, Klima and Bellugi 1979, Lillo-Martin and Klima 1990, Poizner, Klima and Bellugi 1987, Supalla 1978). The

genuine difference between sign languages and spoken languages since, in a sign language, the same hand can point and produce a sign simultaneously.

There is an additional possibility which sign language discourse exploits. The very same pronouns and verbs can point at things, even when the entity being mentioned is not physically present. This ability has a tremendous influence on how signed narratives are structured.

We examined a 6 minute signed narrative told by a man about his experience as a fourth grader at a deaf school. The authorities at the school set up a very fancy classroom exclusively for hard-of-hearing students and provided the hard-of-hearing students with a lot of experiences not provided to the deaf students. This caused a lot of friction between the hard-of-hearing and deaf students, which was ultimately resolved by abandoning the special program.

2. Examples of spatial placement and gestural pointing

The signer associated virtually every entity mentioned in the narrative with an area of space. This poses a substantial problem for the interpretation of signs because he placed 24 entities in space, and some of those 24 often had more than one spatial placement. Our analysis of the tape shows that all of the following entities were placed in the space ahead of the signer: Model Secondary School for the Deaf, Gallaudet University, one experience, 3 schools for the deaf, the West Institute, 2nd grade, 3rd grade, 4th grade, hard-of-hearing students in a classroom, school authorities, carpet, earphones, a music system, a microphone, himself as a hard-of-hearing 4th grader, hard-of-hearing 4th graders as a group, a teacher, Julie Andrews, another town, an event involving going to a movie, a dorm, all students together, positives and negatives. Having this many entities to deal with spatially poses a real problem. How should they be placed and how can either the signer or the addressee keep track of them?

The signer made extensive use of spatial gesturing during the 6 minute narrative. This involved placing elements in space followed by gestures toward them. At times, the signer even gestured toward elements which were never explicitly placed in space.

Although the signer placed elements on both sides of the signing space, we will illustrate here the way that several related entities were set up in the left side of the signing space. Early in the narrative the signer mentions that one experience really stood out in his mind. As he described this experience he held his left hand ahead of his shoulder with an index finger pointing up

---

theoretical position taken in this paper treats such signs as partially linguistically determined and partially gestural.

in the left side of the signing space. This made an association between the hand and the experience being described. The signer takes an abstraction, the experience, and makes it physically present in the form of the 1 handshape held ahead of his left shoulder. This handshape ahead of the shoulder reappears twice more in the narrative with the same association.

Later in the narrative the signer directs a sign toward the left, talking about the location of the school at which the incident took place. This explicitly places the school on the left side of the signing space. Later still the signer pointed up and to the left, above the location of the school, to talk about the authorities at the school. This was done without any explicit mention of the authorities. Thus, reference to authorities is available by pointing above the location of the school. We describe this as the power metaphor (Liddell and Fridman 1995). Later, the signer placed the classroom set up for the hard- of-hearing students on the left side of the signing space. Since the signer sometimes used earlier spatial representations after setting up later ones, there is a big potential for confusion in knowing what is being referred to when the signer points to the left.

What the signer is doing through these placements is making these non-present entities physically accessible. Once these entities are physically accessible, then the signer can direct signs toward the appropriate parts of space, just as if those entities were present.

Model Sec. School	Gallaudet University	one experience	3 schools for the deaf	the West Institute	2nd grade
3rd grade	4th grade	hard-of-hearing students	school authorities	carpet	earphones
music system	microphone	self as hard-of-hearing 4th grader	hard-of-hearing group	a teacher	Julie Andrews
another town	event of attending movie	dormitory	all students together	positives	negatives

Figure 1: A possible solution to keeping track of a large number of referents -- not employed by signers.

Constructing an ASL narrative with numerous referents presents the practical problem of keeping track of all the different entities and their spatial placements. One possible solution to this problem is to produce the spatial equivalent of a communication board by assigning each possible referent a distinct spatial location, as represented in figure 1. But signers do not employ this solution. Not only would it be difficult to remember so many locations, referents and spatial placements, but such a set of placements does not allow for the creation of the locative relationships between referents which play an essential role in surrogate spaces and many token spaces.

What signers do instead is create sequences of simpler spatial representations. In the narrative we examined, the signer created 28 different spatial representations, each one containing from one to four elements.

3. Token and Surrogate Spaces

We divided the spatial representations in this narrative into token and surrogate spaces, two of the three types of spaces proposed by Liddell (1994, 1995). These are each examples of grounded mental spaces, which have all the properties expected of mental spaces, plus the property that the elements of the mental space have physical locations which can be gestured toward (Liddell 1995). We found 15 token spaces and 13 surrogate spaces. These two types of spaces are very different. Figure 2 illustrates a token space.

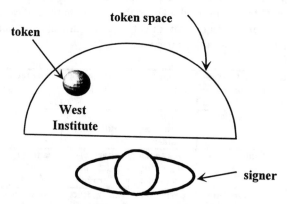

Figure 2: An example of a token space.

The token space is located ahead of the signer. The extent of the token space is illustrated by the semi-circle. It represents a three dimensional space viewed from above the signer. It extends from approximately the level of the waist to as high as the signer's head. A token is an area of the token space associated with some entity. In this representation there is a single token on the left side of the signing space, represented by a sphere. Directing a sign toward the token makes reference to the entity associated with that token. A surrogate space is very different as can be seen in Figure 3.

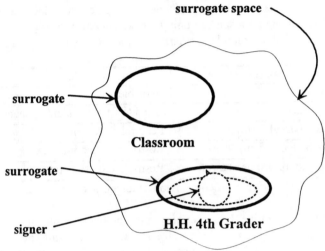

Figure 3: An example of a surrogate space.

The wavy line symbolically represents the extent of the surrogate space. The surrogate space does not have easily describable boundaries, and could be of unlimited size. The surrogate space in figure 3 contains two surrogates: a classroom and a hard-of-hearing 4th grader. In this surrogate space a hard-of-hearing 4th grader is facing a classroom. The physical space which the surrogate space occupies overlaps with the physical space in which the narrator is standing. Thus, the surrogate hard-of-hearing 4th grader is in the same physical space as the signer. Conceptually, however, only the hard-of-hearing 4th grader is facing the classroom. The signer is not. However, the actions of the signer, including signing, are interpreted as those of the hard-of-hearing 4th grader. For example, when the signer directs his gaze toward the location of the surrogate classroom and signs the question meaning "What's going on?", it is interpreted as the question of the hard-of- hearing 4th grader, not a comment from the narrator.

The characteristics which distinguish surrogates and tokens are compared in figure 4. Both types of entities are invisible. Beyond this similarity, tokens and surrogates are quite different. Tokens have a size which allows them to fit in the signing space. Surrogates are full-sized. A surrogate elephant would be as large as an elephant and a surrogate ant would be as small as an ant. Neither a token elephant nor ant would be actual size. Also a surrogate person has physical features such as a head, arms, and trunk, but a token is simply an area of space. Tokens are limited to the space ahead of the signer while a surrogate can be located anywhere. Finally, although a token can only be talked about, a surrogate can serve a 1st, 2nd or 3rd person role in a narrative (Liddell 1995).

Surrogate	Token
Invisible	Invisible
Full-sized	Sized to fit in the signing space
Has physical features	Featureless region
Can be located anywhere	Restricted to signing space
1st, 2nd, or 3rd person role	Restricted to 3rd person role

Figure 4: A comparison of tokens and surrogates

In this narrative the signer solved the problem of spatial placement of the entities being talked about in the narrative by creating the sequence of 28 different mental spaces illustrated in figure 5. The token spaces are drawn as semi-circles and the surrogate spaces have uneven edges. The spaces are numbered in the order that they were created. If a later space is structured in a way which depends on a previous space, a line has been drawn between the two spaces. It is obvious in figure 5 that most of the mental spaces fit into this category. Only 6 of the mental spaces are isolated from the rest in terms of the placement of entities within the mental space. All the rest are structurally related to one another.

The types of motivating factors which link the related mental spaces are illustrated in figure 6. Related elements occurred on the same side of the signing space. For example, the experience was placed on the left. Later the school at which the experience took place was also placed on the left, and even the specific classroom where the experience took place was placed on the left. We refer to this as creating new spaces based on a spatial analogy. In two instances a token space was embedded within a surrogate space. A new space could be created by adding new elements or ignoring old ones. New spaces were created which were not only spatially analogous, but in which the reference of the specific elements showed either a semantic extension or restriction when compared to a preceding space. We also found an example of the "power metaphor" in which signs directed above the location for a school referred to the authorities at the school. This list is not meant to be exhaustive. In fact, we have purposely collapsed some of these categories to give the broadest possible description of the types of relationships between related mental spaces.

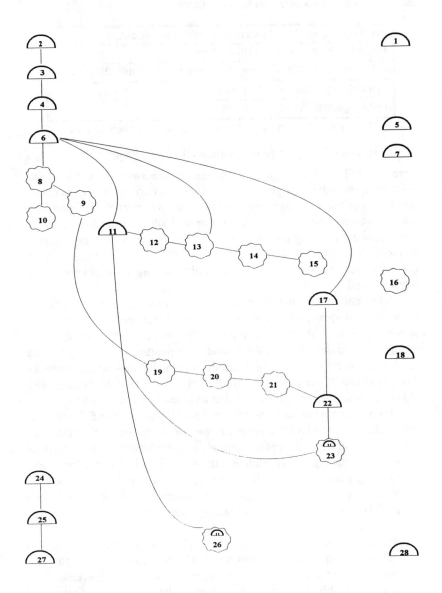

Figure 5: All grounded mental spaces found in the discouse and their structurally motivated connections.

| Creating a space based on analogy with a previous space |
| Embedding one space within another |
| Addition or erasure of elements from a previous mental space |
| Semantic extension or restriction |
| Using space to reflect a metaphor |

Figure 6: Motivating factors in the creation of new spaces

4. A Motivated Sequence of Grounded Mental Spaces

Here we will go through a brief sample of the story with the aim of illustrating the ways that grounded mental spaces are created as the story unfolds. For the most part, the sequences are constructed in a motivated manner, making it possible for the signer and addressee to keep track of what signs are pointing toward at any given time. The following sequence of grounded mental spaces is illustrated in figure 7. As in figure 5, each grounded mental space (GMS) is numbered according to the order in which it was created.

After introducing himself, the narrator explains that an event stands out in his memory, a past experience which he has never forgotten. As previously described, the signer places his weak hand in front of his shoulder and to the left, with the 1 handshape pointing up, thereby making an association between that hand and the memorable experience (GMS 2). The placement of the experience to the left may seem to be unmotivated. However, what happens next shows that its placement is not arbitrary.

The signer next explains that the event took place in North Carolina, at one of the three residential schools for the deaf in the state. He placed the three schools in front of him from left to right. He placed the West Institute to the left by signing WEST while leaning to the left, the Central Institute in the middle by signing CENTER in a neutral position, and the East Institute to the right by signing EAST while leaning to the right. Thus, GMS 3 has a motivation of its own, based on an analogy between the east-west axis and the right-left axis.

It turns out that the experience took place at the school which was placed on the left, the West Institute. The motivation for placing the experience to the left now becomes apparent, since the experience took place at the West Institute which is also on the left. The signer first placed the experience on the left in GMS 2, then placed the school at which the experience took place on the left in GMS 3.

The signer proceeds by explaining that he grew up at the West Institute. He goes on pointing at the token for the West Institute, to the left

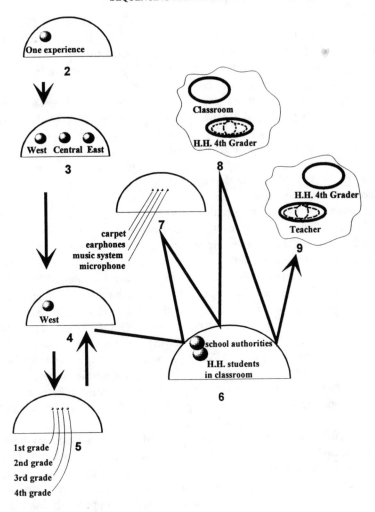

Figure 7: The narrator's progression through the first 9 grounded mental spaces.

at the height of the chest, but from there on the other two institutes are not mentioned nor pointed at. In our analysis, then, a different token space has emerged through the erasure of two tokens. The Central Institute and the East Institute are now absent from GMS 4.

The temporal context of the story comes next. The narrator explains that the events occurred when he became a 4th grader. To express the temporal sequence of having gone through 1st grade to 4th grade, he creates

GMS 5, an ordinal, spatial list created by signing FIRST, SECOND, THIRD, FOURTH G-R-A-D-E while moving his hand from left to right. GMS 5 is not linked through any motivating factor to any previous or following GMS. However, it does have a motivation of its own, a temporal sequence is represented in a linear fashion, from left to right.

Next the narrator describes leaving school at the end of 3rd grade and returning at the beginning of 4th grade. To be produced properly, the signs meaning "leave" and "go back" need to be directed with respect to the location of the token school. But GMS 5 does not contain the school, GMS 4 does. The signer simply signs as if GMS 4 was still present with the school on the left, producing the signs meaning "leave" and "go back" with respect to the token on the left side of GMS 4.

When the hard-of-hearing students go back to school for the beginning of 4th grade they find out that the authorities have assigned them to a separate renovated classroom. The narrator describes this by directing the pronoun PRO up and to the left to identify who made the decision and later in the sentence placing the special classroom below the authorities.[2] No explicit mention is made of the authorities. Only the upward direction of the initial pointing sign tells us that "authorities" did it. The hard-of-hearing classroom token is placed on the left in GMS 6, and the West Institute token was placed on the left in GMSs 3 and 4. We conclude that GMS 6 is based analogically on GMS 4. It contains different elements, but the related elements are placed in a way that parallels the placement in previous GMSs. In this case there is a part/whole relationship between the classroom and the school, and each is placed on the left in their respective GMSs.

The hard-of-hearing students discover that their classroom has been renovated, and many new things have been placed there. The signer lists some of them: a new carpet, earphones, a music system and a microphone for the teacher. However, the signer produces more than a mere list, as he names the different things on the list he also moves his upper body from left to right, associating each element with a left to right spatial placement, creating the GMS 7. As with GMS 5, 7 is not related to any previous or following GMS by any motivating factor. Still, it does have a left-to-right ordinal motivation of its own.

The signer then states that the classroom was very elaborate. To do so he uses a pronoun to point toward the classroom. He signs as if GMS 6

---

[2] Meier (1990) argues that there is no formal distinction between second and third person pronouns in ASL, and used the gloss INDEX to refer to this pronoun. Since the term "index" is used in so many different ways both in ASL studies and in linguistic studies in general, the gloss PRO will be used here to refer to this sign.

were still present. He leans his head and torso to the left, facing the hard-of-hearing classroom token on that same side while signing, making it clear that he is talking about the classroom.

The narrator next expresses the surprise he had as a 4th grader when he saw the changes. However, he does not do this by producing a mere narration of a past event. He performs the reaction he had at the time, as though he were facing the real classroom on the left, and asking what is going on. This creates a surrogate space, GMS 8, which consists of the full sized classroom ahead of and to the left of the surrogate 4th grader. Then the surrogate signer makes a direct quotation of the 4th grader asking what's going on, as he looks at the surrogate classroom to the left. Again we see that related elements are consistently placed across different GMSs. In GMS 6 a token classroom is placed on the left side of the token space. In GMS 8 the hard of hearing classroom is placed on the left side of the surrogate space.

The signer next provides the authorities response to his question. To identify the authorities the signer backtracks again, by pointing up and to the left, taking advantage of the placement of the authorities in GMS 6.

Having identified the authorities, the signer produces the authorities response to the child's puzzlement in the form of constructed dialogue from the authority to the student. To do this the signer creates GMS 9. In this GMS the authority is addressing the student. We know that the authority is now addressing the hard-of-hearing 4th grader because the signer rotates his head and shoulders to the right. This direction is opposite to that used in GMS 8, where the signer faces left to show the 4th grader looking at the classroom. This rightward rotation takes place immediately after pointing at the authorities token in GMS 6. Thus, the return to GMS 6 only lasts for one sign to clarify whose speech is about to be constructed. This way of alternating left and right rotation is a well-established convention of ASL (Padden 1986). It is through this left-right ASL convention for alternating between surrogate spaces that GMS 9 is structured based upon GMS 8.

5. Parallels with spoken language discourse

We have focused on the use of grounded mental spaces in an ASL narrative and we have given a lot of attention to the physical placement of entities within those grounded mental spaces. The signer was faced with the practical issue of how to construct GMSs in order to talk about a large number of entities during a six minute narrative. The signer did it by constructing a large number of spaces. Like non-grounded mental spaces, each of these mental spaces inherits only a partial structure from the event being described. For example, the GMSs in Figure 7 contain only from one to four elements. Although only these few elements were incorporated in the GMSs constructed by the signer, they were sufficient to allow the signer to talk about the events which happened at the school. Our description of sequences of spaces with partial structure is consistent with descriptions of mental space construction in spoken language discourse (Sweetser and Fauconnier 1996). We can see then that if the physical differences between grounded and non-grounded mental spaces are set aside, the two types of spaces share essential properties. This also applies to how mental spaces are related to one another. Sweetser and Fauconnier (1996) describe a typical discourse as involving the creation of a network of spaces through which the speaker moves as discourse unfolds. A "parent" space gives rise to a "child" space, which may itself become a "parent" space, creating a potentially elaborate two-dimensional lattice. Speakers can move in either direction navigating this connection of spaces. Figure 7 is an example of just such a lattice structure and, as we saw earlier, the signer not only moves from "parent" to "child" spaces, but also moves in the opposite direction according to the needs of the discourse. The parallel between the lattice shown in figure 7 and the description of how speakers move through a connection of mental spaces in spoken language discourse is remarkable.

6. Exploiting the modality

Having just described some of the parallels between the ASL narrative and what is known about spoken language discourse, we will now summarize some of the ways that the spatial gestural modality was exploited in the ASL narrative. First, by producing grounded mental spaces, the signer adds immediacy to the elements within those spaces by making them conceptually present. Since these elements occupy positions in space, the signer is able to create analogical mappings across spaces in which those positions remain important. Recall the signer first placed "an experience" on the left side of the signing space in GMS 2. In GMS 3 the signer placed the West Institute on the left. This is where the experience took place. In GMS 6 hard-of-hearing students in a classroom were placed on the left. These are the students who went through the experience. In GMS 8 he imagines himself as a fourth grader actually looking to the left at the classroom as if he were there. The signer was extremely consistent in this type of analogical spatial mapping across succeeding spaces throughout the six minute narrative.

The signer also used space metaphorically by pointing above the classroom to refer to authorities at the school. This is essentially the same metaphor which English speakers use when they talk about Ms. Jones having 6 employees working *under* her. Lakoff and Johnson (1980) find evidence for metaphors based on the meanings expressed in grammatical constructions. For example, the word *under* expresses a spatial relationship in which employees are at a lower level than the boss. Evidence for the metaphor in the narrative we examined comes from the physical placement of entities in GMS 6, since the authorities are physically at a higher level than the students in the classroom. The pronoun which points at the space above the classroom points up, a reflection of the construction of the GMS.[3]

Space was also used to represent the temporal sequence of moving from first grade through fourth grade (GMS 5) as well as to represent a non-temporal list of things added to the classroom (GMS 7). Point of view was also reflected in the type of space created. The leftward placement of the token classroom in GMS 6 reflects an "external" point of view. In that token representation the signer is not conceived as being "there," in or near the classroom. In contrast, GMS 8 places the classroom on the left, but as seen close up, as if being viewed from inside the room itself. This is accomplished by the use of "body shift" which reflects the existence of a surrogate space. In this space the signer demonstrated himself as a fourth grader wondering what was going on as he looked at the classroom.

7. Conclusion

This narrative reveals extensive parallels between the construction and use of mental spaces in the ASL narrative and in spoken language discourse. The individual GMSs described in this paper, like non-grounded mental spaces, inherit only partial structure from conceptualizations serving as the subject of the discourse, contain no grammatical elements, and serve as the cognitive entities which make discourse possible. In constructing the narrative, the signer put successive spaces together in the same ways that spaces are related in spoken language discourse. "Parent" spaces give rise to "child" spaces which successively create a complex two-dimensional lattice of spaces. The signer moves between these spaces in ways that parallel the use of such spaces in spoken language discourse.

There is a tremendous reliance on grounded mental spaces in this narrative. Even entities with the most minor roles in the narrative have spatial associations. This is true even for elements that are mentioned once and never referred to again. Grounding the mental spaces allows the signer to take advantage of the spatial modality. The primary difference between grounded mental spaces and non-grounded mental spaces lies in their

---

[3] ASL pronouns can point in virtually any direction. The way they point is a function of the location of the entity being talked about. This applies regardless of whether the entity being talked about is a real thing, physically present, or an entity in token space or surrogate space.

ability to *additionally* provide spatial placements for their elements. The physical placements allow the signer to express a wide range of meanings including physical relationships, metaphors, spatial expression of temporal relationships, analogical mappings, and shifts in point of view.

References

Fischer, Susan. 1975. Influences on word order change in American Sign Language. In Li, Charles (Ed.) *Word order and word order change.* Austin: University of Texas Press, 1-25.

Kegl, Judy. 1985. *Locative Relations in American Sign Language Word Formation, Syntax, and discourse.* Ph.D. dissertation, MIT, Cambridge, Mass.

Klima, Edward and Ursula Bellugi. 1979. *The signs of language.* Cambridge, MA: Harvard University Press.

Lakoff, George and Mark Johnson. 1980. *Metaphors we live by.* Chicago: University of Chicago Press.

Liddell, Scott K. (1994) Tokens and Surrogates. In Ahlgren, Inger, Brita Bergman & Mary Brennan (Eds.) *Perspectives on Sign Language structure. Papers from the Fifth International Symposium on Sign Language Research.*Durham, England: The International Sign Linguistics Association.

Liddell, Scott K. (1995) Real, Surrogate and Token Space: Grammatical Consequences in ASL. In Emmory, Karen & July Reilly (Eds.) *Language, Gesture and Space.* Hillsdale, NJ: Lawrence Erlbaum Associates.

Liddell, Scott K. & Boris Fridman-Mintz (1995) *Layering spatial representations in an ASL narrative.* Paper presented at New Ways of Analyzing Variation 24 (NWAVE). University of Pennsylvania, Philadelphia.

Lillo-Martin, Diane and Edward S. Klima. 1990. Pointing out the differences: ASL pronouns in syntactic theory. In Fischer, Susan and Siple, Patricia (eds.). 1990. *Theoretical Issues in Sign Language Research*; Volume 1: Linguistics. Chicago, IL: The University of Chicago Press, 191-210.

Meier, R. 1990. Person deixis in American Sign Language. In Fischer, Susan and Siple, Patricia (eds.). 1990. *Theoretical Issues in Sign Language Research*; Volume 1: Linguistics. Chicago, IL: The University of Chicago Press, 175-190.

Padden, C. 1986. Verbs and Role-Shifting in American Sign Language. In C. Padden, ed., *Proceedings of the fourth national symposium on sign language teaching and research.* Silver Spring, MD: NAD.

Poizner, Howard, Edward S. Klima and Ursula Bellugi. 1987. *What the hands reveal about the brain.* Cambridge Massachusetts: The MIT Press.

Sweetser, Eve and Gilles Fauconnier. 1996. Cognitive links and domains: Basic aspects of mental space theory. In Fauconnier, Gilles and Sweetser, Eve. *Spaces, worlds, and grammar.* Chicago, IL: The University of Chicago Press.

Principles of Conceptual Integration

GILLES FAUCONNIER AND MARK TURNER

University of California, San Diego and University of Maryland

In a number of publications, we have argued that in addition to the more familiar mappings that operate in analogy, metaphor, deferred reference (metonymy), and frame projection, there is another cognitive operation, blending, that interacts with these mappings and that is pervasive in many areas of human thought. In this article, we present optimality principles of blending and types of blending networks.

1.   Blending

Blending is in principle a simple operation. It operates on two Input mental spaces to yield a third space, the <u>Blend</u>. The Blend <u>inherits partial structure</u> from the Input spaces and <u>has emergent structure</u> of its own. Here are some of the conditions which are satisfied, when two Input spaces I_1 and I_2 are blended:

1) CROSS-SPACE MAPPING: there is a <u>partial</u> mapping of counterparts between the input spaces I_1 and I_2.

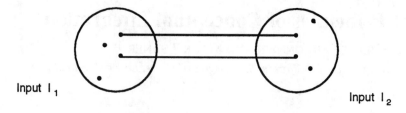

2) GENERIC SPACE: there is a generic space, which maps onto each of the inputs. This generic space reflects some common, usually more abstract, structure and organization shared by the inputs, and defines the core cross-space mapping between them. A generic space does not have to be available prior to the construction of a network. It is often constructed and elaborated along with the other spaces and connections.

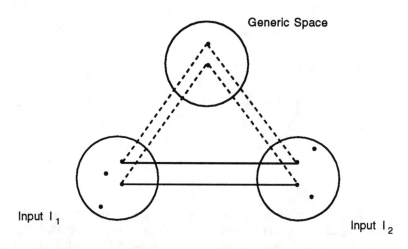

3) BLEND: the inputs I1 and I2 are partially projected onto a fourth space, the Blend.

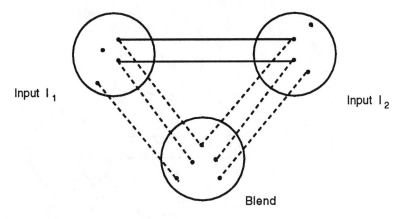

Input I₁

Input I₂

Blend

4) EMERGENT STRUCTURE: the Blend has emergent structure not provided by the inputs. This happens in three (interrelated) ways:

COMPOSITION: taken together, the projections from the Inputs make new relations available which didn't exist in the separate inputs.

COMPLETION: knowledge of background frames and cognitive and cultural models allows the composite structure projected into the Blend from the Inputs to be viewed as part of a larger self-contained structure in the Blend. The pattern in the Blend triggered by the inherited structures is 'completed' into the larger, emergent structure.

ELABORATION: the structure in the Blend can then be elaborated. This is "running the Blend." It consists in cognitive work performed within the Blend, according to its own emergent logic.

Schematically, then, a full four-space Blend looks like this:

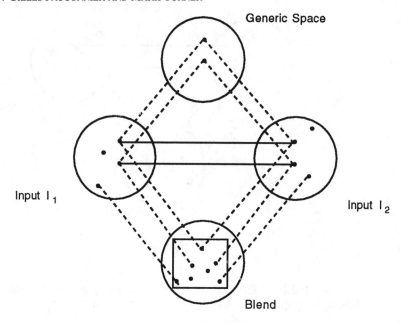

In the diagram, the square stands for the Emergent structure in the Blend. The diagram is meant to indicate that when counterparts are projected into the Blend, they may be fused into a single element, or projected separately.

We document the cognitive operation of conceptual integration, or blending, through a large number of examples taken from a superficially quite diverse array of phenomena, in areas which include puzzle-solving, rhetoric, metaphor, scientific discovery, interface design, grammatical constructions, fictive motion, counterfactual reasoning, and conceptual change.

One of our examples involves a modern catamaran *Great America II* sailing from San Francisco to Boston in 1993, and being compared to a clipper, *Northern Light*, that did the same run back in 1853. The sailing magazine *Latitude* phrases one of its reports as follows:

As we went to press, Rich Wilson and Bill Biewenga were barely maintaining a 4.5 day lead over the ghost of the clipper Northern Light, ...

This expression frames the two boats as sailing on the same course during the same time period in 1993. It blends the event of 1853 and the one of 1993 into a single event. All the conditions outlined above for blending obtain. There is a Cross-space mapping which links the two trajectories, the two boats, the two time periods, positions on the course, etc. Projection to the Blend from the Inputs is partial: the 1853 date is dropped, the 1853 weather conditions, the purpose of the trip, and so on. But the Blend has rich Emergent structure: the boats are now in a position to be compared, so that one can be 'ahead' of the other. This structure itself, two boats moving in the same direction on the same course and having departed from San Francisco on the same day, fits into an obvious and familiar cultural frame, that of a RACE. This yields additional emergent structure by Completion. 'Maintaining a lead' is an intentional part of a race. Although in reality, the catamaran is sailing alone, and the clipper's run took place 140 years before, the situation is described in terms of the blended space, in which, so to speak, the two boats left San Francisco on the same day in 1993, and are engaged in a race to Boston. An explicit referent, the ghost, is set up for the opponent of *Great America* in the blended space. '*ghost*' allows the projection from Input 1 that the clipper no longer (i.e. in 1993) exists. But the starting times are still fused, and it is understood that the 'ghost' is retracing the exact run of the record-holding clipper.

Here is a superficially different example, an analogical counterfactual, which is also constructed in accordance with the above scheme of conceptual integration:

In the 1990s, British Prime Minister Margaret Thatcher - known as the Iron Lady - had a great popularity in the United States. It was common to encounter claims that what the United States needed was a Margaret Thatcher. The response we are interested in is, "But Margaret Thatcher would never get elected here because the labor unions can't stand her." Thinking about this counterfactual requires bringing Margaret Thatcher together with American electoral politics. We must imagine Margaret Thatcher running for president in America, and we must develop enough structure to see the relevant barriers to her being elected. Crucially, the point of this reasoning has nothing to do with the objective fact that it is impossible for Margaret Thatcher to be elected, since she is already head of state, she is not a citizen of the United States, she has no interest in running, and so on. The speaker's point, right or wrong, is that the United States and Great Britain are, despite the obvious similarities, quite different in their cultural and political institutions and will not choose the same kinds of leaders. This point is made by setting up a situation (the "blend") that has some characteristics of Great Britain, some characteristics of the United States, and some properties of its own. For example, in the blend, someone who has not yet been president but is running for president has already had the sort of experience with labor unions that can only be had by a head of state in Britain. The two inputs in this example are the political systems of the United States and Britain, linked by a generic frame of Western democracy. The novel integrated structure, or blend, has Margaret Thatcher campaigning in Illinois and Michigan and hated by the American labor unions. In that blend, Margaret Thatcher is defeated. Because the blend is connected to the rest of the network, the relevant inferences project back to the inputs, yielding the all-important conclusion that the speaker is stressing the disanalogy between the United States and Britain, amounting to the claim that the United States may need a certain kind of leader, but the intricacies of its electoral politics make it impossible for that kind of leader to be elected.

There is a rich tradition of looking at counterfactual examples as simply constructing a possible world that differs minimally from the existing world, but it is clear that this view is inadequate in the case of the Thatcher counterfactual, since these kinds of minimal changes (making Thatcher an American citizen, changing the Constitution to allow her to run, and so on) are beside the point.

Even very simple constructions in language depend upon conceptual integration. A natural way to think about adjectives and nouns is that the adjective assigns a property to the noun, so that "the cow is brown" assigns the property *brown* to *cow*. By the same token, there should a fixed property associated with the adjective "safe" that is assigned to any noun it modifies. Consider the following unremarkable uses of "safe" in the context of a child playing at the beach with a shovel: "The child is safe," "The beach is safe," and "The shovel is safe." There is no fixed property that "safe" assigns to *child, beach,* and *shovel.* The first means that the child will not be harmed, but so do the second and the third - they do not mean that the beach will not be harmed or that the shovel will not be harmed. "Safe" does not assign a property but rather prompts us to evoke scenarios of danger appropriate for the noun and the context. We worry about whether the child will be harmed by being on the beach or by using the shovel. Technically, the word "safe" evokes an abstract frame of *danger* with roles like victim, location, and instrument. Modifying the noun with the adjective prompts us to integrate that abstract frame of *danger* and the specific situation of the child on the beach into a counterfactual event of *harm* to the child. We build a specific counterfactual scenario of *harm* in which *child, beach,* and *shovel* are assigned to roles in the *danger* frame. Instead of assigning a simple property, the adjective is prompting us to perform a conceptual integration where the inputs are, on the one hand, a frame of danger, and on the other, the specific situation of the child on the beach with a shovel. The output of the integration (the blend) is the counterfactual scenario in which the child is harmed. The word "safe" implies a disanalogy between the counterfactual blend and the specific input, with respect to the entity designated by the noun. If the shovel is safe, it is because in the counterfactual blend it is too sharp, but in the specific situation it is too dull to cut.

This process is quite general, as is shown by the fact that the elements in the specific scenario can be assigned to the frame roles differently: in "the shovel is safe," the child is the victim in the blend if we are concerned about the shovel's injuring the child, but the shovel is the victim in the blend if we are concerned about the child's breaking the shovel. Furthermore, any number of roles can be recruited for the *danger* frame. In the counterfactual blend for "the jewels are safe," the jewels are neither victim nor instrument; they have the role *possession* and the *owner* is the victim. If we ship the jewels in packaging, then the counterfactual blend for "the packaging is safe" has *jewels* as victim, external forces as *cause of harm*, and *packaging* as *barrier to external forces*. Other examples showing the variety of possible roles would be "Drive at a safe speed," "Have a safe trip," and "This is a safe bet."

Even more elaborate blends, involving several roles, are constructed for other syntactically simple expressions, like "The beach is shark-safe" versus "The beach is child-safe." In the context of buying fish at a supermarket, the label on the tuna can read, "This tuna is dolphin-safe" to mean that the tuna was caught using methods that prevent accidents from happening to the dolphins. This blend looks more spectacular, but is constructed using the same integration principles as in the unremarkable "safe beach" or "safe trip."

"Safe" is not an exceptional adjective, with special semantic properties that set it apart from ordinary adjectives. It turns out that the principles of integration suggested above are needed quite generally. Even color adjectives, which at first blush look as if they must assign fixed features, turn out to require non-compositional conceptual integration. "Red pencil" can be taken to mean a pencil whose wood has been painted red on the outside, a pencil that leaves a red mark (the lead is red, or the chemical in the pencil reacts with the paper to produce red, or . . .), a pencil used to record the activities of the team dressed in red, a pencil smeared with lipstick, not to mention pencils used only for recording deficits. Theories of semantics typically prefer to work with examples like "black bird" or "brown cow" since these examples are supposed to be the prototypes of compositionality of meaning, but in fact even these examples illustrate complicated processes of conceptual integration.

2. Types of integration networks

In Fauconnier and Turner (in press), we examine a range of projection possibilities for a simple conceptual integration network. This gives rise to a taxonomy of networks, and to a typology of the phenomena that correspond to various formal possibilities. One crucial dimension of this taxonomy is the extent to which spaces in the network share more or less specific frames. Another important, and correlated, dimension is the degree to which each of the inputs provides the basis for the framing in the blend. We find a continuum along these dimensions. The mapping between the inputs may exploit or establish a very specific shared frame, or a highly abstract and schematic topology, or something in between those two extremes. And one input may provide most of the relevant framing, or the two inputs may contribute strongly to the framing of the blend, or we may find an intermediate situation. Along this continuum, some prototypes stand out. The following is a brief description of three important prototypes along this gradient: frame networks, one-sided networks, and two-sided networks.

We call an *organizing frame* for a mental space a frame that specifies the nature of the relevant activity, events, and participants. Examples of organizing frames are *man walking along a mountain path*, *boat sailing along an ocean course*, and *boxers fighting in a boxing ring*. The more abstract frame of *competition* is not an organizing frame, because it does not specify a cognitively representable type of activity and event structure. In particular, we have typical representations of boxing, or sailing, but not of the more general *competition* or *voyage*.

2.1. Frame Networks

A *frame network* is a conceptual integration network in which all spaces - inputs, generic, and blend - share an organizing frame. This is the case for the boat race example in which all spaces have the frame *boat sailing along an ocean course*. It's also the case for the Thatcher example, where all spaces share the frame *Western democracy*. Typically, in a frame network, the common frame F inheres in the more elaborate frame F_B in the blend. In the boat race example, the shared frame *boat sailing along an ocean course* inheres in the more elaborate frame in the blend of *sailboats racing along an ocean course*.

A shared organizing frame provides a straightforward schema to define a cross-space mapping between inputs. This mapping preserves topology at the shared frame level through simple identity. At more specific levels, topology may (and typically will) differ. In the boat race network, one of the elements fits the more specific frame *nineteenth-century clipper on a freight run* and its counterpart fits the more specific frame *late-twentieth-century exotic catamaran on a speed run*. In the blend, some of the more specific features are present, but not others. One of the boats is a catamaran and the other is still a clipper, but the clipper is now engaged in a race instead of a freight run.

2.2. One-Sided Networks

A network is one-sided if the inputs have different organizing frames and one of them is projected to organize the blend.

Simple on-line metaphors that rely mainly on a well-understood frame in one of the inputs (the source) are one-sided networks. For example, in the case of two business competitors portrayed as boxers, the inputs have two different organizing frames (boxing and business), and the blend inherits only one of them (boxing).

In a simple metaphoric blend like this, projection from inputs to blend is highly asymmetric: one of the inputs but not the other supplies the organizing frame and therefore frame-topology. This is why it seems appropriate to call that input the *source input*. The projection of the source frame to the blend carries with it linguistic constructions (e.g., vocabulary) used to evoke the source frame. Of course, there are projections from the target input to the blend that also provide linguistic constructions for the blend, but they refer to elements below the frame level. For example, if the two business competitors are named Murdoch and Iacocca, we may say that "Murdoch knocked Iacocca out": "knocked out" belongs to the frame level of the source while "Murdoch" and "Iacocca" belong to a more specific level in the target.

2.3. Two-sided Networks

A network is two-sided if the inputs are organized by different frames but some topology is projected from both frames to the organizing frame of the blend. Gruen's example of the computer desktop interface is a two-sided network. The two principal inputs have different organizing frames, the frame of office work with folders, files, trash cans on one hand, and the frame of traditional computer commands on the other. In the blend, we find some topology projected from each of these frames, plus inherent topology in the blend itself - icons that move onto other icons, disappear, reappear through clicking, and so on.

The metaphor "digging your own grave" is also a two-sided network with frame structure projected from both inputs. Death and graves come from the source input of the "dying" scenario, but causality and intentionality are projected from the target. In the blended space, digging is unintentional and brings one closer to death, just as making mistakes is unintentional and brings one closer to failure in the target. In the source input, the causal order has the reverse direction: there, it is someone's dying that causes a grave to be dug, and the digging is intentional. The temporal order of events (digging before dying, making mistakes before failing) is also projected from the target input.

Complex numbers are another case of a two-sided network. The inputs are respectively two-dimensional space and real/imaginary numbers. Frame structure is projected from each of the inputs, e.g., angles, rotations, and coordinates from two-dimensional space, and multiplication, addition, and square roots from the space of numbers.

In all these cases, as in most networks, the blended space develops emergent structure of its own, and ends up with a richer specific frame F_B. For example, in the case of complex numbers, multiplication in the blend includes addition of angles. This operation is unavailable in either of the inputs. The input of two-dimensional space doesn't have multiplication; the input of numbers doesn't have angles.

2.4. Framing the Blend

The formal projection possibilities in an integration network result in various framing possibilities for the blend. Four salient cases are 'realistic projected frames', 'realistic emergent frames', 'realistic extended frames', and 'blend-specific emergent frames'.

In a one-sided network like the boxing businessmen, a realistic frame (boxing) is projected from one input to organize the blend.

In the frame network of the regatta example, all spaces share the frame of ocean voyage. Projection to the blend needs to preserve relative time and place, and therefore projects the two boat counterparts to distinct elements in the blend. The blend has two boats on the same course and that pattern is completed into the familiar pattern of a race. The frame in the blend is thus not only ocean voyage, but ocean race. It is emergent, because it is not in the inputs, and it is realistic at the frame level because we know independently that there can or could be ocean races of this kind.[1]

Now consider the case where someone observes that the Vatican seems to be flat-footed in the metaphorical boxing match over abortion and says "I suppose it's hard to bob and weave when you have a mitre on your head." The Pope's competition with an adversary is portrayed as a boxing match, where the Pope is impeded as a boxer by the mitre he is obliged as Pope to wear on ritual occasions, and we interpret this as meaning that his obligation as Pope to remain dignified impedes him in his competition. The organizing frame of the blend is still boxing, but that frame has been extended to include boxing Popes with mitres on their head. Those aspects of the extended frame have been projected from the second input and integrated (by extending the frame) into the organizing frame of the first input, within the blend. The extended frame, although less typical, still counts as realistic, because, in principle, one could fight wearing a robe and a mitre.

Finally, in an example like 'digging one's own grave', the framing of the blend is constructed in terms of elements of one input (graves, digging, and death], but has unrealistic structure (digging results in death, etc.) because of significant frame structure projected from the second input. This

---

[1] It's not realistic at a more specific level, however, because catamarans do not actually race against 19th century clippers.

structure is emergent. It is not an independently available extension of the organizing frame of death and graves. Interestingly, its unrealistic aspect does not seem to impede cognitive processing.

2.5. Blending and Metaphor

There is a theoretical distinction between basic metaphors (Lakoff and Johnson (1980)) and on-line metaphorical blends. Basic metaphors map conceptual domains onto each other at a relatively high level of abstraction (e.g. TIME is SPACE, or STATES are LOCATIONS, or ANGER is HEAT). In metaphorical blends, basic metaphors may give us the deep conceptual motivation for alignments between inputs, and hence cross-space mappings. An actual on-line metaphorical blend typically builds in significant additional structure.

Take the stock example *This surgeon is a butcher*. The statement underscores the clumsiness of the surgeon, and its undesirable effects. But such inferences are not simply transferred from the domain of butchers to the domain of surgery. Butchers are in fact typically quite deft in their own domain of meat-cutting, and their actions in that domain (producing roasts, steaks, and so on) are considered desirable. In an integration network, two input spaces with very partial structures from meat-carving and surgery are mapped onto each other, on the basis of shared generic properties (cutting flesh, sharp instruments, white coat, professional activity, ...). But neither the clumsiness, nor its catastrophic consequences, appear in those input spaces. They emerge in the blend. In the blend, there is projection on one hand of the operating room, the patient, and the surgeon, and on the other of the butcher's tools, the butcher's methods and manner of carving, etc. Emergent structure ensues from simulation of this unusual situation, and we are able to grasp instantly the nefarious effects of the procedure. The resulting failings of the surgeon, represented with considerable hyperbole in the blend, are projected back to the input space of surgery, where they yield an inference of gross incompetence.

This example is clearly a case of a two-sided network. To get the right inferences, we must project frame structure from both inputs to organize the blend. Moreover, since the target is the domain of surgery, the source must be butchers and meat-carving. But the organizing frame in the blend is an extension of the surgery frame (an operating room with a surgeon operating with the gestures and perhaps the tools of a butcher). It is not a butcher shop in which a carcass has been replaced by a patient. This is what we called above a framing of the blend by realistic extension of an input frame. But the extended organizing frame is that of the input ordinarily called the 'target' in metaphor studies.

The point of this example is that an on-line metaphorical blend does not in general reduce to projection of a well-known source frame onto a target. The interpretation in terms of simple unidirectional projection is only possible in the special case of a one-sided network, like the one for the boxing businessmen.

The grave-digging example makes a similar point. We cannot be understanding the target 'financial mistakes and failure' in terms of the source 'grave-digging and death' through direct projection, because the topologies of the inputs in fact do not match (recall that they have different causal, temporal, and intentional structure). But, and this is the crucial point here, a partial cross-space mapping can be established between those inputs by virtue of existing basic metaphors like FAILURE is DEATH, PHYSICAL ACTION (e.g. digging) is GENERAL ACTION.

3. Optimality Principles

A conceptual integration network is constructed dynamically over a period of time, which may be very short (as in the understanding of a joke) or very long (as in the emergence of a new scientific concept, like complex numbers, over several centuries). For the process to be successful, many conditions have to be satisfied. Spaces in the network must be able to run autonomously in certain respects, while remaining connected to the rest of the network. New projections must take place during elaboration. The newly created space, the blend, must have its own integrated emergent structure, while containing relevant information for projection back to the inputs.

In Fauconnier and Turner (in press) we offer evidence for the following general principles. For any given on-line construction of a blend, there will be competition between the principles, and so typically they will only be satisfied to a certain degree.

Integration:

The blend must constitute a tightly integrated scene that can be manipulated as a unit. More generally, every space in the network should have integration.

Web:

Manipulating the blend as a unit must maintain the web of appropriate connections to the input spaces easily and without additional surveillance or computation.

Unpacking:

The blend alone must enable the understander to unpack the blend to reconstruct the inputs, the cross-space mapping, the generic space, and the network of connections between all these spaces.

Topology:

For any input space and any element in that space projected into the blend, it is optimal for the relations of the element in the blend to match the relations of its counterpart.

Good reason:
All things being equal, if an element appears in the blend, there will be pressure to find significance for this element. Significance will include relevant links to other spaces and relevant functions in running the blend.

In a *frame network*, it is relatively easy to satisfy Topology, Integration, and Web simultaneously. The sharing of the organizing frame automatically transfers a rich topology from space to space. Integration is provided in the blend by the elaborated frame F_B, which is already a common, rich, and integrated frame, like *race* or *debate* or *encounter*. The sharing of the frame also preserves automatically the Web connections between spaces.

Although Integration in such networks is typically satisfied at the frame level, it is also typically not satisfied at lower levels of increased specificity. A race between two boats is a fine integration, but the more specific scene of a catamaran racing against a clipper is a poor integration. This discordance has another function. It facilitates the optimality principle of Unpacking by signaling which elements are projected from which input (e.g. the clipper from '1853' and the catamaran from '1993').

In a pure *one-sided network*, as exemplified by the boxing business competitors, Integration in the blend is automatically satisfied because the blend inherits an organizing frame from the source, *boxing*. Topology is satisfied between blend and source for the same reason, and it is also satisfied between blend and target because the basic metaphor of competition as physical combat has aligned the relevant topologies of the two input spaces. Web is similarly satisfied by this shared topology. Unpacking is facilitated just as it was for a frame network by disintegration at sub-frame levels of specificity (e.g. competitors represented in a cartoon as boxing in business suits).

In a two-sided network, Topology, Integration, and Web are not satisfied in such an automatic and routine fashion: it is necessary to use a frame that has been developed specifically for the blend and that has central emergent structure. (This may be why two-sided networks - such as the desktop, complex numbers, and digging your own grave - are often typically thought of as more creative, at least until they become entrenched.) In two-sided networks, there is increasing competition between optimality principles and increasingly many opportunities for failure to satisfy them.

The computer desktop provides an illustration of many of these competitions and opportunities for failure. To satisfy the integration of the two-dimensional screen, we drop the three-dimensionality of office-space, and we don't mind placing the trashcan on the desktop. The position of the trashcan plays no role in the cross-space mapping and can therefore be ignored in the integration.

In contrast, the use of the trashcan both as the container of what is to be deleted and as the instrument of ejecting floppy disks counts as a genuine failure to satisfy Topology and Integration. In the frame elaborated for the blend, the dual roles of the trashcan are contradictory, since one ejects the floppy disk to keep it rather than discard it; for all other operations of dragging one icon to another, the result is that the first is *contained* in the second, but not so in this case, and finally for all other manipulations of icons on the desktop, the result is a *computation*, but in this case it is a physical *interaction* at the level of hardware. The trashcan ejector/container also violates Web, because it results in the floppy disk being sometimes "inside" the world of computer operations and sometimes "inside" the world of the real office. Other interface features that produce similar violations include the command sequence Select-Copy-Paste on word-processing applications. The decomposition of copying into two operations (in the blend) does not map topologically onto real copying in the input of office work, and leads to web violations.

Notice that optimality is a matter of degree. A non-optimal blend, like the desktop, can still be learned and then used fairly automatically. Typically, non-optimality creates maximum difficulties for novices,[2] but can be surmounted by experts.

The fact that in two-sided networks the organizing frame of the blend is not available by extension from the organizing frame of either input increases chances of non-optimality and competition between the principles but also offers opportunity for creativity in attempting to satisfy the optimality principles. Pressure to satisfy optimality principles in highly complex two-sided shared topology networks has historically given rise to some of the most fundamental and creative scientific discoveries. The development of the concept of complex numbers in mathematics is a case in point. The complex number blend turns out to be a two-sided shared topology network. Some key elements in each input have no counterparts in the basic cross-space mapping. The operation of multiplication for numbers has no counterpart in the geometry input, and the angles of vectors in the geometry input have no counterparts in the number input. The blend, however, inherits both the multiplication operation from the frame of the "number" input and the vector angle from the frame of the "geometric" input. This is already enough to make it a two-sided shared topology network, since multiplication in the blend has frame-level topology from the input of numbers while angle in the blend has frame-level topology from the space of geometry. But furthermore, in the blend, multiplication includes addition of angles as one of its constitutive components. This is discovered by running the blend; it turns out to be a highly unexpected essential property of the new concept of number which has emerged. So in this instance, the pressures to satisfy optimality in this two-sided shared

---

[2] In the learning stages, novices will be reluctant to eject a disk through the trash can, for fear of deleting what's on it. They will click Copy instead of Paste or try useless sequences like: Select - Select Insertion Point - Copy.

topology network lead to important mathematical discovery. Jeff Lansing has pointed out to us other marvelous examples of important scientific blends leading to discovery (by Fourier, Maxwell, and Faraday), which suggests that this is a general process. We emphasize that this type of creativity is possible by virtue of the competition of optimality principles and the power of blending to accomodate them.

References

Coulson, Seana (1997). *Semantic Leaps: Frame-Shifting and Conceptual Blending*. UCSD Ph. D. dissertation.

Fauconnier, G. (1997). *Mappings in Thought and Language*. Cambridge: Cambridge University Press.

Fauconnier, G. and M. Turner. 1994. *Conceptual projection and middle spaces*. UCSD: Department of Cognitive Science Technical Report 9401.

Fauconnier, G. and M. Turner. 1996. Blending as a central process of grammar. In *Conceptual Structure, Discourse, and Language*, Ed. Adele Goldberg. Stanford: Center for the Study of Language and Information.

Fauconnier, G. and M. Turner (in press). Conceptual Integration Networks. *Cognitive Science*.

Lakoff, G. and M. Johnson. 1980. *Metaphors We Live By*. Chicago: University of Chicago Press.

Turner, M. 1996. *The Literary Mind*. (New York: Oxford University Press).

Conceptual Integration in Counterfactuals

MARK TURNER AND GILLES FAUCONNIER

University of Maryland and University of California, San Diego

Principles of Conceptual Integration

Conceptual integration—"blending"—is a general cognitive operation used to construct meaning. It is dynamic, supple, and active in the moment of thinking. It interacts with other general cognitive operations. It yields products that frequently become entrenched in conceptual structure and grammar. It often performs new blending on its entrenched products. It is easy to detect in spectacular cases but it is for the most part a routine, workaday process that escapes detection except on technical analysis. It is not reserved for special purposes, and is not especially costly.

In the preceding article in this volume, we have explained principles of conceptual integration (see Fauconnier and Turner, and the citations there). In this article, we demonstrate those principles at work in counterfactuals.

"If Churchill had been Prime Minister in 1938 . . ."

Consider a prototypical counterfactual claim:

—*If Churchill had been prime minister in 1938 instead of Neville Chamberlain, Hitler would have been deposed and World War II averted.*

This counterfactual claim asks us to blend conceptual structure from different mental spaces to create a separate, counterfactual mental space. The input spaces include (1) Churchill in 1938 as outspoken opponent of Germany; and (2) Neville Chamberlain in 1938 as prime minister facing the threat from Germany. To construct the blend, we project parts of each of these spaces to it, and develop emergent structure there.

From the first mental space, the blend takes Churchill. From the second mental space, the blend takes the role prime minister. In the blend, Churchill is prime minister by 1938. The blend is contrary-to-fact with respect to both of its input spaces. The antecedent and the consequent exist in the blended space; neither exists in either of the input spaces.

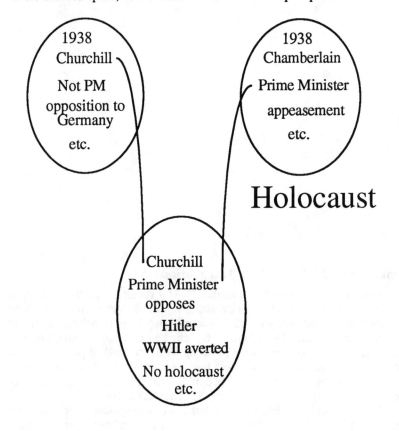

Because the process of blending is largely unconscious, it seems easy, but it is in fact complex. It has many standard features that can be illustrated from the Churchill example.

Blends exploit and develop counterpart connections between input spaces. The space with Churchill and the space with Chamberlain share many identity-counterparts, such as date, England, Germany, Hitler, and tension. Churchill and Chamberlain are additionally frame-counterparts: each is an English political figure, holding a certain political office, with views about Germany.

Counterparts may or may not both be brought into the blend, and may or may not be fused in the blend. Many paired counterparts are brought into the blend as fused units: Hitler in the blend is a single fused entity corresponding to Hitler in each of the inputs but not equal to them—the Hitler in the blend has a different life. Churchill is brought into the blend but not fused with his frame-counterpart, Chamberlain. Chamberlain's political office is brought in but not fused with its frame-counterpart.

The projection from the input spaces is selective. The blend takes from the space with Churchill his opposition to Germany but not his political office or his reputation as having poor judgment of the sort that would prevent him from obtaining a position of leadership. The blend takes from the space with Chamberlain the role *prime minister* and the situation faced by the prime minister in 1938, but not Chamberlain himself or the default knowledge attached to *prime minister* that world leaders facing aggression are concerned greatly to avoid unnecessary war. We frame Chamberlain according to this default knowledge but keep it out of the blend, where we need a prime minister who views conflict as inevitable.

Blends recruit a great range of conceptual structure and knowledge without our recognizing it. Very little of the structure needed for the contrary-to-fact blended space is mentioned. The Churchill blend recruits conceptual frames of world leaders, political aggression, and wars. It recruits the relevant history of Germany and England. These recruitments are needed for the reasoning to work properly in the blend. Academic theories may also be recruited to the blend—game-theoretic interaction during political aggression, or deterrence by "power-maximizing" actors. These recruitments may drive the elaboration of the blend in one direction or another.

Blending is a process that can be applied repeatedly, and blends themselves can be inputs to other blends. Someone might respond to the Churchill counterfactual, "That's only because Hitler was irrational: a more rational Hitler would have seen that his strategic chances were still excellent, and would not have backed down." This new counterfactual blend takes part but not all of the original Churchill blend, and additionally takes part but not all of the characteristics of Hitler from spaces that refer to actual situations. In the new counterfactual hyper-blend, World War II is not averted.

Former prime minister Margaret Thatcher created just such a hyper-blend when she argued that, as leaders of Britain, France, and the United States should have refused to appease Hitler, so Western leaders should refuse to appease aggressors in the war in Bosnia. Thatcher asked members of her audience to take two spaces—the space referring to the situation in Bosnia and the counterfactual space in which Hitler was opposed and the atrocities were averted—as inputs to the construction of a third, blended space in which the Western leaders oppose the aggressors in Bosnia and atrocities are thereby averted. Her policy—"Not Again!"—is anchored in what she takes to be the persuasiveness of the original counterfactual.

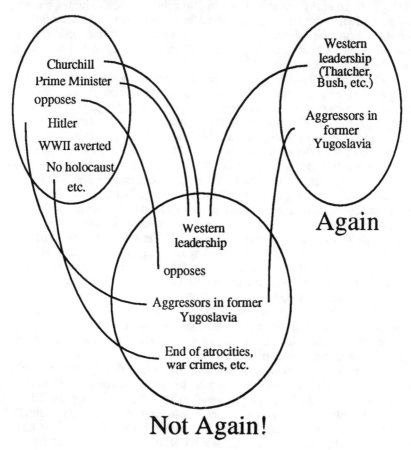

Of course, Thatcher implicitly invited her audience to imagine the counterfactual blend in which Margaret Thatcher is still prime minister during the period in which war breaks out in Bosnia, and the further counterfactual blend in which Margaret Thatcher is prime minister in 1938 and opposes Hitler. In both of these counterfactual blends, the aggressors back down and the atrocities are averted or ended. These two counterfactual blends can be made stronger if they receive projections from the space that refers to the Falklands war, in which Margaret Thatcher is prime minister and is figured as "The Iron Lady," war victor, staunch in her defense of honor regardless of the considerable practical difficulties, courageous adversary of aggressors, enforcer of Britain's policy over vast geographical distances. Thatcher not need refer to the "Falklands" space; her identity evokes it, perhaps more effectively than any mention could.

The "Falklands" space and the two counterfactual blends in which Thatcher faces down (a) Hitler and (b) the aggressors in Bosnia are available to serve as reinforcing inputs to the "Not Again!" space, which represents Thatcher's policy toward Bosnia. Projections of this sort demonstrate the remarkable way in which character—once it has been connected to an actor in a space that has reference—becomes projectable to blends in which that actor faces past or hypothetical situations. In fact, that character becomes projectable to counterfactual blends having to do with what other actors might do or might have done if they possessed that character.

Blends develop structure not provided by the inputs. Typically, the blend is not a simple cut-and-paste reassembly of elements to be found in the input spaces but instead develops considerable emergent structure. Usually, we focus on this additional emergent structure. For example, in the blend, but not in any of its inputs, Hitler backs down and World War II is averted.

Inferences, arguments, and ideas developed in the blend can have effect in cognition, leading us to modify the initial inputs and to change our view of the corresponding situations. A student of historicist patterns that led to World War II might know Churchill's personality well but not have brought what she knows to bear on her conception of appeasement in 1938. The Churchill blend might challenge her to reconsider the causal weight of personality.

How does structure develop in a counterfactual blend? How does structure developed in a blend lead us to reconsider input spaces?

Blends develop by three mechanisms: *composition, completion,* and *elaboration.* We selectively *compose* structure from input spaces into the blend. To do so, we exploit counterpart connections between the input spaces. Partial composition provides a working space for further composition. *Completion* provides additional structure once a few elements have been brought in. A minimal framing of Churchill and Hitler as adversarial heads of state invites us to complete that structure by recruiting any amount of specific or general knowledge we have about personal opposition, international relations, negotiation, and so on. *Elaboration* develops the blend through imaginative mental simulation according to principles and logic in the blend. Some of these principles will have been brought to the blend by completion. Continued dynamic completion can recruit new principles and logic during elaboration. But new principles and logic may also arise through elaboration itself.

Composition and completion often draw together conceptual structures usually kept apart. As a consequence, the blend can reveal latent contradictions and coherences between previously separated elements. It can show us problems and lacunae in what we had previously taken for granted. It can equally show us unrecognized strengths and complementarity. In this way, blends yield insight into the conceptual structures from which they arise.

Composition, completion, and elaboration all recruit selectively from our most favored patterns of knowing and thinking. Consequently, blending is very powerful, but also highly subject to bias. It is hard to evaluate bias in blends, for two reasons. First, composition, completion, and elaboration operate for the most part automatically and below the horizon of conscious observation. Therefore, we rarely detect consciously the infrastructure in the blend that makes it effective. Second, since the emergent structure in the blend comes from our favored patterns of knowing and thinking, we are likely to regard biased infrastructure in the blend as unobjectionable even if we somehow manage to detect it.

For example, in trying to reason about a blend only on the basis of its proper historical structure, we may unwittingly complete the blend with evidence from a later historical moment. In the Churchill counterfactual, we use what we know of 1938. But once we have Churchill as prime minister in the blend, it is impossible to prevent completion from another (covert) input space—Churchill as prime minister later in time. The counterfactual blend in which Churchill opposes Hitler in 1938 is plausible only because we can recruit to it Churchill's great fighting spirit in opposing Hitler during World War II, and we can know of that spirit only because World War II was not averted. Our reasoning in the blend—that World War II might have been averted—depends, therefore, on the occurrence World War II: the blend makes sense to us only because it did not happen. In this way, our ex post knowledge can affect our supposed ex ante reasoning in ways detectable only on analysis. Even the selection of objects of ex ante reasoning can be influenced by ex post knowledge: Had Churchill never been prime minister, it is unlikely that we would think of constructing a blend in which he was prime minister in 1938. Ex post input spaces seep into ex ante counterfactual blended spaces, and in fact prompt us covertly to construct them.

Purposes and Optimality Constraints

The model of conceptual blending, like all scientific models, reveals a set of constraints on the phenomena it describes. It demands mapping between counterparts in inputs, selective projection to the blend, and so on. There are also optimality constraints that pressure blends in one direction or another, as we discuss in the preceding article in this volume. The *integration constraint* requires that blends constitute a tightly integrated scene that can be manipulated as a unit. The *web constraint* requires that manipulation of the blend as a unit maintain the web of appropriate connections to the input spaces easily and without additional surveillance. The *unpacking constraint* requires that the blend alone enable the understander to unpack it to reconstruct the inputs and the connections between spaces. The *topology constraint* requires that any element in a blend that has been projected from an input have relations in the blend that match the relations of its corresponding element in the input.

The weight of an optimality constraint varies with the purpose of the blend. When blending is used to conceive of a new policy, model, or activity (like using the "desktop" interface for operating a computer), the integration constraint may play a dominant role for the blend, since the blend is meant to provide the mental basis for extended integrated activity. In such cases, we usually minimize the projections from the blend back to the input spaces since we usually do not have as a purpose reconceiving or solving for the inputs. Consequently (other things being equal), *web* and *topology* may be relaxed.

Different purposes may in fact require a tightening of *web* and *topology*: an attempt to construct a new consensual policy that is a blend of conflicting policies supported by conflicting parties may require strong *web* and *topology* over just those parts of the inputs cherished by each party, since neither party wishes to yield on central points. Where achieving consensus is a purpose, we may even weaken integration in the blend—producing, for example, a blend less simple or efficient than is cognitively possible—in order to get the conflicting parties to accept it.

In cases where the blend has been constructed with the purpose of casting light on one of the input spaces, *web* and *topology* are likely to dominate, since abandoning relevant connections to the inputs and altering relations between elements may make the blend less useful as an instrument for analyzing the input. Casting light on an input is the principal purpose of counterfactual blends in the social sciences. Pascal's counterfactual statement, *If Cleopatra's nose had been an inch longer, Antony might not have been so infatuated, and the history of Rome and the West might have been entirely different*, is meant to spotlight the potential effect of specific private and personal affairs on large impersonal public political events. The Churchill counterfactual is meant to spotlight the causal role of the leader's personality.

Methodologists, concerned with the widespread (and apparently indispensable) use of counterfactuals in social scientific argument, have proposed criteria for regulating their acceptable use. A survey can be found in Philip Tetlock and Aaron Belkin's introduction to their edited volume, *Counterfactual Thought Experiments in World Politics* (Tetlock & Belkin, 1996). These criteria have been developed in the spirit of making counterfactual spaces a kind of substitute for controlled laboratory experiments. In some sciences, it is possible to design two situations that vary only on the independent variable, to run the two situations experimentally, and to contrast the effects in the two cases. For example, one lab rat (the control) may receive a normal diet while a genetically identical lab rat receives a diet in which fructose has been replaced by glucose. In the social sciences, and especially in reasoning about world events, it is often impossible to run two such situations as an experiment. The methodological substitute for doing so is to contrast the actual situation with an imagined counterfactual situation.

To prevent imagination from running wild in the construction of these counterfactuals, the methodologists have proposed, for example, that counterfactual spaces must be thoroughly specified in their details, especially the details of their causal antecedents and consequents; that they must be consistent with well-established historical facts (e.g., they should require minimal rewriting of the original input spaces; the antecedent should have been recognized historically as an option and should additionally have been possible to bring about; and the antecedents and consequences should be close in time); that they must be consistent with well-established theoretical laws and statistical generalizations; that they must be parsimonious (explain as much as possible with as few assumptions as possible); and so on.

But in fact authors of spotlight counterfactual blends are typically indifferent to these kinds of criteria, because their purpose is to spotlight an input rather than to build a full and detailed simulation of a possible situation. This is very clear in an example like the following:

—*If the Earth were as close to the sun as Venus, life as we know it never would have evolved on our planet.*

This counterfactual blend conforms very badly to the criteria summarized in Tetlock & Belkin, but it is a superb spotlight. Given laws of physics and astrophysics, and given the way the solar system was formed, a planet in the orbit of Venus would necessarily have the size and mineral composition of Venus. The only planet that could be as close to the sun as Venus is one essentially identical to Venus in these respects. For the Earth to form in the orbit of Venus would require violating so many fundamental theoretical laws as to render the solar system unrecognizable to us. Alternatively, if we imagine that the Earth forms in its own orbit but is then somehow moved to the orbit of Venus, we would need a way to move it there and a way to keep it in place during the origin and evolution of life. It would require magic to move it into that orbit and to keep it in place. This counterfactual blend (an Earth-like planet in the orbit of Venus) has not only unimaginable physics but also unspecifiable consequents and antecedents.

But it is an excellent spotlight. The blend is conceptually coherent and easy to build. Mentally, it is easy to move the Earth at the right moment in its planetary history to the orbit of Venus. We all have experience in moving objects from one place to another. The mental space containing Earth and the mental space containing Venus already share elaborate counterpart structure. Earth and Venus are counterparts in those mental spaces. To construct the blend, we need only take partial structure from each of the already highly matched counterparts in the highly matched input spaces, and develop an Earth-as-Venus. It is additionally easy for us to conceive that the sun is a powerful source of heat, and that something a lot closer to a powerful source of heat becomes a lot hotter very quickly. The reasoning works fluidly and properly in the blend. Everything near the Earth's surface would be subjected to extremely high temperatures; yet all forms of terrestrial life known to us die at only marginally higher temperatures; the result is the absence of life. Given the right audience, this spotlight can illuminate something interesting in the input space that contains the Earth: life as we know it may seem marvelously flexible in its adapting to widely varying terrestrial environments, but it requires extremely narrow specifications, relative to the scales of variation that obtain in our solar system.

A similarly illustrative spotlight counterfactual blend is Fauconnier's analogical counterfactual, "In France, Watergate would not have harmed Nixon," which prompts us to build a complicated blend of American political events and French cultural attitudes, in order to spotlight differences in French and American cultural attitudes toward actions taken by politicians. The counterfactual blend is fantastic and even impossible, but the disanalogy between the inputs revealed by the blend superbly spotlights the relevant structure in the inputs.

Spotlights do conform to the constraints that are relevant to their purpose. Since they are constructed to pick out important features—often causal—in an input space, they must obey *unpacking* very well, or the relevant input space may not even be accessible. They must obey *web* and *topology* well enough that the structure in the blend can be connected back to the structure to be spotlighted in the input; but they may purposely violate *topology* where it is the notable difference between the blend and the input that is meant to signal the interesting structure in the input, as when Nixon is *not* harmed in the blend. A spotlight counterfactual blend must obey *integration* over relevant structure, but it can ignore integration for peripheral or subtle structure in the blend that is inconsequential for its spotlight function. In general, an optimality constraint has effect only to the extent that it is needed for accomplishing the purpose of the blend.

Consider next the spotlight counterfactual blend we will call "philosopher in a coma": A woman who had already been in a coma for ten years was raped by a hospital employee, and gave birth to a child. A debate ensued concerning whether the pregnancy should have been terminated. Spotlight counterfactual blends arose such as, "It is right to figure out what she would want. It is wrong to try to figure out what we want." The *Los Angeles Times* article reporting the case ended with a comment by law professor Goldberg. She said,

> —*"Even if everyone agrees she [the comatose woman] was pro-life at 19, she is now 29 and has lived in PVS [persistent vegetative state] for 10 years. Do we ask: 'Was she pro-life?' Or do we ask more appropriately: 'Would she be pro-life as a rape victim in a persistent vegetative state at 29 years of life?' "*

In the blend, the woman is in a persistent vegetative state, but has the reasoning capacities and general information that she would have had at age 29 under ordinary circumstances. The purpose of the counterfactual blend is not to construct a plausible situation in which a woman is reasoning about her inability to reason. The counterfactual blend is offered instead with the purpose of casting light on the element of "choice" in the input space in which the woman is indeed in a coma. Law professor Goldberg is committed to framing this woman as having the right to choose, but what does it mean for a woman in a coma to choose? Her abstract opinion, voiced ten years before her specific dilemma, does not meet our frame for "choice"; the law professor is offering instead an alternative—in the blend, the pregnant woman can make an informed choice about the specific dilemma, and this choice should be projected back to the input to guide our actions.

Guiding our actions through spotlight counterfactual blends is a common goal of political argument, as in the following example:

> —*If Bosnian Muslims were Christians [alternatively: bottle-nosed dolphins], the West Europeans and Americans would never have allowed the slaughter of innocents to go on as long as they did.*

This counterfactual blend has unclear specification of antecedents and consequents, and violates many well-established facts, laws, and generalizations—it would require drastic rewriting of centuries of Mediterranean history to keep Islam out of the relevant geographical area; dolphins live in water and have social organization very far removed from anything underlying human political organization.

But it is potentially a superb spotlight. Although the blending requires intricate unconscious conceptual work involving wild departures from actuality, that intricate blending is well within our competence. Consider the dolphins: we know that fishers are actually harvesting fish, have no animosity toward dolphins, and are killing the dolphins only incidentally, but they have been framed as wanton slaughterers of dolphins. We project only a small part of that frame to the blend, bringing along the associated moral judgments, including the judgment that we, the audience, bear some responsibility for action. By means of the blend, aspects of the "environmental responsibility" frame come to be projected back onto the "foreign policy" frame. In the blend, the dolphins are fused with the Muslims and the fishers with the killers of Muslims. Suppose the audience actually feels, in the blend, some responsibility for taking action, and therefore recognizes that its sense of responsibility varies with the identity of the victims—human versus ocean mammal (or Muslim versus Christian)—and feels ethically uncomfortable that its sympathies would depend upon the identity of the victims. Then the spotlight has led the audience to see something about the causality involved in its attitude, to reconsider its position, perhaps to change the normative frame that motivates and shapes policy, perhaps even to do something. The counterfactual blend flatters the audience, for a rhetorical purpose, by assuming that the members of the audience are moral, responsible, and active in most cases but have atypically been neglectful in this one isolated case.

Let us contrast spotlight counterfactual blends with *reductio ad absurdum* blends, where the purpose is to prove that a blend *must be* counterfactual because of internal disintegration. Here, the blend matches perfectly all the logical requirements on some input space A but has some structure not known to be in A or known not to be in A. The blend is required to meet *integration* absolutely; the logician demonstrates that the blend is disintegrated in containing a contradiction. Such an attempt is not always successful, and failure can result in discovery of new mathematical systems: Following Saccheri, Bolyai, Lobatchevsky, and Gauss put together a blend, essentially of parallel lines that diverge. They elaborated this blended space in great detail, expecting to find a contradiction, but found none. They thereby created hyperbolic non-Euclidean geometry.

A variant of *reductio ad absurdum* has as its purpose to prove something about the input A (assumed to be integrated) by requiring the blend to match all of the logic and known structure of A but including some hypothetical structure X not known to be in A. Again, the blend is required to meet *integration* absolutely; again the logician shows that the blend is disintegrated in containing a contradiction; and now the logician can project an inference back to input A, namely that X cannot be in A. Mathematical examples are prototypical, but this version of *reductio* is common in everyday reasoning, as when we ask ourselves whether it could have been Grace who telephoned a few minutes ago, check the clock to determine that Grace would be driving on the freeway and so would have to have her cellular telephone, observe that she has left her cellular telephone on the table, and so conclude that it was not Grace who called. In this case, blending some of what we know of the world with the hypothesis that Grace called leads us to develop emergent structure in the blend—Grace's having her cellular telephone—which is contradicted by other structure in the blend. The blend is therefore disintegrated, and the hypothesis is therefore ruled out for the input.

The Ubiquity of Counterfactual Blends

We have used spectacular examples to give a demonstration of the principles of conceptual integration in counterfactual blends, but creating counterfactual blends is a routine and usually unnoticed part of everyday reasoning. Consider the following unspectacular examples:

> —*If I were you, I would have done it.* [The speaker is a man. The listener is a woman who at an earlier age had declined to become pregnant.]

> —*I wish I'd had your house. I'd still be living here.* [The speaker and the listener are viewing the remains of the speaker's burned home; the listener owns an adobe home.]

> —*Paul believes he'll get his daughter admitted to Berkeley because he thinks Mary is the dean of admissions.*

> —*Why don't you have a fax machine at home? I do. You could be reading my proposal now.*

> —*Cyprus was meant to have become the Switzerland of the Mediterranean.*

We learn from these examples that grammar provides no simple discriminant of counterfactual thinking. None of them has the linguistic form of an if-then statement whose antecedent is in the past perfect ("If Churchill had been . . ., then"). Grammatical hints of counterfactual thinking are often subtle. They include subjunctivity, main verbs like *wish* or *prevent*, modal verbs like *could*, and adverbs like *not*. Linguistic form often provides no test at all, since the same form can express counterfactuality in one case and not in another—"Max could be in New York, instead of here" evokes a counterfactual blend; "Max could be in New York. Why don't you call him?" does not.

Yet the reasoning in each of these examples requires intricate, orderly, and impressive blending to create a counterfactual space.

References

Fauconnier, Gilles and Mark Turner. This volume. Principles of Conceptual Integration.

Tetlock, Philip and Aaron Belkin, editors. 1996. *Counterfactual Thought Experiments in World Politics*. Princeton: Princeton University Press.

Bound Spaces, Starting Points, and Settings

TUOMAS HUUMO
University of Turku

1. Introduction

Bound spaces are a subclass of mental spaces (see Fauconnier 1994 for the term) that differ from prototypical, autonomous spaces in being conceptually dependent on another entity and existing only with respect to that entity. Linguistically, bound spaces are represented as locations. They are a typical instance of the common linguistic CONTAINER metaphor (in the sense of Lakoff & Johnson 1980): expressions of physical containment are used metaphorically in expressing abstract relations as well. Prototypical bound spaces include internal conditions, mental states, illnesses, and physical conditions, all represented as containers. (1) and (2) are examples of such prototypical bound spaces, in English and Finnish respectively.

(1)   The professor was in a coma / in a hurry / in a bad mood.

(2)   Elmeri oli   flunssa+ssa /   humala+ssa.

       Elmer   was   flu+INE[1] /   intoxication+INE

       'E. had the flu / was drunk' [lit: "was in flu/intoxication"].

---

[1] The following abbreviations are used in the glossings: ADE = adessive, ELA = elative, GEN = genitive, ILL = illative, INE = inessive, PAR = partitive, PL = plural, (number)+PX = possessive suffix.

297

The spatial metaphor of bound spaces obtains even in expressions of a change-of-state: a bound space can for instance be entered by the entity on which it is dependent (3).

(3)   Elmeri   tuli   humala+an.

        Elmeri   came   intoxication+ILL

        'Elmer got drunk' [lit: "Elmer came into intoxication"].

        In spite of their resemblance to autonomous spaces, bound spaces are subject to certain constraints that limit their ability to occur in different syntactic constructions and semantic relations. In this paper I study these constraints with regard to two constructions, both of which require a space-builder to carry a special function. The first is the *reference point construction* (structurally *'In X is Y'*, e.g. *In the back seat is my biology teacher*), which resembles semantically existential constructions, and has the space-builder as the *starting point* (cf. Chafe 1994), i.e. as the *reference point* that is invoked "for purposes of establishing mental contact with another [entity]" (Langacker 1991: 350-351, 552; 1996). In Section 2 I argue, partly on the basis of Huumo (1996a), that bound spaces are not able to function as starting points -- a fact that sets them apart from autonomous spaces such as time and place.

        The second construction type discussed in this paper (in Section 3), is one where the space-builder has the function of establishing a setting where a complex relation unfolds. A setting can be defined as "a global, inclusive region within which an event unfolds or a situation obtains" (Langacker 1991: 553), and thus it may be surprising to find that a bound space can be a setting: if bound spaces are only allowed to contain the entity to which they are bound, then how can they set up a frame within which a whole process unfolds, with the participation of numerous entities? In Section 3 this apparent contradiction is avoided by showing that a bound space, when functioning as a setting, has in fact a double function, setting up two mental spaces simultaneously: first, the bound space,which obeys all the above-mentioned constraints, and second, a *temporal space*, created by highlighting the temporal extension (i.e. duration) of the containment relation between the bound space and the entity that occupies the space. This temporal space, like temporal spaces in general, can fulfil the function of a setting.

        In Section 4, I compare the semantic functions of starting points and settings in general, with the intention to show that a temporal interpretation is only possible with a setting but not with a starting point. This difference is due to the fact that a setting is the frame of a process that unfolds in time, whereas the locative reference-point construction fails to express any temporal processes embedded in the space; thus the space does not have a similar temporal extension.

The main source of the data discussed in this paper is the Finnish language. It has a very rich system for the expression of location (six morphological locative cases), and uses this system extensively in expressing other, nonspatial relations as well.

2. Bound Spaces and Starting Points

It has been argued in Huumo (1996a) that one fundamental constraint that sets bound spaces apart from autonomous spaces is that they are unable to function as the starting points of information presented in existential-like structures. The variation between SVX locative structures (4) and XVS existentials (5) is therefore only observed with autonomous spaces but not with bound spaces, which do not allow the latter (see example 6)

(4)   The motorcycle was beside the shed.

(5)   Beside the shed was the motorcycle.

(6)   * In the coma / in the hurry / in the bad mood was the professor.

In Langacker's (1996) terminology, the crucial difference between constructions like (4) and (5) is that they adopt a different type of *natural path* when approaching the locational configuration consisting of the figure (the motorcycle) and the ground (the shed). A natural path is defined as "any cognitively natural ordering of the elements of a complex structure", and natural paths include phenomena such as the transmission of energy between participants along an action chain, and the temporal sequence of event components, among others. A complex structure subsumes numerous natural paths pertaining to different levels and dimensions of structure. According to this view, an expression like (4) represents an *event participant path* in selecting one participant (the trajector) of the relationship as its starting point. On the other hand, (5) represents a *locational path* in taking the location (the landmark) as its starting point and evoking mental access to the trajector via that location. The event participant path thus relates to the kind of mental access that arises from conceiving of individuals acting in the world, whereas the locational path is connected to the everyday experience of finding things in space.

The inability of bound spaces to function as starting points in expressions like (6) is directly explicable by their non-autonomous nature. Since a bound space is conceptually dependent on the entity situated in it and exists only with respect to that entity, it cannot be used as a reference point in search of the entity in the same sense that autonomous spaces can. A conceptual dependence thus blocks the ability of a space (or of a participant, for that matter) to function as the starting point of the predication.

It is also worth noting that if the space-builder is ambiguous between a bound and an autonomous reading, the bound reading is only natural in the subject-initial construction (7); in the locative reference-point construction a strong tendency exists to assign to it the autonomous reading (8).

(7)   Tyttö   oli   une+ssa.
        Girl   was   dream+INE
        'The girl was asleep'. [lit: in dream].

(8)   Une+ssa   oli   tyttö.

        Dream+INE   was   girl

        'In the dream there was a girl'.

In (7), an internal state of being asleep is attributed to the girl, by using the container metaphor and representing the girl as being inside the domain. In (8), the mental space of the dream is autonomous with respect to the girl: she is not the person having the dream but part of the dream herself.

To sum up: all the examples discussed in Section 2 have spoken in favor of a constraint that prohibits the use of bound spaces as starting points in the locative reference-point construction. When we place a bound space builder in the initial position of this structure, the result is either an ungrammatical sentence (6) or -- if the space builder is ambiguous and has a possible autonomous reading as well -- the expression of a proper containment between the (autonomous) space and an entity.

3. Bound Spaces as Settings

After seeing that bound spaces are unable to function as starting points, it might be surprising to learn that they can nevertheless function as settings in certain constructions (see 9 and 10).

(9)   Humala+ssa   Liisa   riitelee
        Intoxication+INE   Liisa   argues
        pomo+n   kanssa
        boss+GEN   with
        'When she is drunk [lit: "in intoxication"], Liisa argues with
        the boss'.

(10)   Flunssa+ssa   tyttö   lukee   kauhutarino+i+ta.

        Flu+INE   girl   reads   horror-story+PL+PAR

        'When she has the flu [lit: "in the flu"], the girl reads
        horror-stories'.

In (9) and (10), the bound spaces of (Liisa's) intoxication and (the girl's) flu set up a frame for a whole process or relation. In (9), the argument between Liisa and her boss is subordinated to the mental space of her intoxication (i.e. Liisa argues with the boss only when she is drunk); in (10), the girl is predicated to read horror-stories only when she has the flu (with no implications as to her activities under other circumstances). At the same time, however, the bound spaces in these examples remain bound to the subject: in (9), only Liisa (but not the boss) is drunk, and in (10), only the girl has the flu, whereas the horror-stories are of course outside that domain.

We can thus claim that the space-builders of drunkenness and flu here have the double function of setting up two mental spaces simultaneously, one of which is based on the other. The primary space is the bound space, i.e. an internal condition of one entity, while the second one is a *temporal space* which has a scope over the whole relation, i.e. it covers, or "contains" in a metaphorical sense, the whole relation with its participants, and confines the extension of this relation only to the domain it indicates. This temporal space is brought into existence by highlighting the duration of the bound space relation. It is the temporal periods of Liisa's drunkenness and the girl's flu that can function as the settings in (9) and (10). This temporalized bound space thus resembles autonomous temporal spaces (e.g. *today*, *now*, *on Monday*) in that it is able to set up a frame for a whole process.

3.1 Temporal interpretation of nontemporal spaces
The ability of bound spaces to achieve a temporal meaning is not a unique property: in fact, any nontemporal space can achieve a temporal reading in a suitable context (Huumo, 1996b). This can be seen especially clearly in

constructions where a nontemporal space sets up a frame that has a proper temporal relation under its scope. The only way for a nontemporal space to achieve this function is to set up a more extensive temporal space that includes the other temporal space. For instance, when a clause has both temporal and locative space-builders, the temporal space typically has scope over the locative space in limiting the relation between the locative space and the entity situated within it. The spatial relation is thus understood to exist only within the frame set up by the temporal space (see 11).

(11)   On Monday night, Elmer played chess with Lisa in
       Poughkeepsie.

In (11), the temporal space *on Monday night* takes the rest of the predication under its scope, and the spatial relation between the chess-players and Poughkeepsie is subordinated to the temporal space. A locative space-builder, on the other hand, cannot govern a temporal space-builder in the same sense; this is because the relation of an entity to space cannot restrict its relation to time. Only if the locative space is itself temporalized is it able to take a temporal space under its scope. This effect can be achieved by changing the word order so that the spatial element starts the predication (11').

(11') In Poughkeepsie, Elmer played chess with Lisa on
       Monday night.

The interpretation of (11') resembles that of (9). The duration of Elmer's stay in Poughkeepsie is highlighted, and the rest of the sentence, including the temporal space *on Monday night*, is subordinated to it. With this reading, Elmer stayed in Poughkeepsie longer than Monday night alone. The temporal extension of the locative space thus exceeds the limits of the time space.

This variation in scope relations is perhaps best evident in expressions with a discontinuous temporal space; consider (12) vs. (13), originally from Huumo (1996b).

(12)   Viikonloppuisin Elmeri hiihti   Norja+ssa.
       Weekends   Elmer   skied   Norway+INE
       'On weekends, Elmer skied in Norway'

(13)   Norja+ssa   Elmeri hiihti   viikonloppuisin.

      Norway+INE   Elmer   skied   weekends

      'In Norway, Elmer skied at weekends'.

    In (12), the locative relation between Elmer and Norway is, as expected, under the scope of the temporal space. At this time, the time space (*at weekends*) is, however, discontinuous, and this makes the interpretation one where Elmer is in Norway at weekends only (but not on weekdays; see Figure 1).

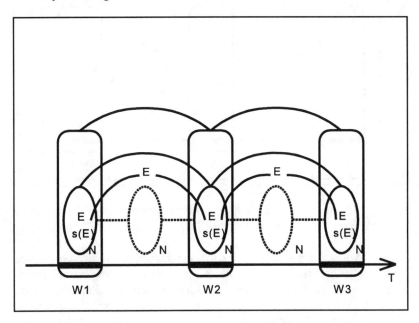

Figure 1. Example (12). The discontinuous temporal space *at weekends* (W1, W2 etc.) sets up a frame for the locative relation between space N (Norway) and entity E (Elmer), who performs an activity s (skiing) while occupying both spaces. Outside W1, W2... etc, there is no predicated relation between E and N.

    In (13), on the other hand, the word order leads to a similar interpretation as in (11'), i.e. one where Elmer's stay in Norway exceeds the temporal space of the weekends, with Elmer spending a longer and continuous period in Norway. His skiing, however, is again subordinated to both spaces. The locative space in (13) thus receives a temporal reading which enables it to have the proper temporal space under its scope (see Figure 2).

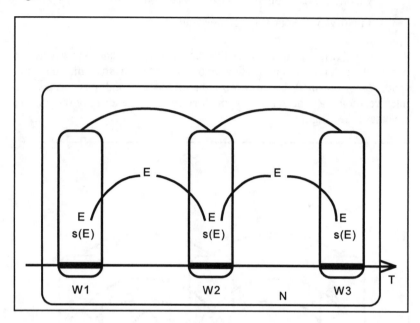

Figure 2. Example (13). The temporalized locative space N (Norway) now has the discontinuous temporal space (W1, W2 etc.) under its scope.

A fundamental factor in the temporalization of a nontemporal space seems to be the tense of the predicate verb. All the above examples with temporalized space-builders have been in the past tense, and indeed it is the case that present tense does not allow nontemporal space-builders to take on a similar temporal interpretation With the present tense, the temporal interpretation is possible only if the sentence is understood as a *generic* predication. Consider (14).

(14) Työmaa+lla   Liisa   riitelee pomo+n   kanssa.

    Worksite+ADE Liisa   argues   boss+GEN+3PX with

    'At the building site, Liisa argues with her boss'.

In 14, the condition that Liisa is at the building-site must be fulfilled for the predication to hold true. With the generic reading, this leads to a temporal interpretation 'Whenever Liisa is at the building-site, she argues with the boss'. Now it is the temporalized space that is discontinuous, in the sense of highlighting only the periods that Liisa spends at the building site. The example is diagramed in Figure 3.

3.2. Temporalization of a bound space

The temporalization of a bound space resembles that of autonomous spaces in all but one important aspect: since a bound space exists only when occupied by an entity, the duration of the containment relation is at the same time the duration of the space's existence. This difference is perhaps best visible in generic present-tense predications. This is illustrated in Figure 4, representing example 9 ('[When she is] drunk, Liisa argues with the boss').

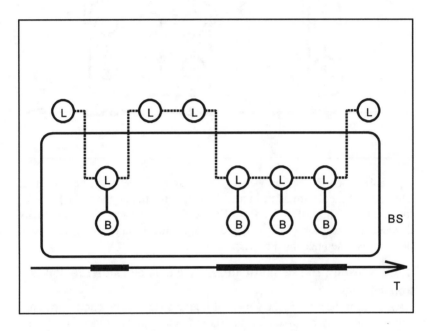

Figure 3. A generic predication with a temporal interpretation of a setting (14). BS = building-site, L = Liisa, B = boss. The predication 'Liisa argues with the boss' is subordinated to the condition of (Liisa's presence at) the building-site.

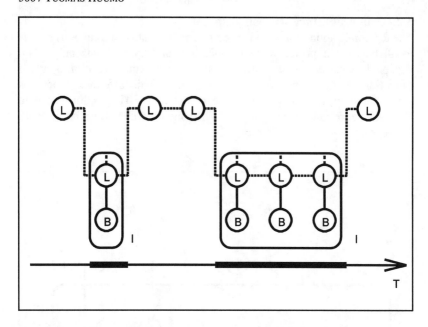

Figure 4. A bound space as a setting with a temporal-generic interpretation. The letter symbols are as in Figure 5, except for the domain I = [Liisa's] intoxication. The difference from Figure 5 is that space I is conceptually dependent on entity L (indicated by the dotted line leading from L to I), and only exists when occupied by L.

4. Conclusion: the semantic difference between starting points and settings

As argued in Section 3, the ability of bound spaces to function as settings can be explained by assuming that they have a double function: in their primary sense they are conceptually dependent on the subject and contain only the subject, but in their secondary sense they establish a temporal space, which functions as a frame for the entire process predicated in the clause nucleus. On the other hand, we saw in Section 2 that bound spaces are not allowed as starting points in locative reference-point constructions (examples 5-6). There thus remains one question to be answered: why cannot locative reference-points (6) be temporalized in the same way as settings (9-10) can?

A fundamental difference between a setting and a starting-point is that a setting contains an entire relation, with several participants interacting with one another, whereas a starting-point contains only one entity. The content of a setting is thus much more complex and variable than the content of a starting-point.[2] This in turn has the consequence that the content of a setting is a process that unfolds through time (as all processes do), but the content of a starting-point is not. We can thus argue that the setting of a process must always have a temporal extension (although it remains implicit in most cases): it is the setting at every moment of the process it contains. This can be neatly illustrated with settings that cover many processes indicated in a complex sentence (*In Norway, Elmer skied at weekends and worked on weekdays*).

In the locative reference-point construction, the duration of the spatial relationship cannot exceed the duration of the process denoted by the verb. The entity in the space is thus there only when participating in the process, and the outermost temporal extension of the whole predication is the time of the process indicated by the verb. In the reference-point construction, then, there is nothing to be placed under the temporal scope of the locative, and the construction provides no independently existing temporal expanse capable of serving as a setting within which a process can be manifested. This can be seen in the fact that settings, but not locative starting-points, can often be replaced with a temporal subordinated clause; e.g. *In England, Elmer fell in love with Lisa* => 'While in England...', but not *In the corner stood the grandfather clock* => '*While in the corner, the grandfather clock stood'.

References

Chafe, Wallace. 1994. *Discourse, Consciousness, and Time: The flow and displacement of conscious experience in speaking and writing*. University of Chicago Press.

Fauconnier, Gilles. 1994 [1985]. *Mental Spaces: Aspects of meaning construction in natural language*. Cambridge University Press.

Huumo, Tuomas. 1996a. "Bound spaces and the semantic interpretation of existentials". *Linguistics* 34 (2), p. 295-328.

----- 1996b. "A scoping hierarchy of locatives". *Cognitive Linguistics* 7 (3), p. 265-299.

Lakoff, George, and Mark Johnson. 1980. *Metaphors We Live By*. Chicago: University of Chicago Press.

Langacker, Ronald 1991. *Foundations of Cognitive Grammar vol. II: Descriptive Application*. Stanford University Press.

----- 1996. "Dynamic Conceptualization". Lecture given at the University of Helsinki, Finland, March 21, 1996.

---

[2] For the terminological distinction between settings and locations in Cognitive Grammar, see Langacker (1991: 300).

Reference Frames: An Application to Imparfait

HENGAMEH IRANDOUST

Université d'Orsay

1. Introduction

Since Partee (1973), the theory of temporal reference in linguistics is essentially based on the assumption that tense is an anaphoric category. The functioning of the French imperfective tense - *imparfait* (IMP) - at discourse level has supported this view in Discourse Representation Theory's (DRT) framework and the so-called anaphoric approach.

Kamp & Rohrer (1983) observe that an IMP sentence denotes a *state*-type predicate that includes the current reference point, previously introduced into discourse by a perfective tense (passé simple - PS or passé composé - PC) or a temporal clause / adverbial. The anaphoric relation between IMP and its antecedent is therefore that of temporal coreference. Thus, in the following example, s2 is interpreted as holding at the same time as the event of the first sentence:

(1)   Pierre entra dans la cuisine (e1=R). Marie faisait la vaisselle (R⊂s2).
      [*Pierre walked into the kitchen. Marie was washing the dishes.*]

Many authors have analyzed IMP as a typically anaphoric tense which always requires an explicit or implicit antecedent. Yet, different opinions have been put forward as to the status of the antecedent and the type of the anaphoric relation.

The point under discussion here is that IMP sentences do not carry a temporal inter-sentential relation, but convey a general interpretative instruction that must be accounted for within the limits of conceptual spaces that result from the episodic structure of texts.

2. Episodes and Reference Frames

As Ehrlich (1988) points out: «While specifying a sentence's truth conditions in terms of its relation to adjacent sentences, Kamp & Rohrer (1983) and Hinrichs (1986) implicitly assume that a discourse is constituted by an indifferentiated string of sentences.»

Obviously, a text is not a set of temporally ordered sentences that are processed sequentially, but a meaningful entity, the propositions of which are connected, explicitly or implicitly, into higher-order structural units intuitively known as *episodes*.

> « Roughly speaking, paragraphs or episodes are characterized as coherent sequence of sentences of a discourse, linguistically marked for a beginning and/or end, and further defined in terms of some kind of 'thematic unity' - for instance, in terms of identical participants, time location or global event or action.» (van Dijk 1982)

Given the episodic structure of narratives, not only must the content of each individual sentence be related to its neighbouring sentences, but it must also be subsumed at a higher level under a central predicate which accounts for the overall conceptual unity of the sequence. As Moens & Steedman (1988) have emphasized: « The episodic partition will quite incidentally define a partial temporal ordering on events, but the primary purpose of such sequences is more related to the notion of a plan of action or an explanation of an event's occurrence than to do anything with time itself.»

In our model, some aspects of which will be presented here, sentences are evaluated with respect to a *reference frame* (RF) which is the conceptual space-time of the events and objects depicted in an episodic sequence. We represent RF as a bipartite structure reflecting the spatial organization of the visual field into foreground (fg) and background (bg). The representation of RF here below shows a temporal-causal figure against a spatial ground:

RF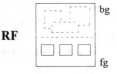

On the assumption that (i) text processing consists of organizing semantic information into macro-units at successively more inclusive levels (van Dijk 1980) and (ii) semantic units imply the construction of mental spaces (Fauconnier 1984), discourse interpretation is represented within this model as the construction of a hierarchical network of reference frames corresponding to different levels of description in a text.

Narratives are processed with respect to an evolving deictic center and therefore at each point a particular RF becomes the current focus space (marked by ⊕). The beginning of a new episode generates a new RF, moves the deictic center and thus modifies the focusing mechanisms. At this point, all the information relative to the previous episode is subsumed by a 'macro-proposition' and transferred to another level of cognitive processing. The formal and linguistic markers that establish a new reference frame are called 'introductors' (Fauconnier 1984).

We consider that in a minimal context, temporal resolution is constrained by our knowledge about situations (sit) - RF's elements - and the interpretative instructions carried by tense: identification, distribution and connexion of these elements within and across RFs. More generally, temporal interpretation can be defined within our framework as a dynamic process that involves immediate inferences as well as high-level operations relative to text macro-processing (see 3.3 and 4).

3. Imparfait: Temporal or Conceptual ?

In DRT's system and its extensions, the temporal referent of an IMP predicate is defined as a state. However, in (1), we perceive Mary's activity as a dynamic process. The [± dynamic] character of a situation is an intrinsic property of the situation itself and is not conveyed by tense. Moreover, contrary to English, Aktionsarten and grammatical aspect do not interact in French (Smith 1986). An IMP sentence can denote all type of situations: states, processes, actions or events.

In fact, IMP does not denote a stative situation but presents its referent as being a part of the global *state of affairs* that holds at a given point in the text. All events take place against a ground, explicit or not, and this is what IMP predicates give evidence for. In (1), Pierre's coming in (sit1) occurs in a wider world structure where other states and events hold or are in progress. One of these background elements, and probably the most relevant, is Mary's activity (sit2). Thus, the IMP sentence partially defines the PS event's underlying context and can therefore be considered as its spatial extension. This is the most classical use of IMP and results in a discourse relation which is generally called *Background*:

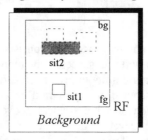

Background

It will be argued here that the reason for which IMP is considered as an anaphoric tense is that the situation it identifies must be integrated into an accessible RF. Consequently, the only conditions that constrain the use of IMP are its conceptual relevance to the foreground event and the whole episode for which it gives background information.

We will give evidence of this by comparing our definition of IMP with the one provided by the anaphoric accounts in the light of some problematic cases where (a) IMP is unacceptable even when coreference with a temporal antecedent is possible; (b) IMP is not coreferential with its antecedent; (c) no antecedents are available.

3.1 IMP ruled out despite a temporal antecedent

Let us examine the following examples:

(2)   Quand il ouvrit la porte de la cuisine, * elle grinçait. [*When he opened the kitchen's door, it creaked.*]

(3)   Il ouvrit la porte de la cuisine. Elle grinçait. [*He opened the kitchen's door. It creaked.*]

If the antecedent of IMP is the event time of the previous sentence, then why is it that IMP is ruled out in (2) where it is precisely this moment that has been emphasized?

The existence of a temporal anchoring point does not justify the use of IMP because IMP predicates do not refer to times but to frames. In constructions like (2), the when-clause provides a temporal frame for the event of the IMP clause. The latter can give a description of this frame by pointing out any of its elements. This excludes the door's creaking which is an effect or an aspect of the anchoring event itself. In (3), the first sentence does not establish a frame, but simply reports a fact. Thus, the IMP sentence characterizes the frame implied by the occurrence of the PS event.

The antecedent of IMP is therefore not a moment, but the global context that holds at that moment. This also explains why topicalized adverbials that emphasize the properties (length, endpoints) of a temporal interval are not allowed in IMP sequences:

(4)   Toute sa vie / pendant toute sa vie / dès le début de son règne et jusqu'à la fin, Napoléon *souffrait de maux d'estomac. (Anscombre 1992) [*All his life / during all his life / from beginning to end of his reign, Napoleon suffered from stomach aches.*]

The object IMP refers to is not a temporal entity, but a global context which may be temporally identified. The difference of acceptability between (4) and (5) hereafter:

(5)   En 1801, Napoléon souffrait de terribles maux d'estomac. [*In 1801, Napoleon suffered from awful stomach aches.*]

is that in (4), the antecedent specifies the temporal structure of an interval, while in (5), it simply localizes a frame in time. In the second case, the IMP predicate describes the conditions that held at the time specified by the adverbial and thus gives a global characterization of the RF corresponding to that temporal location. However, adverbials such as the ones in (4) would be felicitous when used to demarcate two periods within the same reference frame as in:

(6)   Pendant toute l'année, Napoléon voyageait, mais à Noël, il se reposait. [*During the whole year, Napoleon travelled, but at Christmas, he rested.*]

Also, the identification of a frame is not a sufficient condition for the use of IMP if its predicate cannot be interpreted as a significant property of such a frame. Example (7) below is ruled out because of the disproportion between the temporal dimensions of the antecedent-frame and the single event of getting married:

(7)   L'année dernière, *Jean se mariait. (Ducrot 1979) [*Last year, Jean got married.*]

An IMP predicate must be able to partially 'cover' the background space of the RF to which it is related. This is why in cases like (5) or (6) the combination adverb + IMP results in an iterative effect. Generally speaking, the IMP/RF part-whole relation is acceptable when the IMP element is understood in the context as a characteristic feature of the frame in question.

In all cases, it is always the entire frame and not its temporal coordinates that functions as the antecedent of IMP. An IMP predicate does not *refer* to a given temporal moment, but presents its content as a property of the context that pertains at that moment.

3.2 Non coreferential IMP

In the following examples, the IMP situations are not coreferential with their antecedents:

(8)   Jean attrapa une contravention (sit1). Il roulait trop vite (sit2). (Molendijk 1993) [*Jean got a ticket. He drove too fast.*]

(9)   Jameson éteignit la lumière (sit1). Il faisait nuit noire car les volets étaient fermés (sit2). (Hinrichs 1986) [*Jameson switched off the light. It was pitch dark around him because the blinds were closed.*]

Clearly, we cannot make the necessary inferences about temporal relations solely on the basis of linguistic information, as it had been suggested in DRT's framework. One of the alternatives to the anaphoric approach is the Segmented Discourse Representation Theory (SDRT) which favors an important role for pragmatics. Lascarides and Asher (1993) claim that temporal relations are resolved as a by-product of reasoning about *coherence relations* that can be derived by means of world knowledge. In (8) and (9), the relations that hold between the two utterances would be *Explanation* and *Result* which entail two different temporal relations: sit2 < sit1 and sit1 < sit2.

But although we need to exploit real knowledge for temporal interpretation, we still have to account for the factors that determine the choice of tense. Within SDRT's system, not only does the treatment of tense as an anaphoric category become unnecessary, but, by avoiding this problem, we also do away with one of DRT's major concerns, that is explaining the contribution of tense to discourse representation.

Vet (1992) and Molendijk (1993) maintain the coreference constraint and argue that the temporal simultaneity expressed by IMP does not only apply to the time of the previous event but sometimes to a temporal interval that has either been presupposed or implied by it. This of course covers all the possible temporal relations encountered in PS / IMP sequences, but does not explain why temporal simultaneity between (sit2) and the interval presupposed by (sit1), as suggested by Molendijk (1993), allows (8) but not (10):

(10)   Jean attrapa une contravention (sit1). * Il roulait avec plaisir (sit2).

        (Berthonneau & Kleiber 1993) [*Jean got a ticket. He drove with pleasure.*]

Berthonneau & Kleiber (1993) propose a new anaphoric solution according to which an IMP sentence presents its denoted state or event as a « part » of a past situation viewed as a whole. Thus, in (8), the IMP predicate describes an element, the cause in this case, of the global situation described by sit1: the reporting of an offence. While driving too fast seems to be a good reason for getting a ticket, driving with pleasure is not.

Molendijk (1996) integrates these general coherence principles into his rules and argues that the temporal simultaneity condition must be preserved given that (11) is unacceptable although a causal relation can be observed:

(11)   Jean attrapa une contravention (sit1). * Il brûlait un feu rouge (sit2). [*Jean got a ticket. He went through a red light.*]

But Molendijk's solution is problematic in that it explains the unacceptability of these sequences by the absence of coherence relation sometimes between IMP and its textual antecedent (sit1), as in (10), and sometimes between IMP and its temporal antecedent (the interval presupposed by sit1), as in (11).

Nevertheless, it is a fact that the use of IMP cannot be accounted for only in terms of conceptual relations even when they are specific enough as in Berthonneau & Kleiber's account. As to SDRT, although the right temporal ordering of events can be predicted, not only does the case of (11) remain unresolved, but we also fail to explain why the *Explanation* relation can be successfully derived in both (8) and (11) with a different sequence of tense:

(12)   a. Jean a attrapé une contravention (sit1). Il a roulé trop vite. / Il a brûlé un feu rouge (sit2). [*Jean got a ticket. He drived too fast. / He went through a red light.*]

b. Jean a attrapé une contravention (sit1). Il avait roulé trop vite. / Il avait brûlé un feu rouge (sit2). [*Jean got a ticket. He had driven too fast. / He had gone through a red light.*]

The fact is that these discourse relations are *co-determined* by tense and must therefore be defined in terms of specific configurations of conceptual spaces. An IMP situation is always a background element that can potentially characterize the global context that holds at a given point in the text. As we saw in the previous section, the single event of going through a red light (example 11) cannot be considered as a characteristic feature of the RF which preceded the one introduced by the PS event.

For Blakemore (1987), consequence can either refer to a causal effect or to a logical conclusion. The explanation relation expressed by a PS or PC / IMP sequence is always of the second type, that is an inferential relation of premise and conclusion. The only acceptable causal schemata, as in (8), are those in which the IMP proposition describes the *conditions* that led to the occurrence of the foreground event.

In (8), the IMP sentence presents the causal element as a property of an implicit RF which in an earlier episode gave ground for the event of getting a ticket (fig. 1). The situation is quite different in (12a) where sit2 is interpreted as a punctual occurrence which immediately entails sit1.

This causal effect relation is viewed as holding within the same reference frame (fig. 2). In (12b), the pluperfect predicate (plus-que-parfait - PQP) refers to an earlier episode in the same way as IMP, but unlike the latter, the PQP element is viewed as an occurrence whose resulting state underlies the PC event observed in the current RF. This relation is generally called Flashback (fig. 3). These different configurations can be represented as follows:

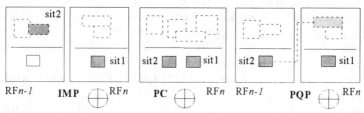

RF*n-1*   **IMP** RF*n*   **PC** RF*n*   RF*n-1*   **PQP** RF*n*

Fig. 1: Logical Conclusion   Fig. 2: Causal Effect   Fig. 3: Flashback

Let us now reexamine (10). Our knowledge frames which lead to the inference of a causal relation in (8) and (11), preclude the possibility that driving with pleasure be a reason for getting a ticket. This does not imply the incoherence of the sequence by itself since some other discourse relation may hold between the two utterances. Yet, it is the impossibility to recover a causal link that rules out (10).

An event such as getting a ticket has an incidental character and can raise implicit questions that are expected to be answered in the following propositions. By using IMP in the second part of the utterance, the subject conveys his intention of describing the circumstances that held before, during or after the event of getting a ticket. But the situation *driving with pleasure*, which most probably refers to the previous frame, is not a relevant context description. The inferential computations the hearer performs are based on his knowledge of situations as well as the relational instructions conveyed by tense. We expect an *Explanation* relation because IMP provides background information.

The *Result* relation in (9) where IMP is used to depict a state that follows the occurrence of a PS event, is still more restrictive. The presence of a transitional event cannot justify the use of IMP by itself, as the following example shows:

(13)   Paul tomba de la falaise. * On le ramassait avec les deux jambes fracturées.
(Berthonneau & Kleiber 1993) [*Paul fell off the cliff. He was picked up with two fractured legs.*]

In fact, in sequences like (9), IMP does not express a consequence as we understand it in causal relations. It rather depicts a new state of affairs as perceived by one of the characters of the story. The IMP situation in (9) is oriented by Jameson's point of view and is understood as a representation of his consciousness.

Ehrlich (1988) shows that the cohesive device of referential linking is at least one means by which the continuation of a particular episode or, in this context, a particular character's RST (Represented Speech and Thought) is signalled. Example (13) is ruled out because this type of construction requires that the IMP sentence refer to a dominant NP of the first sentence. In (9), this condition is fulfilled and the IMP sentence presents its situation as an element of the reality space (R) of the first proposition's agent (a1):

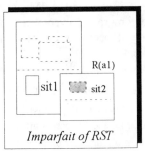

Imparfait of RST

Such reality spaces are represented in auxiliary RFs and are considered to be an integral part of the main episode, the RF of which is currently focused.

3.3 IMP without an antecedent

It is very frequent to find IMP right in the beginning of a story, which seriously compromises the anaphoric thesis:

(14)   Nous étions à l'étude quand le proviseur entra, suivi d'un nouveau habillé en bourgeois et d'un garçon de classe qui portait un grand pupitre. (Flaubert, Madame Bovary) [*We were in the study room when the principal entered, followed by a new student dressed like a bourgeois and an attendant who carried a big desk.*]

Kamp & Rohrer (1983) explain the use of IMP in (14) as a stylistic device «which exploits the presupposition that the reader should already have a temporal reference point to which the event or state presented by the sentence can be anchored.»

Our intuition is, and literary theoricians (Hamburger 1986, Vuillaume 1990) seem to agree, that we do not relate narrated events to any previously identified moment. We rather project ourselves in an imaginary space-time that is completely disconnected from our self-centered world. For the reader, the narrative universe is not parallel to the real one, but becomes, in the process of reading, *the* reality.

The only presupposition the author may have concerns our familiarity with the conventional structure of stories. Kintsch (1979) argues that story comprehension involves a 'schema-based inference' in which readers expect a narrative superstructure. More specifically, text information is hierarchically organized by topic function into macro-propositions that are used to fill in empty 'slots' corresponding to macro-categories such as, exposition, complication, resolution, etc.

All stories comprise a setting description that establishes the initial frame against which a temporal-causal figure is shown. In (14), it is this 'expected', but not yet specified RF, that IMP characterizes. In fact, pragmatically speaking, it is always the IMP sentences that provide an anchoring point for the foreground events and not the contrary, but of course background material becomes relevant only in relation with a significant foreground event.

The following passage is a more detailed setting description:

(15) D'une longue planche posée sur le tronc d'un chêne, Delphine et Marinette avaient fait une balançoire. Quand l'une touchait la terre, l'autre se trouvait si haut perchée que le monde lui paraissait bien plus grand. Marinette ne pouvait pas s'empêcher d'avoir peur un peu. Elle riait quand même, et avec la main, elle faisait des signes à une petite poule blanche qui la regardait depuis le seuil du poulailler. (Marcel Aymé, Les Contes du Chat Perché) [*Delphine and Marinette had made a swing from a plank and the trunk of an oak tree. When one of them touched the ground, the other one went so high up that the world seemed much bigger to her. Marinette could not help being scared a little. Still she laughed and made signs to a small white hen who watched her from the poultry.*]

Once again, there are no temporal anchoring points for the IMP occurrences. The pluperfect is considered to be anaphoric itself and is therefore ruled out as a possible antecedent. On the other hand, as we can notice, all of the IMP predicates are action descriptions and cannot be assimilated to states even though they cannot be sequentially ordered in time. The relation that holds between these situations is some kind of spatial parallelism. Each of the IMP elements stands in a part-whole relation with the story's initial RF which is built and extended by means of a metonymical process.

We can conclude that IMP situations are descriptive elements that convey information about the spatial ground of an accessible RF. The latter may be explicitly identified by an adverbial expression, merely implied by the occurrence of a foreground event, or inferred on the basis of text knowledge.

4. Imparfait de Rupture

Contrary to descriptive IMP, *imparfait de rupture* (IR) presents its predicate as achieved and therefore moves narrative time forward:

(16) Je me secouai, outré de colère contre lui, et je répondis sèchement: «Je vous remercie, mais je crois que j'ai déjà assez voyagé ; il faut maintenant que je rentre en France». Le surlendemain, je *prenais* le bateau pour Marseille. (Sartre, La Nausée) [*I shook myself up, madly angry at him, and answered: «Thank you but I think I have done enough travelling; I have to go back to France now». Two days later, I took the boat for Marseilles.*]

Our view is that, imparfait de rupture, as its name suggests, is a stylistic device by which the narrator creates an episode juncture. IMP and IR respectively characterize a « given » and a « new » RF. While IMP propositions provide background information for the current episode and are integrated into an already salient RF, IR propositions close the current episode, yield a new RF and thus provoke a focus shift. Since IMP sentences cannot trigger temporal movement by themselves, the juncture is marked on the text surface by a discontinuity in time.

It has been argued (Ducrot 1979, Tasmowski 1985) that the use of IR is crucially dependent on an adverbial that not only introduces a new reference point in discourse and thus provides IR with a temporal anchoring point, but also functions as the topic of the sentence. It seems, however, that the role of this temporal expression is above all to signal a new significant moment in the main line of the story. By using IR in (16), the narrator does not characterize the time 'two days later', but tells us that from that point on, the course of events took a new turn. The departure, whose temporal location happens to be 'two days later', prompts a new frame for the episode which will take place in France.

The topical function of the adverb is not due to its position, but lies in its ability to introduce a reference frame for the development of a new discourse segment. In other words, IR's textual antecedent is always an introductor.

The technique used in (16) can be called a 'macromove' since it explicitly introduces a new temporal frame and reinitializes the episodic memory. But IR can mark the transition in a more subtle way, as in:

(17) Une nouvelle affaire ? demanda sa femme. Un crime semble-t-il, avenue du Parc Montsouris.

Il *enroulait* la grosse écharpe autour de son cou, *endossait* son pardessus, *saisissait* son chapeau. (Simenon, Maigret et l'Affaire Nahour)

[- *A new case ? his wife asked. It seems to be a crime, Parc Montsouris*

> *avenue.*
>
> *He rolled his big scarf around his neck, put on his overcoat, took his hat.*]

The construction of a reference point, as Tasmowski admits, becomes a little far-fetched for such IR sequences in which no adverbials are mentioned. In fact, the paragraph break, which is one of the basic introductors, creates the temporal discontinuity necessary for the use of IR. In (17), the IR occurrences depict the tense atmosphere that precedes Maigret's investigation.

The difficulty raised by IR sentences is that they denote single occurrences that can always be replaced with simple pasts. Yet, the same sentences conjugated with PS would be interpreted as a simple sequence of actions. By using IR, the narrator does not mean to report an event chronology, but to communicate, beyond the temporal dimension, the underlying narrative structure. The combination 'introductor + IR', as illustrated by (16) and (17), is a linguistic cue which clearly indicates to the reader that he has reached the complication[1] of the story, and that he must therefore discard the previous RF and generate a new one.

Although IR occurrences create time movement, they do not have the status of foreground events. Rather than the facts themselves, the narrator expresses their consequences, that is the atmosphere they create or the new circumstances to which they lead. In fact, the introductor and the event-type predicate make the new reference frame accessible, but then IMP relegates this event to the background and presents it as a property of the frame. This configuration can be represented as follows:

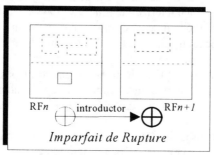

---

[1] IR can also signal the resolution, as in:

Dès le lendemain, on *s'occupait* à faire venir une nouvelle pompe à incendie. (André Dhôtel, Le pays où l'on arrive jamais) [*The next day, we got busy bringing in a new fire engine.*]

or both the complication and the resolution:

Comme elle avait été à l'Opéra, une nuit d'hiver, elle rentra toute frisonnante de froid. Le lendemain, elle *toussait.* Huit jours plus tard, elle *mourait* d'une fluxion de poitrine. (Maupassant, Les Bijoux) [*Since she had been to the Opera by a winter night, she came back shivering from cold. The next day, she coughed. Eight days later, she died of pneumonia.*]

Clearly, IR does not have an inter-sentential function. It is used to delimit two macro-categories. This specific use of imparfait shows the best why temporal interpretation must be sensitive to the episodic partition and the macro-processing of narratives.

5. Conclusion

Through the analysis of imparfait, we have attempted to show that the episodic structure of texts involves the construction of reference frames and that tense conveys specific instructions for the configuration of such reference frames.

We accounted for the different discourse relations observed in IMP sequences by reasoning in terms of conceptual spaces and compared our results with the ones provided by the anaphoric approach. Our conclusion is that an IMP situation characterizes the reference frame that is present in the reader / hearer's episodic memory and must therefore be viewed as a property of the global context that pertains at a given point in the text.

References

Anscombre, J.-C. 1992. Imparfait et Passé Composé : Des Forts en Thème et Propos. *L'Information Grammaticale 55*: 43-53.

Berthonneau, A.-M. & G. Kleiber. 1993. Pour une Nouvelle Approche de l'Imparfait: L'Imparfait un Temps Anaphorique Méronomique. *Langages 112*: 55-73.

Blakemore, D. 1987. *Semantic Constraints on Relevance*. Oxford: Blackwell.

van Dijk, T.A. 1980. *Macrostructures. An Interdisciplinary Study of Global Structures in Discourse, Interaction and Cognition*, Hillsdale: Erlbaum.

van Dijk, T.A. 1982. Episodes as units of Discourse Analysis, in D. Tannen, ed., *Analyzing Discourse: Text and Talk*. Washington: Georgetown University Press.

Ducrot, O. 1979. L'Imparfait en français. *Linguistische Berichte 60*: 1-23.

Ehrlich, S. 1988. Referential Linking and Tense. *Journal of Pragmatics 14*: 57-75.

Fauconnier, G. 1984. Espaces Mentaux: Aspects de la construction de sens dans les langues naturelles. Paris: Editions de Minuit.

Hamburger, K. 1986. *Logique des Genres Littéraires*. Paris: Seuil.

Hinrichs, E. 1986. Temporal Anaphora in Discourses of English. *Linguistics and Philosophy 9*: 63-82.

Kamp, H. and C. Rohrer. 1983. Tense in Texts, in R. Bäuerle, R. Schwarze, and A. von Stechow, eds., *Meaning, Use and Interpretation of Language*. Berlin: de Gruyter, 250-269.

Kintsch, W. 1979. On Comprehending Stories, in M.A. Just and P.A. Carpenter, eds., *Cognitive Processes in Comprehension*. Hillsdale, N.J., Erlbaum, 33-62.

Lascarides, A. and N. Asher. 1993. Temporal Interpretation, Discourse Relations, and Common Sense Entailment. *Linguistics and Philosophy* 13: 179-206.

Moens, M. and M. Steedman. 1988. Temporal Ontology and Temporal Reference. *Computational Linguistics 14.2*: 15-28.

Molendijk, A. 1993. Présuppositions, Implications, Structure Temporelle, in C. Vetters, ed., *Le Temps de la Phrase au Texte*. Lille: Presses Universitaires de Lille, 167-191.

Molendijk, A. 1996. Anaphore et Imparfait: La Référence Globale à des Situations Présupposées ou Impliquées. *Chronos 1, Actes du Colloque Anaphore et (In)cohérence*, Anvers, 109-123.

Partee, B.H. 1973. Some Structural Analogies Between Tenses and Pronouns in English. *Journal of Philosophy 70*: 601-609.

Smith, C. 1986. A Speaker-Based Approach to Aspect. *Linguistics and Philosophy* 9: 97-115.

Tasmowski-de Ryck, L. 1985. L'Imparfait Avec et Sans Rupture. *Langue Française 67*: 59-77.

Vet, C. 1992. The Temporal Structure of Discourse: Setting, Change and Perspective, in S. Fleischman and L.R. Waugh, eds., *Discourse Pragmatics and the Verb. The Evidence from Romance*. London, N.Y.: Routledge, 7-25.

Vuillaume, M. 1990. *Grammaire Temporelle des Récits*. Paris: Edition de Minuit.

Viewpoint Shifts in Narrative

ILANA MUSHIN

State University of New York at Buffalo

1. Introduction

This paper is an examination of one particular mode of viewpoint representation in narrative - the representation of speech as direct speech - and how it should be modeled in a cognitive account of narrative structure.[1]

Theories of narrative structure in linguistics and psychology have been concerned primarily with the organization of narrative in terms of its temporal structure or plot structure (see for example, Labov 1972, Polanyi 1989 in linguistics; Rumelhart 1975, Mandler & Johnson 1980 in psychology; Genette 1980, Prince 1982 in Narratology). Recently, however, there has been an increasing interest in the development of theories which can account for patterns of viewpoint and shifts in point of view in narrative (Sanders 1994, Cutrer 1994 in mental space theory; Duchan et al 1995 in deictic shift theory).

In 1.1 I present a general characterization of 'narrative viewpoint' and discuss where direct speech (DS) fits into this larger frame. Section 1.2

---

[1] This paper developed out of many fruitful discussions with Gilles Fauconnier and David Zubin. I would like to thank them both for their input and advice. Thanks also to Jean-Pierre Koenig, Wendy Baldwin and the anonymous reviewer for comments on various earlier drafts.

gives a brief description of a representation for DS in narrative that has been proposed using Fauconnier's (1994 and elsewhere) mental space approach. In section 2 I present some data from actual narrative texts which provides evidence for the need to modify the existing mental space representation, if it is to successfully represent narrative viewpoint structure in a cognitive model. Section 3 is my proposal for a revision of the existing mental space representation of viewpoint spaces from a linear to a multidimensional representation.

1.1 A Characterization of Narrative Viewpoint

Narrative viewpoint involves the degree to which parts of the story are represented as 'objective' descriptions of the things and events in the storyworld, or as 'subjective' thoughts, perceptions and words of the characters in the story.[2]

Subjectivity is a gradient notion which can be characterized along two axes. First there is the issue of *domain*, which asks whether the information in question can be potentially known to anyone in the storyworld, or only known to a particular character in the story. Information that can be known or witnessed by anyone is information in the *public* domain. Thoughts and perceptions of characters in the story are in the *private* domain. *Private* information is more subjective than *public* information.

The other dimension, relevant to the notion of subjectivity in discourse, is *origin of information*. Information that is deictically centered with one of the story characters is more subjective than information that is deictically centered elsewhere. According to this characterization, the most subjective information will be private information deictically centered with one of the characters in the story.

Narrative information can be represented as expressing differing degrees of subjectivity and thus different viewpoints. (1) - (3) are some examples from the corpus used for this study (Macedonian - South Slavic).

---

[2] See Wiebe (1990) for a similar approach to the notion of subjectivity in narrative discourse

(1) 2ab:

I	nevestata	nekako	i	padna	kako	krivo,	kako
and	*bride*	*somehow*	*3DAT*	*feel*	*how*	*crooked*	*how*

uvreda.	Zoshto	lebot	da	i	se	napraj	taka
upset	*why*	*bread*	*to*	*3DAT*	*REFL*	*make(D)*[3]	*like. that*

'And the bride somehow feeels frustrated and upset. Why did her bread turn out like that?'

(1) is an example of represented thought. The question '*Why did her bread turn out like that?*' is interpreted as what the bride was thinking as she was feeling frustrated and upset. The information is in a *private* domain since only that character has access to the information in the storyworld. Furthermore the information is deictically centered with the character whose thoughts are being represented. This mode is thus subjective in terms of domain and origin of information.

(2) 3bc:

Bila	nekoja	nevesta	mlada.	Mesila	leb.	Svekrvata	poshla	na
be(I)	*some*	*bride*	*young*	*knead(I)*	*bread*	*M-in-law*	*go(I)*	*LOC*

pazar.
market

'There was a young bride. She had kneaded some bread. The mother-in-law had gone to market.'

(2) is an example of 'narration'. The information that there was a bride, she had kneaded some bread and that her mother-in-law had gone to the market, is in a *public* domain, since anyone who is present at that time and place in the storyworld could have knowledge of such information. In terms of origin, the information is not deictically centered at a particular character, nor at a particular vantage point within the storyworld. Narration is thus 'objective' in terms of domain and origin of information.

---

[3] There is a contrast in past tense forms in Macedonian. (D)efinite past in used when speakers are able to 'confirm' the event described by the proposition. (I)ndefinite past is used when speakers are not necessarily able to 'confirm' the event described in the proposition. See Friedman (1986) and elsewhere for a more thorough treatment of this important contrast in Macedonian.

(3) 1bc:

I	mu	rekla,	"Mamo,	mene	lebot	ne	mi	se,
and	*3DAT*	*say(I)*	*mother*	*1DAT*	*bread*	*NEG*	*1DAT*	*REFL*

ne	se	pogodi.	Se	napraje	kako	zhila."
NEG	*REFL*	*make.well(D)*	*REFL*	*make(D)*	*how*	*sinew*

'And she said to her, "Mother, my bread did not work out for me. It turned out like sinew."'

(3) is an example of DS. The information in quotation marks is interpreted as what this character in the story said at a specific time in the story, as she said it in the storyworld. The first clause of the passage introduces the speech event and designates the reported speaker.

The information in DS is in the *public* domain, since anyone at that time and place in the story has access to the information by virtue of hearing it. In this sense, DS is an 'objective' representation. However, the content of speech in DS is deictically centered with the reported speaker, a specific character in the story world. In this sense, DS is a 'subjective' representation.

Table 1 summarizes the characterization of the different modes in terms of subjectivity.

Table 1: Modes of Viewpoint Representation

MODE	DOMAIN	ORIGIN
Represented Thought	private	character
Narration	public	not character
Direct Speech	public	character

The representation of DS in general theories of narrative structure has been problematic, since as I have shown here, DS can be characterized as both objective and subjective. Labov (1972) does not even attempt to represent DS, but simply characterized it as 'evaluation' (anything that does not advance the narrative, nor is an 'objective' description of the storyworld). Polanyi (1989), who continues along Labovian lines, suggests that the matrix clause be represented on the narrative timeline (as 'advancing' the narrative), but that the content of speech should not be connected. Under this interpretation, the matrix clause is a separate type of structure from the content.

One of the aims of this paper is to present evidence that shows that the matrix clause and content of speech need not be separated in this way - that both form part of a unified DS structure and that both need to be incorporated into the 'narrative timeline'.

1.2 DS Representation in Mental Space Theory

The issues discussed in this paper build on some existing analyses of viewpoint in narrative which are based in Fauconnier's (1985) mental space theory.

The mental space approach has proven useful for representations of discourse which seek to include the dimension of narrative viewpoint. The theory is designed to be able to track propositional information through different belief spaces and so represent how information is distributed through different viewpoints. It is a useful approach for the purpose of representing what is public and what is private in the discourse world. The approach can also be used to represent information in terms of its deictic orientation. Sanders (1994) uses this approach to distinguish differences in use of epistemic modals in narrative. Cutrer (1994) applies the mental space framework to tense and tense sequences.

Cutrer (1994) also discussed the representation of speech in narrative. Figure 1 is her proposal for the general representation of a DS passage:

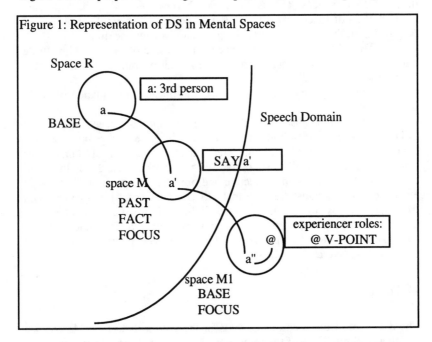

Figure 1: Representation of DS in Mental Spaces

Space R

a: 3rd person

BASE

a

Speech Domain

SAY a'

space M a'

PAST
FACT
FOCUS

experiencer roles:
@ V-POINT

@

a"

space M1
BASE
FOCUS

Each space represents the propositional content of some narrative information which has a particular 'profile', indicated with primitives like BASE, VIEWPOINT, FACT, PAST, FOCUS. BASE spaces are those which code particular deictic centers. The deixis of spaces which are directly connected to a BASE space are interpreted relative to that BASE, and no other.

According to Cutrer, verbs of saying in DS open up a 'speech domain', the first space of which is a new BASE. In figure 1, space R represents the deictic center of 'narration' (with no propositional content). Space M is the matrix clause of DS which contains the predicate SAY which opens up the speech domain and establishes the new BASE space at space M1. The 'a' represents the referent who is the reported speaker, who is third person outside of the speech domain. The connection of 'a' with '@' in space M1 signals that the referent of 'a' is now the deictic center for that speech domain.

While Cutrer's mental space based approach to narrative representation is concerned with the representation of viewpoint and viewpoint shift - an improvement over frameworks that are only concerned with temporal structure - for the purposes of representing the viewpoint structure of DS in narrative it is limited in the following ways:

a) DS is characterized as a *linear shift* in domains, as marked by the different BASE spaces. The use of a speech verb means that the following configuration of spaces *shifts* to a different domain. The implication is that only one narrative viewpoint can be represented at any one time.

b) The discourse is represented at a 'micro' level with little consideration given to 'macro' structures like the overall temporal structure or rhetorical structure.[4]

The main concern of this paper is a) - the linear representation of shifts in viewpoint.

As I showed in subsection 1.1, the representation of speech in narrative as DS encodes aspects of both subjective and objective viewpoints, but this conclusion was reached without reference to any actual discourse. The obvious question at this stage is "what evidence is there that DS conceptually encodes both subjective and objective information?" or "what evidence is there against the view that DS codes a linear shift in viewpoint from matrix clause to content of speech?" In the following section I present some data which supports the hypothesis that DS is understood as simultaneously representing more than one viewpoint in terms of conceptual structure.

2) The Data

The data come from a corpus of texts in the Bitola dialect of Macedonian which are all retellings of the same story. The original story was a personal account of what happened to the narrator when she was first married and living with her husband's family in rural Macedonia. Her mother-in-law told

---

[4] It was not Cutrer's aim, however, to represent discourse at a macro level.

her to bake some bread and it turned out badly and the narrator was worried about the mother-in-law's reaction (Mothers-in-law are notorious in traditional Macedonian society). Contrary to the narrator's expectations, the mother-in-law was nice about it. This story was recorded and played to different women who were asked to retell the story to other women who were then asked to retell the story to another set of women. Thus some of my texts are retellings of the story constructed from hearing the original version and some of my texts are versions constructed from hearing a retold version.

The advantage of this type of corpus is that it is possible to compare information in one version of the story and how it was linguistically manifested, with the manifestation of that information in the reconstructed version. It is thus possible to compare variations in the representation of information in terms of viewpoint representation.

In the following subsections I present two types of evidence from the use of DS in the corpus for the representation of DS as a simuleneity of different viewpoints: the retelling of direct speech as a narrative event (2.1) and the properties of matrix clauses of DS (2.2).

2.1 DS as Narrative Event.

A comparison of information coded as DS in one version with subsequent versions shows that DS is often retold as an 'objective' narrative event which incorporates information from the 'subjective' content of speech into the objective structure. (4) and (5) are examples of this phenomenon:

(4) VS:

I	**reche**	"Nevesto	lebot	da	go	mesish	Da	go	naprajsh
and	*said(D)*	*bride*	*bread*	*to*	*3m*	*knead*	*to*	*3m*	*make*

Opechete	go	so	svekorot	Eve	i	Verka	e	doma
cook	*3m*	*with*	*F-in-law*	*Here*	*also*	*Verka*	*be*	*home*

Sve	napraj	gotovo	da	bide	Znajsh	ti	kako"
evrythng	*make*	*ready*	*to*	*be*	*know*	*2sg*	*how*

'... and said, "Bride, knead the bread to make it. Cook it with the father-in-law. Verka is also at home. Make everything to be ready. You know how."'

is retold as

(4')1ab:

I	sega	svekra	mu	mu	objasnuva	kako	se	mesi
and	*now*	*M-in-law*	*3DAT*	*3DAT*	*explain*	*how*	*REFL*	*knead*

leb.	Ili	mu	reche	da	mesi	leb
bread	*or*	*3DAT*	*say*	*to*	*knead*	*bread*

'And now her mother-in-law is explaining to her how bread is kneaded. Or (rather) she told her to knead bread.'

and

(4'') 2ab:

E	natalala	svekrvata	da	mesi	leb.
3sg	*compel(I)*	*M-in-law*	*to*	*knead*	*bread*

'The mother-in-law compelled her to knead bread.'

(5) VS:

Dobro	**Rekov**	Majko
good	*say(D)*	*mother*

'"OK", I said, "Mother."'

is retold as

(5') 1ab:

I	ovaa	snaata	zedi	da	mesi	leb.
And	*this*	*D-in-law*	*take*	*to*	*knead*	*bread*

'And this daughter-in-law takes to kneading bread.'

and

(5'') 2ab:

Ovaa	nevestata	zela	leb	da	mesi
this	*bride*	*take(I)*	*bread*	*to*	*knead*

'This bride took on the task of kneading bread.'

The retold narrative event may express that there was a speech event in the previous telling, as in (4), or it may express some inference concerning the actions of the story character, given what she said, as in (5). where the Bride's affirmation of the Mother-in-law's instructions implies that she took on the tasks that the Mother-in-law had given to her. So retelling information coded as DS in one version as a narrative event in the next version amalgamates the information in the matrix and in the content of speech. This is evidence that it is not the case that DS is interpreted as a speech event in the narrative by virtue of the matrix clause alone as is assumed in Labovian analyses.

The evidence from story retelling also highlights the need to represent DS as a unified structure which is an 'objective' event in the narrative but which 'subjectively' emanates from a particular story character. This differs however from the current mental space approach which separates DS into matrix and content on the basis of their deictic differences and represents DS as a shift between viewpoints.

2.2 Matrix Clauses

Evidence for a parallel rather than linear representation of narrative viewpoints in DS comes from the distribution of matrix clauses.

Most discussions on the representation of speech in discourse assume a fixed DS structure where the matrix clause 'introduces' the content of speech (e.g.. Banfield 1982, Coulmas 1986). This assumption strengthens the view that DS codes a shift in viewpoints which is marked by the matrix clause and that it is the matrix clause that 'connects' the whole DS structure to the narrative sequence.

The problem is that in actual discourse there is considerable variation in the position and use of DS. (6) - (8) are some examples which show the considerable variation in position and frequency of matrix clauses in my corpus.

(6) 1ab:

Snaata   **mu**   **veli** "Lebot   majko   ne   mi   se   pogodi.
D-in-law   *3DAT*   *say*   *bread*   *mother*   *NEG*   *1DAT*   *REFL*   *make.well(D)*

Nekako   zhilosan   mi   e"
somehow   *veiny*   *1DAT*   *be*

I   **ovaa svekrvata**   **mu**   **veli** "Ako   Snao   ako   e   zhilosan"
and DEM   M-in-law   *3DAT   say*   *EXCL D-in-law*   *if*   *be*   *veiny*

'**The daughter-in-law says to her**, "The bread, mother, did not work out for me. For me it is somehow vein-like." **And this mother-in-law says to her**, "It doesn't matter, Daughter-in-law, if it's veiny."'

(6) represents the prototypical case where each DS passage is introduced with a matrix clause that identifies the reported speaker.

(7) 3ab:

I	koga	si	doshla	svekrvata
and	*when*	*REFL*	*come(I)*	*M-in-law*

"Shto	naprajvte	go	mesivte	lebot"
what	*make(D)*	*3m*	*knead(D)*	*bread*

'And when the mother-in-law returned, "What have you two done? Did you knead the bread?"'

(7) is an example of a DS passage that did not have a matrix clause at all. Clearly the shift in deixis, voice quality and the context are enough to code a chunk of discourse as DS. Note however that even without the matrix clause, the DS passage is still interpretable as an observable event in the storyworld.

(8) 2bc:

I	sega	sednuvale	go	gleda	lebot.	**Mu**	**veli**	**na**	**nevestava,**
and now		*sit(I)*	*3m*	*look.at*	*bread*	*3DAT*	*say*	*LOC*	*bride*

Ne	sakala	da	e	navredi.	**Mu**	**veli,**	"Mnogu	ubav"
NEGwant(I)		*to*	*be*	*upset*	*3DAT*	*say*	*very*	*good*

Nekoja	dobra	bila"	Mnogu ubav	lebot"	**reche,**	"Nevesto"
someone good		*be(I)*	*very good*	*bread*	*say(D)*	*bride(VOC)*

I	"Za	potamu"	**reche,**	"Ushte	poubav	kje	go
and	*BEN*	*later*	*say(D)*	*still*	*better*	*will*	*3m*

naprajsh.	Kje	mesish"	**mu**	**veli.**
make(2sg)	*will*	*bake(2sg)*	*3DAT*	*say*

'And now as they were about to sit down, she looks at the bread. **She says to the bride,** (She didn't want her to be upset) **She says to her,** "Very nice." She was a good woman. "Very nice bread," **she said,** "Bride." **And** "Later on," **she said,** "You will make it even better. You will bake," **She says to her.**'

(8) is an extreme example that shows that there is no real syntactic restriction on the occurrence of the matrix clause - it may occur anywhere within and around the content of speech. The significance of (8) is that despite the occurrence of more than one matrix clause, the content of speech is conceptually a single event in the narrative. It is not interpreted as four

or five separate speech events, as is indirectly suggested by linear representations of DS in discourse.[5]

There is clearly more to the story of matrix clauses than there is space to discuss here. In written language, the matrix clause is often required for describing the manner of speaking, a function less needed in spoken narrative, where the teller of the story can act out the different manners and emotions of the speaking characters. There were only three different verbs of speaking used in my corpus and only one of those implied manner of speaking (*vika* 'shout, call').

The matrix clause can also be used to disambiguate reported speakers. (6) is an example of this function. However, once speakers have been established, this function is redundant. Furthermore, there are many ways of establishing the identity of a reported speaker without using a matrix clause, as (7) shows.

Deictically, matrix clauses do code the occurrence of a speech event from an 'objective' perspective, temporally 'mirroring' the subjectively coded content of the speech event (the flow of speech of a story character as they said it at that time in the story). My characterization of the matrix clause as a 'mirror' differs from earlier characterizations which suggested that the matrix clause coded a *shift* in viewpoint. I suggest that one of its function is to overtly maintain the duality of viewpoints which is inherently there already in the use of DS. The fact that speakers do interpolate passages of DS with matrix clauses, regardless of the syntactic and informational structure of the subjective content of speech, is evidence for this parallelism.

The retelling of DS as an objective narrative event and the use of matrix clauses in my corpus have been presented as evidence that the conceputalization of DS involves a simultaneous represetation of subjective and objective viewpoints. The current mental space architecture, illustrated in figure 1 therefore requires some modification.

3) The Proposed Representation: Parallelism of Viewpoints

In this section I present my revised mental space representation of narrative viewpoints. The representation maintains many of the structures of the original architecture, illustrated in figure 1. The main difference is the modelling of simultanous viewpoints at a macro-level of discourse.

Figure 2 is a representation of the kind of structure that would be built based on the section of narrative in (6).

---

[5]Although the current 'linear' mental space architecture does allow for connections back to already established spaces, enabling the same space (here the content of speech) to be accessed repeatedly.

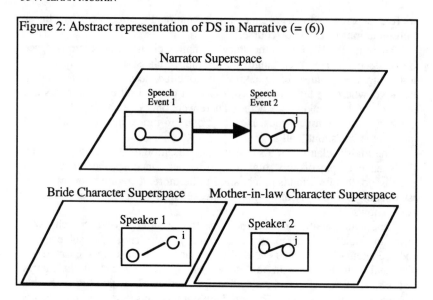

Figure 2: Abstract representation of DS in Narrative (= (6))

Figure 2 should be viewed as *multidimensional* rather than hierarchical. Each 'level' in the figure represents a different plane, each with its own deictic profile: the identity of every conscious character in the story. The narrator superspace represents the objective report of the sequence of events and description of the storyworld and everything in it. Each box within the superspace represents the propositional content of each narrative event (including stative descriptions of things that are true at that time in the storyworld), reflecting the assumption that there is a mental construct of a narrative timeline in the narrator superspace.

In DS, the information coded in the content of speech is represented in the superspace of the reported speaker. *At the same time*, the information that DS is an event in the narrative is represented as an equivalent box in the narrator superspace. Propositional information that is coded in the matrix clause, like manner of speech or identity of speaker, is represented in the narrator superspace. If there is no matrix clause, this box is empty of propositional content.

I have represented the connection between the subspaces with indices. Thus the relationship between 'speaker' spaces and 'narrator' spaces should be thought of as equivalent structures in parallel dimensions.

(6) is a conversational exchange between the characters of the Bride and the Mother-in-law. The information that there are two speaking events in the narrative is represented in the Narrator superspace. These event spaces in the narrator space are coinexed with the propositional content of speech of these speech events (Bride: "The bread, mother, did not work out for me.". Mother-in-law: "It doesn't matter, daughter-in-law, if it's veiny..."), which build their own configuration of mental spaces.

Both versions of the mental space model of narration can represent the domain and origin of information, the two important facets of viewpoint representation. Both models also represent the mental space configuration of propositional information in the text.

The main difference between the Cutrer's canonical mental space representation and the one presented here is the representation of narrative superspaces which run in parallel with each other and are coindexed. The original model required shifting from one viewpoint to another (and perhaps back again). The revised model thus captures the fact that the direct speech mode of representation involves the simultaneous representation of objective and subjective viewpoints in narration. This revised model should be useful for modelling other complex configurations of viewpoints.

As a theory of conceptual structure, the mental space framework should be able to model the conceptualization of discourse at all levels. The use of superspaces to represent narrative viewpoints is an application of mental space theory to modelling discourse macrostructure (i.e. its temporal, rhetorical and viewpoint structure). Figure 2 is an overall representation of the storyworld, modeling the narrative timeline and the relationship of the conscious SELF of each story character to that timeline. Figure 1 is a local representation of the shift in deictic orientation (i.e. tense) at a particular point in the text, and it's consequences for the interpretation of viewpoint at that point.

This last point highlights the fact that Cutrer and I have approached the issue of DS representation with different goals in mind. However I have shown here that a mental space approach developed for the purposes of modeling local grammatical forms, and their relationship to viewpoint in a text, can be modified to model the overall conceptualization of narrative text, which includes a conceptualization of viewpoint structure as much as it involves a mental representation of temporal structure.

6) References

Banfield, A. 1982. *Unspeakable Sentences: Narration and Representation in the Language of Fiction.* Boston: Routledge & Kegan Paul.

Coulmas, F.(ed.) 1986. *Direct and Indirect Speech.* Berlin: Mouton de Grutyer.

Cutrer, M. 1994. *Time and Tense in Narrative and Everyday Language.* Doctoral Dissertation, University of California, San Diego.

Duchan et al 1995. *Deixis in Narrative: a Cognitive Science Approach.* Hillsdale: Lawrence Erlbaum

Fauconnier, G. 1994. *Mental Spaces: Aspects of Meaning Construction in Natural Language.* Cambridge: CUP.

Friedman, V. 1986. Evidentiality in the Balkans: Bulgarian, Macedonian, and Albanian, in W. Chafe & J. Nichols, eds., *Evdentiality: The Linguistic Coding of Epistemology.* Norwood: Ablex.

Genette, G. 1980. *Narrative Discourse.* (translated by Lewin, J.E.) Oxford: Basil Blackwell

Labov, W. 1972. The Transformation of Experience in Narrative Syntax. In *Language in the Inner City: Studies in the Black English Vernacular.* Philadelphia: University of Pennsylvania Press. 354-396.

Mandler, J.M. & Johnson, N.S. 1977. Remembrance of Things Parsed: Story Structure & Recall. *Cognitive Psychology* 9. 111-151.

Mushin, I. 1994. The Function of Direct Speech in Retelling. *CLS* 30.

Polanyi, L. 1989. The Structure of Stories. In *Telling the American Story.* Cambridge: MIT Press. 15-42.

Prince, G. 1982. *Narratology: The Form and Functioning of Narrative.* Janua Linguarum 108. The Hague: Mouton.

Rumelhart, D.E. 1975. Notes on a Schema for Stories. In Bobrow, D.G. & Collins, A. (eds), *Representations and Understanding: Studies in Cognitive Science.* New York: Academic Press. 211-236

Sanders, J. 1994. *Perspective in Narrative Discourse.* Doctoral Dissertation, Univeriteit Brabant, Tilburg.

Wiebe, J. 1990. *Recognizing Subjective Sentences: a Computational Investigation of Narrative Text.* Doctoral Disseration, State University of New York, Buffalo.

Blending and Other Conceptual Operations in the Interpretation of Mathematical Proofs

ADRIAN ROBERT*

University of California, San Diego

1 Introduction

Insights[1] from cognitive semantics suggest that conceptual mapping and combination processes play a role at several levels in natural language interpretation. It has been proposed by Lakoff (1987) and Johnson (1987) that such correspondence-making plays a role not only in communicative but in reasoning processes, and, in particular, mathematical reasoning. This proposal suggests that abstract mathematical concepts are grounded in experientially-based image schemas, and reasoning with the concepts proceeds according to the correspondences we make between the properties of the grounding schemas and the specific configurations arising in mathematical situations.

*Department of Cognitive Science; University of California, San Diego; La Jolla, CA 92093-0515; arobert@cogsci.ucsd.edu.
[1] In formulating the ideas contained in this paper I benefited from discussions with Gilles Fauconnier.

The present paper carries this proposal forward by examining in detail how the concepts specified in mathematical definitions are grounded and how they are manipulated in mathematical proofs. As will be shown, proofs are generally not sequences of precise propositions that follow logically from one another as the folk psychological conception would have it, but sets of instructions directing the interpreter to form correspondences between conceptual domains. It is the pattern of mentally observed consonance and/or dissonance arising from the resulting transfer of structural information that leads the interpreter to be convinced of the validity of a proof's conclusion.

The theory of *blended spaces* developed by Fauconnier & Turner (1994) provides a useful framework for studying this conceptual correspondence-making in mathematics and relating it to similar processes in language. This framework has been applied to analyze phenomena at several levels in language ranging from grammar to discourse, as well as certain types of literary analogies and mathematical conceptual developments. Since it is described elsewhere in this volume in the paper by Fauconnier & Turner, we do not explain it further here.

2 The Grounding of Mathematical Concepts

2.1 The Distinction Between Formal and Informal Mathematics

Before discussing mathematical grounding it is necessary to draw a distinction between *formal* and *informal* mathematics (see Lakatos, 1976, pp. 1–5). *Formal mathematics* as a program was originated by David Hilbert (1899/1959)[2] in response to pressures which will be discussed in Section 4.2 and was most thoroughly developed by Whitehead & Russell (1910/1925). It is done within a *formal system* made up of a collection of symbols, a set of axioms or strings of the symbols, and a set of rules specifying how new strings may be derived from old. A *theorem* is a string that has been derived through a sequence of rule applications starting from one of the axioms, and its *proof* is simply the sequence of strings produced by the applications. A theorem can provide the starting point (in place of an axiom) for new proofs. To verify a proof, it is merely necessary to check that the preconditions for the given rule's application are satisfied at each step, and original theorems can be produced simply by the selecting applicable rules and applying them in sequence starting with axiom or theorem.

---

[2]It has its earliest roots, however, in Euclid's axiomatic approach in the *Elements*, and Peano's (1889) development of symbolic shorthand for proof notation was an important precursor (see discussion in Bell (1945) on pp. 333–4, 558–9).

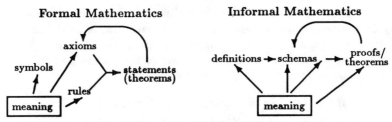

FIGURE 1 Formal and Informal Mathematics

Notice that the production of proofs and theorems is essentially internal to the system: valid chains of applications depend only on the form of the rules and axioms, not on what the symbols stand for. As formal mathematics is typically employed, the symbols *do* stand for external entities or concepts; this is the route by which formal mathematics may be applied to understand and predict phenomena in the experiential world. But the properties of these experiential concepts play a role only in initially determining the forms of the axioms and rules, and subsequently no reference is made to these properties in determining whether a given proof is valid. This latter task is easily automated, and in fact all present machine-based theorem proving systems (see review by Bundy (1983) and Farmer et al. (1995) for a recent example) operate within the formalist program.

This stands in stark contrast to *informal mathematics*, the only form of mathematics extant prior to Hilbert and still the predominant form today. It is the familiar pure mathematics studied in high school and university courses, in which concepts are defined making reference via natural language to schemas and intuitions deriving from everyday experience and then reasoned with in proofs according to their resulting properties. A theorem is a (possibly complex) statement of relationship between defined concepts, and a proof is a sequence of statements of relationship between defined concepts. The validity of each step in a proof is verified by reference to the properties of the concepts. Thus, there is no two-stage separation of *meaning* (by which is simply meant connection to everyday experience) from *mathematical manipulation* as in the case of formal mathematics. The differences[3] are schematically illustrated in figure 1.

---

[3] In fact there is something of the informal meaning-concept connection that does play a role in formal mathematics, which is that *the ways in which strings of symbols and rule conditions interact* are grounded in experience in the same way that informal mathematical schemas are. The difference is that in formal mathematics this is not the level of meaning of concern to the mathematician. See discussion in Section 4.2 below.

The predominant folk psychological model of mathematical activity corresponds more or less with formal mathematics as it has been described, however in the remainder of this paper we focus on informal mathematics – except in Section 4.2 where the formal and informal versions are compared with one another.

2.2   The Grounding of Informal Mathematical Concepts

In mathematical discourse (textbooks, lectures, etc.), concepts are specified by natural language definitions which make reference to natural concepts or schemas (i.e., those available as a result of commonplace experience) but modify them in one or both of two ways, referred to as *truncation* and *extension*. Truncation is aptly illustrated by some of Euclid's original definitions in the *Elements* (trans. Heath, 1956, p. 153):

1.   A **point** is that which has no part.
2.   A **line** is breadthless length.
5.   A **surface** is that which has length and breadth only.
8.   A **plane angle** is the inclination to one another of two lines in a plane which meet one another and do not lie on a straight line.

What is crucial in definitions 1,2,5 is that there is nothing in the world we know that corresponds to the objects they describe. In the real world, all examples of lines have width and even depth, all examples of points have some extension, and all examples of surfaces have depth. Yet the *concepts* of location, length, and breadth *do* exist independently in the mind as useful generalizations for organizing experience. Euclid's definitions, therefore, invite us to consider a very strange yet imaginable kind of objects – those which possess only certain subsets of the attributes which objects possess in the real world.

The subsequent text in the *Elements* explores the relationships between hypothetical instances of the defined objects. We are able to comprehend and understand these relationships because the concepts like length and location that exist in our minds possess a rich network of relational connections with other concepts. We know without Euclid having to tell us, for instance, that points have locations, and lines have locations and orientations. Thus, when definition 8 is given, we understand exactly what is being referred to, for we well know that two directed lengths, when they meet, will do so with a certain quantitative relationship between their directions, and when Euclid later asks us to consider a means for constructing an equilateral triangle from a line segment using compass and straight-edge, we are able to easily see that it works as he describes.

Truncation alone, however, does not fully explain the grounding of Euclidian geometry, let alone other branches of mathematics. The notion of *extension*, based on the idea that we trust certain procedures to result in certain situations, is also necessary. The notion of CONGRUENCE, for example, is based on the imagined possibility of placing figures over one another and noting their correspondences. Based on our own experiences in abstractly similar situations, we understand that such operations could conceivably be performed, even though they never will. Similarly, the notion of NUMBER is based on the idea that certain regular correspondences are maintained in imaginary augmenting and reducing operations on collections of abstract entities just as they are in our experiences with real objects. This kind of grounding is discussed by the philosopher Philip Kitcher (1984) as based on a notion of an "ideal agent" operating in "supertime", and is described by Lakoff (this volume) as involving metaphorical mapping from our schemas for agentive manipulation onto the relevant abstract symbols and structures.

Thus, the properties of mathematical concepts derive from the properties of already-possessed perceptual and motor schemas grounded in experience. Although the schemas are combined and modified in novel ways, the interactive characteristics which, as will be seen below, play the crucial role in mathematical reasoning, are all based on these grounded intuitions. We suggest that the mathematical concepts themselves achieve some independent cognitive reality of their own through processes of entrenchment.

3 Blending in the Interpretation of Mathematical Proofs

In this section, the argument will be made that the interpretation and verification of mathematical proofs involves mapping the general schematic components of defined concepts onto the specific elements of an imagined configurational situation. As mentioned in the introduction, this process is similar to what is proposed to occur in metaphor in language, in which a general schema is applied to understand relations between elements in a particular content domain. We begin by examining the nature of proof in informal mathematics.

3.1 The Nature of Proof in Informal Mathematics

A mathematical proof is a sequence of statements which ultimately lead the reader to perceive a valid connection or relationship between a theorem's conditions and its consequences. This is accomplished by breaking down the relationship, which may be quite complex, into simpler relationships and guiding the reader in such a way that he may convince himself that each of them is true. This process of guided observation has been likened by the mathematician G.H. Hardy (1928) to pointing out the features of a distant mountain range for observation, except that the observed objects are internally imagined instantiations viewed by the mind's eye.

The instantiations are constructed by reference to the mathematical schemas discussed in Section 2, directed by what are termed *introducing* statements. These typically take the form "Let x be a y", as in "Let E be a set" or "Let x be an element of E". The interpretation of such statements involves mapping a label or an imagined entity onto the slot of a given schema; the resulting "meaning" is an *imagined instantiation* of the schematic slot, an object held in mind with certain properties.

Inference statements state a relationship between schemas and instantiations held in mind which it is up to the interpreter to verify for himself. The interpretation of these statements generally involves constructing a mapping between the slots of the schema(s) and the elements of the instantiation(s) and observing that no dissonance or mismatch arises. Sometimes a further inference must be drawn based on the structure of the resulting construction.

Each of the different types of statement is marked in proof discourse by a particular key word or phrase (marked in bold in the analysis below in Table 2).

3.2 Mental Operations in Interpreting Proof Statements

In both introducing and inference statements, interpretation involves making mappings and forming blends using structures from background knowledge and previous discourse, looking for dissonance or its absence, and drawing structural inferences. For any given statement, several of these elementary operations are required. Through introspection on the interpretation process, it is possible to identify the operations performed in interpreting any given statement and classify them. The types of elementary operations found thusfar through the examination of statements from proofs in analysis and algebra are listed in Table 1, below. The contents of the table are explained in detail in the context of an analysis of an actual mathematical proof in the next subsection.

3.3 Analysis of a Proof in Mathematical Analysis

Table 2 below contains the analysis of the first half of a proof in elementary point-set topology taken from Rudin (1976, p. 34). This book is a standard text used in introductory college courses in mathematical analysis. Point-set topology deals with the properties of sets of points

Table 1: Elementary Mental Operations for Proof Interpretation

CLASS	#	OPERATION
instantiating	1)	imagine entity exemplifying or satisfying a schematic slot
blend	2)	imagine entity involving blended combination of schemas/frames (usually embedding of extant, focused entity into a new frame)
focus	3)	focus on an element/substructure in an imagined schema, usually specified by a subschema
	4)	shift focus to structure present (focused on) in previous discourse – triggered by a) text, either explicitly or semiexplicitly (e.g., symbol in text is part of substructure of a previously given schema), or b) implicit cue
	5)	shift focus to a previous structure with new substructural detail (a, b variants as for #4)
observational	6)	(related to #4) blend in structure from previous discourse as substructure in current focused blend
blend	7)	blend a schema specified by text with contents in given context; 7': blend schema counterfactual to text with present contents
	8)	recall a previous blend and, using the same schema, add new substructure on instantiation side and map over to a new part of the schema
inspection	9)	note presence or absence of conflict/dissonance in immediate situation
	10)	note conflict with structure previously present in discourse
	11)	draw relevant schematic inference/notice relevant schematic implication
	12)	work sequentially through an analogy, verifying compatibility in mapping and drawing a resulting inference

in spaces that are generalizations of the coordinate spaces on which mathematical functions are defined.

In the table, the text of each step of the proof is given in the left-hand column, with the statement-type keyword in bold type. The second column lists the associated functional category of each step as given in Table 1 above. In the third and fourth columns the mental operations required to interpret the step (and accept its validity if it is an inference) are delineated. The third column lists the operation type under the classification in Table 2, and the fourth column provides a short description of how the operation is applied in the given situation, with all mathematical schemas marked by capitalization. The complete text of the proof as it appears in the book is given below. Note that there are no illustrations or diagrams associated with this proof, nor with any other in Rudin's text.

<u>Thm. 2.23</u>: *A set is open if and only if its complement is closed.*

First, suppose E^c is closed. Choose $x \in E$. Then $x \notin E^c$, and x is not a limit point of E^c. Hence there exists a neighborhood N of x such that $E^c \cap N$ is empty, that is, $N \subset E$. Thus, x is an interior point of E, and E is open.

Next, suppose E is open. Let x be a limit point of E^c. Then every neighborhood of x contains a point of E^c, so that x is not an interior point of E. Since E is open, this means that $x \in E^c$. It follows that E^c is closed.

In the remainder of this subsection, the interpretation of the first three steps of the proof is explained in detail, in order to provide a clear picture of the interpretation of both introduction and inference steps.

In the first substep of step 1, or step 1.1, we call to mind the schema for SET and combine it with the label 'E'. This can be analyzed using the blended spaces framework as in figure 2a. This blend is similar to the caused-motion example analyzed by Fauconnier & Turner (1994) in that the left-hand side contains a general schema and the right-hand side contains specific content items, in this case a single label and an attached entity standing schematically for the thing to be labeled. The "meaning" arrived at is that of a *specific instantiation* of the entity (called for by the right side) described by the schema (structure mapped from the left side).

In step 1.2, we blend the COMPLEMENT schema with two arguments (figure 2b). The first of these is the already-extant instantiation E, an entity compatible with one of the slots in the COMPLEMENT schema, and the second is 'E^c', another label. The result is that we have two instantiations held in mind, with a particular relationship between them specified by the schema.

In step 1.3, focus is shifted to this new entity, 'E^c', which has just been specified in relation to the previously focused E. This prepares the way for step 1.4 (not illustrated, but similar to 1.2), in which additional structure is given to the instantiation 'E^c' by mapping it into a compatible slot in the CLOSED schema.

In step 2.1 (see figure 3a), focus is shifted back to the SET instantiation E, triggered by the reference in the text. In step 2.2, focus is shifted a second time, to substructure of the SET schema that has just been recalled, and in step 2.3, a blend similar to that in step 1.2 is made associating the label 'x' with an instantiation of this substructure.

Thusfar, the operations have involved generating instantiations held in mind and bound to certain properties. The result is that an imagined configuration has been set up and in the next step (step 3) an observation is made on it. The text of the step states that a certain relationship that has not been specified in the preceding construction holds. The interpreter must look for evidence of the relationship in what is held in mind.

In step 3.1, focus is shifted back to the embedding of E and E^c into the COMPLEMENT schema. In step 3.2, a blend is constructed

Table 2: Analysis of a proof.

#	STEP	FUNC.	OP	DESCRIPTION
1.	First, **suppose** E^c **is** closed.	introduce	1	instantiate an entity (labeled 'E') in SET schema
			2	embed this in COMPLEMENT schema
			3	shift focus to another part of the schema (the complement, labeled E^c)
			2	embed this part in CLOSED schema
2.	**Choose** x∈E.	introduce	4a	return focus to 1a: E in SET schema
			3	focus on POINT subschema
			2	imagine instantiation ('x')
3.	**Then** x∉E^c,	infer	5a	recall previous embedding of E into COMPLEMENT schema
			7	blend ∉ schema with arguments x,E^c
			9	see that no conflict/dissonance arises
			7'	counterfactually blend ∈ schema with arguments x,E^c
			9	note that dissonance does arise
4.	**and** x is not a limit point of E^c.	infer	7'	blend LIMIT POINT schema with x, E^c
			4b	recall E^c CLOSED blend from 1d
			8	blend x (with contextual property LIMIT POINT) as subcontent into this
			11	draw inference x∈E^c (schematic implication)
			10	note conflict with x∉E^c in earlier step
5.	**Hence** there exists a neighborhood N of x such that E^c∩N is empty,	infer	7	blend NEIGHBORHOOD schema with x
			7	blend INTERSECTION schema with neighborhood and E^c
			4a'	embed into LIMIT POINT schema
			7'	counterfactually assume INTERSECTION nonempty
			11	draw inference that x is a LIMIT POINT
			10	note dissonance with previous step
6.	**that is,** N⊂E.	infer	4a'	from prior focus on N,E^c (as disjoint), recall COMPLEMENT schema
			3	use schema to shift focus to E
			2	blend SUBSET schema with args E,N
			9	note absence of dissonance
			7'	counterfactually assume N extends out (not SUBSET) of E
			11	draw inference (using COMPLEMENT schema) that N∩E^c nonempty
			10	note dissonance with step 3
7.	**Thus,** x is an interior point of E,	infer	7	blend INTERIOR POINT schema with x,E
			6	bring N (with context ∋x, ⊂E) in from previous discourse
			9	note precondition satisfaction (absence of dissonance)
8.	**and E is open.**	infer	7	blend OPEN schema with x,E
			6	bring in x INTERIOR POINT from previous step
			9	note precondition satisfaction (dissonance absence)

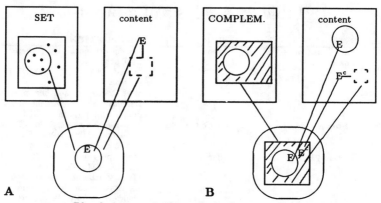

FIGURE 2 Blends in step 1 of proof. A: Step 1.1. B: Step 1.2.

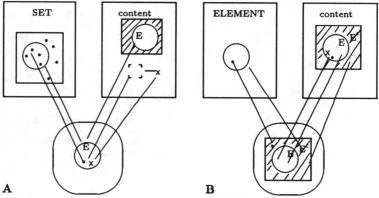

FIGURE 3 Blends in steps 2-3 of proof. A: Step 2.2. B: Step 3.4.

using the $\notin$ schema on the left-hand side and the instantiations x and E^c on the right-hand side. The difference between this type of blend (type 7) and blends of type 1 and 2 is that ALL content items on the right-hand side have prior bindings, hence the situation regarding potential mappings is more restricted. In this case, the restrictions do not generate a conflict with the specifications for the slots being mapped to in the $\notin$ schema, and this lack of dissonance is what is noted in step 3.3.

In most cases when similar slot-filler blends are made in natural language (as when mapping arguments into a construction), such an absence of dissonance suffices to accept the constructed meaning without further (or any) thought. However in mathematics, experience proves that dissonance may sometimes exist in such cases without being noticed (see following section), and one important check to eliminate this possibility is to construct the counterfactual blend and see that dissonance *does* exist in this case. Thus, a mathematician verifying the given proof would perhaps also carry out steps 3.4 and 3.5, attempting to construct a blend using a schema contrary to the specified one ($\in$ instead of $\notin$) and observing that conflict arises (from the structure of the COMPLEMENT schema) which prevents the mapping from being formed (see figure 3b).

4 Discussion

4.1 Parallels and Differences Between Mathematics and Language

The preceding analysis has shown that interpretation of natural language and mathematical proofs exhibit several parallels. In both cases the structures manipulated are ultimately grounded in experience, we can identify conceptual mapping and blending operations in the construction of meaning, and the retrieval of structures from discourse context and background knowledge is often required. An important difference, however, is that conscious awareness of underlying conceptual operations is greater in mathematics than language. One reason for this is that the schemas employed in blends in the former case are conceptually novel structures that have been consciously constructed by mathematicians, rather than subconsciously acquired from regularities in linguistic and extralinguistic experience. Another reason is that whereas in language it is generally only the results of blending that are attended to, in mathematics conscious attention must be paid to whether or not constructed blends actually *work* – that is, whether or not dissonance arises as a result of the mapping.

4.2 Understanding Trends in the Development of Mathematics

Owing to the parallels in grounding and manipulation, interpretation in informal mathematics is subject to some of the same difficulties inherent in language. In particular, there are two potential sources of miscommunication leading to disagreement over the validity of theorems and proofs, depending on whether the problem lies with the schematic entities or their manipulation.

The problem with schemas lies in their specification via natural language definitions. If the wording of a given definition is not sufficiently precise, there may be more than one conceptual schema that is compatible with it. In this case different mathematicians may be using the same terminology to refer to different schemas with different interactive properties, leading to confusion and disagreement over which relationships hold.

The second kind of difficulty arises in the manipulation of schemas that occurs in proofs. As shown in the preceding section, instantiations must be mapped into slots and their eligibility for the slots verified. Often several factors (required properties) bear on such eligibility, and as the situation grows more complex, it becomes more difficult to hold everything clearly in mind without making any oversights. The more complex the schemas and their slot requirements, the more difficult and error-prone these kinds of operations will be.

During the 18th and particularly the 19th centuries, awareness of these difficulties led to modifications of both mathematical concepts and the complexity of the inference steps used in their manipulation (Bell, 1945[4]). Mathematical concepts were defined more precisely and by appeal to simpler schemas from ordinary experience.

These simplifications to concepts in turn affected reasoning in proofs, it being easier to handle concepts and examine the interactions of their properties when they are simpler. And when the concepts were complex, mathematicians were more careful to split reasoning into smaller steps with less needing to be verified in each step. This was the basis of the trend towards increasing rigor in mathematics.

The culmination of these trends of increasing precision and rigor came at the beginning of the 20th century, with the development of the formal mathematical program by Hilbert (1899/1959) and its most thorough implementation to date, within a symbolic logic framework, by Whitehead & Russell (1910/1925). Although the immediate stimulus for the development of Hilbert's program was the apparent existence of conflicts between the different types of non-Euclidean geometry that had been discovered (see Bell, 1945, chapter 15 (pp. 332–5), chapter 23), it would not have occurred without the stage having been set by the trends.

5 Conclusions and Future Directions

In this paper, a description of the grounding of mathematical concepts in everyday experience elaborating on ideas of Lakoff and Johnson has been put forth, and some proposals have been made as to how these conceptual structures interact in the interpretation of mathematical proofs, based on Fauconnier & Turner's blended spaces framework. The analysis resulting from this proposal highlights two important observations. First, the cognitive operations involved in interpreting proofs do

[4]This book, though inaccurate in some technical details, provides an excellent survey. See in particular chapters 13 and 23.

not seem qualitatively different from those involved in ordinary natural language, and, second, the structure of these operations is generally more consciously accessible in mathematics than in language.

This suggests that one direction to extend the present work would be to utilize the analysis of mathematical discourse as a *window* on processes in natural language interpretation. For example, the fine detail of patterns of reference to discourse context is accessible to introspection in mathematical proof, and it was even possible to classify focus-shifts and blending operations on this basis. Another area which might potentially benefit is the understanding of acceptability constraints for conceptual mappings (see Turner, 1991). Such constraints are highly accessible to introspection in mathematical reasoning, because it is often the question of whether a given mapping is acceptable or not that is focused on in verifying a proof step.

This analysis might also serve as a window on human reasoning in general. We suggest that interpretive reasoning in mathematics proceeds by the coordinated interaction of schematic structures – by means of structure mapping, focus-shifting, and dissonance searching. To the extent that reasoning in other domains such as science or law is similar to that in mathematics, this would provide a structured way of conceptualizing the underlying cognitive processes in those domains.

References

Bell, E.T. 1945. *The Development of Mathematics.* New York: McGraw-Hill.

Bundy, A. 1983. *Computer Modelling of Mathematical Reasoning.* New York: Academic Press.

Farmer, W.M., J.D. Guttman, and F.J. Thayer. 1995. Contexts in Mathematical Reasoning and Computation. *J. Symbolic Computation* 19:201–16.

Fauconnier, G., and M. Turner. 1994. Conceptual Projection and Middle Spaces. Technical Report 9401. Department of Cognitive Science, University of California, San Diego. available from http://cogsci.ucsd.edu.

Hardy, G.H. 1928. Mathematical Proof. *Mind* 38:1–25.

Heath, T.L. (ed.). 1956. *The Thirteen Books of Euclid's Elements.* New York: Dover Publications.

Hilbert, D. 1959. *The Foundations of Geometry.* La Salle, Ill.: Open Court Pub. Co. originally published Grundlagen der Geometrie, 1899.

Johnson, M. 1987. *The Body in the Mind.* Chicago: University of Chicago Press.

Kitcher, P. 1984. *The Nature of Mathematical Knowledge.* Oxford: Oxford University Press.

Lakatos, I. 1976. *Proofs and Refutations.* Cambridge: Cambridge University Press.

Lakoff, G. 1987. *Women, Fire, and Dangerous Things.* Chicago: University of Chicago Press.

Peano, G. 1889. *Principii di Geometrica Logicamente Eposti.* Torino: Fratelli Bocca.

Rudin, W. 1976. *Principles of Mathematical Analysis, 3rd Edition.* New York: McGraw-Hill.

Turner, M. 1991. *Reading Minds.* Princeton, N.J.: Princeton University Press.

Whitehead, A.N., and B. Russell. 1925. *Principia Mathematica, 2nd Edition.* Cambridge: Cambridge University Press. 1st Edition published 1910.

Part V

Semantics/Pragmatics Interface

The Distribution of Generic Objects: Lexical Semantics vs. Pragmatics[*]

WILLIAM BYRNE

University of California, San Diego

1. The Problem

At least since Christopherson (1939), researchers have been aware of the fact that so-called 'generic' or kind-denoting direct objects are restricted to certain environments. For example, in the Spanish sentence in (1), the object *el salmón* refers to the genus Salmon; however, the same object NP has no such interpretation in (2). ('#' indicates that the example is only interpetable in very specific contexts.)

(1) Pedro detesta <u>el salmón</u>.
     Pedro hates the salmon
     'Pedro hates salmon (generic).'

(2) #Pedro come <u>el salmón</u>.
     Pedro eats the salmon

As recognized more recently by Lawler (1972), Declerck (1987) and Laca (1990), the examples in (1) and (2) show that the verb class involved is

---

[*] I would like to thank John Moore, Adele Goldberg, Farrell Ackerman, Gilles Fauconnier, Almerindo Ojeda, and Chris Barker for their helpful comments. All remaining errors are my own. This paper was supported in part by a UCSD Academic Senate grant.

relevant to the distribution of generic objects. In particular, on the neutral reading, it seems that psychological verbs such as *detestar* 'hate' readily take generic objects while activity verbs such as *comer* 'eat' disallow them.

However, it has also been recognized, most notably by Laca (1990), that this generalization does not hold up for the full range of data. After all, there are many cases in which activity verbs allow generic objects in neutral contexts; for example, in (3-4), the direct objects readily take on the generic reading despite the fact that they occur with the activity verbs *comer* 'eat' and *perseguir* 'chase'. (*a*, as in *a los gatos* in (4), marks animate specific DOs in Spanish.)

(3) Pedro come <u>los vegetales</u> crudos. (adapted from [28a] Laca 1990)
     Pedro eats the vegetables raw
     'Pedro eats salmon (generic) raw.'

(4) Los perros persiguen a <u>los gatos</u>.
     the dogs chase the cats
     'Dogs chase cats (generic).'

Moreover, further investigation shows that almost any sentence that disallows the generic object on the neutral reading, such as the one in (2), will allow it when considered in the appropriate context, as we will see shortly.

The goal of this paper therefore is to give a unified analysis of the distribution of generic objects that can account for the full range of data, taking into consideration both the cooccurrence of generic objects with certain verb classes as well as their occurrence in the other environments mentioned. The analysis is based on the idea that this distribution is predictable when we take into account certain principles of construal. In particular, generic objects are found in sentences that are construed as expressing an inherent or stable relationship between the grammatical subject and object. This type of construal is referred to here as a *characterizing relation* and differs from what I call the *characterizing property*, which only expresses an inherent or stable characteristic with respect to the grammatical subject.

I will also show that, whether or not a sentence is construed as involving a characterizing relation as opposed to a characterizing property depends on two different types of information. In some cases, the lexical semantics of the verb seems to be responsible for the relational vs. property reading of the sentence. However, in other cases, the interpretation is a result of the speaker's pragmatic knowledge.

2. Background

In this section I cover the background material that will be relevant to our discussion of generic and nongeneric NPs.

2.1 The Upward Entailment Test

Lawler (1972) shows that generic NPs fail to show the usual monotonicity effects in upward entailing contexts (as pointed out to him by Herb Clark). In other words, when speaking of kinds, one cannot generalize from subset to superset. For example, (5a) includes the generic subject *Coyotes* and does not entail the sentence in (5b).

(5)   a.   <u>Coyotes</u> have bushy tails.

-/->   b.   <u>Mammals</u> have bushy tails.

In contrast, sentences with non-generic objects do show upward entailment. In this way, (6a), in which *coyotes* has an existential rather than a generic interpretation, entails (6b).

(6)   a.   There are <u>coyotes</u> in the field.

—>   b.   There are <u>mammals</u> in the field.

We see then that bare nouns in English are inherently ambiguous in that they may have either a generic or a non-generic interpretation. By using the upward entailment test, we can distinguish the two readings in identical syntactic environments. For example, comparing the bare plural direct objects in (7), we find that (7a) does not entail (7b). We can assume then that these direct objects are generic. However, since (8a) does not entail (8b), we assume that these direct objects are not generic.

(7)   a.   Sam hates <u>salmon</u>.   (Generic Objects)

-/->   b.   Sam hates <u>fish</u>.

(8)   a.   Sam eats <u>salmon</u>.   (Non-generic Objects)

—>   b.   Sam eats <u>fish</u>.

2.2 English vs. Spanish

In Spanish, the generic/non-generic distinction shown in (7) and (8) is overt, as generics in this language are represented with definite NPs; that is, they are marked by the definite articles *el* and *la*, or the plural *los* and *las*, as shown for example in (9a). The nongeneric, nonspecific counterpart is represented with the bare noun in Spanish, as shown in (9b).

(9)   a.   Pedro detesta <u>el salmón</u>.
           'Pedro hates salmon (generic).'

      b.   Pedro come <u>salmón</u>.
           'Pedro eats salmon (non-generic).'

Given this overt distinction, I will be using Spanish examples throughout.

2.3 *Characterizing* vs. *Particular* Sentences

I will focus on the distribution of generic objects in what I will call *characterizing* sentences following Krifka et.al. (1995) which contrast with *particular* sentences. Characterizing sentences describe inherent properties or relationships and therefore make no reference to any particular time or place. Typical examples involve copulas as in (10) or other lexically stative verbs such as *love*, as shown in (11).

(10)   Kim is tall.

(11)   Sandy loves the Padres.

However, as noted by Dahl (1975), Carlson (1989), and Langacker (1995) among others, characterizing sentences may also be formed using activity verbs, as shown in (12).

(12)   Pedro speaks French.

This type of sentence abstracts away from the individual events on which it is based. In this way, it can serve to predicate a property of the individual or kind it describes in the same way a predicate nominal or adjective does; thus, (12) is often interchangeable with *Pedro is a speaker of French* .

In contrast to characterizing sentences, particular sentences report on specific events or occasions and involve either adjectives that describe transitory states, as in (13), or verbs with perfective aspect, as shown in (14). (In terms of Carlson 1977, characterizing sentences involve *individual-level* predicates while particular sentences involve *stage-level* predicates.)

(13)   Zelda is drunk.

(14)   Fred broke his leg.

Although generic objects are found in particular sentences, as shown in (15), they seem to be licensed for different reasons in this environment than those relevant to characterizing sentences. Furthermore, bare nouns often cannot take on a generic interpretation in particular sentences, as shown in (16). Therefore, I will not be discussing this type of example here.

(15)   The early settlers exterminated the dodo (generic).

(16)   The early settlers exterminated dodos (non-generic only).

3. Distributional Facts

3.1 Psych Verbs vs. Activity Verbs

Recall that (1-2) (repeated below as (17a-b)) show the distinction between psych verbs and activity verbs. That is, psych verbs such as *detestar* 'hate' readily allow generic objects in neutral contexts, as in (17a), while activity verbs such as *comer* 'eat' in (17b) do not. On the other hand, as shown in (18a-b), these two verb classes behave in the exact opposite manner with respect to the nongeneric bare objects: The bare NP *salmón* is ungrammatical in (18a) but fine with the activity verb in (18b).

(17)   a.   Pedro detesta el salmón.
            'Pedro hates salmon (generic).'

(17)   b.   #Pedro come el salmón.
           Pedro eats the salmon

(18)   a.   *Pedro detesta salmón.

       b.   Pedro come salmón.
           'Pedro eats salmon (nongeneric, nonspecific).'

3.2   Subject-Object Pairs

Looking now at (19-20), we see that whether or not a direct object can get a generic reading sometimes depends on the subject NP that it is paired with. For example, the object *los gatos* 'cats' in (19) cannot get a generic reading. However, if we change the subject NP to *los perros*, as in (20a), *los gatos* readily takes on a generic interpretation. Still, the generic object is not required in this context, as shown in (20b).

(19)   #Mi hijo persigue a los gatos.
       My son chases the cats

(20)   a.   Los perros persiguen a los gatos.
           'Dogs chase cats (generic).'

       b.   Los perros persiguen gatos.
           'Dogs chase cats (nongeneric).'

3.3   Secondary Predications

Moving on to the examples in (21) and (22), we find that sentences with secondary predications also license the generic object in neutral contexts. As shown in (22), without the the depictive adjective *crudos* 'raw', activity verbs such as *comer* 'eat' do not license generic objects in neutral contexts.

(21)   Pedro [$_{VP}$ come [los vegetales] [crudos]].
       Pedro eats the vegetables raw
       'Pedro eats vegetables (generic) raw.'

(22)   #Pedro come los vegetales.
       Pedro eats the vegetables

4. Relations vs. Properties

From the data shown above, we see that there are two types of transitive characterizing sentences: those with generic objects, which are marked by the definite NP in Spanish, and those with nongeneric nonspecific objects, which show up as bare NPs. This distinction is seen respectively in (20a) and (20b) above. In what follows I will point out the different meanings associated with each sentence-type as indicated by their logical entailments. Afterward, I will show that these distinct meanings correspond to the speaker's construal of the situation in one of two alternate ways.

4.1 Distinctions in Meaning

Sentences with generic objects simultaneously express a generalization about their object as well as their subject and suggest a certain type of interaction between the two participants. In contrast, sentences with the nongeneric bare object NPs merely express a generalization about their subject. Thus, if we look at the entailments of (23a), which involves a generic object, we can conclude both that there is something about Pedro that causes him to hate salmon, as in (23b), and that there is something about the kind Salmon that causes Pedro to hate it, as in (23c).

(23) a. Pedro detesta <u>el salmón</u>.
          'Pedro hates salmon (generic).'

—> b. *Pedro is such that he hates salmon.*

—> c. *The kind* Salmon is such that Pedro hates it..

In contrast, if we look at the entailments of (24a), which involves a bare object, we can only conclude that Pedro is a salmon eater, as shown in (24b). (24c) is not entailed as it does not follow from (24a) that there is something about salmon that causes Pedro (to want) to eat it.

(24) a. Pedro come <u>salmón</u>.
          'Pedro eats salmon (nongeneric nonspecific).'

—> b. *Pedro is such that he eats salmon.*

-/-> c. *The kind Salmon is such that Pedro eats it.*

This difference is even more striking when the sentences are identical except for the fact that one has a generic object and the other has a nongeneric bare object, as illustrated in (25-26) (repeated from 20a-b above):

(25) a. Los perros persiguen a <u>los gatos</u>.
          'Dogs chase cats (generic).'

—> b. *The kind Dogs is such that they chase cats.*

—> c. *The kind Cats is such that dogs chase them.*

(26) a. Los perros persiguen <u>gatos</u>.
          'Dogs chase cats (nongeneric nospecific).'

—> b. *The kind Dogs is such that they chase cats.*

-/-> c. *The kind Cats is such that dogs chase them.*

In (25), we get two entailments; that is, from (25a) it follows both that there is something about dogs that makes them want to chase cats, as shown in (25b), and that there is something about cats that triggers this chasing reflex in dogs, as in (25c). However, from (26a) it only follows that Dogs are cat chasers, as given in (26b). (26c) is not entailed. (The reader is reminded that only the Spanish examples are unambiguous, so trying to get the right entailments from the English glosses may be misleading.)

4.2 Alternative Construal-types

As mentioned above, I claim that the different meaning types associated with (25) versus (26) correspond to the speaker's construal of the situation in one of two alternate ways. Below I will give a schematic illustration of these construal types. Then, in §5, I will go on to show how this claim will account for the distribution of generic objects as presented in §3.

Abstracting away from any particular sentences, the two construal-types available to the speaker when considering transitive characterizing sentences are illustrated in Figure 1 and Figure 2. (The diagrams are not meant to follow the conventions of any particular theory).

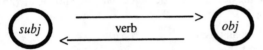

experiences, w.r.t. object, state   triggers in subject state of
of verb or reflex to engage in   verb or reflex to engage in
activity described by verb   activity described by verb

Figure 1: Characterizing Relation

Figure 1 represents what I am calling a *characterizing relation* and, as shown by the arrows, indicates that sentences associated with this construal-type involve a sort of two-way predication. That is, they express a stative interaction between the participants involved. In particular, the subject experiences the state described by the verb or a reflex to engage in the activity described by the verb with respect to the object; and, at the same time, the object triggers this state or reflex in the subject. Both the subject and object are highlighted since, semantically, both are the target of predication or 'Subjects' in the Aristotelian sense (see Kuroda 1992).

Figure 2 below represents what I am calling a *characterizing property*.

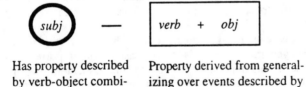

Has property described   Property derived from general-
by verb-object combi-   izing over events described by
nation   verb-object combination

Figure 2: Characterizing Property

In contrast to characterizing relations, characterizing properties only make a generalization about the subject. Therefore, only the subject is highlighted in Figure 2. Furthermore, in the case of transitive sentences, the property predicated of the subject is derived from generalizing over the events described by the verb-object combination. Thus, as indicated in the rectangular area, this type of transitive sentence is analyzed as involving a complex predicate in which the direct object combines with the verb.

That the verb-object combination shown in Figure 2 forms a complex predicate is reflected more clearly in languages like Hungarian, where the bare noun is incorporated with the verb to express the property reading. For example, to get the property reading of *Pedro eats fish* in Hungarian, the bare noun *halat* 'fish' is incorporated into preverbal position, as shown in (27a), literally 'Pedro fish-eats'. However, incorporation cannot be used for characterizing relations in Hungarian, as shown in the ungrammatical (27b). Instead, relations are expressed in Hungarian just as they are in Spanish; that is, they include the definite generic object NP, as shown in (28) (Examples from E. Kiss, p.c.).

(27)   a.   Pedro halat eszik.   (Property)
            Pedro fish-eats
            'Pedro eats fish.'

       b.   *Pedro halat utal.
            Pedro fish-hates

(28)   Pedro utalja a halat. (Relation)
       Pedro hates-def the fish
       'Pedro hates fish (generic).'

4.3 Summary

To summarize so far, I have proposed that there are two types of construal available to the speaker with respect to the interpretation of transitive characterizing sentences: characterizing relations and characterizing properties. In making this distinction, I have shown that there is a correlation between sentences with generic direct objects and characterizing relations on the one hand and between sentences with nongeneric bare objects and characterizing properties on the other. Thus, the following generalization will account for the distribution of generic objects: Generic objects are only found in sentences that have the characterizing relation construal.

We are now ready to take a closer look at the examples given earlier to show that this generalization holds in each case. More importantly, we will investigate the factors that are responsible for the association of a particular sentence with either the characterizing relation or the characterizing property construal. With psych verbs, we will find that their lexical semantics are responsible for their strong compatibilty with the relational construal. In the case of activity verbs, we will see that the context and pragmatic knowledge available to the speaker will determine when a sentence is associated with the relational vs. the property construal-type.

5. Lexical Semantics vs. Pragmatics

5.1 The Lexical Semantics of Psychological Verbs

As I pointed out earlier, psych verbs always take generic objects in neutral contexts and disallow bare NPs. Thus, the examples in (29a) and (30a) are fine when uttered outside of any particular context while (29b) and (30b) are ungrammatical.

(29) a.   Los niños detestan las espinacas.
          'Kids hate spinach (generic).'

—>   *Kids are such that they hate spinach.*
—>   *Spinach is such that kids hate it.*

      b.   *Los niños detestan espinacas.

(30) a.   Los chistes groseros divierten a los niños.
          'Dirty jokes amuse children (generic).'

—>   *Dirty jokes are such that they amuse children.*
—>   *Children are such that they are amused by dirty jokes.*

      b.   *Los chistes groseros divierten niños.

Examining the lexical semantics of this verb class shows that the characterizing relation is built into their meanings. In particular, they are lexically stative and select for arguments that have the semantic roles of experiencer and stimulus. For example, in (29a), the subject *Los niños* 'children' is the experiencer and the direct object *las espinacas* 'spinach' is the stimulus. Given these semantic roles, we construe this sentence as saying, on the one hand, that there is something about children that causes them to hate spinach; that is, they 'experience' detestation for spinach. And, on the other hand, it says that there is something about the nature of spinach that makes children hate it; that is, spinach 'stimulates' this detestation in children. Thus, the interaction between the experiencer and stimulus forces a relational reading. In particular, a generalization is made both about the grammatical subject as well the object and therefore the sentences are compatible with the generic object even in neutral contexts. Furthermore, given that the property reading is not available, the bare NP as in (29b) and (30b) are not permitted in direct object position. (Note that the experiencer and stimulus may also occur in the reverse order, as seen in (30a), where the grammatical subject *los chistes groseros* 'dirty jokes' is the stimulus and the object *los niños* 'children' is the experiencer.)

5.2 Activity Verbs

In contrast to psych verbs, we have seen that, ceteris paribus, activity verbs are incompatible with generic objects in neutral contexts; that is, they are not immediately associated with the relational reading in the way that psych verbs seem to be. However, when a sentence is associated with certain pragmatic knowledge or when it is imbedded in certain contexts, activity verbs readily take generic objects. As we will see, the pragmatic knowledge or contexts that license the generic objects are those that will enable the interlocuter to contrue the sentence as involving a characterizing relation.

5.2.1 Conventionalized Relations

Consider next the examples listed in (31) and (32). In (31a) and (32a), the verb cooccurs with a generic object and the sentences are construed as characterizing relations; yet this is not the case in (31b) and (32b).

(31) a. Los perros persiguen a <u>los gatos</u>.
          'Dogs (generic) chase cats (generic).'

—> *Dogs are such that they chase cats.*
—> *Cats are such that dogs chase them.*

     b. #Mi hijo persigue a <u>los gatos</u>.
          my son chases the cats

(32) a. El sol blanquea <u>la ropa de algodón</u>.   (≈[43a] Laca1990)
          the sun bleaches the clothes of cotton
          'The sun bleaches cotton garments (generic).'

—> *The sun is such that it bleaches cotton garments.*
—> *Cotton garments are such that the sun bleaches them.*

     b. #María blanquea <u>la ropa de algodón</u>.
          María bleaches the cotton clothes

This is explained by the fact that the pragmatics associated with the subject-object pairs in (31a) and (32a) give rise to a relational reading but the pairs in (31b) and (32b) do not. Let us take (31a-b) first. Because of the pragmatics associated with cats and dogs, i.e. the conventional belief that they are arch enemies, (31a) can be construed as describing a state of affairs in which dogs have an inherent reflex to chase cats and, crucially, in which cats have an inherent quality that triggers this reflex in dogs. On the other hand, one is hard-pressed to get the same kind of interpretation for (31b). That is, out of context, it is hard to imagine an inherent chasing relationship that should necessarily hold between a specific child and the Cat species, which is why (31b) cannot license the generic object.

The same type of explanation can be made for the examples in (32). To be specific, the bleaching described in (32a) is a result of the physical properties of both the sun and cotton garments. Thus, (32a) describes a stative interaction between the two rather than just a property of one participant or the other. Thus the state of affairs is construed as a characterizing relation and licenses the generic object. On the other hand, there is no reason for us to construe (32b) as describing a necessary bleaching relationship between María and cotton garments. Therefore, (32b) is incompatible with the relational reading and disallows the generic object in neutral contexts.

5.2.2 Secondary Predications

Let us now take a look at the examples in (33). As shown, (33a) involves the depictive adjective *crudos* 'raw' and licenses the generic object unlike its counterpart in (33b) which lacks a secondary predication.

(33) a. Pedro come <u>los vegetales</u> crudos.
          Pedro eats vegetables (generic) raw.'

—> *Pedro is such that he eats vegetables raw.*
—> *Vegetables are such that Pedro eats them raw.*

      b. #Pedro come <u>los vegetales</u>.
          Pedro eats the vegetables

Again, the claim is that the pragmatics associated with secondary predications are what give this sentence the characterizing relation construal. To be more specific, depictive predicates as used in (33a) in effect describe 'specialized' ways of doing things. In this case, it describes a specialized way of eating vegetables, namely, raw. Furthermore, a particular way of eating is often reserved for particular <u>kinds</u> of things. That is, we normally eat some foods raw, such as cookie dough and sushi, while others we eat cooked. It is in this light, then, that secondary predications allow the two-way relational reading in neutral contexts. In other words, because of the use of a secondary predication, in (33a) the speaker is saying both that Pedro is the type of person that eats vegetables raw, and that there is something about vegetables that makes Pedro want to eat them raw. This, in turn, licenses the generic object.

5.2.3 Specific Contexts

Finally, as I mentioned in the introduction, almost any transitive sentence can license a generic object provided it is found in the appropriate context, that is, in a context where the characterizing relation construal is appropriate. To show this, let us consider (34) which does not allow the generic object in neutral contexts.

(34) #María mata a las cucarachas.
      María kills the cockroaches

From what I have said so far, in order to get the relational interpretion for (34), there would have to be a situation in which roaches trigger some kind of inherent reflex in María to kill them. These conditions are easy enough to imagine. For example, let us say that María unknowingly moves into to a new apartment infested with roaches. She finds them so disgusting and kills them so often that she develops a reflex for doing so, even when she sees them in a restaurant or outdoors. In this context, it is appropriate to use (34) in order to emphasize that María is obsessed with killing cockroaches *and* that there is something about cockroaches that triggers a reflex in her to kill them.

364 / WILLIAM BYRNE

6. Conclusions

To conclude, I have shown that there are two different types of construal that can be associated with transitive sentences. On the one hand, characterizing *relations* describe an inherent or stable relationship between two individuals or kinds. As we have seen, sentences that involve a characterizing relation make a generalization about both their grammatical subject as well as their object. On the other hand, characterizing *properties* describe an inherent or stable characteristic of a single individual or kind. Therefore they only make a generalization about the grammatical subject. As it turns out, generic objects are only found in sentences that are construed as characterizing relations.

I have also shown that whether or not a sentence is construed as involving a characterizing relation depends on two different types of information. In the case of psych verbs, their lexical semantics seem to directly match the characterizing relational construal. Because of this, generic objects are interpretable in sentences with psych verbs even in neutral contexts. In the other cases, we have seen that whether or not the sentence can have a characterizing relation construal is based on context and pragmatic knowledge.

References

Carlson, Gregory, 1977. *Reference to Kinds in English.* Doctoral dissertation, University of Massachusetts Amherst.

Carlson, Gergory, 1989. On the Semantic Composition of English Generic Sentences, in G.Chierchia, B. Partee, and R. Turner, eds., *Properties, Types and Meaning, II,* 167-192. Dordrecht: Kluwer Academic Publishers.

Christophersen, P. 1939. *The articles. A study of their theory and use in English.* Copenhagen: Munksgaard.

Dahl, Östen, 1973. On Generics, in Edward Keenan, ed., *Formal Semantics of Natural Language,* 99-111. Cambridge: Cambridge University Press.

Declerck, Renaat, 1987. A Puzzle About Generics. *Folia Linguistica* 21: 143-153.

Krifka, Manfred, J. Pelletier, G. Carlson, A. ter Meulen, G. Chierchia and G. Link. 1995. Genericity: An Introduction, in G. Carlson and J. Pelletier, eds., *The Generic Book,* 1-124. Chicago: University of Chicago Press.

Kuroda, S.-Y., 1992. *Japanese Syntax and Semantics.* Dordrecht: Kluwer.

Laca, Brenda, 1990. Generic Objects: Some More Pieces of the Puzzle. *Lingua* 81: 25-46.

Langacker, Ronald W., 1995. Generics and Habituals. Paper presented at *Conceptual Structure, Discourse, and Language I,* UC San Diego.

Lawler, John, 1972. Generic to a Fault. *Proceedings of the Eighth Regional Meeting of the Chicago Linguistics Society,* 247-258. Chicago: Chicago Linguistics Society.

Meaning and Context: German *aber* and *sondern**

JEAN-PIERRE KOENIG AND BEATE BENNDORF
State University of New York at Buffalo

Introduction

What is a possible word meaning? What is the range of meaning distinctions to which particular words can be sensitive? Such questions have been at the forefront of research in lexical semantics in recent years (see Talmy 1985, 1988, Pinker 1989, Jackendoff 1990, Bach 1995). These questions are typically addressed in the context of the meaning of verbs or spatial prepositions; the major issue is then one of event- or spatial relation packaging: what kinds of events or spatial relations can be denoted by verbs or prepositions and what parts of our conceptualization of events and spatial relations is lexicalized by verbs or prepositions in different languages? In this paper, we want to contribute to this debate on the limits of lexical meaning by examining another kind of words, conjunctions, and a different kind of meaning, than types of eventualities, one more akin to pragmatics in nature. Our goal is to assess the kinds of constraints on their contexts of occurrence words can impose. Said differently, we are interested in the kind of pragmatic content that individual words can conventionally encode. We concentrate on two German conjunctions *aber* and *sondern*, both of which are generally translated by *but*, and one aspect of their meaning which has hitherto gone unnoticed. We show that *aber* and *sondern* are sensitive to meaning distinctions of a kind that has not been previously recorded: they impose different constraints on the type of inferential processes via which

365

interpreters derive interpretations of utterances in which they occur. The conclusion we draw— which constitutes a fact not previously observed, to our knowledge— is that the meaning of lexical items can make reference to and distinguish between R-based and Q-implicatures, in the terminology of Horn (1984).

1.Q- and R-maxims and the neo-Gricean view of the interaction between semantics and pragmatics:

The issue of the possible pragmatic content of words we raised in the introduction arises out of the 'classical' view of the relationship between sentence-types and interpretations put forth in Grice (1975, 1989). According to this view, the interpretation of utterances proceeds in two steps. In a first step, a decontextualized, linguistic convention-driven semantic meaning is computed. To simplify, this first step can be analyzed as a function which takes as input a lexicon and a set of combinatory rules and returns expressions of a suitable logical language. In a second step, the interpretation of the utterance-token is derived. This second step takes as input the output of the first step— i.e. logical expressions—, as well as general conversational maxims and particular world beliefs shared among the speech participants, and derives the contextual interpretation of utterances.

For Grice himself, a crucial component of this second step is the addition[1] of inferences licensed by general conversational maxims to the linguistically-licensed meaning of utterance types. Grice called such inferences conversational implicatures. By distinguishing between sentence meaning and interpretations derived via conversational maxims, Grice intended to capture the difference between conventionally-driven and non-conventionally-driven aspects of utterances' interpretations. Formally, we can model this second step of the interpretation of utterances as follows.

Conversational maxims are additional axioms of a suitable formal language. Conversational implicatures are then simply inferences drawn from the propositions expressed linguistically, the axioms representing the conversational maxims, and (optionally) world knowledge accessible to the speech participants. In other words, an utterance's implicatures differ from its semantic entailments in the kind of premises one uses to derive them:

---

[1] The effect on interpretation of Grice's conversational maxims is not always additive. It can also be to reverse or otherwise modify the literal meaning of a sentence, as in instances of irony, metaphor, and so forth. Such additional effects are not relevant to the issues discussed in this paper.

only logical axioms are used to derive the latter, whereas conversational axioms are also used for the former (see Hirschberg 1985 for an example of such a formalization of Grice's program).

Whereas the fundamental division between entailments and implicatures is widely accepted, there has been much discussion regarding the proper number and formulation of the conversational maxims governing the contextual interpretation of utterances. One influential reformulation of Grice's original description is due to Horn (1984, 1989). Horn argues that Grice's maxims can be reduced to two general principles, the Q- and R-principles, as he calls them.[2] These two principles are defined as follows (see Horn (1989, p.194)):

Q-maxim:

'Make your contribution SUFFICIENT: Say as much as you can (given both QUALITY and R).

R-maxim:

'Make your contribution NECESSARY: Say no more then you must (given Q).

The second maxim is as an economy maxim: speakers should leave out of their utterances what they can reliably expect their addressees to be able to infer. The first maxim is a minimal commitment maxim: speakers should be assumed to commit themselves to the minimum amount of information consistent with the meaning of the utterance. The R-maxim is at play when we infer from an utterance of *I lost a finger* that it is my finger that I lost (example from Horn 1984, see also Atlas and Levinson (1981)). The implicature that the lost finger was mine need not be made explicit by speakers: hearers can be reliably expected to add this piece of information on their own, given the R-maxim. The Q-maxim is at play when we infer from an utterance of *John bought 5 CD's* that John bought 5 CD's and no more. Again, speakers need not make explicit the implicature that *only* 5 CD's were bought: hearers can be reliably expected to add this piece of information, given the Q-maxim.

---

[2] Sperber and Wilson (1986) purport to reduce the number of maxims even further to one general Relevance maxim. But their notion of relevance involves the weighting of two separate conditions: (i) the number and informational weight of inferences one can draw from the utterance's meaning and (ii) the cost of these inferences. Sperber and Wilson's notion of relevance therefore also includes *two* competing conditions, as does Horn's model based on Q- and R-maxims.

An implicit assumption of this neo-Gricean research program is that Q-based implicatures and R-based implicatures are on a par. Both should be distinguished from entailments as well as inferences which can be drawn from world-knowledge. The class of inferences which are drawn from utterances is thus divided into three subclasses: logical inferences, conversational implicatures, and world-knowledge based deductions. The table in 1 summarizes the differences between the three kinds of deductions. As can be seen in the table, differences between the three classes of deductions reduces to differences in the kind of premises used to derive them. Different sets of premises are used to derive each class of inferences. All three classes use logical axioms and rules of inference.[3] But conversational implicatures add as premises suitable formalizations of the Q- and R-maxims. Deductions based on world-knowledge add as premises propositions taken from a knowledge base.[4] For ease of reference, from now on we call these various classes of inferences L-, Q-, R- and W-inferences respectively.

The classification of inferences summarized in table 1 is widely accepted within the neo-Gricean community. As we show in the next section, the semantics of *aber* and *sondern* challenges this tripartite classification of inferences. They group together sets of inferences which cut across the tripartite classification represented in table 1.[5] *Sondern* groups together inferences based on Q-maxims and logical entailments; *aber* groups together inferences based on R-maxims and world knowledge.

---

[3] Of course, different logical systems use different axioms and different rules of inference. Such differences are not relevant to the issues discussed in this section.

[4] In the table, we assume, for simplicity, that deductions based on world-knowledge do not encompass conversational implicatures as premises.

[5] More precisely, as discussed below, *sondern* requires its first conjunct to include a metalinguistic negation, and metalinguistic negations crucially distinguish between R- and Q-implicatures.

	Logical inferences: L-inferences	Conversational Implicatures		Deductions based on world-knowledge (W-inferences)
		Q-inference	R-inference	
Logical axioms and rules of inferences	✓	✓	✓	✓
Gricean maxims — Q-maxim	No	✓	No	No
R-maxim	No	No	✓	No
Knowledge-base	No	No	No	✓

Table 1

2. The meaning of *aber* and the pragmatic content of lexical semantics:

As is well-known, many languages encode what is expressed by *but* in English in at least two different manners (see Anscombre and Ducrot 1977, 1983, Lang 1984, among others). Languages such as English or French use basically one conjunction to mark the idea of contrast between two propositions: *but* in English, *mais* in French. Languages such as German and Spanish, on the other hand, use two different conjunctions to mark the same meaning: *aber* and *sondern* in German, *pero* and *sino* in Spanish. We begin this section by a brief description of the meaning of *aber*. Our description is inspired by Anscombre and Ducrot's analysis of French *mais*

(1977, 1983).[6] We then turn to the hitherto unnoticed sensitivity of *aber* to the distinction between Q- and R-inferences.

Intuitively, as many scholars have noticed (see Lakoff 1971, Anscombre and Ducrot 1977, 1983, Lang, 1984, Blakemore 1989 among others), the basic function of *aber* is to contrast two propositions. Sentences (1)-(2) illustrate this contrastive function of *aber*. We call the two propositions which *aber* contrasts α and *not* α.

(1)   Jana ist nicht groß, aber eine gute Basketballspielerin.
        Jana is not tall but a good basketball player.

(2)   Jana ist nicht groß, aber das ist nicht schlimm.
        Jana is not tall, but that does not matter.

In (1), for example, what is being contrasted are the propositions expressed by 'She is not a good basketball player' (our α) and 'She is a good basketball player' (our *not* α). Note that α and *not* α do not have to be the propositions expressed by the two sentences conjoined by *aber*. Whereas *not* α corresponds to the proposition expressed by the second conjunct in (1), this is not the case for α and the first conjunct. Similarly, in (2), the contrasting propositions might be— depending on the particular context of utterance— 'We should not add Jana to the team' (our α) and 'We should add Jana to the team' (our *not* α).

This last example illustrates another important property of the two propositions which utterances containing *aber* contrast: their identity is underdetermined by the meaning of sentences in which they occur. Various contextual conditions— including the particular beliefs speakers assume to be mutual beliefs— influence the choice of α's and *not* α's in particular situations. In what follows, we reserve the symbol α and *not* α for the two contextually determined contrasting propositions. We use p and q for the

---

[6]Since we concentrate in this paper on the interaction between the meaning of *sondern* and *sondern* and Gricean Maxims, we cannot go into the details of Anscombre and Ducrot's description of the uses of French *mais* which correspond to German *aber*. Suffice it to say that their description is couched within their general 'rhetorical' theory of linguistic meaning— what they call 'Argumentation Theory' (see their (1983) book for details). Because of empirical and epistimological doubts on the viability of Argumentation Theory, we refrain from adopting as is their definition of the meaning of *mais/aber* and recast their insight in a dynamic, 'logical' approach to meaning. Despite significant technical differences, we believe the spirit of our definition to be very similar to theirs.

propositions expressed by the first and second clauses conjoined by *aber*. The upshot of examples such as (1)-(2), then, is that although α is related to p and *not* α to q, they cannot be identified with p and q. The question then arises of the kind of semantic or pragmatic relationships which can exist between α and p.

Intuitively, α in (1) (the proposition expressed by 'she is not a good basketball player') follows from p (the proposition expressed by 'she is small'), if we make the assumption that small people are not good basketball players. Similarly, α in (2) (the proposition expressed by 'We should not add Jana to the team') follows from p (the proposition expressed by 'she is not tall'), if we make the assumptions that people only want to add to their teams good players and that small people are not good basketball players. Finally, *not* α in this case (the proposition expressed by 'We should add Jana to the team') follows from q (the proposition expressed by 'it doesn't matter'), given the assumption that if arguments against somebody's proposed course of action are irrelevant, one should *ceteris paribus* follow the proposed course of action.

To model the observed dependency of the interpretations of utterances containing *aber* on the speech participants' assumptions about the world, we borrow the concept of common ground from the work of Stalnaker (1979), Heim (1983), Chierchia (1995), and others. The common ground is defined for the time being as the set of assumptions about the way the world is mutually believed (or taken to be so) by speech participants. We can now give a more precise (preliminary) definition of the semantic contribution of *aber*:

(3)   *A aber B*

- Context checking: (i) there is a proposition α which is (generically) entailed by p together with the common ground; (ii) there is a proposition *not* α which is (generically) entailed by q together with the common ground.

- Context change: add p, q, and *not* α to the common ground.

We have now defined the notion of contrast which *aber* marks: two propositions one of which is the negation of the other. We have also defined the relationship between the contrasting propositions and the propositions directly expressed by the two sentences conjoined by *aber*. The contrasting propositions must be (generically) entailed by the common ground and the two propositions directly expressed by the two conjoined sentences.

Several comments on this definition are in order. First, there are many ways to define the notions of common ground and generic entailments. For our purposes, it suffices that there are "generic" entailments— i.e. generic propositions from which other propositions can be derived. How such generic propositions and their entailments are ultimately modeled is not our concern (see Carlson and Pelletier 1995 on the notion of generic propositions). Similarly, we assume the common ground to be defined (for now) via a set of propositions (some of which generic) which are mutually believed (or taken to be so) by the speech participants.

Second, we define the semantic contribution of *A aber B* in terms of a context-update view of meaning made popular by Stalnaker's (1979) seminal article and represented in work such as Heim (1983) and Chierchia (1995), among others. In such a view, meanings are viewed as ways to check or update the context or common ground— i.e. the set of possible worlds compatible with the common ground. As is typically the case with words carrying presuppositions (in the broad sense of the term), our particular definition of the effects on the common ground of *aber* comprises two parts, a context-checking and context updating part. Felicitous uses of *aber* require the existence of two generic entailments, α and *not* α from *p*, *q*, and the common ground. It also requires adding to the common ground *p*, *q*, and *not* α.[7]

Let's apply our definition of the semantic contribution of *aber* to an example, which we borrow from Ducrot (p.c.):

(4)   Marc: Laß uns einen Spaziergang machen
                  Let's go for a walk
        Eric: Das Wetter ist gut, aber meine Füsse tun weh
                  The weather is nice, but my feet hurt

α here is paraphraseable (under one contextual interpretation) as 'I'd like to go for a walk' and *not* α by 'I wouldn't like to go for a walk.' *p* (the proposition expressed by 'the weather is nice') (generically) entails α in contexts where the proposition 'If the weather is nice, one likes to go for a walk' is part of the common ground. The context checking conditions on *A*

---

[7] Adding propositions to the context or common ground in this approach to meaning is equivalent to intersecting the set of possible worlds compatible with what is currently mutually believed and the set of possible worlds in which the proposition to be added is true.

aber B are satisfied; the propositions expressed by p, q, and *not* α can be added to the common ground.

Note that our definition of *aber* is (partly) asymmetric: aside from p and q, only *not* α is added to the context. α belongs to the 'working sheets' of the computation of the meaning of the utterance, but does not affect the new common ground created by the utterance in (4). By distinguishing between context-checking and context-updating, we model both the symmetric and asymmetric facets of the semantics of *aber*. With respect to context checking, the two conjuncts behave symmetrically: both must generically entail a proposition, given a common ground. With respect to context updating, the two conjuncts behave asymmetrically: of the two propositions which must be generically entailed by the common ground, p, and q, only one (*not* α) is added to the common ground and is thus relevant to subsequent conversational turns.

The definition of the meaning of *aber* in (3) merely recasts Anscombre and Ducrot's intuitions within a dynamic view of meaning. But it is inexact as is. In particular, the expression '(generically) entails' we used to characterize the relationship between p and α is too broad. Not all kinds of (generic) inferential relations between p and α are possible. Consider sentences (5) and (6):

(5)   *Marc: Jana ist groß, aber sie ist klein.
        She is tall but she is short.

(6)   *Sie ist groß, aber riesig.
        She is tall but a giant.

Clearly, we can logically infer (L-infer) α ('she is not small') from p ('Jana is tall') in (5). The context-checking condition mentioned in (3) is apparently satisfied. Still, (5) is ungrammatical. Similarly, in (6), we can infer via the Q-maxim (Q-infer) α 'she is only tall'— i.e. not very tall— from p 'she is tall'. Again the context-checking condition seems satisfied and we expect (6) to be grammatical. But it is not.

The contrast between (1)-(2) and (5)-(6) is not isolated. It ranges over the whole gamut of L-inferences and Q-implicatures (Q-inferences in our terminology). In all cases where α is Q-inferred from p, the sentence is ungrammatical. We give a few other examples in (7)-(9):[8]

---

[8] In all examples to follow, we subscript *but* in the translation of German examples with either *aber* or *sondern* to indicate the German word it translates.

(7)   *Sie mochte ihn, aber liebte ihn

She liked him, but_{aber} loved him

(The Q-inference 'she didn't love him' is α, *not α* is 'she loved him')

(8)   *Sie kaufte drei Bücher, aber vier Bücher

She bought three books, but_{aber} four books

(The Q-inference 'she didn't buy four books' is α, *not α* is 'she bought four books')

(9)   *Ich bin in der Lage das zu tun, aber ich werde es tun

I am able to do it, but_{aber} I will do it

(The Q-inference 'I will not do it' is α, *not α* is 'I will do it')

The conclusion is clear. The proposition α mentioned in (3) cannot be related to p via either L- and Q- inferences.[9] The reverse is true of R- and W-inferences— *aber* welcomes them. Example (1) we discussed above illustrates W-inferences: inferring that Maria is a bad basketball player ($=$ α) from the fact she is small ($= p$) requires us to use as an additional premise a culture-bound belief that (typically) small people are not good basketball players. In our terminology, α is W-inferred from p.

(10)   Gestern habe ich ein Buch verloren, aber nicht meins.

I lost a book yesterday, but_{aber} not mine.

(11)   John hat gestern getrunken, aber keinen Alkohol

John had a drink yesterday, but_{aber} it was not an alcoholic one.

---

[9] Garcia Negroni (1995) discusses an interesting class of examples involving French *mais* which seem to contradict this generalization:

(i)   Pierre est riche, mais RICHE   Heavy stress on 'RICHE'
        Pierre is rich, but REALLY rich

Corresponding examples are impossible in German, according to our informants. Examples such as (i) are still puzzling, given the otherwise similarity in the meaning of French *mais* and German *aber*. Our explanation of these data is similar to Garcia Negroni's. What *mais* 'cancels' in (i) is the R-implicature that Pierre's degree of wealth is ordinary, i.e. that Pierre is an ordinary wealthy man. Such 'normality' implicatures are characteristic of R-implicatures (see Horn 1984), suggesting that (i) does not provide a counterexample to our hypothesis that α cannot be L- or Q-inferred from p.

Sentences (10) and (11) show that R-inferences can indeed relate p and α. Following Atlas and Levinson (1981) and Horn (1984), I assume that the proposition that the speaker lost his book yesterday ($= \alpha$) is R-inferrable from the proposition that the speaker lost a book yesterday ($= p$). Intuitively, hearers of (10) might infer *ceteris paribus* that the book was the speaker's by reasoning that speakers can leave out the specification of whose book it was and hope the hearer can recover that information. In other words, if we hold the premise that (cooperative) speakers leave out of their utterance information they expect their addressees to be able to recover, we can infer from the first conjunct of (10) that the book was the speaker's. It is this R-entailed proposition which the second conjunct of an *aber* sentence contradicts. Via the same reasoning, the proposition expressed by the first conjunct of (11) R-entails that the drink was an alcoholic beverage, a proposition which is negated by the second conjunct.

To summarize, we can characterize the possible inferential relations between p and α as in (12). (13) gives a suitably revised definition of the meaning of *aber*.

(12) p and α can be related via (a chain of) generic W-inferences or R-inferences. They cannot be related via (a chain of) L-inferences or Q-inferences.

(13)   *A aber B*   (Revised formulation)

- Context checking: (i) p, together with the common ground (generically) R- or W-entail a proposition α; (ii) q, together with the common ground, entails $\neg\alpha$.

- Context change: add p, q, and *not* α to the common ground.

The definition of the semantic content of *aber* in (13) is theoretically significant. It presents new evidence relevant to the broad questions we mentioned in the introduction. First, the lexical meaning of *aber*, as stated in (13) refers to what the Gricean pragmatic component is supposed to do (Q- or R-inferences). The very fact that the lexical semantics of *aber* must make reference to what is generally considered the province of pragmatic processes challenges the traditional view of a strict division between semantics and pragmatics. Of course, we are not the first ones to point out the need to loosen the division between semantic and pragmatic processes (see Carston 1988, Recanati 1994 among others). Many studies have suggested that the semantics of natural languages include underspecified meanings to be determined pragmatically. In particular, it underlies recent work on the meaning of particles and conjunctions (see

Ducrot 1984, Kay 1990, Michaelis 1992 *inter alia*). According to this research, the interpretation of particles is only partially specified grammatically. Some aspects of their interpretation is left open and must be filled pragmatically. The semantics of *aber* summarized in (13) confirms the findings of this research tradition.

But there is a second, more fundamental way in which the semantics of *aber* challenges the Gricean view that the computation of the conventional meaning of sentences precedes— and is the input to— the pragmatic determination of utterances' contextual interpretations. The meaning of *aber* not only introduces variables whose values can only be specified pragmatically, it imposes constraints on the pragmatic processes by which the values of these variables are to determined. R- and W-inferences are appropriate means of deriving α, L- and Q-inferences are not. Words such as German a*ber* suggest that the meaning of individual words can include the specification of which kinds of inferences must be drawn from utterances containing them. It's not only that lexical semantics can explicitly leave something for pragmatics to do, it can tell pragmatics what kind of tools to use!

Finally, by lexically distinguishing L- and Q-inferences from R and W-based inferences, the meaning of *aber* sets up a new lower bound on the variety of semantic distinctions individual words can encode: not only must metalinguistic notions such as 'inference' be among the semantic vocabulary available to lexical semantics, distinctions among types of inferences and types of premises use to draw these inferences must also be countenanced.

3. *Sondern*, metalinguistic negation, and what speakers say.

Although the argument is more indirect, the meaning of the second German conjunction which can be translated as English *but* corroborates one of the theoretical consequences we draw from the meaning of *aber*: the neo-Gricean grouping of Q- and R-inferences to the exclusion of L- and W-inferences is not warranted. But, first, we must describe the meaning of *sondern*. As is well-known, the first conjunct of sentences containing *sondern* must include a negation. As argued convincingly by Anscombre and Ducrot, the purpose of the first conjunct of a *sondern* sentence is to challenge a prior utterance; the second conjunct then (typically) presents a correct formulation the addressee should have used instead. Not all aspects of a previous utterance can be challenged in the first conjunct of a *sondern* sentence, though. Consider (14)-(19).

(14) Jana ist nicht groß, sondern klein.

Jana ist not tall but$_{sondern}$ small

(15) Jana mochte ihn nicht, sondern liebte ihn.

Jana didn't like him, but$_{sondern}$ loved him.

(16) Jana hat nicht drei Bücher gekauft, sondern vier Bücher.

Jana didn't buy three books, but$_{sondern}$ four books.

(17) *Jana ist nicht klein, sondern eine gute Basketballspielerin

Jana is not short, but$_{sondern}$ a good basketball player

(18) *Gestern habe ich ein Buch verloren, sondern nicht meins.

I lost a book yesterday, but$_{sondern}$ not mine.

(19) *Sandra and Tom haben ein Klavier gekauft, sondern sie haben es nich zusammen gekauft.

Sandra and Tom bought a piano, but$_{sondern}$ they did not buy it together.

The first conjunct of a sentence containing *sondern* can negate L- or Q-inferences of the proposition expressed by its positive counterpart (henceforth *p'*), as (14) and (15)-(16) show. The first conjunct of (14), for example, negates that Jana is tall, a trival L-inference from *p'* (i.e. 'Jana is tall'). Simarly, the first conjunct of (15) and (16) negates Q-inferences of *p'* (i.e. 'Jana only liked him' and 'Jana only bought three books' respectively). But the first conjunct of a sentence containing *sondern* cannot negate W- or R-inferences of *p'*, as (17) and (18)-(19) show.

In this respect, the behavior of *sondern* is the mirror image of that of *aber*. The contrast between *sondern* and *aber* is summarized in the minimal pairs in (20)-(23).

(20) a. Sie ist nicht groß, sondern klein.

She is not tall, but$_{sondern}$ small   L-inference

b. *Sie ist groß, aber klein.

She is tall, but$_{aber}$ small

(21) a. *Sie ist nicht groß, sondern das macht nichts.

She is not tall, but$_{sondern}$ that does not matter   W-inference

b. Sie ist groß, aber das macht nichts.

She is tall, but$_{aber}$ that does not matter

(22)   a. Sie ist nicht groß, sondern riesig

She is not tall, but$_{sondern}$ gigantic   Q-inference

b. *Sie ist groß, aber riesig

She is tall, but$_{aber}$ gigantic

(23)   a. *Gestern habe ich nicht ein Buch verloren, sondern nicht meins.

I lost a book yesterday, but$_{sondern}$ not mine.   R-inference

b. Gestern habe ich ein Buch verloren, aber nicht meins.

I lost a book yesterday, but$_{aber}$ not mine.

Sentences (20)-(23) show that whereas *aber* requires α and p to be related via either R- or W-inference, *sondern* requires the relationship between p' (the positive counterpart of p) and what is being challenged to be one of L- or Q-inference. The constraints on the target of the negation that must be included in the first conjunct of a *sondern* sentence can be used to make the same point we made with respect to *aber*: Q- and R-inferences are not on a par contrary to the neo-Gricean claim. But the argument is more indirect here because the restriction on the negation's target is not a unique, lexical property of *sondern*. Whereas it is legitimate to ascribe to the lexical meaning of *aber* the requirement that α must be derived from p via W- or R-inferences, the corresponding target of negation constraint for *sondern* follows from the metalinguistic nature of the negation its first conjunct contains. Sentence (24) below demonstrates the metalinguistic nature of the negation included in the first conjunct of a sentence containing *sondern*:

(24)   Es heißt nicht [økonamiʃ], sondern [økonomiʃ]

It's not [økonamiʃ], but$_{sondern}$ [økonomiʃ]

As in other instances of metalinguistic uses of negation (see Horn (1985)), the negation present in the first conjunct of sentences containing *sondern* can target not only implicatures, as in (15) and (16) above, but also the pronunciation (or otherwise conventional properties) of utterances.

Confirmation of the metalinguistic nature of the negation present in the first conjunct of *sondern* sentences is provided by an interesting syntactic difference between *aber* and *sondern*. *Aber* can occur sentence initially in German, as (25) shows. In other words, the first conjunct need not be expressed syntactically. We analyze these sentences in the same way we did before, although, since there is no first conjunct, p here corresponds to a proposition describing a perceptually salient event or is otherwise provided by the context.

(25)   Aber laß das!

      But$_{aber}$ stop that (sic)

(26)   *Sondern laß das!

      But$_{sondern}$ stop that

By contrast, *sondern* does not allow such linguistically implicit first conjuncts. In particular, *sondern* cannot open a discourse (see (26)). If the first conjunct of sentences containing *sondern* involves a metalinguistic negation, this difference is easily accounted for. For a proposition to be metalinguistically negated, it must be present in the discourse context and the objection registered by speakers of sentences containing *sondern* must also be expressed. If the function of the first conjunct of sentences containing *sondern* is to object to an utterance already present in the context, a sentence containing *sondern* can hardly be used as the first turn of a conversation. Hence the contrast between (25) and (26).

    Assuming, now, that the negation contained in the first conjunct of sentences containing *sondern* is used metalinguistically, we are prevented from ascribing to the meaning of *sondern* the contrast between (14)-(16) and (17)-(20). Metalinguistic negation— irrespective of its inclusion in a sentence involving *sondern*— does not allow the basis of the negation to be a R-inference, as already noticed by Horn (1984) in another context. Horn contrasts, for example, the following two sentences:

(27)   He didn't eat 3 carrots— he ate 4 of them.   (his (10a))

(28)   She wasn't able to solve the problem.   (his 11a))

      (≠ She was able to solve it, but didn't)

Whereas metalinguistic negation can cancel utterances' Q-implicatures ('He only ate 3 carrots' in (27)), it cannot cancel R-implicatures ('She solved the problem' in (28)). Since the contrast between (14)-(16) and (17)-(19) stems from the presence of a metalinguistic negation, not *sondern per se*, we cannot directly use *sondern* as further evidence that some lexical items distinguish between R- and Q-implicatures.

    But the semantics of *sondern* can indirectly be used to make the same point: it is part of the nature of metalinguistic negation, we claim, to distinguish between Q- and R-implicatures. It thus suggests, as the semantics of *aber* did, that R- and Q-inferences do not form a natural class, contrary to the neo-Gricean claim summarized in table 1. Our analysis directly challenges Horn's (1984, 1985) account of the same facts. Horn suggests that the fact that metalinguistic negation cannot bear on R-inferences follows from general considerations and need not be stipulated as part of the import of metalinguistic negation. Horn's explanation of the restriction on metalinguistic negation exemplified in (27)-(28) is as follows.

In both sentences (27) and (28), Horn reasons, the non-metalinguistic interpretations of the negated propositions means 'less' (information-theoretically speaking) than their positive counterparts ('He ate three carrots or more', and 'she was able to solve the problem, but might not have solved it respectively'). In the case of (27) the negated proposition can be paraphrased as 'he ate less than 3 carrots' and in (28) as 'she wasn't even able to do it (let alone dit it)'. But in (27), the stronger proposition that he ate 4 carrots is given and directly contradicts this interpretation, thus, triggering a reinterpretation of the first conjunct in which the negation is understood metalinguistically. In (28), no contradiction arises: the negation of the R-implicature (that she didn't solve the problem) is not incompatible with the ordinary negation (that she did not have the ability to solve the problem). There is therefore no need for reinterpreting the negation as a metalinguistic implicature canceller. A Horn-style account of the data in (15)-(23) would, then, be perfectly compatible with the claim that Q- and R-implicatures form a natural class of inferences. R-implicatures cannot be metalinguistically negated simply because negating sentences which implicate them never triggers the reinterpretation process via which metalinguistic uses arise. The observed difference between R- and Q-implicatures does not follow from the semantics or pragmatics of negation, but from the absence of any reinterpretation-triggering contradiction in the case of sentences such as (28).

One drawback of Horn's (1984) explanation is its claim that logical contradiction is at the root of the reinterpretation of an ordinary use of negation as metalinguistic. If, as Horn (1985) argues and example (24) illustrates, metalinguistic uses of negation can bear on non-propositional aspects of utterances (or even non-linguistic vocalizations), metalinguistic interpretations of negation cannot depend on discovering logical inconsistencies. The question then remains why can L-, Q-inferences or inadequate pronunciations be cancelled via metalinguistic negation, but not R-inferences? We claim that the impossibility to metalinguistically negate W- and R-inferences stems from the nature of metalinguistic negation, which thus provides further evidence that R- and Q-inferences do not form a natural class.

Why, then, do Q- and R-inferences behave so differently under metalinguistic negation? Recent work in psycholinguistics by R. Gibbs and his associates (see Gibbs and Moisse (1996)) provides an answer, we believe. Their experiments show that hearers' understanding of what was *said* in an utterance can include Gricean implicatures. But, their data suggest that hearers crucially distinguish between R- and Q-implicatures. Only the latter are included in people's judgments of what speakers *say* by their utterances.[10] Subjects when presented with sentences such as (29) judge the Q-implicature that John has only three dogs part of what the speaker said. But, when presented with sentences such as (30), they do not deem the R-implicature that Robert broke his own finger part of what the speaker said by uttering the sentence. If this is true, the fact that the former but not the latter can be metalinguistically negated should come as no surprise. Through a metalinguistic negation, speakers challenge the appropriateness of some aspect of a previous utterance. What is challenged must be "part" of the utterance, either via its pronunciation, syntax or its conveyed meaning. If hearers deem Q-implicatures— but not R-implicatures— part of what was said, they can only challenge via a metalinguistic negation the former: one cannot challenge that which one does not assume to be part of a speaker's utterance.

(29)   John has three dogs.

(30)   Robert broke a finger last night

Even more interestingly, sentences for which subjects included R-implicatures in what they thought speakers said (see (31a) and (32a) from Gibbs and Moise) correspond to utterances on the putative R-implicatures of which metalinguistic negation *can* bear, as (31b) and (32b) show (uttered as answers to a. and b. respectively).

(31)   a. It will be a while before Tom arrives.

         b. It won't be a while before Tom arrives, he's coming right now.

(32)   a. Christmas is still some time away

         b. Christmas isn't still some time away, it's right around the corner.

---

[10] This last point is not Gibbs and Moise's interpretation of the results. They are puzzled by the fact that some, but not all implicatures are judged part of what speakers say. They do not notice that the difference in hearers' judgments parallel the distinction between Q- and R-implicatures.

(31a) and (32a) trigger the (putative) R-inferences that neither Tom nor Christmas will arrive soon. Both inferences were considered by Gibbs and Moise's subjects part of what the speaker said; both can be polemically negated.[11]

What metalinguistic negation targets, then, is what hearers consider part of speaker's utterances,[12] on either phonological, syntactic, or semantic grounds. Non-conventionalized R-implicatures— like W-inferences— are culture-dependent: they are not part of the 'conventions' of what is communicated. By contrast, Q-inferences are based on a general condition on the amount of information hearers can cooperatively take speakers to be responsible for. They are part of the 'convention' of what is communicated. Consider Horn's (1984) following two examples of R-implicatures:

(33)   Mort and David took a shower

        $\vDash_R$ They took separate showers

(34)   Mort and David bought a piano

        $\vDash_R$ They bought a piano together

The different R-inferences licensed by (33) and (34) stem from our distinct beliefs about events of piano-buying and shower-taking. In our culture, we are more likely to buy pianos together and take showers alone. What *aber* requires then, is a relation between *p* and *α* dependant on particular beliefs. With *sondern* and metalinguistic negation in general, just the opposite is true: what can be challenged is what speakers commit themselves to by virtue of linguistic conventions or our general assumptions about the nature of conversational interactions. Hearers judge that Q-implicatures are part of

---

[11] Horn notices this fact already with respect to *drink* which in English means *drink an alcoholic beverage*. Note that German speakers we interviewed do not allow metalinguistic negation to bear on the corresponding R-implicature of *drinken*, as (19) shows.

[12] As Horn (1985) convincingly shows, metalinguistic negation can also be used to object to expressions that are not linguistic in nature. For the purposes of this paper we restrict ourselves to instances of metalinguistic negation which bear on linguistic utterances. Our description can be generalized to non-linguistic vocalizations, if popular songs are treated as conventions of sorts— i.e. if we assume one can be right or wrong about a tune. Pointing out something is wrong in somebody's expression (be it linguistic or not) would then be what underlies all instances of metalinguistic negation.

what was said because the interpretation of the sentence they can cooperatively assume the speaker is committing herself to is the (minimal) Q-implicated interpretation. They do not judge (non-conventionalized) R-implicatures part of what was said because they depend on culture-bound beliefs that are not part of the conventions of language or conversations.

To conclude, the fact that metalinguistic uses of negation distinguish between R- and Q-implicatures confirms what *aber* already suggested: the traditional neo-Gricean classification of inference-type summarized in table 1 must be reorganized. Q- and R-implicatures do not form a natural class. Rather, the major division of inference-type is between cultural, belief-bound, and non-cultural, non-belief bound inferences. In that respect, Q-inferences and L-inferences are on a par: they are not culture-bound, they only depend on universal principles of logic and communicative behavior. Table 2 summarizes the classification of inference-types to which *aber* and *sondern* (via metalinguistic negation) are sensitive.[13]

| | | Quasi-logical inferences | | Deductions based on world-knowledge: W-inferences |
		L-inferences	Q-inferences	
Quasi-Logical axioms and rules of inferences	Logical axioms	✓	✓	✓
	Q-maxim	No	✓	No
Knowledge-base		No	No	✓

Table 2

---

[13] ✓ (No) in a cell indicates what kinds of premises can (cannot) be used for various kinds of inferences . As sentences (31a) and (32a) suggest, some R-implicatures are conventionalized or short-circuited, to borrow a term from Morgan (1978). In such cases, R-implicatures differ from W-implicatures. But, then, they are not live implicatures anymore.

Conclusion:

We began our paper by asking what kinds of meaning distinctions can be encoded in words. What our study of German *aber* and *sondern* suggests is that the range of meaning distinctions is larger than previous studies in lexical semantics have suggested. Distinctions in inference-types must be among the vocabulary of semantic primes from which lexical items can draw. But the nature of the meaning distinction lexically encoded in *aber* is of wider theoretical significance. It shows that lexical semantics can be sensitive to distinctions hitherto believed to only be relevant to the contextual interpretation of utterances. This lexical sensitivity further challenges the 'pipeline' model of interpretation originally proposed by Grice, according to which pragmatic interpretation follows semantic decoding. The semantics of *aber* refers to the inner workings of the pragmatic component and constrains the pragmatic interpretation of sentences that contain it.

The meaning of *aber*, and its contrast with metalinguistic negation and the meaning of *sondern*, also suggest that the neo-Gricean classification of inferences is not warranted: Q- and (non-conventionalized) R-inferences are not on a par; they are more similar to logical entailments and world-knowledge-based inferences respectively than to each other. As we showed our 're-classification' of inferences to which utterances can lead is further supported by recent psycholinguistic work: Q-implicatures— but not R-implicatures— are part of what listeners deem 'said' by the utterance of a proposition.

Acknowledgments

We are grateful to Holger Diessel and Arthur Merin for their comments on a previous version of this paper. All remaining errors are ours.

References

Atlas, J. and S. Levinson (1981) "It-Clefts, Informativeness, and Logical Form," in Cole, P., ed., *Radical Pragmatics*, Academic Press, New York, 1-21.

Anscombre, J., & Ducrot, O. (1977). Deux *mais* en français? *Lingua, 43*(1), 23-40.

Anscombre, J., & Ducrot, O. (1983). *L'argumentation dans la langue*. Bruxelles: Pierre Mardaga.

Bach, E. (1995) "Word-Internal Semantic Relations in Wakashan," in Burgess, C., K. Dziwirek and D. Gerdts, eds., *Grammatical Relations: Theoretical Approaches to Empirical Questions*, CSLI, Stanford, 1-13.

Blakemore, D. (1989). Denial and contrast: A relevance theoretic analysis of *but*. *Linguistics and Philosophy, 12*(1), 15-37.

Carlson, G. and F. Pelletier (1995) *The Generic Book,* Chicago University Press, Chicago

Carston, R. (1988) "Implicature, Explicature, and Truth-Theoretic Semantics," in Kempson, R., ed., *Mental Representations: The Interface Between Language and Reality,* Cambridge University Press, Cambridge, 151-181.

Chierchia, G. (1995). *The Dynamics of Meaning.* Chicago: Chicago University Press.

Fauconnier, G. (1985). *Mental Spaces.* Cambridge, MA: MIT Press.

Garcia Negroni, M. M. (1995) "Scalarité et Réinterprétation," in Anscombre, J., ed., *Théorie Des Topoi,* Kimé, Paris, 101-144.

Gibbs, R. and J. Moise (in press) "Pragmatics in Understanding What is Said," *Cognition.*

Grice, P. (1975) "Logic and Conversation," in Cole, Peter and J. Morgan, eds., *Syntax and Semantics 3: Speech Acts,* Academic Press, New York, 41-58.

Grice, P. (1989) *Studies in the Way of Words,* Harvard University Press, Cambridge, Mass.

Heim, I. (1983). On the Projection Problem for Presuppositions. In D. Flickinger & et al. (Eds.), *Proceedings of the Second West Coast Conference on Formal Linguistics* (pp. 114-125). Stanford: Stanford University Press.

Hirschberg, J. (1991/1985). *A Theory of Scalar Implicature.* New York: Garland.

Horn, L. (1984). Toward a New taxonomy for Pragmatic Inference: Q-based and R-based Implicature. In D. Schiffrin (Ed.), *Meaning, Form, and Use in Context : Linguistic Applications (GURT '84).* Washington: Georgetown University Press.

Horn, L. (1989). *A natural history of negation.* Chicago: Chicago University Press.

Jackendoff, R. (1990). *Semantic Structures.* Cambridge, Mass.: MIT Press.

Kay, P. (1990). Even. *Linguistics and Philosophy, 13*(1), 59-111.

Kay, P. (1992). The inheritance of presuppositions. *Linguistics and philosophy, 15*(3), 333-379.

Kratzer, A. (1981). The Notional Category of Modality. In H. Eikmeyer & H. Rieser (Eds.), *Words, Worlds, and Contexts* (pp. 38-74). Berlin: Walter de Gruyter.

Lakoff, R. (1971). 'If's, and's and but's about Conjunction. In C. J. Fillmore & D. Landendoen (Eds.), *Studies in Linguistic Semantics.* New York: Holt, Reinhart and Winston.

Lang, E. (1984). *The semantics of coordination.* Amsterdam: John Benjamins.

Michaelis, L. (1993). "Aspect and the Semantics-Pragmatics Interface: the Case of *Already". Lingua* 87: 321-339.

Morgan, J. (1978) "Two Types of Convention in Indirect Speech Acts," in Cole, P., ed., *Syntax and Semantics 9: Pragmatics,* Academic Press, New York, 261-280.

Nunberg, G. (1978) "The Pragmatics of Reference," Bloomington: Indiana University Linguistics Club.

Pinker, S. (1989). *Learnability and Cognition*. Cambridge, Mass.: MIT Press

Rapaport, W. (1986) "Logical Foundations for Belief Representation," *Cognitive Science* 10, 371-422.

------, S. Shapiro and J. Wiebe (1995) *Quasi-Indexicals and Knowledge Reports*. Technical Report, vol. 95-17, Center for Cognitive Science, SUNY at Buffalo, Buffalo.

Recanati, F. (1993) *Direct Reference: From Language to Thought*, Blackwell, Cambridge.

Reyle, U. (1993) "Dealing with Ambiguities by Underspecification: Construction, Representation, and Deduction," *Journal of Semantics* 10, 123-179.

Segal, E. and J. Duchan (In press) "Interclausal Connectives as Indicators of Structuring in Discourse," in Costermans, J. and M. Fayol, eds., *Processing Interclausal Relations for the Production and Comprehension of Text*, Lawrence Erlbaum Associates, Hillsdale, NJ.

Stalnaker, R. (1979). Assertion. In P. Cole (Ed.), *Syntax and Semantics vol.9: Pragmatics* (p. 3150322). New York: Academic Press.

Talmy, L. (1985) "Lexicalization Patterns: Semantic Structure in Lexical Forms," in Shopen, T., ed., *Language Typology and Syntactic Description, Vol.3: Grammatical Categories and the Lexicon*, Cambridge University Press, New York.

------ (1988) "Force Dynamics in Language and Cognition," *Cognitive Science* 12, 1, 49-100.

Wilson, D., & Sperber, D. (1986). Inference and Implicature. In C. Travis (Ed.), *Meaning and Interpretation*. Oxford: Basil Blackwell.

On Sentence Accent in Information Questions

KNUD LAMBRECHT AND LAURA A. MICHAELIS

University of Texas, Austin and University of Colorado, Boulder

1. Introduction[1]

This study concerns the formal and pragmatic principles which govern the placement of sentence accent in English information questions (IQs). Examples of variability in accent placement are given in (1-3):

(1) [I went to the mall with Audrey yesterday.]

    a.   What did you BUY?

    b.   What did AUDREY buy?

(2) [I heard you went to France.]

    a.   What CITIES did you visit?

    b.   What cities did you VISIT?

(3) a.   Who ate my COOKIES?

    b.   Who ATE them?

    c.   WHO ate them?

---

1   For various suggestions we would like to thank Matthew Dryer, Kevin Lemoine, Bill Raymond, and David Zubin. Special thanks go to Jean-Pierre Koenig for penetrating comments on a previous version.

We presume that the relevant principles cohere with a theory of INFORMATION STRUCTURE. This theory concerns the morphosyntactic and prosodic encoding of the topic, focus and activation statuses of referents in discourse.

We will refer to the following information-structure concepts as defined in Lambrecht 1994:

(4) PRAGMATIC PRESUPPOSITION: The set of propositions lexicogrammatically evoked in a sentence which the speaker assumes the hearer already knows or is ready to take for granted at the time the sentence is uttered.

(5) PRAGMATIC ASSERTION: The proposition expressed by a sentence which the hearer is expected to know or take for granted as a result of hearing the sentence uttered.

(6) FOCUS: The component of a pragmatically structured proposition whereby the assertion differs from the presupposition.

(7) TOPIC: A referent which a proposition is construed to be about in a given discourse; a proposition is about a referent if it conveys information which is relevant to, and increases the addressee's preexisting knowledge of, this referent.

We distinguish three kinds of pragmatic presupposition, which correspond to different kinds of assumptions a speaker may have concerning the addressee's state of mind at the time of an utterance. All three are lexicogrammatically coded in sentence structure. The distinctions among these three presupposition types will play a crucial role in the argument presented in this paper:

(8) TYPES OF PRAGMATIC PRESUPPOSITION:

a.	Knowledge presupposition	(KP)
b.	Consciousness presupposition	(CP)
c.	Topicality presupposition	(TP)

KNOWLEDGE PRESUPPOSITIONS (KPs) concern the assumed knowledge state of an addressee at the time of utterance. KPs are what linguists typically have in mind when they use the term '(pragmatic) presupposition'. CONSCIOUSNESS PRESUPPOSITIONS (CPs) concern the assumed temporary activation states of the representations of denotata in the addressee's mind. A mental representation of a denotatum can be in one of three states: active, accessible, or inactive (Chafe 1987, Lambrecht 1994:Ch.3). TOPICALITY PRESUPPOSITIONS (TPs) concern the assumed statuses of referents as topics of current interest in the discourse.[2]

---

[2] The distinction between KP and CP is explicitly drawn also in Dryer 1996. However, Dryer does not allow for a separate category of topicality

In accordance with Lambrecht (1994), we distinguish beween TOPIC STATUS and ACTIVATION STATUS of a referent. An ACTIVE referent is one which is currently 'lit up' among the inventory of referents known to speaker and hearer at speech time. An active referent is often coded by a pronoun. A TOPICAL referent is one which, due to its discourse salience, represents a predictable or expectable argument of a predication. A referent whose topic role in a predication is predictable to the point of being taken for granted at utterance time will be called a RATIFIED TOPIC. A ratified topic necessarily represents an active referent. However an active referent does not necessarily represent a ratified topic. Thus a pronominally coded (hence active) denotatum may be focal rather than topical, as in the asssertion *YOU are responsible*.

Concerning the notion of PRAGMATIC ASSERTION in (5), it is important to understand that it does not coincide with the common use of 'assertion' in which this term designates the kind of speech act expressed by declarative, as opposed to interrogative or imperative, sentences. The pragmatic assertion expressed by a sentence can be thought of as the effect a sentence has on a hearer's knowledge state. As we argue below, this knowledge state is affected by interrogative and imperative as well as by declarative utterances.

The FOCUS of a proposition is that denotatum whose occurrence in the proposition makes an utterance into an assertion, i.e. which makes it possible for an utterance to constitute a piece of information. Like topic, focus involves a pragmatic RELATION between a denotatum and a proposition. But unlike topic, focus is by definition an unpredictable element of a proposition. Notice that 'focus' is NOT defined in terms of prosody.

IQs present a challenge to a theory of information structure. Their prosodic structure cannot be described in terms of the function that is ordinarily attributed to sentence accent, namely focus marking. In order to understand the problem of IQ prosody, we first need to understand the function of sentence accent in general.

We assume the following general principles for ACCENT PLACEMENT (for detailed discussion see Chapter 5 of Lambrecht 1994):

(9) GENERAL ACCENT-PLACEMENT PRINCIPLES:

(i) THE DISCOURSE FUNCTION OF SENTENCE ACCENTS: A sentence accent indicates an instruction from the speaker to the hearer to establish a pragmatic relation between a denotatum and a proposition. An utterance must have at least one sentence accent to be informative.

---

presupposition (TP). As we argue below, the proper analysis of IQ prosody crucially relies on the difference between KP and TP.

(ii) GENERAL PHRASAL ACCENT PRINCIPLE (GPAP): A phrasal accent marks the right boundary of a pragmatically construed portion (whether topical or focal) of a proposition.

(iii) DISCOURSE CONDITION ON UNACCENTED REFERENTIAL CONSTITUENTS: A referential constituent is unaccented iff the speaker assumes that the referent is a ratified topic in the proposition at the time of utterance.

(iv) THE PRINCIPLE OF PREDICATE-ARGUMENT ASYMMETRY: arguments with inactive denotata necessarily receive an accent; predicates with inactive denotata may remain unaccented (Schmerling 1976, Selkirk 1983).

Regarding Principle (9i), it is important to understand that the pragmatic relation whose establishment is signaled by the sentence accent can be either a FOCUS RELATION or a TOPIC RELATION. In other words, the denotatum of an accented constituent can be focal or topical. Following Lambrecht 1994, we will use the term TOPIC ACCENT to refer to a sentence accent which falls on a constituent whose denotatum has a topic relation to the proposition but whose topic status has not yet been ratified at the level of the sentence and which therefore does not fall under Principle (9iii). A crucial diagnostic in identifying a topic accent is that it coexists with a focus accent on the predicate.

A topic accent may signal ratification of a recently activated or accessible referent as the topic of a new proposition. This is the case in the B responses of (10):

(10)   A: Remember that guy MOE?
          B: Yeah. His WIFE was a NUT.
          B': MOE was a NUT.

In the B responses the VP *was a nut* expresses the focus. The subjects *his wife* and *Moe* are unratified topics: Moe's wife has not been mentioned before (but is accessible for topichood via the marriage frame), and Moe, who was activated and introduced in focus position in the previous utterance, is not yet taken by the speaker to be an approved topic of discussion. In both cases, the topic accent is assigned by Principle (9iii). The important point for our purposes is that the accent which appears on the subject NP does NOT signal focus. We know this because the actual focus accent appears as predicted at the right boundary of the VP focus domain.

The different accent placement principles in (9) are illustrated in (11):

(11)   A: Did you lose one of your CONTACTS?
          B: I'm not WEARING my contacts.
          B': #I'm not wearing my CONTACTS.

In A's utterance, the pragmatically construed portion is the focal predicate. The accent falls at the end of the VP via (9ii). The verb, though focal (hence unratified), may remain unaccented, in accordance with (9iv). The topical subject *you* remains unaccented via (9iii). In B's utterance, the verb receives the accent by default because the NP *my contacts* is unaccentable via (9iii): the NP referent counts as a ratified topic (hence the pragmatic ill-formedness of B').[3]

Following Lambrecht (1994), we distinguish three types of focus-articulation: ARGUMENT FOCUS (AF), PREDICATE FOCUS (PF), and SENTENCE FOCUS (SF). The three types are exemplified in (12):

(12)   a.   SOCIETY's to blame.   (ARGUMENT FOCUS)

          b.   I slipped on the ICE.   (PREDICATE FOCUS)

          c.   Your SHOE's untied.   (SENTENCE FOCUS)

The three types express three basic communicative functions: providing the unidentified argument in a presupposed open proposition (AF, IDENTIFICATIONAL function); predicating a property relative to a given topic (PF, TOPIC-COMMENT or CATEGORICAL function); introducing a new discourse referent or expressing an event involving such a referent (SF, PRESENTATIONAL or THETIC function).

For the present analysis, the relevant focus-articulation type is the AF type in (12a). The information structure of (12a) is represented in (12a'). We represent here only those pragmatic features which are relevant for distinguishing the three focus types. The term 'focus domain' refers to the maximal phrasal constituent which contains the focus:

(12a')   INFORMATION STRUCTURE OF (12a): *SOCIETY's to blame.* (AF)
            Context: He should be pardoned.
            Presuppositions:
                  KP: x is to blame (for his crimes)
                  CP: KP 'x is to blame' is active
                  TP: KP 'x is to blame' is ratified
            Assertion: x = society
            Focus: society
            Focus domain: NP

Sentence (12a) is an IDENTIFICATIONAL assertion. It K-presupposes a propositional function of the form *x is to blame;* the focus portion is the

---

3   As observed by Jean-Pierre Koenig (p.c.), the question arises as to why the referent of *contacts* in (11) necessarily counts as ratified at second mention while the referent of *Moe* in (10) does not. The answer to this question lies in the inherent information-structural difference between subjects and objects. The object noun *contacts* occurs in the unmarked sentence-final focus position. If accented, the object noun would necessarily be construed as focal, leading to pragmatic ill-formedness. The sentence-initial subject NP *Moe* in (10B), however, occupies the unmarked topic position. Whether accented or not, it is naturally construed as topical since the focus is marked by the accent on the final VP constituent *NUT.*

argument which is substituted for the variable: 'society'; this argument distinguishes the K-presupposition from the assertion (cf. Jackendoff 1972). The assertion is the establishment of an identity relation between the focus and the missing argument in the KP. The sentence accent falls on the focus NP via Principle (9i). The rest of the sentence is unaccented because the denotatum 'x is to blame' is taken to be active and ratified.

We are now in a position to address the prosodic problem posed by IQs. As mentioned earlier, the sentence accent in IQs does not appear to mark focus. Notice, for example, the question-answer pair in (13):

(13)   A: What did Mom BUY?
        B: Mom bought a JACKET.

(13')   Presupposed: 'Mom bought x.'

In A's question, accent falls on the predicate *BUY*, even though the thing bought, rather than the buying, is the unknown element. Nevertheless, the *wh*-constituent of an information question seems to be the focus, since IQs have essentially the same information-structure representation as declarative sentences with argument-focus articulation. A's question in (13) presupposes a propositional function of the form 'Mom bought x', just as (in the given context) the assertion *Mom bought a JACKET* in B's answer presupposes the propositional function 'Mom bought x'.

Thus IQs violate the default interpretive principle that a lone sentence accent is a focus accent (Lambrecht 1994). Culicover and Rochement (1983), as well as Selkirk (1984), actually claim that an accent such as that on *buy* in (13) is a focus accent, but this analysis doesn't seem to make much sense: if *buy* is within the knowledge presupposition, it can't also represent new information.

In the remainder of this paper, we will attempt to accomplish two things. First, we will defend the analysis of WH-elements in IQs as focus constituents, against, for example, Erteshik-Shir (1986), who presumes that focus is not relevant to the analysis of IQs (Section 2). Second, we will propose a general algorithm for the assignment of sentence accent in IQs (Section 3).

2. Focus and IQs

According to the definition in (6), focus is that element within a proposition which makes an utterance into an assertion. However, a question word provides strictly speaking no new propositional information relative to what is presupposed. Nevertheless, cross-linguistic studies, such as that recently conducted by Raymond and Homer (1996), reveal that question words in IQs consistently show up with the formal trappings of focus arguments.

Take for example Basque, according to Manandise 1988. The default word order in Basque is APV (agent - patient - verb). The default word order is shown in (14). However, an argument-focus constituent must appear in immediate preverbal position, as shown in (15). (16) reveals that the Basque IQ construction is formally analogous to the declarative AF construction:

the questioned constituent appears necessarily in immediate preverbal position:

(14)   Mikelek   liburu   bat   irakurri   du.
           Michael.E   book   one.A read.Perf Aux.Pst
           "Michael has read one BOOK."

(15)   Bonba   Mikelek   egin   zuen.
           Bomb-the.Sg.A Michael.E make.Perf Aux.Pst
           "MICHAEL made the bomb."

(16)   Bonba   nork   egin   zuen.
           Bomb-the.Sg.A who.E make.Perf Aux.Pst
           "Who made the bomb?"

Essentially the same situation obtains in the Mayan language Mam, as described by England (1983) or in Hungarian (cf. Comrie 1981, Horvath 1986).

Another piece of evidence for the formal similarity between question words in IQs and argument-focus constituents comes from spoken French, where interrogative QU-expressions often appear in the focus position of a cleft construction:

(17)   C'est QUOI que tu fais?
           it-is what that you do
           What are you DOING?

Since c'est-clefts (like it-clefts) mark the clefted constituent as focal, it follows that the interrogative expression QUOI in (17) is the focus of the sentence. The use of cleft constructions for IQs is a common crosslinguistic phenomenon (cf. e.g. Demuth 1987 on Sesotho). It is also found in English, with fronting of the clefted WH-constituent (*What is it (that) you're doing?*). We will return to the use of clefts in IQ constructions in Section 3.

French offers a third argument in favor of the identification of the question word as the focus of an IQ. In spoken French the question constituent may also quite naturally appear *in situ*, as in (18a):[4]

(18)   a. Tu as acheté QUOI?   b. J'ai acheté une VESTE.
          you have bought what   I have bought a jacket
          'What did you BUY?'   'I bought a JACKET.'

As the comparison with the corresponding declarative in (18b) shows, the QU-word of the question appears in the same position, and with the same prosodic (and intonational) features, as the argument focus of the answer.

The characterization of WH-expressions as foci is entirely consistent with our definitions of focus and assertion in (5) and (6). For example, the

---

4   Notice that, unlike its literal gloss in English, (18a) is NOT an echo question.

propositional content of the IQ in (1a) *What did you buy?* functions as a pragmatic assertion in the sense that after hearing the question the addressee knows more than before, namely that the speaker wants to know the identity of the thing that the addressee bought. As a result of hearing the utterance, the addressee's knowledge state is changed. It is the substitution of the focus *what* for the variable in the presupposed propositional function that creates the change. We can say that utterance of a WH-question pragmatically asserts the desire of the speaker to know the identity of the referent inquired about via the WH-expression. (For a comparable analysis see Rochemont 1978.)

Now that we have established that question words can reasonably be treated as the foci of the IQs in which they appear, let us discuss the principles underlying the assignment of sentence accent in IQs.

3. Sentence-Accent Assignment in IQs

The general questions here are the following: (i) what is the pragmatic role of sentence accent in IQs if it is not to mark the focus; and (ii) why does this non-focal accent fall where it does? Our answer to these questions relies crucially on the distinction we drew earlier between FOCUS ACCENT and TOPIC ACCENT.

Let us look again at our initial examples of accent-placement variability in IQs. Example set (1) is repeated in (19):

(19)   [I went to the mall with Audrey yesterday.]

    a.   What did you BUY?

    b.   What did AUDREY buy?

The accents in (19) fall not on the focus constituent but instead on material within the presupposition. For example, a declarative that corresponds to the IQ in (19a) (*What did you BUY?*) could be something like *You bought a TIE.* In the declarative version, unlike the IQ, accent falls on the focus NP; it does not fall on the verb. Since in the IQ the accent does not fall on the focus constituent, we assume that the sentence accent is a TOPIC ACCENT.

In posing an IQ, the speaker is signaling that a mutually known (open) proposition is an appropriate topic for further inquiry. For example, we might represent the topic-focus articulation of (19a) as in (20):

(20)   [you bought x]$_{TOP}$ is [what?]$_{FOC}$

Depending on the utterance context, the topic 'you bought x' may have to be ratified, in which case the constituent expressing it will carry an accent (as it does in (19a)).

We postulate that the placement of sentence accent in IQs is determined by the DIFFERENTIAL STATUS of the KNOWLEDGE PRESUPPOSITION (KP) and the TOPICALITY PRESUPPOSITION (TP) at the time of the utterance. Whatever portion of the KP whose topic status is not yet ratified at the time of speech will appear as an accented constituent in the sentence. This analysis allows us to account for accent placement in IQs with essentially the same principles as in declarative sentences. In a declarative sentence the focus accent signals a denotatum that distinguishes two propositions, the assertion and the presupposition. In an IQ the accent also signals a denotatum that distinguishes two propositions, namely the KP and the TP. In the declarative, the accent signals an intended change in the KNOWLEDGE state of the addressee; in the IQ it signals an intended change in the addressee's mental state with respect to the current TOPIC of conversation.

Let us now look at the way in which our proposal applies to our three example sets. (19a') contains a representation of the information structure of (19a). (19a) is compatible with more than one pragmatic construal, depending on which portion of the topic denotatum expressed in the KP is taken to be already ratified at utterance time. We distinguish three different contexts:

(19a') Sentence: *What did you BUY?* (= (19a))
        Contexts:
             (i) I went to the mall with Audrey yesterday.
            (ii) I went to the mall with Audrey yesterday and stole
                  something.
           (iii) I went to the mall with Audrey yesterday and bought
                  something.
        Presuppositions:
            KP: you bought x
            TP: (i) 'you' is ratified topic
                  (ii)/(iii) 'you did something (at the mall)' is ratified
                       topic
        Assertion: x = what?
        Focus: what

The Assertion line expresses the notion, discussed in Section 2, that the information conveyed by an IQ is the communication of the speaker's desire to know the identity of the missing argument in the open proposition.[5]

In (19a) the topic accent falls at the end of the predicate via Principle (9ii). In the case of context (i), only the subject referent is ratified. Following Ladd (1978), we can call this the BROAD construal. Context (ii) results in a NARROW construal, in which the buying act is contrasted with a specific alternative mentioned in the context. This type of construal is often referred to as 'contrastive'.[6]

---

[5] In (19a') and below we have omitted representation of the CP. Since the crucial factor in determining the presence or absence of an accent in IQs is topic ratification, and since a ratified topic necessarily has an active referent, CP and TP always coincide in the relevant respect.

[6] It has been suggested to us (Len Talmy, p.c.) that the narrow reading of (19a) is INTONATIONALLY distinct from the broad reading. Following Ladd 1978:213, Selkirk 1984:198f., Lambrecht 1994, we distinguish between the

As for context (iii), its compatibility with the prosodic structure of (19a) may seem surprising. Since the context sentence explicitly mentions the addressee's buying activity at the mall, the denotatum of *buy* is naturally taken to be activated in B's reply and the verb should not receive an accent. We claim that the accent on the verb in context (iii) has the same function as that on the noun *MOE* in (10B'): the speaker ratifies the propositional topic 'addressee bought something' which was introduced as a predicate-focus assertion in the context utterance. Since this topic is not yet ratified, (9iii) cannot apply and an accent is required.

Let us now compare (19a) with (19b). (19b') shows the information structure of (19b):

(19b') Sentence: *What did AUDREY buy?*   (= (19b))
        Context: I went to the mall with Audrey yesterday and bought
                   some shoes.
        Presuppositions:
            KP: Audrey bought x
            TP: 'someone bought x' is ratified
        Assertion: x = what?
        Focus: what

In (19b), the noun *AUDREY* receives the accent via (9iii), since, unlike the pronoun *you* in (19a), its referent is not yet a ratified topic. The verb *buy* remains unaccented via (9iii) because the propositional topic 'someone bought something' is both discourse-active and ratified.

The fact that the propositional topic 'someone bought something' counts as ratified in (19b) requires an explanation. What makes this topic more ratified than the propositional topic 'you bought something' in context (iii) of (19a)? In other words, why is the verb *buy* unaccented in (19b) but accented in (19a)? We offer the following explanation. Unlike (19a), at the time (19b) is uttered the speaker already knows what the addressee bought. The question asked in (19a) *What did you BUY?* would be a non-sequitur in the context described for (19b). Now since in (19b) Audrey's buying activity is contrasted with the addressee's, the denotatum 'buy' is necessarily taken as ratified. Hence the lack of accent on the verb.

It is important to acknowledge that in (19) the subjects (*you* and *Audrey*) are TOPIC expressions. These questions are about the referents of the subject NPs, which were mentioned in the immediately preceding utterances. In asking the questions, the speaker wants to increase his knowledge concerning the subject referents and their activities. The only difference between *you* in (19a) and *AUDREY* in (19b) is that the referent

---

information function of sentence accents and the EXPRESSIVE use of intonation contours. While we acknowledge the possibility of distinguishing the two readings intonationally, we maintain that narrow construal does not require special intonational marking.

'you' is already ratified while the referent 'Audrey' is only accessible and requires ratification as a topic. Hence the accent on the proper noun. This accent does NOT entail focus status of the referent, as claimed e.g. by Culicover & Rochement (1983). The focus is in all cases 'what'.

The non-focal status of 'Audrey' in the proposition can be demonstrated with syntactic tests. Consider first the English detachment construction in (21a) and its colloquial French equivalent in (21b):

(21)   [I went to the mall with Audrey yesterday and bought some shoes.]

    a. A: And AUDREY, what did SHE buy?
        B: AUDREY (she) bought a TIE.

    b. A: Et AUDREY, elle a acheté QUOI?
        B: AUDREY elle a acheté une CRAVATE.

Left-detachment is generally acknowledged to be a topic-establishing device. In (21), the accent on the left-detached NP *AUDREY* in speaker A's question has the function of activating the topic 'Audrey', while in speaker B's declarative reply the function of the accent on the NP is to ratify this topic. The topic function of 'Audrey' is more obvious in the French version in (21b): here we have no difficulty analyzing AUDREY as a topic NP because the interrogative word *QUOI* appears in situ, hence receives the focus accent via (9ii), just like it does in B's answer. It would make little sense to claim that 'Audrey' is a topic in French, but not in English.

Another syntactic test demonstrating non-focus status of *AUDREY* in (19b) is clefting. If *AUDREY* were an argument focus in (19b), it should be possible to make it the focus of an *it*-cleft. Notice the facts in (22):

(22)   a. What is it that Audrey bought?
      b. *What is it Audrey who bought?
      c. *What is it that it is Audrey who bought?

As (22a) shows, the WH-expresssion itself can be clefted, as expected from our analysis of WH-words as argument foci. However it is impossible to cleft the subject NP *AUDREY*, as shown in (22b-c), independently of whether the WH-constituent itself is clefted or not. We conclude that both in (19a) and in (19b) the subjects are topic expressions.

Let us now turn to the analysis of the sentences in (2), repeated as (23).

(23)   [I heard you went to France.]

    a. What CITIES did you visit?
    b. What cities did you VISIT?

These sentences differ from the ones in (19) in that the WH-word functions here as a determiner within an NP rather than as an argument of the verb. In (23a'), we see a representation of the information structure of (23a). As in (19a), there is more than one possible construal, depending on the context:

(23a')   Sentence: *What CITIES did you visit?*   (= (2a))
       Contexts:
           (i)   I heard you went to France.
           (ii) I heard you went to France and visited some Roman ruins.
       Presuppositions:
           KP: you visited x cities
           TP: (i) 'you' is ratified
                  (ii) 'you visited some place (in France)' is ratified
       Assertion: x cities = what cities?
       Focus: what

In both construals of (23a), the accent falls on the nominal constituent whose denotatum distinguishes the KP from the TP: *what CITIES*. The subject *you* is unaccented by Principle (9iii). In the broad construal (i), the verb *visit* remains unaccented in accordance with Principle (9iv).[7] In the narrow construal, in which 'cities' contrasts with 'Roman ruins', *visit* is unaccented because its denotatum is part of the ratified topic 'you visited some place (in France)'.

The information-structure representation of (23b) is given in (23b'). Again we represent two possible construals:

(23b')   Sentence: *What cities did you VISIT?*   (=(23b))
       Contexts:
           (i)   I heard you went to France and visited various cities.
           (ii) I heard you avoided Paris on your trip to France.
       Presuppositions:
           KP: you visited x cities
           TP: (i) 'you' and 'cities' are ratified
                  (ii) 'you did something with respect to cities (in France)'
                     is ratified
       Assertion: x cities = what cities?
       Focus: what

In (23b), both the subject 'you' and the object 'cities' are ratified topics at the time of utterance. Both constituents are therefore unaccentable by (9iii). The accent falls on the verb by default. Construal (i) of (23b) is analogous to construal (iii) of (19a): the KP, though activated in the context, does not yet count as ratified, hence a topic accent is required. Context (ii) results in a

---

[7]   We are finessing the question of the exact conditions under which the accent on an object argument may include the predicate denotatum in its pragmatic scope, as it does in (23a). We assume that the answer to this question has to do with the degree to which the verb-object combination is semantically predictable. For example in (23a) the combination of the argument 'city' with the predicate 'visit' is recoverable from the 'traveling frame', which includes the visiting of sites when touring foreign countries. We leave this issue for further research.

narrow construal, in which the denotatum of the verb *VISIT* contrasts with the denotatum 'didn't visit' which is implied by the context sentence.

We now turn to our third set of examples, repeated here for convenience:

(24)   a.   Who ate my COOKIES?

        b.   Who ATE them?

        c.   WHO ate them?

This set is different from the first two in that the WH-word is here the subject. This entails that there is no overt syntactic difference between the declarative and the interrogative versions of these sentences.

Item (24a') represents the information structure of (24a). Again, we mention two readings, one broad, one narrow:

(24a')   Sentence: *Who ate my COOKIES?* (= (24a))
         Contexts:
            (i)   The jar is empty!
            (ii) I know someone ate my chocolate.
         Presuppositions:
            KP: x ate my cookies
            TP: (i)   -------
                   (ii) 'someone ate something of mine' is ratified
         Assertion: x = who?
         Focus: who

In (24a) the topic accent falls on the noun via (9ii). In Context (i) the entire KP 'x ate my cookies' needs to be ratified. The verb may remain unaccented in accordance with Principle (9iv). In Context (ii) the verb is unaccented because its denotatum is part of the ratified topic 'someone ate something of mine'.

(24b') contains the information structure of (24b):

(24b')   Sentence: *Who ATE them?* (= (24b))
         Contexts:
            (i)   My COOKIES are gone!
            (ii)   I don't care who MADE my cookies.
         Presuppositions:
             KP: x ate my cookies
            TP: (i)   referent 'them' (my cookies) is ratified
                    (ii) 'x did something with respect to my cookies' is
                         ratified
         Assertion: x = who?
         Focus: who

In (24b) the accent falls on *ATE* by default: the pronoun *them* codes a ratified topic. It is therefore unaccentable by Principle (9iii). In the broad construal (i), only the referent of *them* is ratified. In the narrow construal (ii), both this referent and some activity involving it is ratified. The denotatum 'ate' is construed as contrasting with the denotatum 'made' in the context sentence.

Finally, (24c) illustrates the marked prosodic pattern in which the sentence accent falls on the WH-word itself. We will argue that this pattern is appropriate just in case at utterance time the entire knowledge presupposition has already been ratified as a topic of further inquiry, i.e. just in case KP and TP coincide. The pattern thus follows in a straightforward fashion from Princple (9iii), according to which ratified topic constituents remain unaccented.

One situation in which the KP is construed as a ratified propositional topic and in which the WH-word gets accented involves a METALINGUISTIC speech act: the WH-expression receives the accent because the speaker wants to express the fact that she uttered the same IQ before but got an unsatisfactory reply. This somewhat trivial case is illustrated in (25):

(25)   I didn't say YOU ate them, I said WHO ate them.

The information structure of (25) is represented in (25'):

(25')   Sentence: *WHO ate them?*   (= (24c))
          Context: I didn't say "YOU ate them", I said ...
          Presuppositions:
              KP: x ate my cookies
              TP: KP 'x ate my cookies' is ratified
          Assertion: x = who?
          Focus: WHO

Unlike the examples analyzed so far, the point of the utterance in (24c) is not to ratify the propositional topic expressed in the KP ('x ate my cookies'). Rather at the time the question is uttered, the KP is already taken for granted at the topicality level, i.e. KP and TP coincide. As a result, no topic-ratification accent is required. The accent falls therefore on the only element in the sentence which is not contained in the KP, namely the focus expression *WHO*.

A different pragmatic motivation for accenting the WH-expression in an IQ is illustrated in (26), a variant of context (iii) in (19a):

(26)   A: I went to the mall and bought something. (= (19a), (iii))
          B: I KNOW you bought something. WHAT did you buy?

The crucial difference between speaker B's reply in (26) and that in (19a) (*What did you BUY?*) lies in the fact that in (26) speaker B has already established the propositional topic 'you bought something' in the preceding sentence ("I know you bought something"). As a result, this propositional topic counts now as both active and ratified at the time the question is asked. The sentence portion expressing it must therefore remain unaccented, given Principle (9iii). This entails that only the WH-word can receive the accent. The information structure of the relevant sentence in (26) is represented in (26'):

(26')   Sentence: *WHAT did you buy?*
          Context: I KNOW you bought something.
          Presuppositions:
              KP: you bought x
              TP: KP 'you bought x' is ratified topic
          Assertion: x = what?
          Focus: **what**

In (26), the reason for accenting the WH-word is not metalinguistic, as it was in (25). The point of B's question in (26) is to make A aware that the proposition 'I bought something' which A took to be a pragmatic assertion is in fact already K-presupposed for the addressee.

There are other discourse motivations for using this marked prosodic pattern, which we cannot go into here. We are also ignoring important INTONATIONAL differences (falling vs. rising) between different kinds of sentences with accented WH-expressions. However we claim that all sentences with accented WH-expressions have one essential pragmatic feature in common: the accent falls on the WH-expression because at the time of utterance the K-presupposed propositional function is taken for granted at all three presuppositonal levels.

It is worth pointing out that the denotatum of a WH-expression can hardly be said to be "more focal" or to convey "newer information" when the question word is accented as in sentences in which it is not accented, contrary to what is claimed e.g. by Culicover and Rochemont (1983). Nor does it seem informative to say that the WH-denotatum is more "dominant" in these cases, as claimed by Erteshik-Shir (1986), unless dominance is defined in terms of accentuation, in which case the dominance argument becomes circular. The reason for the presence of a sentence accent on a WH-word is fundamentally the same as in declarative sentences in which the focus accent has "moved leftward" via Principle (9iii): the accent falls where it does not because the denotatum of the accented constituent is pragmatically more important, but because the accent has no other place to go, given the unaccentable nature of the element or elements to its right. The accent falls on the WH-word not for ICONIC reasons but by DEFAULT.[8]

4. Conclusion

It seems reasonable to propose that IQs instantiate a GRAMMATICAL CONSTRUCTION, in terms of Fillmore and Kay 1994. They have idiosyncratic prosodic properties: they require the marking of topic rather than focus status, but they permit the prosodic marking of focus in contexts like those in (25) and (26). At the same time, IQs appear to inherit general prosodic properties: an account of the placement of sentence accent in IQs requires reference to general principles which are also invoked by the declarative constructions. IQs are a clear illustration of the proposition that

---

8   For the notion of 'default accent' see in particular Ladd 1978.

a construction is not reducible to a set of interacting general principles, but instead represents an intersection of highly general and highly particular constraints on the pairing of form and meaning.

References

Chafe, Wallace. 1987. Cognitive Constraints on Information Flow. In R. Tomlin, ed., *Coherence and Grounding in Discourse*. Amsterdam: Benjamins.

Comrie, Bernard. 1981. *Language universals and linguistic typology*. Chicago: Chicago University Press.

Culicover, Peter & Michael Rochemont. 1983. Stress and Focus in English. *Language* 59:1. 123-165.

Demuth, Catherine. 1987. Pragmatic functions of word order in Sesotho acquisition. In R. Tomlin, ed., *Coherence and grounding in discourse*. Amsterdam/Philadelphia: John Benjamins.

Dryer, Matthew. 1996. "Focus, pragmatic presupposition, and activated propositions." Journal of Pragmatics 26. 475-523.

England, Nora C. 1983. *A Grammar of Mam, A Mayan Language*. Austin: University of Texas Press.

Erteshik-Shir, Nomi. 1986. WH-Questions and Focus. *Linguistics and Philosophy* 9:2. 117-150.

Fillmore, Charles and Paul Kay. 1994. *Construction Grammar Coursebook*. UC Berkeley ms.

Horvath, Julia. 1986. *Focus in the theory of grammar and the syntax of Hungarian*. Studies in Generative Grammar, vol. XXIV. Dordrecht: Foris Publications.

Jackendoff, Ray. 1972. *Semantic Interpretation in Generative Grammar*. Cambridge, MA: MIT Press.

Ladd, D., Robert Jr. 1978. *The structure of intonational meaning: evidence from English*. Bloomington: Indiana University Press.

Lambrecht, Knud. 1994. *Information Structure and Sentence Form*. Topic, focus, and the mental representations of discourse referents. Cambridge: Cambridge University Press.

Manandise, Esmérelda. 1988. *Evidence from Basque for a New Theory of Grammar*. New York: Garland.

Raymond, William R. & Kristin Homer. 1996. The Interaction of Pragmatic Roles and Thematic Structure in the Selection of Question Form. Paper presented at *BLS* 22.

Rochemont, Michael. 1978. *A theory of stylistic rules in English*. PhD dissertation, University of Massachusets.

Schmerling, Susan F. 1976. *Aspects of English sentence stress*. Austin: University of Texas Press.

Selkirk, Elisabeth O. 1984. *Phonology and Syntax: The Relation between Sound and Structure*. Cambridge, MA: MIT Press.

A Non-Syntactic Account of Some Asymmetries in the Double Object Construction*

Maria Polinsky
University of California, San Diego

Introduction

In the double object construction in English, some grammatical behaviors give superiority to the recipient, and others to the patient (the so-called object asymmetries). Some of these asymmetries are also found in other constructions involving double complements. The question then arises: Why do double complements show recurrent asymmetries? I am going to propose an explanation for several of the recurrent asymmetries based on the semantic-pragmatic status of double complements. Such an account contrasts with the usual view of object asymmetries as representative of the syntactic status of the double object. If, as I show, certain syntactic behaviors reflect the semantic/pragmatic status of objects within a construction, the question that will arise is of the extent to which these behaviors are definitional for grammatical relations.

The paper is structured as follows. Section 1 presents a brief overview of the relevant constructions and section 2 describes several object asymmetries. Section 3 discusses crucial semantic characteristics of the double object construction that will form the basis of my analysis. In section 4, I examine

* I am grateful to Chris Barker, Bernard Comrie, Hana Filip, Adele Goldberg, Jack Hawkins, Ron Langacker, and especially Knud Lambrecht for their comments. All errors are my responsibility.
Abbreviations: DAT - dative construction; DOC - double object construction; IS - information structure; NPI - negative polarity item.

the information structure of the double object construction. Section 5 applies the semantic findings to the resolution of several object asymmetries. For considerations of space, I will focus only on prototypical ditransitives with verbs such as *give* or *show*.

1. Relevant constructions

A double object construction (DOC) is one where two objects are not distinguished by any overt marking, as in (1a):

(1) a. The royal divorce gives 58m people who have little in common
recipient
something to talk about (*Economist* 3-9-96)
patient

The only characteristic that distinguishes the objects in this construction is their order, which is fixed. The DOC can be compared to a construction in which the objects are differentiated by overt marking; in English, this is the so-called dative construction (DAT below), as in (1b). Constructions such as (1a) and (1b) are linked together under the name of the Dative alternation.

(1) b. The royal divorce gives something to talk about to 58m people who have little in common

The semantic roles of the two objects in DOC may vary depending on the semantics of a verb and on a given language. However, a typical ditransitive construction describes a transfer, either actual or intended, of a possession or of some kind of effect related to that possession (Green 1974; Pinker 1989; Jackendoff 1990; Goldberg 1992; Langacker 1991). In this transfer, a crucial role is played by the recipient—an agentive participant other than the agent of transfer; the active and often willing[1] involvement of this participant ensures that the transfer is successful. The typical object of transfer is described as the patient. Bearing in mind the multiplicity of roles of the two objects, I will be referring to the first object in (1a) as recipient and the second as patient because these roles frequently occur in DOC.

It is well-known that the so-called dative alternation illustrated by (1a) and (1b) is not absolutely correlative; some specific cases require that DOC be used, while others require DAT. Thus, a number of set expressions tend to occur only in DOC, and this is shown by the contrast between (2a) and (2b):[2]

---

[1] Often, but not always; see section 3 below.

[2] Note that the patient, not the recipient, forms a set expression with the ditransitive—and despite that, can be separated from its host by the recipient nominal (Hudson 1992: 262; Nunberg et al. 1994: 525-8).

(2)   a.   Fergie gave the royal family a kick/a headache/grief
       b.   */?Fergie gave a kick/a headache/grief to the royal
             family

The contrast between (3a) and (3b) illustrates the opposite tendency: some events can be encoded only by DAT:

(3)   a.   Maria gave birth to Jesus
       b.   *Maria gave Jesus a/the/Ø birth

2.   Object asymmetries

Although the two objects in DOC look alike, they show multiple asymmetries which have been studied in great detail in formal frameworks with respect to English and less so to Bantu languages (Barss and Lasnik 1986; Jackendoff 1990; Larson 1988; 1990; Johnson 1991; Runner 1995; Koji 1996; Bresnan and Moshi 1990).

In this paper, I won't present an exhaustive list of object asymmetries but will focus on those which are accounted for in a uniform manner. The effects are grouped in the following way: first, those according to which the recipient is a higher-ranking NP, then the ones according to which the patient ranks higher.

Contrary to many existing accounts, I insist that object asymmetries not be treated as all-or-nothing effects. Rather, many asymmetries should be stated as implications of the following form:

(4)   If effect E applies to object A, then effect E also applies to object B

2.1. Effects which give superiority to the recipient. These effects include: passive, scope relations, variable pronoun binding, optional deletion, pronominalization, and control of reflexives and reciprocals.

The failure of the all-or-nothing principle is evident with *passivization* because English shows significant dialectal variation in passives of DOC. Thus, there are speakers of English who accept both (5b) and (5c), speakers who accept only (5b), and speakers who may occasionally accept a patient passive as in (5c). Crucially, there are no speakers who accept (5c) without accepting (5b).

(5)   a.   John gave Mary a book
       b.   Mary was given a book by John
       c.   A book was given Mary

The implication then is as follows: In any dialect of English, if the patient in DOC can become the subject of a passive, the recipient can become the subject of a passive, too.

(6)   Recipient passive   >   Patient passive

A full explanation of passive asymmetry will remain beyond the scope of this paper. However, passivization is important here because it illustrates the importance of the implicational approach to asymmetries.

Next, if the objects in DOC are quantified, the first quantifier takes wide scope, as shown in (7a) where *every* has wide scope but *two photos* don't. The "control" DAT in (7b) is scope-ambiguous.

(7) a. I showed every critic two photos
         "For every critic X, I showed X two photos"
         * "For two photos X, I showed them to every critic"
     b. I showed a photo to every critic
         "For every critic X, I showed X a photo"
         "For photo X, I showed it to every critic"

(8a) illustrates the so-called scope freezing, where again, the second object cannot take scope over the first. In (8b), both scope interpretations are available.

(8) a. John assigned some student every problem
         "For student X, John assigned him every problem"
         * "For every problem X, John assigned it to some student"
     b. John assigned every problem to some student
         "For student X, John assigned him every problem"
         "For every problem X, John assigned it to some student"

The first NP, as a quantified NP, can serve as the antecedent for the pronoun in the second object, as shown by (9a).[3] In no event can the quantified patient bind a variable pronoun in the recipient, which is illustrated by the ill-formed (9b).

(9) a. What is giving everyone$_i$ their$_i$ biggest headache?
     b. *I denied its$_i$ owner each paycheck$_i$

Next, recipient is superior to patient in accessibility to *optional deletion*; thus, while (10a) is fine, (10b) is impossible except for the incongruous reading that John was given to someone else:

(10) a. I gave/sent a book
     b. *I gave/sent John

---

[3] (9a) presents an additional problem for formal accounts: according to May (1985); Larson (1988; 1990), the only allowable interpretation for (9a) should be the one whereby *what* takes scope over *everyone*. Meanwhile, (9a) is at the very least ambiguous and CAN have the interpretation whereby *everyone* has wide scope (Kuno 1991: 266).

Some of the verbs that appear in DOC, particularly verbs of speaking, permit the deletion of the patient, as in (11a). But as with the previous effects, these verbs follow the implicational generalization because they also allow the deletion of the recipient shown in (11b):

(11) a. I told/asked Mary
      b. I told the news/asked my question

This suggests another implication. If the patient of DOC can undergo optional deletion, the recipient of DOC can undergo optional deletion, too:

(12) Recipient deletion   >   Patient deletion

Pronominalization, illustrated in (13), operates along similar lines; the recipient has clear priority in accessibility to pronominal expression but if the patient can be pronominalized at all, as in (13c-e), then the recipient has to be pronominalized as well, within the same construction.

(13) a. I gave them advice
      b. *I gave John it
      c. ??I gave him them
      d. ?I gave them it
      e. I gave them that

Two other effects that give preference to the recipient over the patient in English include the control of a reflexive (14) and licensing of the element *other* in *each other* (15). Thus:

(14) a. I showed Mary$_i$ herself$_i$ in that picture
      b. *I showed herself$_i$ Mary$_i$ in that picture
(15) a. The committee denied John and Bill a meeting with each other
      b. *The committee denied each other a meeting with John and Bill

2.2. Effects which give superiority to the patient. These effects include Wh-word licensing, relativization, and the licensing of negative polarity items.
     For *Wh-word licensing*, given dialectal and idiolectal variation in English, the implicational formulation is again preferable to the all-or-nothing one. Thus, in any dialect of English, if the recipient of DOC can license a Wh-word, the patient must license it, too.

(16) Patient Wh-word > Recipient Wh-word

Accordingly, all speakers accept (17a), few speakers accept (17b), but no speaker accepts (17b) without accepting (17a).

(17)   a.   What did John give Mary?

           b.   ?/*Who did John give a book?

Wh-word asymmetry remains the same in innocent Wh-questions, as in (17), and in complicated extractions out of an NP, as in (18):

(18)   a.   The prep school gave this child of humble beginnings a veneer of education (*LA Times* 2-12-96)

           b.   What did the *LA Times* say (that) the prep school gave this child of humble beginnings a veneer of __?

           c.   *What did the *LA Times* say (that) the prep school gave this child of __ a veneer of education?

There is experimental evidence for the superiority of the patient over other arguments in the licensing of *Wh*-words. In their study of parsing of *Wh*-questions in English, Hickok *et al.* (1992) show that even *Wh*-phrases that are semantically implausible as the patient of the matrix verb are nonetheless reactivated in that position. Such a patient-oriented re-activation of the *Wh*-phrase was observed in particular with three-place predicates including *give*. A more recent experimental study by Boland *et al.* (1995) confirms the implicational approach. In that study, sentences with object control verbs and ditransitive verbs were parsed starting with the patient interpretation but then were judged to make sense as long as the Wh-phrase could be plausibly interpreted as at least one of the verb's arguments. This suggests that the bias to initially interpret a Wh-phrase as the patient of a ditransitive is again a matter of degree.

Relativization is often likened to Wh-word licensing as a subtype of extraction (e.g. Chung 1994: 11-14). In English, the patient in DOC relativizes easily (19a), while relativization of the recipient is questionable at best (19b):

(19)   a.   the candy that John gave the little girl

           b.   ?/*the little girl that John gave (the) candy

The next effect concerns the behavior of negative polarity items—expressions whose distribution is restricted to negative contexts. NPIs can be licensed by the second object of DOC but not by the first:

(20)   a.   I'll be amazed if Donald gives Ivana a red cent

           b.   */?I'll be amazed if Donald gives a red cent to Ivana

The effects reviewed for English are summarized in Table 1. How can we account for these asymmetries? A syntactic explanation has been investigated extensively, whereby the asymmetries were accounted for in terms of the relative dominance of the two objects, and different executions of this idea have been proposed by Larson (1988; 1990) and Koji (1996), on the one hand (VP-shell analysis), and Johnson (1991) and Runner (1995) on the other (small clause analysis).

Table 1.   English double object construction: Object asymmetries

EFFECT	SUPERIOR OBJECT
Passivization	Recipient
Scope relations	Recipient
Pronoun binding	Recipient
Optional deletion	Recipient
Pronominal expression	Recipient
Licensing of Wh-elements	Patient
Relativization	Patient
Licensing of negative polarity items	Patient
Verb + Obj set phrase	Patient

Objections to these analyses include several points, one of which is that scope asymmetries do occur in a large family of double complements and cannot be accounted for in terms of relative dominance effects. Particularly telling are the data on double PP complements (Jackendoff 1990; Kuno and Takami 1993).

Some examples are given in (21), which illustrates that the second PP but not the first can license *any*; and in (22), which illustrates the pronominal anaphor asymmetry (see Jackendoff 1990a):

(21) a. I talked about none of the boys to any of the girls
      b. *I talked about any of the boys to none of the girls
      c. *gifts from any of the boys to few of the girls
(22) a. I talked about every girl$_i$ to her$_i$ mother
      b. *I talked to her$_i$ mother about every girl$_i$

The examples in (23) are interesting because the asymmetry here occurs between a core argument (patient) and an adjunct (an element within an adverbial clause). They underscore that the differences between double complements are relative, not absolute, in nature—licensing *any* is not a universal property of the patient in DOC; rather, it is a property in which the patient has superiority over the recipient. As (23a) shows, this superiority can be taken over by some other expression (Runner 1995: 90):

(23) a. John gave Mary nothing at any of the events
      b. *John gave Mary anything at none of the events

In Polinsky (forthcoming) I also show that many of the asymmetries shown in Table 1 recur across languages and are thus associated with DOC and not with language-specific phenomena.

In the next two sections, I am going to present an explanation whereby specific effects observed in DOC are successfully accounted for in terms of the interaction between the semantics of the construction and its information structure.

3. Semantics and pragmatics

3.1. Pragmatic presupposition. The account presented below relies on the notion of pragmatic presupposition. Following Kempson (1975), pragmatic presupposition is defined as a proposition about which the speaker and hearer are expected to have some shared knowledge and/or one which they can successfully activate at the time of utterance.

The disjunction on successful activation is particularly important here; I am making a distinction between those presuppositions which must be activated for the utterance to make sense and those presuppositions which can be triggered by some other presuppositions. Note that the distinction between activated shared knowledge and triggerable shared knowledge also parallels the discourse-model distinction of Evoked or Discourse-Old entities on the one hand, and Inferrables on the other (Prince 1992, and many others).

My proposal is that the recipient in DOC is associated with the pragmatic presupposition of independent existence *at least prior* to the event of transfer. The independent existence prior to the event of transfer immediately explains the ill-formedness of example (3a) above: Jesus did not exist prior to his own birth; similarly, the expression *give rise* cannot occur in DOC.

It has been noticed that the recipient in DOC is often a willing participant (e.g., Goldberg 1992). The presupposition of independent existence is linked to this volitionality: to be volitional, a participant has to have independent existence, although not all independently existing participants have to be volitional (Dowty 1991: 572-3). The fact that some participants can be characterized as independently existing but not as volitional allows us to explain the observed actual instances of DOC where the recipient is inanimate and, thus, non-volitional, as in (24), or where its volitionality is irrelevant, as in (25):

(24)   I gave the house a new coat of paint
(25)   Bill gave the driver a speeding ticket

3.2. Recipient vs. agent. The description of the recipient as independently existing underscores its similarity to the subject (agent) of transfer, but there are also important differences.

It is the agent but not the recipient that initiates the event of transfer; the recipient has will only over the end point of transfer—cf. Langacker's characterization of the recipient as the active respondent in the target domain of transfer (1991: 324-7). Accordingly, the recipient cannot stop the transfer as it develops but can refrain from completing it (Oehrle 1977: 206):

(26)   I handed her a cigarette but she wouldn't take it

The presupposition of independent existence associated with the agent is normally generated by the speaker, and this can be shown by the oddity of examples such as (27) where the speaker contradicts herself (Kempson 1975):

(27)   #The mayor of Wynx visited the exhibition but there is no mayor of Wynx

Meanwhile, the presupposition of existence associated with the recipient may be generated either by the speaker or by the agent of transfer. This follows from Green's observation (1974) that in DOC—as opposed to DAT—the agent and the recipient must exist at the same time and the agent must know that the recipient exists[4] (see also Pinker 1989: 221). Compare:

(28)   a.   I bought a ring for my wife in case I should decide to marry
       b.   #I bought my wife a ring in case I should decide to marry

The oddity of (28b) is due to the conflict between the presupposition that the wife already exists inherent in the meaning of the construction and the congener which cancels this presupposition.

In example (28a), the speaker and the agent of transfer are identical. The speaker can even create a mental space in which the existence of the recipient could be presupposed, and this is shown by (29), where double object construction is used in a hypothetical utterance:

(29)   If I had a daughter, I would teach her/my daughter to play scrabble

When the agent of transfer is not the speaker, what matters is whether or not the agent presumes that the recipient exists. The speaker, in the meantime, can disagree with that presupposition. This is shown by example (30), where the existence of God is Mary's perspective, and the congener '...but there is no God' is compatible with the speaker's perspective:

(30)   Mary told God her sorrows   but there is no God
       Mary's viewpoint: G exists   *Speaker's viewpoint*: G does not exist

Thus, the presupposition of existence associated with the agent of transfer can be generated in a different way than the presupposition of existence

---

[4]Green describes the meaning of DOC as involving a component "X intends Y to have Z" and argues that "intend" has the presupposition "X believes Y to exist".

associated with the recipient. The existence of the recipient is in the eye of the agent, and if the speaker is different from the agent, the speaker prompts the hearer to blend these separate mental spaces (as in Fauconnier 1994). The details of such an analysis still have to be worked out but examples as in (30) point in the general direction of applying the blending approach to DOC.

3.3. Recipient vs. patient. The next question concerns the difference between the recipient and the patient. The major difference is that the existence of the recipient prior to the event of transfer is presumed, while the existence of the patient is not. This is corroborated by two pieces of evidence. First, as is well known for English and confirmed by cross-linguistic data, verbs of creation are typical as DOC predicates (Jackendoff 1990b: 196 for English); the existence of the patient is incompatible with the semantics of such verbs. If the patient is not created for the transfer, then at least its state is dramatically changed (it changes ownership), which is also incompatible with independent existence. Second, verbs of destruction normally fail to appear in DOC (Polinsky, forthcoming), unless used in metaphors (Goldberg 1992); the meaning of verbs of destruction presupposes the existence of the patient prior to the (unfortunate) event, and this results in semantic incompatibility.

Since the recipient's existence is presumed and the patient's does not have to be, the recipient can serve as a *reference point* for accessing the patient. This means that the identity of the recipient is established first and is construed as independent of other entities, and the identity of the patient is established indirectly, via the identity of the recipient (cf. Langacker 1993: 5-14).

This interpretation is fully consistent with the analysis of successful transfer as resulting in the possession relation between the recipient and the patient or cancellation of such relation as with *deny* or *refuse* (Green 1974: 103; Goldsmith 1980; Pinker 1989: 155; Jackendoff 1990b; Langacker 1991; Goldberg 1992). In the possession relation, the conceptual asymmetry between the possessor and possession can be generalized as the asymmetry between the reference point—identified as an independent and directly accessible entity—and the entity which is accessed indirectly, via the reference point.

In DAT, on the other hand, there is no implication of a successful transfer; thus, the goal does not necessarily enter into a possession relation with the patient. They both exist independently and neither can serve as a reference point for accessing the other.[5]

---

[5]For the discussion here, I have assumed the concept of the reference point as a given. Although not related directly to this paper, I would like to state the following questions related to the more general theory of reference points:
    (i)   what features make a reference point accessible?

The asymmetry between the recipient and the patient in terms of the presupposition of existence also accounts for the specificity effects which have been noticed for English (Runner 1995: 116). In (31), the preferred interpretation is that the doctor is specific though indefinite, and that the speaker (who is also the agent of transfer) has this specific doctor in mind. The specificity effect can be predicted from the presupposition of existence associated with the recipient.

(31)   I sent a doctor the letter

Note that specificity should not be identified with definiteness. Specificity relies on the presupposition of existence; if defined as an informational status, and not as a formal category (for the distinction, see Prince 1992: 299-303), definiteness requires that the referent of the NP be uniquely identifiable to the hearer. Unique identifiability is often due to prior shared knowledge or to the activation of a referent in discourse; thus, it derives from pragmatic presupposition of existence but is not its necessary corollary. Thus, the recipient in DOC has to be specific but does not have to be definite.

To conclude, the crucial generalizations about the nominals of DOC are as follows: The recipient in the DOC is associated with the pragmatic presupposition of existence, subordinate to the pragmatic presupposition in regards to the subject of transfer. The recipient serves as the reference point in the identification of the patient. The patient is underspecified in that it is not directly associated with pragmatic presupposition and can therefore be associated with pragmatic assertion.

4. Linking pragmatic presupposition to information structure

My next step is to argue that the asymmetry in the pragmatic presupposition between the two objects translates into their asymmetry in the information structure (IS) of the double object construction.

That the contrast between the double object and dative construction has discourse consequences was shown early on by Erteschik-Shir (1979; also Erteschik-Shir and Lappin 1979). Erteschik-Shir introduced the notion of dominance to account for discourse characteristics. Her notion of dominance can be compared to that of assertion, especially because she establishes the dominant constituent on the basis of the so-called "lie test" which is similar to the application of negation to the assertive component of utterance.

(ii)   given several candidates for a reference point within a construction,
        what makes A a better reference point than B?
I suggest, in an attempt to answer (i), that the accessibility of a reference point depends on the pragmatic presupposition of independent existence associated with a given participant (although that might not be the only factor).

However, contrary to the account presented here, Erteschik-Shir insists that dominance is an absolute category.

In this section, I show that the objects in DOC differ in their relative status in the IS. As the notions of topic and focus play an important role in the IS representation, let me start with explaining my understanding of these notions.

My approach is close to Lambrecht's (1994) in that both topic and focus are defined as content-based, not formal, categories. For such an analysis, topic and focus are defined at the semantic level of the pragmatically structured proposition, not at the grammatical level of the syntactically structured sentence. However, this does not preclude a theory in which the semantic categories topic and focus are linked, via gradual linking rules, to structural positions.

Since topic and focus are understood as conceptual, not formal categories, pragmatic presupposition plays an important role in their definition. Topic is defined as an entity which is within the scope of a pragmatic presupposition at the time of the utterance. Accordingly, if an utterance has several pragmatic presuppositions, it can have several topic elements, ordered in accordance with the strength of the respective pragmatic presupposition. This is similarly captured in the distinction between several degrees of prominence in cognitive grammar (Langacker 1991).

In the definition of focus, I follow Lambrecht (1994: 213) for whom focus differs from assertion and is represented as the relationship between presupposed and non-presupposed information. In other words, focus is the semantic component of a pragmatically structured proposition whereby the assertion differs from the presupposition.

Given the association between the recipient and the presupposition of existence and the absence of such an association for the patient, the recipient must be superior to the patient in topicality; conversely, the patient is superior to the recipient in focusing. Such a characterization relies on the relative ranking of the recipient and patient in IS. This relativity is particularly welcome given that differences in topicality exist between the agent and the recipient. Topicality differences between the agent and the recipient were noticed by Givón (1984), who suggested the terms primary and secondary topic, but did not fully explain that distinction. My presupposition analysis gives Givón's generalization a conceptual motivation: the presupposition of existence is stronger for the agent than for the recipient, and the agent is expected to be more topic-prominent than the recipient.

Overall, the topical prominence of NPs in DOC follows the scale in (32):

(32) *Degrees of prominence in the double object construction:*
  agent   recipient   patient
  <—   topicality increasing
                    focusing increasing   —>

It has been shown that the relationship of an expression to preceding discourse is an important dimension of its semantic value. Topicality, as a dimension of discourse prominence, is known to be linked to the ability of an expression to represent old information. In her discourse study of English dative alternation, Thompson (1990; 1995) shows that in DOC, the recipient is old information in 92% of all cases, while the patient is old information in about 30% of all cases. In DAT, the goal is old information only 18% of the time. These statistics confirm the scale in (32).

The next step is to link the order of double complements to their IS distinctions. It is well known that word order is sensitive to IS distinctions and often serves to reflect them. In English, the general tendency is for topic to precede focus. As a particular realization of this tendency, in double complements, regardless of their argument or adjunct status, the more topical complement precedes the less topical one; this is reflected in their fixed order. Note that the order in DOC is much more rigid than in DAT; in DAT, the patient, if sufficiently heavy, can follow the goal (Kuno and Takami 1993: 129-34).[6] Let me reiterate that the relative and not the absolute IS status of objects is important, because the recipient is inferior to other nominals which have a higher degree of topic prominence (e.g. agent/subject of transfer). Likewise, the patient, which in a "bare" DOC is likely to be focus, can be "outfocused" by a different focus constituent in a DOC complicated by adjuncts. In English, where focused constituents tend to be situated at the left periphery of an utterance (Hawkins 1994: 184-8), this is reflected in the order of the patient and the adverbial (Runner 1995: 98), cf. (33a) and (33b):

(33) a. He faxed the committee his last letter of recommendation
          reluctantly
          focus
      b. ?He faxed the committee reluctantly his last letter of recommendation

Assuming that (33a) and (33b) are both uttered without emphatic accent (Ladd 1980), the reason (33b) is ill-formed is that the inherently more focused adverbial is in a less focused linear position than the object *letter*.[7]

5 Explaining the asymmetries

Given the proposed match between the semantic and the information structure of DOC, we can now predict that those "grammatical" behaviors which are sensitive to topicality will give superiority to the recipient because it is more topical than the patient. On the other hand, those "grammatical" behaviors which are sensitive to the focus status will give superiority to the patient. In

---

[6]In Polinsky (1995; forthcoming), I also show strong cross-linguistic word-order patterns which encode IS distinctions between double complements.

[7]The information structure of DAT should be subject to a separate analysis, but lack of space prevents me from doing that here.

this section, I will analyze several asymmetries that can be resolved by reference to IS distinctions.

Two disclaimers are in order here. First, unless indicated otherwise, the DOC in questions have no emphatic accent. Emphatic accent indicates contrast, and contrastive IS may be superimposed upon neutral IS (Polinsky, forthcoming). Second, the analysis proposed here works for non-embedded DOC. Once a DOC is embedded under a quantifier or a world-creating predicate (e.g., *doubt; promise*), the analysis has to be expanded in order to account for the properties of the matrix before accounting for the properties of the embedded construction.

Wh-word licensing can be explained in the following way. Wh-questions target focus—speaker and hearer share the knowledge of a proposition and the Wh-word represents an element missing from that proposition or supplemental to it. Often Wh-word licensing is even used as a procedure to establish the focus. Since in DOC, the patient is superior to the recipient in focusing, the asymmetry in Wh-word licensing (16) is adequately explained.

Relativization is patterned after Wh-word licensing for a purely formal reason—most relative pronouns in English are related to Wh-words. Although Wh-word licensing is inherently sensitive to focus and relativization is not, what matters is the formal similarity between relative pronouns and Wh-words. Therefore, as long as Wh-word licensing gives priority to the patient, relativization does the same. This is true cross-linguistically of those languages where relativization patterns with Wh-word licensing (Polinsky, forthcoming). Crucially, if a language's relative pronouns are not related to Wh-words, relativization in DOC can differ from Wh-word licensing (e.g. in Bantu, see Bresnan and Moshi 1990; in Korean, see Kozinsky and Polinsky 1993). Thus, the explanation of relativization in DOC is not semantically-based, but it draws on the formal parallels between relativization and an extraction effect which *is* motivated by information structure.

Next, *optional deletion* and *pronominalization* can be explained as sensitive to topic; both apply to those elements of IS that have already been activated and are accessible to speaker and hearer. More topical information is easily backgrounded, which explains why the recipient is more easily deleted. Pronominal topic expressions identify the referent anaphorically or deictically and serve as a grammatical link between the topic and the proposition.

Of special interest are examples such as (13d, e), where two pronominal objects occur. This is not precluded by this analysis because both objects can represent background information; again, it is the relative status of objects that matters, which effectively rules out examples such as (13b), where the patient is backgrounded but the recipient is not.

Pronominal relations whereby the first object may antecede a pronoun in the second object but not vice versa can be explained as a particular case of the pronominalization of a more topical complement. Besides, under the pronominal reference as in (34a), the first object explicitly serves as a reference point for the identification of the second object. If, on the other hand, the second object is coindexed with a pronominal within the first object (34b), this contradicts the less topical status of this second object and inappropriately marks it as a reference point for identifying the first object. In (34a), the unknown (the referent of the second object) is identified by the known (the referent of the first object); in (34b), the unknown is assumed as a reference point for the known, and the result is incongruous (examples from Barss and Lasnik 1986: 348)

(34) a. I showed every trainer$_i$ his$_i$ lion
      b. *I showed its$_j$ trainer every lion$_j$

The asymmetry in the control of *reflexives* and *reciprocals* in English can be explained on more formal grounds. English reflexives and reciprocals contain a pronominal element, which obeys the regularity just described. However, just as with relativization, the asymmetry is not inherent to reflexives and reciprocals but draws from the formal link between pronominals and reflexives/reciprocals.

Van Valin (1993; 1995) and Kuno (1991) have both presented evidence that *scope effects* are determined by an interaction of semantic and discourse factors. Of these factors, topicality is most significant. A topicalized element has wider scope than a non-topicalized element for the following reason: the topicalized element is established in the information territory of both speaker and hearer; therefore, it can serve as a reference point. The construal of the subsequent element relies on the association between this subsequent element and the reference point. To put it differently, the identification of the new element is facilitated by linking it to the reference point, hence the preferred (but not necessarily the only) interpretation of the two referents as scope asymmetrical. Since the recipient in DOC is superior to the patient in topicality, it is predicted to take wide scope.

Given that linear order reflects IS distinctions, we can expect that the first complement will tend to take wider scope than the subsequent complement(s) because of its higher topicality. Experimental results on scope asymmetries (Kurtzmann and MacDonald 1993; Tunstall 1996) suggest that there is a strong preference for wide scope on the first quantifier; wherever possible, this bias is actualized. The preservation of the bias in constructions where no structural hierarchical relations between phrases can be established suggests that we are dealing with a cognitive salience asymmetry that projects into the IS.

We can now look at the problem from a different angle and ask the following question: can the patient in DOC take wide scope over the recipient at all? It turns out that the topicalization of the patient can change the scope asymmetry described so far. In (35a), the recipient expectedly takes wide scope. However, in (35b), where the patient is topicalized by fronting, the asymmetry can disappear. Thus the patient takes wide scope in interpretation of the sentence (for some speakers, this is the only interpretation, for others, the sentence is scope ambiguous):

(35)   a.   Heidi Fleiss offered all her clients many of her services
             "For all HF's clients, it is true that they were offered many services"
             * "There were many services such that HF offered them to all her clients"
       b.   Many of her services Heidi Fleiss offered all her clients
             "There were many services such that HF offered them to all her clients"
             ?"For all HF's clients, it is true that they were offered many services"

Finally, the presupposition/assertion distinction explains the *licensing of NPIs* by the second complement. The semantics of the English *any* differs from the semantics of other universal quantifiers (such as *every, each*) in that *any* does not have to carry the pragmatic presupposition of existence (McCawley 1993: 36-40, 164-5, 170-1, 177, 199). Existence can be inferred, but this is strictly an inference.

Since *any* does not carry the pragmatic presupposition of existence, its occurrence in the position of the recipient in DOC creates a conflict with the required presupposition of the existential commitment, and this explains why sentences such as (36) are ill-formed.

(36)   *I gave anybody nothing

On the other hand, the patient in DOC does not have to be associated with the presupposition of existence, and its expression by *any* or other NPIs is fully licensed.

Similarly, in other double complements, the first complement is topical, and has to be under the scope of the presupposition of existence. The use of a negative polarity item in such a position would contradict the presupposition of existence, hence the ill-formedness of example (20b) above.

To summarize, I have demonstrated that several object asymmetries in the double object construction derive from the IS of the construction, which in turn, is consistent with the overall semantics of this construction. Since asymmetries between complements result from these differences in IS status and since IS is expressed by word order, my results are consistent with Jackendoff's idea that linear order must be included among the possible reasons for anaphoric relations. My conclusions differ from Jackendoff's in that I propose that linear order reflects IS rather than having a self-fulfilling role.

Two other questions arise from these results. First, can we explain other effects in precisely the same manner? The answer is probably no. Some effects are likely to have other explanations and it is also very likely that a number of effects will have multiple motivations. The discussion of such effects is beyond my scope but let me still note that multiple motivation would be required to account for the object asymmetries in passivization and control of depictives.

The second question is: What do these results tell us about the nature of syntactic tests? A number of effects (extractions, Wh-word licensing, scope phenomena), which are conventionally used as "standard" syntactic behaviors, have been shown to have a non-syntactic motivation.[8] This suggests that such effects may at least be less definitional to grammatical relations than we tend to think they are. This has important consequences for theory and warrants a re-examination of a number of conventionally used syntactic tests. It is likely that many of these tests will survive the scrutiny, so there still is hope for autonomous grammar.

To conclude, this paper has argued for a semantic motivation for several object asymmetries and thus shown that properties commonly assumed to constitute the core of grammatical (or syntactic) behaviors can be determined by semantics and information structure. These findings strongly suggest that language theory should integrate information structure as a component of representation (cf. Vallduví 1992; 1995). The information structure component should be related to the lexical-conceptual component and to syntax via multiple linking rules.

References

Barss, Andrew, and Howard Lasnik. 1986. "A Note on Anaphora and Double Objects." *Linguistic Inquiry* 17: 347-54.

Bresnan, Joan, and Lioba Moshi. 1990. "Object Asymmetries in Comparative Bantu Syntax." *Linguistic Inquiry* 21: 147-85.

Boland, Julie; Michael K. Tanenhaus; Susan M. Garnsey, and Greg Carlson. 1995. "Verb Argument Structure in Parsing and Interpretation: Evidence from Wh-Questions." *J of Memory and Language* 34: 774-806.

Chung, Sandra. 1994. "Wh-Agreement and "Referentiality" in Chamorro." *Linguistic Inquiry* 25: 1-44.

Deane, Paul. 1991. "Limits to Attention: A Cognitive Theory of Island Phenomena." *Cognitive Linguistics* 2: 1-63.

Dowty, David. 1991. "Thematic Proto-roles and Argument Selection." *Language* 67: 547-619.

Erteschik-Shir, Nomi. 1979. "Discourse Constraints on Dative Movement." In Talmy Givón, ed. *Syntax and Semantics. Vol. 12: Discourse and Syntax*, 441-67. New York: Academic Press.

---

[8]See Deane (1991) for similar conclusions regarding extractions.

Erteschik-Shir, Nomi, and Shalom Lappin. 1979. "Dominance and the Functional Explanation of Island Phenomena." *Theoretical Linguistics* 6: 41-86.

Fauconnier, Gilles. 1994. *Mental Spaces: Aspects of Meaning Construction in Natural Language*. Cambridge: Cambridge University Press.

Givón, Talmy. 1984. "Direct Object and Dative Shifting: Semantic and Pragmatic Case". In Frans Plank, ed. *Objects. Towards a Theory of Grammatical Relations,* 151-82. London-Orlando, Fla.: Academic Press.

Goldberg, Adele E. 1992. "The Inherent Semantics of Argument Structure: The Case of the English Ditransitive Construction." *Cognitive Linguistics* 3: 37-74.

Goldsmith, John. 1980. "Meaning and Mechanism in Grammar." *Harvard Studies in Syntax* 3: 423-49.

Green, Georgia. 1974. *Semantics and Syntactic Regularity*. Bloomington: Indiana University Press.

Hawkins, John A. 1994. *A Performance Theory of Order and Consistency*. Cambridge: Cambridge University Press.

Hicock, Gregory; Eduardo Canseco-Gonzalez; Eric Zurif, and Jane Grimshaw. 1992. "Modularity in Locating Wh-Gaps." *J of Psycholinguistic Research* 21: 545-61.

Hudson, Richard. 1992. "So-called 'Double Objects" and Grammatical Relations." *Language* 68: 251-76.

Jackendoff, Ray. 1990a. "On Larson's Analysis of the Double Object Construction." *Linguistic Inquiry* 21: 427-56.

Jackendoff, Ray. 1990b. *Semantic Structures*. Cambridge, Mass.: MIT Press.

Johnson, Kyle. 1991. "Object Positions." *Natural Language and Linguistic Theory* 9: 577-636.

Kempson, Ruth. 1975. *Presupposition and the Delimitation of Semantics*. Cambridge: Cambridge University Press.

Koji, Fujita. 1996. "Double Objects, Causatives, and Derivational Economy." *Linguistic Inquiry* 27: 146-73.

Kozinsky, Isaac, and Maria Polinsky. 1993. "Causee and Patient in the Causative of Transitive." In Bernard Comrie and Maria Polinsky, eds. *Causatives and Transitivity,* 177-240. Amsterdam: John Benjamins.

Kuno, Susumu. 1991. "Remarks on Quantifier Scope." In Heizo Nakajima, ed. *Current English Linguistics in Japan,* 261-87. Berlin-New York: Mouton de Gruyter.

Kuno, Susumu, and Ken-ichi Takami. 1993. *Grammar and Discourse Principles*. Chicago: University of Chicago Press.

Kurtzman, Howard S., and Maryellen MacDonald. 1993. "Resolution of Quantifier Scope Ambiguities." *Cognition* 48: 243-79.

Ladd, D. Robert. 1980. *The Structure of Intonational Meaning: Evidence From English.* Bloomington: Indiana University Press.

Lambrecht, Knud. 1994. *Information Structure and Sentence Form: Topic, Focus, and the Mental Representations of Discourse Referents.* Cambridge: Cambridge University Press.

Langacker, Ronald W. 1987-1991. *Foundations of Cognitive Grammar.* Vol. 1: *Theoretical Prerequisites.* Vol. 2: *Descriptive Applications.* Stanford: CSLI.

Langacker, Ronald W. 1993. "Reference-point Constructions." *Cognitive Linguistics* 4: 1-38.

Larson, Richard. 1988. "On the Double Object Construction in English." *Linguistic Inquiry* 19: 335-91.

Larson, Richard. 1990. "Double Objects Revisited: Reply to Jackendoff." *Linguistic Inquiry* 21: 589-631.

McCawley, James D. 1993. *Everything That Linguists Always Wanted to Know About Logic.* Chicago: University of Chicago Press.

Nunberg, Geoffrey, Ivan Sag, and Thomas Wasow. 1994. "Idioms." *Language* 70: 491-538.

Oehrle, Richard. 1977. Review of Green 1974. *Language* 53: 198-208.

Pinker, Steven. 1989. *Learnability and Cognition: The Acquisition of Argument Structure.* Cambridge, Mass.-London: The MIT Press.

Polinsky, Maria. 1995. "Double Objects in Causatives." *Studies in Language* 19: 129-222.

Polinsky Maria, forthcoming. *Double Object Constructions.*

Prince, Ellen F. 1992. "The ZPG Letter: Subjects, Definiteness, and Information Status." In William C. Mann and Sandra Thompson, eds. *Discourse Description: Diverse Linguistic Analyses of a Fund-Raising Text,* 295-326. Amsterdam: John Benjamins.

Runner, Jeffrey. 1995. *Noun Phrase Licensing and Interpretation.* Ph. D. Dissertation, University of Massachusetts at Amherst.

Thompson, Sandra. 1990. "Information Flow and "Dative Shift" in English." In Jerold A. Edmondson, Crawford Feagin, and Peter Mülhäusler, eds.*Development and Diversity: Linguistic Variation Across Time and Space,* 239-53. Arlington: Summer Institute of Linguistics.

Thompson, Sandra. 1995. "The Iconicity of "Dative Shift" in English." In Marge Landsberg, ed. *Syntactic Iconicity and Freezes: The Human Dimension,* 123-46. Berlin—New York: Mouton de Gruyter.

Tunstall, Susanne. 1996. *Processing Quantifier Scope in Dative Sentences.* Paper presented at the LSA Annual Meeting, San Diego, January 1996.

Vallduví, Enric. 1992. *The Informational Component.* New York: Garland.

Vallduví, Enric. 1995. "Structural Properties of Information Packaging in Catalan." In Katalin É. Kiss, ed. *Discourse Configurational Languages,* 122-52. Oxford: Oxford University Press.

Van Valin, Robert, Jr. 1995. *Focus Structure and Syntax: Solving Problems of So-called 'Abstract Syntax'.* Paper presented at the International Conference on Functional Approaches to Grammar. University of New Mexico, Albuquerque, July 1995.

From Hypothetical to Factual and Beyond: Refutational *si*-clauses in Spanish Conversation[*]

SCOTT A. SCHWENTER

Stanford University

1. Introduction

A popular assumption about conditional sentences is that their protases ('if' clauses) are hypothetical in nature: they characterize an unrealized, but possible state of affairs that is advanced as a frame of interpretation for another state of affairs in the conditional apodosis ('then' clause). The state of affairs in the protasis may either cause the state of affairs in the apodosis, as in *If you stare at the computer screen you'll go blind*, or it may enable it to happen, as in *If it snows, we'll go skiing*. The hypothetical nature of conditionals like these has often been used to distinguish them from other, similar constructions, like temporals. Consider, for instance, the views of Snitzer Reilly (1986:312): "the speaker's attitude toward the antecedent event or state, believing it to be fact or merely supposing the possibility of its existence, is the criterial feature distinguishing the basic *when/if* structures".

It is clear from recent research (e.g. Athanasiadou and Dirven 1996), however, that the uses of conditionals in natural language extend well

---

[*] Parts of this paper were presented previously at Stanford University and the Universitat de València. Many thanks to the audiences there for many helpful comments. Special thanks to my Spanish informants for being so willing to talk, and also to my colleagues in Valencia, especially Manuel Pérez Saldanya and Salvador Pons, for helpful suggestions and warm hospitality. The fieldwork this research is based on was supported in part by a Graduate Research Opportunity grant from Stanford University.

beyond the familiar, hypothetical conditional that makes reference to relations between possible states of affairs. In particular, a number of studies have focused on the "given" or "factual" status that the protasis can often assume. As one example, Sweetser (1990) has shown how the typical hypothetical, or in her terms, "content" conditional differs along several parameters from other conditional types, which she labels "epistemic" and "speech act". One crucial difference is that only the latter two types of conditionals allow "factual" protases.

In this paper, I examine a set of "factual" uses of a conditional structure in conversation, and outline some implications for a theory of conditionals. In brief, the main claim of the paper is that any attempt to limit conditionals to the domain of irrealis modality--a commonly accepted view (cf. Akatsuka 1985; Palmer 1986)--is misguided, since conditionals incorporating realis propositions are also commonly found.

The phenomena of interest are extended uses of a conditional protasis marked by *si* 'if' in Spanish, examples of which are culled from spontaneous conversational data collected during 1994 and 1996 in Alicante, Spain (ALC). These protases are used independently, i.e. without an overt apodosis, although there are full conditional sentences that perform similar functions. The discourse function of this independent structure can be best described as "refutational", because it is used by speakers to reject or deny the validity of some aspect of another speaker's utterance(s) in conversation.

2. Refutational *si*-clauses

Refutational *si*-clauses in Spanish are always declarative in form, and in the indicative, not subjunctive, mood. They nearly always have declarative intonation--not the non-final intonation of a conditional protasis--and may also have increased loudness when used to strongly refute some aspect of a prior utterance. The use of refutational *si* is quite easily distinguishable from the *sí* of affirmation: the first *si* cannot be stressed nor followed by a pause, while the second *sí* can and often is. In addition, the vowel of "conditional" *si* is often reduced and may even be devoiced.

Functionally, Spanish refutational *si*-clauses reflect speaker assessments of what is "acceptable in a (particular) discourse context". Just as a protasis postulates a background for the interpretation of the apodosis in a conditional sentence, refutational *si*-clauses highlight the pragmatic assumptions that underlie conversation. Speakers use these clauses to point to infelicities in conversation, and to challenge their interlocutors by denying and questioning the latters' often implicit beliefs. More specifically, refutational *si*-clauses may pick out certain aspects of a prior utterance (including its implicatures or presuppositions) or other parts of the preceding discourse, and suggest a dissonance between the prior utterance and a discourse model, which is not presupposed (or judged as such by the speaker) by all of the participants.

Here, I will outline four separate but related uses of refutational *si*-clauses, all of which represent speaker commentary on discourse appropriateness. The first type, exemplified in (1) and (2), is an objection to some aspect of the propositional content, and makes reference to assumptions that the speaker[1] considered to be shared, common knowledge among the group of interlocutors.

(1)   [Talking about some friends returning from a trip]

    Y: Espero que lleguen sin problemas.

        'I hope that they arrive without problems.'

    L: Si ya han llegado.

        'SI they've already arrived.'[2]

                                                    (ALC)

(2)   A: Creo que Javi ha aprobado el examen: estará contento.

        'I think Javi has passed the exam: he must be happy.'

    B: Si lo ha suspendido.

        'SI he has failed it.'

                                                   (ALC)

In example (1), the main verb of "hope" and the subjunctive verb form in the subordinate clause of Y's utterance leads L to infer that Y is talking about a future event, i.e. Y assumes that the friends have not arrived yet. L's response refers explicitly to the status of the friends' arrival; in fact, she points out, they've already arrived. In (2), A reasons from what she thinks to be the case--the belief that Javi has passed his exam--to a conclusion based in his success, namely that he must be happy as a result. B's response in (2) takes issue with the "passing" part of A's prior utterance and goes on to provide a revision of it which also nullifies A's ensuing conclusion.

A second class of uses is employed to object to scalar implicatures that are evoked by particular utterances in context. Thus, in this case it is not the proposition that is being objected to, but rather the implicatum that may be associated with it (cf. Horn 1985).

---

[1]When referring to "the speaker" here, I am talking about the utterer of the refutational *si*-clause in the example.

[2]I have opted not to translate refutational *si* into English. It is certainly not translatable by *if*. Perhaps the closest equivalent would be *but*, but this translation is also difficult at times as well as problematic for other reasons (cf. Schwenter 1996).

(3)   [H and M are talking about their son, whose math teacher has
       just sent home a note about his poor performance in the class.]
       H: Pues, parece que va a suspender matemáticas.
           'Well, it looks like he's going to fail math.'
       M: Si va a suspenderlas todas.
           'SI he's going to fail all of them.'

                                                                    (ALC)

(4)   [B looks strangely at a glass of purple Kool-Aid]
       B: ¿Qué es eso?
           'What is that?'
       A: Es el que te gusta a ti.
           'It's the one that you like.'
       Q: Si a ella le gustan todos los sabores.
           'SI she likes all of the flavors.'

                                                                    (ALC)

In (3), H says something that he believes to be true, but yet potentially
implicates something false, i.e. that his son is going to fail math and none
of his other school subjects. M draws the inference that this is what H is
trying to say, and goes on to refute the upper bound ("math and only
math"). M points out that, in fact, their son is going to fail all of his
courses, not just math. M may also be denying the possible "surprise"
quality of H's contribution, i.e. its communicative effects as a novel
"conclusion" that H is drawing about his son. Likewise, in (4), A and Q are
trying to get B (age 6) to eat and drink at mealtime. A's response to B's
query potentially implicates that there is one and only one kind of Kool-Aid
that appeals to B's tastes. Q, probably in an effort to get B in an even more
positive frame of mind towards eating and drinking, amplifies A's response
to include all flavors of Kool-Aid. This amplification effectively invalidates
the implicature that arose from A's response.
    The third type of refutational *si*-clause may refer to wider sociocultural
"norms" of behavior. The speaker who utters such a *si*-clause is presenting
its contents as justification for his or her actions or words, especially when
others are (implicitly) questioning those actions or words.

(5)   [C walks past Q (age 22), who is watching cartoons on TV]
       C: Q, ¿qué estás viendo? ¿dibujos?
              'Q, what are you watching? cartoons?'
       Q: ¡Si no hay nada más!
              'SI there is nothing else!'

C: Vale.

       'OK.'

(ALC)

(6)   [Y runs into an open door, banging hard against it.]

      Y: ¡Me cago en la puta leche!

          'I shit in the damn milk! [a very strong expletive]'

      A: Che mamá, por favor.

          'Gee mother, please.'

      Y: Si es que me he hecho mucho daño.

          'SI it's that I hurt myself badly.'

(ALC)

In (5), C asks a question that, on the surface, requests confirmation of what she believes she has witnessed while walking by, namely that Q is watching cartoons on television. Q's reaction to C's question(s), is focused on C's possible motivations for asking the question, and shows implicit recognition of the popular belief that consumers of cartoons are typically children and not 22-year-old adults like herself. Thus, Q anticipates that the purpose of C's utterance is actually to convey criticism or ridicule, or enable these to be conveyed in light of Q's response. In essence, Q is requesting temporary exemption for her actions, which are justifiable since, she claims, there is nothing else on TV at the moment. C's response, *Vale* 'OK' demonstrates that she accepts R's justification and grants the exemption that R has sought. Similarly, in (6), Y presents a justification for her earlier expletive-laden utterance, to which her daughter A had objected. The *si*-marked clause describing the results of her collision with the door is the background that led to the outburst in Y's prior utterance, and is presented as a condition under which saying such words can be considered acceptable. At the same time that Y's response justifies her own actions, it also refutes the validity of A's objection to Y's use of "foul language". In both examples, then, part of what the speakers are trying to convey via the *si*-marking is their awareness of having broken some norm, which is justifiable due to the conditions under which the norm was broken.

Finally, refutational *si*-clauses can also be used for "pure" metalinguistic negation, e.g. to comment on and "rectify" a pronunciation, choice of register or dialect, etc. that the speaker deems to be unacceptable (cf. Horn 1985). This use is also very much concerned with "norms": such rectifications are not concerned with real-world "facts", but rather social attitudes about "correct" language use.

(7)　　B:　No encuentro mi medicina [medeθina].

　　　　　　'I can't find my medicine ["incorrectly" pronounced].'

　　　　L:　Si es medicina [mediθina].

　　　　　　'SI it's medicine ["correctly" pronounced].'

(ALC)

(8)　　A:　Mañana tengo que dar clase, sobre la GENEOLOGÍA

　　　　　　'Tomorrow I have to teach a class, about geneology.'

　　　　R:　Si se pronuncia GENEALOGÍA. ¿Cuántas veces te lo tengo
　　　　　　que decir?

　　　　　　'SI it's pronounced genealogy. How many times do I have
　　　　　　to tell you?

(ALC)

In (7) L corrects the pronunciation of B (age 6), who pronounces the second vowel of *medicina* as [e] instead of [i]. In (8) A produces an [o] instead of an [a] in the third syllable of the word *genealogía*, and is corrected (and chastised) by R. The *si*-marked clauses in both responses are evaluative, based in speaker beliefs about "correct" pronunciation. Nevertheless, the *si*-marking lends a sort of authority to the proposition, conveying the message "you can't and shouldn't say it that way" to the interlocutor.

　　The examples above show clearly that propositions marked by *si* in its refutational use differ greatly from the hypothetical nature of protases in the prototypical conditional sentence. Indeed, it seems that speakers consider the content of these clauses to be "factual", reflective of some aspect of what they perceive to be "reality". Although it is not always possible to reconstruct a conditional apodosis to accompany these independent uses of *si*-clauses (cf. Bello 1984[1847]), to the extent that it is, one can imagine an implicit question like "How could you/Why would you say/think/believe such a thing?". This reflects the challenge to discourse appropriateness that respondents are posing to their interlocutors in each of the examples above. In terms of Sweetser's (1990) tripartite division of conditionals, these uses most closely resemble her class of speech-act conditionals, in which "the performance of the speech act represented in the apodosis is conditional on the fulfillment of the state described in the protasis" (1990:118). The speech act is the question left implicit by the utterance of the refutational *si*-clause within the discourse context.

3. Conditionals, "facts", and (ir)realis

Despite seemingly "factual" examples like those just surveyed, there has been widespread agreement in the literature about the irrealis nature of conditionals. The standard view is that conditional protases can express a range of modal attitudes within some region of a gradual scale of epistemicity. That region, however, is to be located entirely within the irrealis domain, which itself has a gradual quality. As an exemplar of this view of conditionals, consider the following classification of conditionals in (9), based on Akatsuka (1985). This classification is also compatible with those of other theorists interested in both epistemicity and conditionals, such as Givón (1982) and Comrie (1986).

(9) **MORE IRREALIS**

      | NEGATIVE CONVICTION

      | ('I know that this is not the case.')

      | UNCERTAINTY ('I don't know if this is the case.')

      | SURPRISE or NEWLY-LEARNED INFORMATION

      | ('I didn't know this until now!')

    LESS IRREALIS

By contrast, what is **excluded** from expression in a conditional is the entire domain of **REALIS** or, more concretely, the speaker attitude of:

(10)   POSITIVE CONVICTION

            ('I know that this is the case.')

Matching up the irrealis attitudes in (9) with conditional sentence types is a fairly straightforward task. Negative conviction is the attitude typical of past counterfactual conditionals, where the speaker is hypothesizing about a past situation, and how things might have been different under different conditions, as in (11a). The attitude of uncertainty is to be found in the typical hypothetical conditional that predicts a future state of affairs (11b). where the speaker does not know if it will rain tomorrow. Finally, the attitude of surprise or newly-learned information is shown in (11c), where the content of the protasis is hearsay based on speaker A's prior utterance.

(11)   a.   Si hubiera llovido, nos habríamos mojado.

          'If it had rained, we would have gotten wet.'

    b.   Si llueve mañana, nos vamos a mojar.

          'If it rains tomorrow, we're going to get wet.'

    c.   [A is looking out the window, but B isn't]

        A: Está lloviendo.

            'I think that it's raining.'

        B: Si está lloviendo (como tú dices), no podemos ir.

            'If it's raining (as you say), we can't go.'

The key example for the irrealis account of conditionals is (11c). Although speaker B may not doubt A's claim that it is raining, the *si*-marking is possible because this is newly-learned information, and also because B is not a direct experiencer of the falling rain (Akatsuka 1986:341). Once B goes to the window to see the rain for herself, the *si*-marking is no longer possible. Such a shift from the role of external observer who is repeating hearsay to that of direct experiencer of the situation is consonant with a shift from the irrealis to the realis domain of knowledge.

The Spanish *si*-clauses in section 2 appear to be counterexamples to such a classification of conditional protases, since the content they express is clearly considered realis by the speaker: the speaker knows or believes that the content of the clause "is the case". One might therefore argue that these uses merely reflect the existence of a homonymous *si* in Spanish, which marks assertive declarative clauses for emphasis. This approach to "marginal" uses of *si* has been assumed by a number of previous analyses, e.g. those found in grammars of Spanish (cf. Butt and Benjamin 1994).

However, before tackling the question of the status of refutational *si*-clauses, it is instructive to examine some other "marginal" uses of conditionals, in both Spanish and English, which also appear to express positive conviction in the realis domain. One type that is quite common to journalistic and academic registers fits into a pattern that Horn (1991) has labelled "concession/affirmation". In this pattern, a conditional structure highlights a rhetorical contrast between two propositions. Example (12) displays a summary of prior commentary and a transition to a contrastive but related comment about the other team. In (13), the author concedes that there are problems with the book, but that, overall, the book is an important contribution to the field.

(12)   [During the broadcast of a basketball game; the announcer has
         been talking about Unicaja's undefeated record on their
         home court]
         Bueno, si Unicaja no ha perdido ningún partido en su cancha, el
         Real Madrid ha perdido dos.
         'Well, if Unicaja hasn't lost a game on its court, Real Madrid has
         lost two.'

                                                                (TVE2, 2/96)

(13)   [From a book review; the author of the review has just finished
         discussion of two main problems in the theory advanced in the book]
         If some of the steps in this, which was once called "A
         programmatic sketch" have proved mistaken, nevertheless we
         would not know that they were so without the clarity of the
         exposition and the many empirically testable hypotheses with
         which we are presented.

                                                        (Traugott, Forthcoming)

More relevant to the refutational *si*-clauses in section 2 above, there are also full-form speech-act conditionals (Sweetser 1990) that present a challenge to the hearer in the face of the "fact" in the *si* clause. The typical purpose of this "fact" is to somehow bias the interpretation of the speech act in the apodosis. In (14) and (15), the *si*-marked protasis is used as a frame of interpretation for the question in the apodosis; what is implied by these questions is rather obvious given the contexts in which they are asked.

(14)   [Z is drinking a glass of cola, poured from a new bottle that has

   just been opened]

   Z: Está desbravada ya.

      'It's flat already.'

   C: ¿Cómo va a estar desbravada si la acabas de abrir?

      'How could it be flat if you just opened it [the bottle]?'

(ALC)

(15)   [From a newspaper ad for an airline, showing pictures of two

   identical toy planes]

   Estos dos aviones son exactamente iguales. Si son exactamente

   iguales, ¿por qué pagar más por uno que por otro?

   'These two planes are exactly the same. If they are exactly the same,

   why pay more for one than for the other?'

(*El Mundo*, 1/96)

The assumed nature of the protasis in each example is clear: in (14) the act of opening the bottle is manifest to the participants, while in (15) the planes' "sameness" has just been asserted. The "factual" status of these conditionals provides a plausible link to refutational *si*-clauses; note particularly that if the apodosis in (14) were dropped, the protasis left standing would function in the same way as any of the *si*-clauses in section 2.[3] Hence, there is no need to posit a "homonymous" *si*--this marker can perform near identical functions in both full-form and "reduced" conditionals.

   The uses of *si* (or *if*) illustrated in this section do, however, call for some clarification as to the role of the protasis. Put simply: the "condition" in a conditional sentence--in all cases--is a condition on an **utterance**. The relationship of the protasis' propositional content to the external world (considered factual, hypothetical, or whatever) is independent of this condition. That is, conditions on the speaker's own (or the hearer's) utterance do not have to be "hypothetical" in the "real world", unlike conditions on future states of affairs, which are unpredictable. Therefore, classifying conditionals by different degrees of "knowing", as Akatsuka and others have done, does not appear to be useful. Conditionals can span the whole

---

[3]The "postposed" protasis in (14) may be an even stronger link to the refutational *si*-clause since, in this position, the protasis is typically realized with declarative intonation.

continuum of speaker "knowledge". Thus, we must seriously question the widely-held belief that conditionals (i.e. their protases) are always "irrealis".

4. (Non-)Assertion and Commitment

A general function of *si* or *if* is to encode a **possibly** true assumption that the speaker is not presenting as his or her own belief (Dancygier 1993). The "presentation" aspect of this function is key, since, as we have seen, it is not necessarily the case that the speaker does not believe the assumption to be true. These conditional protases may mark assumptions that are considered "hearsay" as in (11c) above, but whose validity are not being doubted by the speaker. In addition, these protases may also consist of inferences drawn from utterances in context (16), or of "common/obvious/assumed knowledge" (17). All three of these types of protases are non-assertive (cf. Lunn 1989; Mejías-Bikandi 1994) and concerned with the type of evidence that the speaker holds:

(16) [friends talking about a movie that they had previously planned to go see]

A: He leido la crítica, dicen que es un petardo.

'I read the review of it, they say it's a bomb.'

B: Si ya no quieres verla, iremos a otra.

'If you don't want to see it anymore, we'll go to another one.'

(17) [math teacher teaching class multiplication; they learned addition earlier]

Profesor: Si 2+2 son 4, ¿cuántos son 2x2?

Teacher: 'If 2+2 is 4, what's 2x2?'

The "common/obvious/assumed" status of the protasis in (17) is especially relevant for an account of refutational *si*-clauses. Indeed, it appears that speakers (like those in section 2) are attempting to present their responses as having this status: the *si*-marking lends the proposition a sense of "indisputable fact", even when what is involved are speakers' evaluative attitudes and assessments (cf. the "metalinguistic" examples (7) and (8)). Furthermore, beyond this piece of discourse analytic speculation, there is additional evidence to support this interpretation of the status of refutational *si*-clauses.

The first piece of evidence comes from native speakers of Peninsular Spanish--the source of the data presented in this paper. Their interpretations of speakers' intent in employing a refutational *si*-clause is that its purpose is often to put down or reprimand their interlocutor(s) for purportedly not being aware of something obvious (call it X). However, the *si*-marking implies that this X is not simply the individual viewpoint of the speaker, but rather a perspective shared by many or all relevant persons: the speaker is saying "everybody knows that X (is true)" and implying "why don't you?". The marking establishes a means for the speaker to evade responsibility as the unique source for the epistemic evaluation of X.

A second piece of additional evidence comes from collocational restrictions: *si*-clauses are pragmatically strange (and, in my data, not found) with other devices that attenuate or "hedge" speaker commitment to the proposition, e.g. epistemic parentheticals like English *I think* (18) [=(3)], or modal verbs (19) [=(2)]:

(18) [H and M are talking about their son, whose math teacher has

just sent home a note about his poor performance in the class.]

H: Pues, parece que va a suspender matemáticas.

'Well, it looks like he's going to fail math.'

M: Si va a suspenderlas todas, #creo yo/#digo yo/#me parece.

'SI he's going to fail all of them, #I think/#I say/#it seems to me.'

(ALC)

(19) V: Creo que J ha aprobado el examen: estará contento.

'I think J. has passed the exam: he must be happy.'

T: #Si puede/debe haberlo suspendido.

'#SI he could/must have failed it.'

(ALC)

The modal contribution of *si* in examples like (18) and (19) creates a clash with other modal elements, like parentheticals and modal verbs, that reduce speaker commitment to the truth of (or strength of speaker belief in) the proposition. Again, the *si*-marking lends the content of the clause a modal overlay of "common/obvious/assumed" knowledge that cannot be hedged as to its truth or factual status.

Speakers are in fact strongly committed to the truth or "factuality" of the propositions conveyed by refutational *si*-clauses, because they see these propositions as constituting "knowledge" that the hearer should also know, or points of view that the hearer should share. The prototypical domain of a conditional is non-assertion, and *si* is the prototypical marker of this domain. But certain uses, such as those of refutational *si*-clauses, may intrude into the pragmatic domain of assertion, which may also be reflected in the form (including intonation) of the construction. So why mark these declarative clauses with *si*? My view is this: the *si*-marking of the clause permits the speaker to present an asserted proposition **as if it were assumed**, implying that it **should have been assumed**. This view finds support in the pragmatic structure of all types of full conditional sentences: even a hypothetical protasis must be assumed with respect to the apodosis, because the interpretation of the apodosis is made only within the background provided by the protasis (cf. Sweetser 1990:126).

Thus, the key to understanding the use of refutational *si*-clauses in Spanish, and the "factual" reading of the *si*-marked protasis in conditional sentences, lies in a more complete understanding of why speakers decide **not** to assert something. As shown by examples (11c), (16), and (17) above, propositions marked by *si* in full conditionals may be "not asserted" for a variety of reasons.[4] However, the distance that speakers wish to signal between themselves and these propositions, e.g. when marking some content as hearsay, is not only in the direction of weakened commitment to the veracity of the propositional content being conveyed. This distance may also be conceived as applying in the seemingly opposite direction, toward a stronger commitment to the propositional content, e.g. when the "factuality" of this content is beyond question. This strengthened commitment, however, is "external" to the speaker in the sense that he or she is not presenting the proposition as if it were a subjective personal belief, but rather as an objective fact that constitutes "common/obvious/assumed" knowledge. In other words, the "commitment" that speakers make to some propositional content should not be considered with respect to "truth" or truth conditions, but rather to their own beliefs. Speakers thus have the option of presenting a proposition as not being their own personal belief, but as known to be objectively "factual", i.e. a proposition that all persons **must** believe or know. This sort of presentation is but another way to distance yourself from sole responsibility for a proposition. Nonetheless, the fact that you are presenting it as a corrective measure to someone else's discursive behavior--behavior that you have assessed to be inappropriate for some reason--will lead hearers to infer that you also believe the proposition to be true.

5. Conclusion

Recent studies have shown how conditionals express much more than logical connections between propositions which are true or false. This paper contributes to this line of research by attempting to further weaken the link between conditionals, hypotheticality, and other irrealis notions. Conditionals and their offspring (like refutational *si*-clauses) are not used only to predict or hypothesize, but also to talk about social and group norms, discourse appropriateness, and interlocutor expectations. These are all attitudinal realms that speakers treat very much as "factual" and realis. The irrealis "look" of conditionals is actually a by-product of protasis marking; in fact, the essence of *si* or *if* is not hypotheticality, but non-assertion, which is a strategy that speakers employ for diverse means, including the "masking" of their own views as shared, assumed, or obvious.

---

[4]Note that I have not said, as others have (cf. Dancygier 1993), that the **propositions** are "unassertable". Rather, I see this non-assertion as the result of strategic speaker choices about how to structure texts and arguments. The reasons underlying these choices are deserving of much closer analysis (cf. Schwenter 1997).

References

Akatsuka, Noriko. 1985. Conditionals and the Epistemic Scale. *Language* 61:625-39.

Akatsuka, Noriko. 1986. Conditionals are Discourse-bound, in E.C. Traugott et al., eds., *On Conditionals*, 333-51. Cambridge: Cambridge University Press.

Athanasiadou, Angeliki and Rene Dirven. 1996. Typology of *if*-clauses, in E. Casad, ed., *Cognitive Linguistics in the Redwoods*. Berlin: Mouton de Gruyter.

Bello, Andrés. 1984[1847]. *Gramática de la lengua castellana*. Madrid: EDAF.

Butt, John and Carmen Benjamin. 1994. *A New Reference Grammar of Modern Spanish*. 2nd. ed. London: Edward Arnold.

Comrie, Bernard. 1986. Conditionals: a Typology, in E.C. Traugott et al., eds., *On Conditionals*, 77-99. Cambridge: Cambridge University Press.

Dancygier, Barbara. 1993. Interpreting Conditionals: Time, Knowledge, and Causation. *Journal of Pragmatics* 19:403-34.

Givón, Talmy. 1982. Evidentiality and Epistemic Space. *Studies in Language* 6.23-49.

Horn, Laurence R. 1985. Metalinguistic Negation and Pragmatic Ambiguity. *Language* 61:121-74.

Horn, Laurence R. 1991. Given as New: When Redundant Affirmation Isn't. *Journal of Pragmatics* 15:313-36.

Lunn, Patricia V. 1989. Spanish Mood and the Prototype of Assertability. *Linguistics* 27:687-702.

Mejías-Bikandi, Errapel. 1994. Assertion and Speaker's Intention: A Pragmatically Based Account of Mood in Spanish. *Hispania* 77:892-902.

Palmer, F.R. 1986. *Mood and Modality*. Cambridge: Cambridge University Press.

Schwenter, Scott A. 1996. The Pragmatics of Independent *si*-clauses in Spanish. *Hispanic Linguistics* 8:316-51.

Schwenter, Scott A. 1997. The Pragmatics of Conditional Marking: Implicature, Scalarity, and Exclusivity. PhD Dissertation, Stanford University.

Snitzer Reilly, Judy. 1986. The Acquisition of Temporals and Conditionals, in E.C. Traugott et al., eds., *On Conditionals*, 309-31. Cambridge: Cambridge University Press.

Sweetser, Eve E. 1990. *From Etymology to Pragmatics*. Cambridge: Cambridge University Press.

Traugott, Elizabeth Closs. Forthcoming. Review of C. Lehmann, Thoughts on Grammaticalization: A Programmatic Sketch. *Journal of Linguistics*.

Index